The Bonds of Inequality

The Bonds
of Inequality

Debt and the Making of the American City

DESTIN JENKINS

THE UNIVERSITY OF CHICAGO PRESS

CHICAGO AND LONDON

The University of Chicago Press, Chicago 60637
The University of Chicago Press, Ltd., London
© 2021 by The University of Chicago
Published 2021
Printed in the United States of America

31 30 29 28 27 26 25 24 23 22   1 2 3 4 5

ISBN-13: 978-0-226-72154-5 (cloth)
ISBN-13: 978-0-226-81998-3 (paper)
ISBN-13: 978-0-226-72168-2 (e-book)
DOI: https://doi.org/10.7208/chicago/9780226721682.001.0001

Library of Congress Cataloging-in-Publication Data

Names: Jenkins, Destin, author.
Title: The bonds of inequality : debt and the making of the American city /
Destin Jenkins.
Other titles: Debt and the making of the American city
Description: Chicago ; London : The University of Chicago Press, 2021. |
Includes bibliographical references and index.
Identifiers: LCCN 2020037872 | ISBN 9780226721545 (cloth) |
ISBN 9780226721682 (ebook)
Subjects: LCSH: Municipal bonds—California—San Francisco—History—
20th century. | Finance, Public—California—San Francisco—History—20th century. |
Debts, Public—California—San Francisco—History—20th century. | Municipal
government—California—San Francisco—Finance—History—20th century. |
Equality—Economic aspects—California—San Francisco. | San Francisco (Calif.)—
History—20th century.
Classification: LCC HJ9205.S3 J36 2021 | DDC 336.3/4409794610904—dc23
LC record available at https://lccn.loc.gov/2020037872

♾ This paper meets the requirements of ANSI/NISO Z39.48-1992
(Permanence of Paper).

Contents

Figures and Tables

Figures

Tables

Abbreviations

ACNB	Anglo California National Bank
BART (BARTC/ BARTD)	Bay Area Rapid Transit (Commission/District)
BISD	Bond Investment Securities Division of Bank of America
BOA	Bank of America
BSC	Bond Screening Committee of San Francisco
DBB	*Daily Bond Buyer*
HHFA	Housing and Home Finance Agency
MFOA	Municipal Finance Officers' Association of the United States and Canada
MUNI	San Francisco Municipal Railway
SFBC	San Francisco Bond Club
SFBG	*San Francisco Bay Guardian*
SFHA	San Francisco Housing Authority
SFRA	San Francisco Redevelopment Agency

Introduction

The history of inequality in twentieth-century America is, in part, the history of municipal debt. Yet historians rarely note the centrality of the bond market to the production of inequality. Similarly, voters, confronted with a bond measure, seldom recognize that a question about municipal financing is also a question about inequality. There is a general lack of awareness, both in the academy and among the wider public, that municipal debt has proven to be a durable means of structuring racial privileges, entrenching spatial neglect, and distributing wealth and power. American cities, paragons of democracy, have become dependent on financiers, rating agencies, and the bond market for their most fundamental responsibilities: the provision of infrastructure and social services to their citizens. In turn, granting outsized political power to the holders of municipal debt can and does reshape the social contract between local governments and their residents. At the center of the decision to borrow is an ethical and political choice—deciding who and what is worthy of debt—with profound material consequences. The cumulative impact of these choices is nowhere more evident than in San Francisco, one of the most unequal cities in one of the wealthiest states in America.

Although San Francisco assumed considerable debt to fund development following World War II, not all areas of the city saw equal investment. By the late 1960s, the southeastern neighborhood of Hunters Point was "on the other side of the freeway," badly in need of recreational investment to prevent children from playing "on steep, rocky hillsides—or in the streets, between cars."[1] Despite repeated bond measures to upgrade San Francisco public schools, by 1969 some 1,200 elementary school children, many of them black, were still shunted into "temporary" classrooms built just after the war.[2] Black third graders received instruction under leaky roofs and inside dreary classrooms whose fiberglass windows generated "a cruel glare."[3] The long-term social impact of these years of neglect on black children was incalculable, and it was measured in more than dollars and cents. In September 1966, San Francisco became the latest American city jolted by the urban rebellions sweeping the nation. Municipal officials increasingly recognized that the mere threat of a riot raised the cost to borrow, as lenders prize little more than stability. There was now a pragmatic as well as a moral imperative to improve the infrastructural quality of life in Hunters Point. In November 1968, city officials hoped voters would agree by passing a $6.4 million bond measure that would pay for parks in the divested neighborhood.

The bond measure was no handout. Black people, as taxpayers, had long serviced debt that delivered parks to residents of other neighborhoods and helped turn San Francisco into a consumer playground for residents and visitors alike. As campaign supporters clarified, black residents of Hunters Point "also pay their taxes—even if they haven't received a just share for their money." Local supervisors, assemblymen, congressmen, big-name judges, real estate magnates, religious leaders, and others who supported the measure offered a sobering historical assessment: it had been seventeen years since "a single City penny" had been spent on a new park in the area.[4] The spate of postwar bond issues for transportation, streets, water and sewage systems, schools, and playgrounds elsewhere in the city had deepened inequality. Yet when offered a chance to make amends, enough San Franciscans voted "no." The November 1968 measure failed by a narrow margin. But even had it passed, the measure would have exacerbated the inequality of wealth and power. As one critic of an earlier measure implored, "Vote NO on Bond Profits for Wealthy Tax Evaders."[5]

These routine bond drives illustrated the production of inequality on two levels. The first was at the level of a local referendum, either through the discriminatory use of funds approved by voters or through the circumvention of voter approval entirely, typically to pursue pet projects that hardly benefited the wider public. The second was at the level of the bond market, a network of state and local government borrowers who secure huge chunks of funds, and banks, investors, credit rating analysts, and sellers of information who stake their fortunes on the infrastructural needs of everyday Americans. Bankers collect underwriting fees, bondholders collect principal and tax-exempt interest—income backed by layers of guarantees—and analysts and information brokers collect subscription fees. Borrowers became dependent on a set of actors whose drive for higher interest payments clashed with cities' desire to borrow as cheaply as possible. Both expressions of inequality fed off each other. And both expressions expose the kinds of tensions San Francisco and other cities were forced to navigate. Rejection of a local bond measure crystalized the infrastructural advantages afforded to white San Franciscans. Rejection left unaddressed the infrastructural frustrations and inequalities that conditioned the urban riots. Yet approval, while addressing some infrastructural needs, would reroute taxpayer dollars upward to bondholders who used municipal debt to shield their capital from federal taxes. Approval extended the gaze of lenders and made cities more vulnerable to the capricious criteria of bond financiers and bond raters. Whatever the outcome, cities lost. The result was that the municipal bond market was an untoward game where the stakes of public spending rewarded the bond industry and benefited white Americans.

By exploring the making of bondholder power, we can see how lenders came to rule over cities. Their power was amplified in many ways: through New Deal banking reform, the nesting of bond financiers in urban government, and the reliance of city technocrats on the opinions of those who sought to protect bondholder interests at the expense of residents' social welfare. To residents, cities are homes, families, neighbors, jobs, amusement, and dangers. But to bondholders they are just capital. Of course, if lenders did not fork over billions of dollars to finance parks, playgrounds, schools, and sewage systems, cities as residents know them would not exist. Yet there was always a tension between those calling for services and those who examined such demands in terms of yield, creditworthiness, bond prices, and tax revenues—a tension that played out in racially and economically unequal ways. The ideology and politics of the bond market helped to literally underwrite easier urban lives for white Californians. San Francisco pursued projects like transportation to benefit mostly white, white-collar workers; parking garages to attract white suburbanites to the city; and improvements to arts and entertainment infrastructure aimed at a bourgeoning white middle class. It was no coincidence that some of the same people who urged San Franciscans to approve a given bond measure were the same bond financiers who underwrote it.

This story moves from a fleeting moment of low interest rates just after the Second World War to the emergence of a new political economy of American capitalism in the 1980s, a period when high interest rates punished cities already reeling from rounds of retrenchment. To focus on the social and political economic history of municipal debt during these years is to see how city finance officers parlayed with credit analysts to effectively insulate debt policy from popular pressure; how San Francisco's infrastructure was built to benefit privileged whites even as it was paid for by all citizens (often regressively); and how municipal debt made cities into interchangeable entities in the eyes of investors.

A bond is much more than a financial instrument issued by borrowers, rated by credit analysts, purchased by financiers, and sold to investors. A bond entails indebtedness, a condition entangled with governance and democracy, social welfare and capitalism. By exploring the relationships between bond financiers and municipal technocrats, urban infrastructure and bondholder guarantees, interest payments and retrenchment, democracy and creditworthiness, and racism and finance, we can see that a city is never the product of its own making. Ultimately, distant institutions and actors place profound constraints on local conditions of possibility. The inequality of race and space, wealth and political power, and infrastructure and services makes dreadful sense once we engage the trajectory of a bond, whether rejected by voters or conveyed into the hands of wealthy investors who, as Marx once remarked, exercise a "preferential claim" on the future revenues extracted from the many.[6]

Political and social histories of inequality in twentieth-century America have been largely written through a handful of metanarratives. Scholars have wielded the concept of *deindustrialization* to explain the eclipse of an older model of industrial capitalism and, with it, the impoverishment of innumerable towns; to account for (black) male unemployment and racialized poverty in the Rust Belt; and as a way of discussing the mobility of capital and its impact on workers in the United States and beyond.[7] The *white flight* story goes something like this: Whether lured by federally guaranteed mortgages or lower taxes, or seeking refuge from the encroachment of racial Others, in the postwar decades white people fled to the suburbs. In taking their tax dollars with them, white Americans depleted urban coffers. The rise of black political power and of nonwhite politicians generally sparked a backlash among the white people who remained. In these accounts, white flight created huge fiscal gaps between revenues and expenditures that made cities hollow prizes for their nonwhite inheritors.[8] Another well-worn metanarrative underscores the *neoliberal* ascendancy of economists, former black power advocates, business groups, and the intellectual progeny of Friedrich von Hayek during the "age of fracture." Market ideology became the default response to urban fiscal woes, compelling neoliberals in charge of the city to impose what the market wanted: budget cuts, service reductions, hiring freezes, and layoffs.[9] A slightly different version of this story exists in which *the market* is treated as a liberating force. Cities are imagined as "venture capitalists" seeking to harness markets "to circumvent controls and constraints imposed" by federal and state governments. In this telling, inequality would be far worse if not for the magic of the market.[10]

As powerful and ubiquitous as these narratives are, postwar San Francisco does not always fit them. Indeed, deindustrialization cannot account for the decline of public infrastructure and services, the budgetary pressures, the hierarchy of expenditures, and the turn to regressive revenue sources. The City by the Bay did not experience the same degree of white flight to the suburbs as other cities did. And although a diverse succession of elected officials implemented structural adjustment from the 1970s onward, describing them as "neoliberals" does not account for why they all settled on similar programs. But San Francisco's experience does make the financial forces and institutions acting on all American cities particularly visible. As we will see, much of the inequality with which historians and sociologists have been concerned was tied up with a city's ability to borrow, and with the terms and strings attached. For example, credit rating analysts might penalize a city because of the mere specter of white flight and the calcification of multiple racial ghettos. Put simply, postwar inequality was very much rooted in the political economy and sociality of municipal debt.

While the postwar history of San Francisco seems to challenge dominant assumptions about the construction and reinforcement of racial inequality, it actually is the exemplar of what political philosopher Charles W. Mills has called the trick of color-blind liberalism, "seemingly colorless, but actually white." There, even as racist representations were repudiated, the city's institutions, practices, and social norms furthered "illicit white racial advantage."[11] The city's liberalism was not one thing but many.[12] And there were certainly racist conservatives who sought to dissuade San Franciscans from borrowing for the benefit of black people. But their political clout was relatively limited. Hence, the reinscription of racial inequality cannot reasonably be placed at the steps of conservative-populists seeking to pare down expenditures for minorities across the Bay Area.[13] The kinds of dispossession experienced by black renters in the Fillmore neighborhood, for example; the disparity between the allocation of bond funds for white and black schools; and the inequality of recreational space between much of the city and Chinatown did not occur despite the city's liberalism but because of it.

Investigating this history can shed new light on the older question of who rules in and over cities, and how. That question was posed most forcefully by political theorist Robert H. Dahl in his 1961 classic, *Who Governs?* Dahl was concerned with how the "great inequalities in the conditions of different citizens" interacted with the "creed" of liberal democracy. How, that is, political and wealth inequality related to "the most widely distributed political resource—the right to vote." Dahl rightly anticipated the increased importance of "technicians, planners, [and] professional administrators" in shaping the postwar "politics and policies of city governments."[14] Nevertheless, he missed a tension that had been apparent well before the 1950s and was independent of whether mayors, aldermen, or bureaucrats were administering urban policies: as one observer noted nearly one hundred years ago, "The American theory of government is that any person elected to public office is fully competent to perform the duties of that office. As a matter of fact, the average municipal official is not a match for the skilled bond buyer."[15]

Our understanding of urban governance has not adequately taken account of the power asymmetries between elected and appointed experts, on the one hand, and the buyers, peddlers, raters, and holders of debt, on the other. This power imbalance is a specific, if overlooked, slice of the much larger tension between the nation's belief in democratic institutions expressed through the vote, and the acknowledgment that governing power has favored elites. Although Marxists have grappled with explanations for the persistence of elite power, they have been content to ascribe the subversion of democratic governance to the "needs of capital."[16] While theorists of urban pluralism were right to push back on simple tales of elites dictating electoral politics, the pluralist story of fragmented and decentralized power does not hold when we try to understand how bonds were screened before they appeared before the public, or, indeed, whether bond issues came before voters at all.[17] In focusing on how urban publics engage with their voting power and the relationship of voting to bond referenda, I hope to update Dahl's take on the relationship between democracy and inequality and between democracy and capitalism.

Urban historian Michael B. Katz implored scholars to search for an alternative to "public failure as the master narrative of urban history." Over the past twenty years or so, histories of postwar urban America have been largely structured around two poles, with scholars tracing the "rise" and "fall" of different locales. It was almost as if any given city were exchangeable with another within a general story of how federal policy contributed to the collapse and failure of Chicago, Detroit, or Oakland. Writers on the political left and right, Katz maintained, effectively agreed on this basic story. And because urban historians "stopped looking for a counter-narrative," their histories might prove a "gift" to the political right. Showing that public policies fueled the growth of the ghetto or the racial wealth gap between cities and suburbs could abet "the campaign to reduce the size and influence of government and privatize public functions."[18] The project of austerity and privatization has proven successful in part because the master narrative of urban history makes it difficult to demand the use of federal financial power to circumvent the local inflections of racism.

My objective is not to let the federal government or public policy makers off the hook. Nor is it to traffic in nostalgic renderings of midcentury federal policy as some idealized moment merely blemished by "unfortunate" trade-offs with racist Southern Democrats. Rather, this book takes an important step toward a counternarrative by showing that the breakdown of public housing does not make sense without exploring bondholder guarantees; the revenue problems of major American cities do not make sense without considering escalating fixed expenditures for debt-service payments; and the prioritization of some infrastructural projects and the steady decline of others is not legible without discussing the evaluative rubrics of bond rating agencies. So many of the social, fiscal, and political ills of American cities can be traced, in a fundamental way, to structural dependence on the municipal bond market. And as we shall see, when urban historians underscore the failure of the federal government, they chime with stories told by bond financiers and credit analysts threatened by federal power. Federal failure is also the bankers' story.

It is customary to encounter polemics of how debt burdens future generations. It is less common to think about how the past is leveraged to sell investors on the present and future potential of a borrower. Because the quantitative metrics used to evaluate local governments were reflections of past borrowing decisions (for instance, total bonded debt), selling investors on future guaranteed revenue streams was predicated on telling pared-down histories. To see bond financiers and credit analysts as amateur historians is to explore how some cities are deemed exceptional and others suspect. More to the point, these renderings could expand or constrict the market for borrowers. A 1936 report from the Anglo California National Bank (ACNB) of San Francisco illustrates that profound power.[19]

Investment analysts working for the ACNB treated San Francisco's fiscal conservatism as a transcendent quality. It was what allowed the city to survive the "acid test" of the Great Depression. But behind this evaluation was an older history of debt expansion and severe contraction. During the first half of the nineteenth century, state governments issued bonds in aid of canals and railroads. The panic of 1837 and bond defaults of the 1840s precipitated the passage of strict limits on state indebtedness. Throughout the remainder of the nineteenth century, local governments took the lead in financing infrastructure. The overall share of state government debt fell from 86 percent in 1838 to 10 percent in 1890. During this period, the local share of government debt rose from 12.5 to 40 percent.[20] During the 1850s, San Francisco officials borrowed at remarkably high interest rates; debt-service payments soon occupied a large chunk of expenditures. Infrastructural investment at costly rates weighed heavily on the emerging political regime. In response to the economic depression of the 1870s, the San Francisco Board of Supervisors instituted a dollar limit tax rate through dramatic cuts in expenditures for streets, schools, and sewers, on the one hand, and a steadfast refusal to contract new debt, on the other. These decisions were part and parcel of a pay-as-you-go approach to municipal finance. The piecemeal construction of physical infrastructure was funded out of current real and personal property tax revenue.[21] During the late nineteenth century the pay-as-you-go model was "adhered to almost universally" in San Francisco and beyond.[22]

The older model could not—indeed, was not meant to—keep up with new patterns of residential settlement. Not only did residents living in newer sections of San Francisco experience higher tax burdens during the 1890s, but the pay-as-you-go model also failed to deliver essential water, sewage, and fire services, as well as educational facilities, to them. Composed of business and neighborhood improvement groups, "self-conscious progressive reformers" argued that by enacting cuts in municipal departmental expenses and higher assessments on public corporations, the city could deliver these infrastructural improvements through municipal debt yet keep the general property tax rate low.[23] By contrast, the *San Francisco Chronicle* staunchly opposed getting "the bond mill running."[24] Municipal debt was a menace, the paper avowed, and progressivism promised to "make it fatally easy for the city to run into debt."[25] Long before municipal debt was serviced through regressive taxes and before homeownership was made more widely available, local governments taxed affluent property holders to retire debt. Between 1860 and 1905, close to 84 percent of San Francisco's revenues were derived from real and personal taxation.[26] As "a distinct menace," the *Chronicle* argued that an expansion of municipal debt would drive "the property-holder out of existence."[27]

That the ACNB detailed the credit profile of San Francisco indicated that the progressives had won, though it would take some time to assess the nature of the prize. Between 1897 and 1936, the city's total bonded debt increased from $180,000 to more than $167 million.[28] Progressive reformers ushered in a conceptual shift whereby municipal bonds were seen not as conduits of extravagance but as tools of progress. Progressives sought to break local monopoly control over water, electricity, and transportation by leveraging financial markets to borrow from investors. In some instances, municipal debt helped cities achieve ownership of public utilities. The Charter of 1898 established limits on debt-service payments, interest rate ceilings, and ratios between indebtedness and the assessed valuation of property. Through charter reform, San Francisco established enough administrative safeguards to keep the "bond mill" from rotating at an ever-accelerating pace. Equally consequential, the charter upheld the two-thirds threshold required for voters to approve certain kinds of municipal bonds.[29] The result was that a minority of voters in general, and antidebt advocates in particular, could maintain "an effective veto power," as historian Philip J. Ethington has observed.[30] The two-thirds rule had important consequences for how the city would develop, the strategies employed to get around that threshold, and the confidence of bondholders in investing in San Francisco.

When bond buyers agreed to lend their capital for up to thirty years through the purchase of San Francisco debt, they made a bet that the city's future was safe, stable, and supportive of the economic growth essential to delivering principal and interest payments. By the mid-1930s, the ACNB asserted that San Francisco stood at "the center of an extensive metropolitan area backed by a rural region as large as the New England group of states." The Bay Area was responsible for a substantial portion of California's total crop value, boasted a favorable climate conducive to agricultural production, and generated over half of California's gold, cement, oil, and natural gas. San Francisco's stature within a wider metropolitan economy was the legacy of a much older pattern of economic development.

San Francisco sits at the northern tip of a peninsula between the San Francisco Bay and the Pacific Ocean. The proximity to water allowed the city to assume other economic roles not long after the Gold Rush. Steamers and clipper ships from New York, Panama, and Australia debarked at newly constructed docks where longshoremen carried merchandise to the city's warehouses. Merchants used San Francisco's harbor and inland waterways to "dominate," in one historian's words, "the all-important commerce with California's interior." By the end of the 1860s the city's merchants exported grain to Liverpool and countries in the Pacific.[31] Merchants also helped move manufactured goods from the East Coast to miners working not too far from San Francisco.[32] Manufacturers and the workers they employed helped transform the city's landscape. By 1860, industrialists had built iron and brass foundries, machine shops, boiler and gas works, flour- and sawmills, meat packing plants, and distilleries and breweries.[33] With merchant activity came financiers who set up shop between Montgomery and Market streets.[34] In short order, San Francisco joined Boston, New York, and Philadelphia as the only American cities with discernible financial districts.[35] By 1936, the ACNB could appropriately assert that this inheritance made San Francisco "the financial center of the West," home to some of the nation's largest banks, the Twelfth District Federal Reserve Bank, and one of the more "active regional stock exchanges" in the country.

The ACNB observed that visiting bankers "return[ed] almost invariably sold on San Francisco municipal securities" but lacked "the data necessary to convince their skeptical associates." However, there was something else to the Bank's report on San Francisco debt at a time when the bond market was relatively prostrate. Local bankers and credit analysts were helping to transform the city's image as one wrecked by unprecedented labor power. As early as 1919—not coincidentally, as American workers went on strike around the country—one municipal bond theorist explained to bankers, "There is good reason for not buying the bonds of a city cursed with frequent strikes."[36] The failure of bond referenda in San Francisco during the 1930s signaled a clash between business groups who opposed the issuance of debt to acquire public utilities, on one side, and an empowered labor movement hoping to use municipal debt for full employment, on the other.[37] During the General Strike of 1934, San Francisco was effectively shut down for four days; the police attacked striking longshoremen, killing some and badly wounding others. The labor militancy of maritime and hotel workers continued well into the 1930s. Labor agitation throughout the 1930s threatened San Francisco's borrowing reputation, which, in turn, undermined an emergent vision of shared prosperity through economic growth. In response, "San Francisco's financial elite," notes historian William Issel, helped broker a rapprochement between labor and capital. In a way, the absence of explicit commentary on this recent history in the ACNB's report signaled peace. At the very least, the report hinted at a public relations campaign to sell the city to investors through the suffocation of some details and the amplification of others.

If by 1936 San Francisco's economy was diversified, its population was not. The ACNB proclaimed that the city was "predominantly native white with less than 7% of other races." In the bankers' minds, white settlers became natives; nonwhites born in San Francisco were indefinitely foreign. ACNB bankers perhaps took comfort in the stabilizing influence of the "right" kind of fiscally conservative white people who could discipline white ecological refugees arriving from the Dust Bowl region seeking relief. But there is another way to look at the Bank's brief discussion of the city's demographics. We tend to imagine cities as big, durable, self-contained entities. But urban populations are transitory. And the dynamism of a city could prove a particular challenge for the holder of a long-term debt obligation. Of great concern to bond financiers and bond raters throughout the mid-twentieth century was whether a city experienced population loss, and, if so, *which* kinds of people left the city and *who* remained. Population growth and decline became ways of talking about race and class; bankers leaped from population declines, plateaus, and upticks to observations about revenues and expenditures; proper ratios between the two were folded into determinations of creditworthiness, lending conditions, and interest charges. Demographics were facts of life, but they could also function as metonyms, a way of avoiding yet signaling the racial and class character of a city. During the 1930s, then,

San Francisco scored well. But in a society in which African Americans were discriminated against and blackness was treated as a penalty, how would San Francisco, among other destinations of the Great Migration, fare in the bond buyers' calculus over the postwar period?

In this book the usual cast of characters familiar to urban historians—unions, local chambers of commerce, real estate moguls, newspaper editorial boards—play a supporting role. Instead, municipal technocrats and creditors, along with people who experienced the downstream effects of debt, are the main actors. Here, city controllers and accountants, bondholders and lenders, bond financiers and the peddlers of debt, and credit analysts and bond raters loom large. Of all these groups, only municipal finance officers are rooted in their home city. The rest—the analysts, lenders, and bankers—can be located anywhere.

Out of the political tremors of the 1930s emerged the modernization of the municipal bond market, and the respective roles of bankers and municipal technocrats in tapping the savings of investors to meet the infrastructural needs of borrowers. By and large, New Deal banking reforms reconfigured finance capitalism.[38] Until the mid-1970s, however, the municipal bond market was hardly regulated. Borrowers and financial institutions did not face the same level of oversight as their counterparts within the corporate securities market.[39] Even after the uptick in "sharp and fraudulent" banking practices, some of which led to "massive investor losses," the Municipal Securities Rulemaking Board, established in 1975, was little more than a paper tiger.[40] Indeed, New Deal reforms are equally notable for what they did not do. Through the Banking Act of 1933 (Glass-Steagall), commercial banks were still able to buy and resell US Treasury obligations and the general obligation bonds of state and local governments.[41] By 1940, nearly 70 percent of commercial bank investments were in US government obligations. That year, commercial banks owned 38.6 percent of all US government debt, as well as $3.6 billion in state and local government bonds, which "exceeded bank owned private sector bonds for the first time."[42] The famed Glass-Steagall Act, which separated investment from commercial banking, allowed both commercial and investment banks to continue to serve as lender to the American state. The act allowed for the continued distribution of financial power among the private sector; public infrastructure and social services would continue to be financed along a public-private axis.[43]

A most crucial segment were the bond financiers who underwrote and invested in municipal debt. Who were they? Why did bankers spend their days buying, selling, investing, and socializing? Business historians and practitioners of the "new" history of capitalism have often answered these kinds of questions by studying entrepreneurs or firms. However, the policing of corporate archives and the waves of mergers and acquisitions over the twentieth century have meant that even these histories have relied too heavily on the neat, performative annual reports of firms. The upshot is a picture of a rational economic actor in sole pursuit of capital disembodied from the cultural, social, and political practices of the firm's employees. Bond financiers as a class were shaped through participation in syndicates, clubs, and other trade organizations; through a shared culture and technical knowledge; and through a vigorous attempt to maintain their role as critical intermediaries.

Although they linked borrowers to lenders, in effect, firms like Moody's Investors Service, and the Bond Buyer, among other sellers of financial information, helped augment creditor power. They did the work of monitoring quantitative changes in debt and the political experiments that might impinge on creditor claims. Whereas credit rating agencies specialized in turning infinite differences into a standardized letter grade, and the Bond Buyer played the part of daily surveillance, both segments helped bondholders secure information on dynamic entities: cities. Through their ratings and daily catalogs, these firms not only offered a record of past borrowing behaviors but also monitored the current operations and future prospects of a city.

Bond downgrades were only the most dramatic instance of an everyday power relationship. In this book, we meet the individual rating analysts who did the work of evaluating the credit profile of borrowers. This is largely possible because, surprisingly, for much of the twentieth century, just a handful of people did the work of rating the bonds of thousands of municipal borrowers. "The staff at Moody's did not exceed four people at any time between 1920 and 1935, and available information was skimpy," explained one student of municipal debt.[44] Very little had changed by the late 1960s. Though supported by clerks and "a varying number of trainees," Standard & Poor's municipal bond department had a staff of just nine analysts. At Moody's, the "scrutiny and detailed evaluation" fell on the shoulders of twelve full-time analysts.[45] These were the people on whom American cities relied to deliver on the infrastructural promises of urban life.

By disaggregating the creditor class, we can explore shifting relations among its segments, from the financiers who viewed bond ratings with skepticism to the investment bankers who defended their turf against the encroachment of commercial bankers seeking to underwrite revenue bonds. But despite these internal squabbles, collective bondholder power and bondholder supremacy nevertheless emerged. Bond financiers, bond attorneys, and credit appraisers and raters, along with trade outlets such as the *Daily Bond Buyer* were part of a municipal fraternity that safeguarded and advanced the interests of bondholders.

It is telling that when bond buyers perused industry trade outlets or purchased the dry reports of bond rating agencies, they focused heavily on San Francisco's debt-collecting apparatus and the powers of the controller's office. Finance officers (controllers, accountants, and the like) were most central to maintaining investor confidence and managing distributionary conflicts over public spending. City finance officers were fueled by the idea that only those trained to the level of expertise, who possessed a body of technical knowledge about the ins and outs of debt finance, should make direct spending decisions. As appointees, they used their access to state power to administer "sound" debt policy. Although the practice of turning to the municipal bond market was well established by 1945, there was nothing intuitive about borrowing. Nor was the soundness of debt policy politically neutral. Through organizations such as the Municipal Finance Officers' Association of the United States and Canada (MFOA), San Francisco technocrats learned from credit rating analysts, bankers, and bond attorneys how to insulate debt from various "pressure groups." They learned how to differentiate city debt from the bonds of other borrowers. They heard how accommodating the needs of lenders would help lower borrowing costs. In the end, city technocrats who were members of MFOA viewed bankers and credit rating analysts as their accomplices.

Individual financiers who possessed the technical know-how became nested in urban government. Serving on advisory boards, committees, and councils at the local level, and appointed to governing bodies that helped spearhead urban renewal, public housing, and rapid transit projects, bond financiers not only screened what voters saw at the ballot; they also steered public spending decisions toward projects that expanded the finance, insurance, and real estate sectors and abetted white people's control of urban life.

Financiers could not maintain this influence without something of a cross-class compromise managed by city finance officers. Along with the reconstruction of the municipal bond market, New Deal reforms conditioned the "rights consciousness" of white Americans in new ways.[46] During the early twentieth century, as one historian has observed, there was little consensus "that urban services were a right and that they should be financed through a redistributive system." The Great Depression pushed working-class whites towards a "tentative acceptance of an activist government" that protected people like themselves.[47] At the same time, postwar middle-class whites asserted their right to housing, public schools, streets, and arts and entertainment, which became part of an expansive package of white rights. The racial welfare state, of which infrastructure and social services were a crucial part, became acceptable only insofar as the allocation of borrowed funds helped secure white rights while keeping taxes low. In addition to managing the external impressions of San Francisco's credit reputation, then, city finance officers massaged the battles over public spending. It was a task made more difficult by rising black political power, tax revolts, and other challenges to the inequality of debt.

The postwar period cannot be treated as an undifferentiated moment. Infrastructural needs remained persistent, but the years between 1945 and 1965 offered borrowing conditions dramatically different from those that came after.

When the federal government made income on its own debt obligations taxable in 1941, it provided a virtual monopoly on tax exemption to state and local governments. Low interest rates lured borrowers to the municipal bond market. In the spring of 1946, for instance, more than a few cities were able to borrow a chunk of funds maturing in twenty years at less than 1 percent.[48] Low-cost borrowing was much needed. Serving as an administrative headquarters for the army and navy and a major shipbuilding and repair center, San Francisco saw war production cause "a mass in-migration which is without duplicate since the days of gold," explained one of the city's largest landlords.[49] The influx of people taxed city streets, roads, and playgrounds, some of which had not been upgraded in years. The infrastructural backlog was also due to the postponement of borrowing for nonwar purposes. Whereas prewar annual state and local government capital outlays registered at $2.5 billion, that number fell to $700 million in 1944.[50]

The infrastructural pressures on San Francisco and other cities coincided with the attempt by investors to shield their capital from federal taxation. In 1951, for example, the federal marginal tax rate on individual incomes of $50,000, $100,000, and $1 million was roughly 54, 67, and 87 percent, respectively.[51] The pressure to improve deteriorating infrastructure and the search for tax shelters powered the reconfiguration of the built environment. The municipal bond market had seen 3,300 new issues of long-term bonds totaling $1.2 billion in 1946. Some twenty years later, state and local governments nearly doubled the number of bond issues, raising about $11.1 billion. During those same years, short-term debt financing rose from 567 new issues totaling $741 million to a little more than 1,900 issues amounting to more than $6.5 billion. All told, state and local indebtedness had risen from $16.5 billion in 1945 to $99 billion by July 1965.[52]

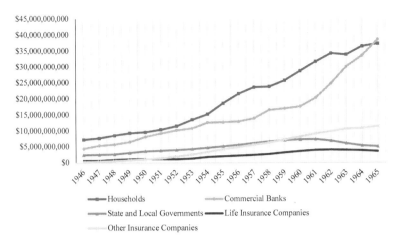

FIGURE 0.1 Major holders of state and local government debt, 1946–1965. Originally treated as a residual category, "households" included individuals and nonprofits serving individuals. "Other Insurance Companies" included fire and casualty insurance and the "insurance activities of fraternal orders."

Source: Joint Economic Committee, Subcommittee on Economic Progress, "State and Local Public Facility Needs and Financing: Volume II," 89th Cong., 2nd sess., December 1966, 40.

One banker reflected on how the needs of borrowers and investors transformed the bond business. Municipal bonds were "an underdeveloped product in an underdeveloped market" during the late 1940s. Recognizing the premium of tax exemption and the allure of government guarantees, "Investment banking firms with small bond departments expanded and those with none started departments." Commercial banks entered in full force to develop an expansive white-collar workforce.[53] They also responded to high tax rates on investment income by stepping up their purchase of municipal debt. Sometimes they held onto these bonds. Other times they resold bonds to wealthy individuals and institutional investors (figure 0.1).

These numbers fail to capture a national tragedy. During a moment of historically low interest rates, black neighborhoods were continuously deemed unworthy of debt. The twenty-year moment when money was cheap is marked by what I call the infrastructural investment in whiteness. What was new was not the state's investment in whiteness, per se, but its class inflections. During the late nineteenth century, local governments invested in public infrastructure, but largely for white elites through a system of privatized development.[54] The New Deal amplified the state's investment through an *intraracial* cross-class compact.

By 1948, state and local government capital outlays reached $3.7 billion, much of it evident through construction expenditures for everything from highways to streets, schools to hospitals, sewage treatment to water systems, electric utilities to transportation, parks to urban renewal.[55] The emphasis on construction created new political space for organized labor.

While the debt story of organized labor in the 1930s is one in which empowered unions turned out large numbers of voters to secure passage of or torpedo a bond measure, after the war labor was folded into a progrowth coalition. Labor was on board with the model of growth predicated on residential and commercial redevelopment.[56] And for close to twenty-five years that is where labor remained, voting on bond measures that kept the white working class—and, more precisely, members of segregated building trades—employed in the construction of innumerable capital improvement projects. White workers built the infrastructure on which the white middle class depended for their enjoyment of San Francisco. The expansion of a segregated pie for white workers and white consumers required borrowing from wealthy white investors who, in turn, secured tax-exempt interest income. Put simply, the decision by the federal government to forgo tax revenue from bondholders (by allowing tax exemption) in turn allowed cities to deliver on their promises to white middle-class and working-class Americans. Bond financing effectively racialized both the distribution of income and the resources directed toward cities and select neighborhoods. At the same time, this racial compact was predicated on the denial of such facilities and services to San Francisco's black and brown residents, on their dispossession and displacement, on their exclusion from building trades, on their unequal access to the arts, and on rerouting their tax dollars to service debt.

Immediately following the war, "just about all of the advantage of tax exemption was being retained by state and local government borrowers." Still, there were early signs of a shift in the balance of power. Between 1946 and 1957, interest rates rose from 1 to 3½ percent on long-term, highly rated issues. The yield on municipal debt was relatively small, but the uptick during these years was greater than on corporate debt.[57] If marginal differences made for accumulation, they also made for disruption. Rising interest rates might force city technocrats to postpone bond offerings, delaying much-needed infrastructure projects for a restless public. By 1964, president Lyndon B. Johnson responded to the blatant contradiction between affluence and poverty, but the infrastructural promise of the Great Society hardly had a chance to succeed. If there was ever an inflection point, the credit crunch of 1966 was it.

As the low-interest-rate regime came to an end and the urban fiscal crisis intensified, the antagonism between governments and lenders was laid bare. Across the nation, and across a variety of municipal borrowers, the cost to borrow upended infrastructure projects. Some were forced to cancel bond offerings. Others failed to receive bids altogether. When large government units pared down long-term borrowings by nearly $1.4 billion in 1966, close to 80 percent of the reductions were "attributed to high interest rates."[58] As bondholders collected higher tax-exempt interest payments, cities, agencies, authorities, and districts were forced to devote larger chunks of their budgets to fixed debt-service payments, revenue that might have otherwise gone toward schools and public-housing projects. It was in the crucible of high interest rates and dependence on lenders that the deterioration of urban infrastructure accelerated.

Bond rating analysts and financiers had long worked to constrain the welfare state. From the late 1960s onward, however, they did so much more heavy-handedly. With the urban fiscal crisis, major American cities became questionable investments. White labor criticized regressive taxation and disrupted services through strikes. Looking from afar, lenders came to see the bloc that had proven so essential to floating new bond issues as partially responsible for urban instability. Moreover, black folks and residents of Chinese descent staged a revolt of sorts, calling for greater expenditures for their communities and a redistribution of the burdens of debt. Leading financiers and analysts responded by arguing that an unsustainable imbalance between revenues and expenditures, not to mention the radical demands of "labor and minorities," was to blame for the crisis.

The September 1966 riots that began in southeast San Francisco soon placed the city between a rock and a hard place. The urban crisis raised the cost to borrow. One way to lower it was by selling bonds. But the attempt to sell the public on debt collided with a property tax revolt against select bond measures. Despite their broad range of support from constituencies as diverse as merchants, athletes, labor unions, and civic groups, bonds for playgrounds and street lighting failed. For those closest to the bond drive, racism and the two-thirds voter threshold that protected the rights of property were too much to overcome. Later faced with the dilemma of supporting elementary school bonds or busing black children to white schools, San Franciscans voted against taking on debt. Even a bond measure for public schools, which would have invested funds in schools throughout the city, was considered a "black issue" and was rejected. In ways that ultimately unlocked greater profits for underwriting banks, the city's answer to bond failure was to rely ever more on debt that voters had not approved.

Although differentiation among cities was an old game, the stakes heightened as New York City's extravagant debt woes morphed into national fears of a fiscal contagion during the 1970s. Whereas San Francisco sought to become the Wall Street of the West in the 1950s, the existential goal was to now show that San Francisco was unlike New York. That meant striking down "profligate" spending and imposing cuts. California's Proposition 13 of 1978 accelerated the program of structural adjustment, which, paradoxically, meant adjusting the long-term obligations to local residents while maintaining long-term commitments to bondholders. Populist-conservatives and others contributed to draconian spending cuts, sell-offs, infrastructural scale-backs, and higher public transportation fares, water rates, and recreational user fees. But ultimately it was the outlook of creditors, their access to capital, and the structural dependence of local governments on their services that gave their attack on the racial welfare state greater force.[59]

By the 1980s, a hostile federal posture and the emergence of a new political economy pinched cities further. The Reagan administration effectively told cities they were on their own. This pushed San Francisco and other municipal borrowers further into the lion's den. The cost to borrow to upgrade streets battered by inclement weather, or to fix underfunded public schools, was somewhere between 10 and 14 percent. Indeed, the choice for cities around the country had become a simple, if dire one: cancel bond offerings, borrow at sky-high rates, or issue debt instruments that offered greater guarantees to lenders. When Moody's downgraded San Francisco bonds in the spring of 1980, it revealed how even this ostensibly exceptional city, insulated as it had been from deindustrialization and white flight, and buttressed by a relatively strong tax base, could be penalized, not for missing quantitative targets but due to a supposed climate of uncertain voter support. It wasn't that too much democracy was a bad thing, but the uncertainty of democracy itself was brought to bear on the city's credit standing. But the relative amount and outcomes of democracy were beside the point. In what was perhaps the clearest sign of bondholder power, few people questioned why Moody's could penalize urban publics in the first place.

Calling this situation "hegemony" overstates the case; "bondholder supremacy" is more appropriate. But to see how supremacy emerged from innumerable bondholder losses during the 1930s, to understand the paradox of debt as remedying racial and spatial inequality in ways that exacerbates the inequality of wealth and power, we must engage the critical and understudied world of municipal debt. It is the making of that world to which we now turn.

PART I
Rule of Experts

1. Management

Municipal finance officers assumed the unenviable task of managing the fallout from the Great Depression. By any measure, the early 1930s were brutal. Gross national product slumped, the durable goods industry saw a sharp downturn, and iron and steel production fell by 60 percent from precrash levels. Foreclosures on defaulted home mortgages reached epic proportions—250,000 in 1932 alone. By 1933, nearly thirteen million workers were unemployed.[1] To make matters worse, the Great Depression delivered a significant blow to the municipal bond market, which had been a key means by which cities delivered on the infrastructural promises of progressivism. In the early twentieth century, political candidates had run on a platform of spending "vast sums for drainage, for streets, for the protection of life and property, for schools, for museums, for galleries, for parks."[2] With bonds treated as a tool of civic progress and issued in aid of real estate speculation and overdevelopment, "every ten years brought practically a doubling" in municipal debt between 1903 and 1932.[3] Suddenly, the virtual collapse of the banking system disrupted the ability of cities to improve water and sewage systems, schools, and roads. Highly rated municipal bonds fell into default, bond offerings were canceled, and bond sales were delayed.[4]

Borrowing difficulties were compounded by questions over how to distribute the shrinking pie of municipal resources. Large taxpayers went on strike; real estate interests and other owners of real property, many of whom had convinced local governments to essentially borrow on their behalf during the 1920s, no longer thought it fair to pay taxes.[5] Tax delinquencies depleted the pot of funds from which bondholders were paid, which, in turn increased the likelihood of default. Compared to other classes of debt, the percentage of municipal bonds in default was relatively low: by 1932, 2 percent of the $18.2 billion in outstanding municipal debt was in default, compared to 19 percent of the $7.5 billion in foreign bonds. Nevertheless, when a municipal government defaulted, its finance officers were forced to negotiate with attorneys working on behalf of bondholders. There was "no lack of organization among creditors.

Approximately two hundred bondholders' protective committees were functioning in 1935."[6]

Fiscal difficulties, bondholder pressure, and the absence of intergovernmental support effectively meant that municipal finance officers had to choose between fulfilling their obligations to creditors, on the one hand, and maintaining educational activities and local health, fire, and police services, as well as extending relief to ordinary Americans, on the other hand. Each option came with severe consequences: payments to bondholders meant a curtailment of government services, and directing funds away from bondholders toward city services would damage the borrowing reputation of the defaulting city.[7] But for many bankers, this was not a choice at all. One journalist rightly noted that as major bondholders, bankers had "a stake in the entire field of public credit." Many of the nation's leading bankers, themselves seeking to stay afloat, thus concluded that bondholders must be paid and unbalanced budgets met by "paring expensive expenditures."[8]

City reliance on the private bond market had proven extraordinarily disruptive, and whatever the decision, the choice between retrenchment and incurring the wrath of bondholders threatened the long-term viability of cities themselves. Yet during capitalism's greatest crisis, New Deal banking reforms rekindled this public-private partnership and provided a number of lifelines that would shape the arc of postwar urban governance and the reconfiguration of the built environment.

The Glass-Steagall Act of 1933 still let commercial banks behave like investment banks, but only when investing in, and buying and reselling, certain classes of government debt. The Home Owners' Loan Corporation not only aided the revival of the housing market but also, through loans, helped to remake the credit standing of municipal governments dealing with unpaid taxes.[9] The Reconstruction Finance Corporation lubricated the municipal bond market by helping defaulted borrowers refinance older debts and, in some cases, selling debt to banks that might benefit from tax-exempt interest income in the short run and profit from resale in the future. Finally, the Public Works Administration (PWA) pushed the progressive use of debt in Keynesian directions. Beginning in 1933, the PWA stimulated employment and economic development through large-scale infrastructure projects and encouraged a new form of "state-building" through the creation of public authorities with the power to issue debt.[10]

Through the Municipal Finance Officers' Association of the United States and Canada (MFOA), municipal technocrats underwent something of a modernization process. Founded in 1906, after a few name changes, the Chicago-based organization emerged as MFOA in 1932. By January of the following year, executive director Carl H. Chatters claimed a sizable membership of controllers, accountants, and other public finance officers from twenty-five to thirty states and nearly two hundred cities.[11] In addition to the quarterly publication of *Municipal Finance*, MFOA sponsored conferences throughout the United States and Canada. Through the organization, those in command of the public purse could read extensive histories of municipal bond defaults.[12] They could discover alternative sources of municipal revenue.[13] When the organization did not propose legislation, or its members were not before Congress offering expert testimony, MFOA helped to standardize the accounting and management policies of local governments. In 1938, for instance, MFOA published a manual describing San Francisco's finance and accounting procedures. The City by the Bay was selected "because its finance and accounting procedures are clean cut, complete, and effective; because lines of authority are clearly defined; and lastly because it is one of the few public bodies which has already reduced departmental instructions to written form." Through a close collaboration with controller Harold J. Boyd, his chief assistant controller Harry D. Ross, and senior accountant Raymond J. Rock, MFOA highlighted a particularly strong model for other cities.[14] San Francisco finance officers learned from their colleagues around the country and contributed to the development of the profession by explaining the intricacies of borrowing, accounting, and city management.[15]

In no small part, technocratic knowledge was also shaped by the advice of creditors. One of the social consequences of permitting financiers to underwrite the infrastructural provisions of the state was that bankers, credit analysts, and bond attorneys explained debt administration, as well as the likes, wants, and demands of lenders. They did so as contributors to MFOA publications and as invited guests to its national conferences. It was not uncommon for members of MFOA to draw on reports penned by the credit reporting agency Dun & Bradstreet. A. M. Hillhouse, a leading voice in the modernization project, welcomed "a closer relationship . . . between debt administrators and reliable investment banking firms." The "counsel of dealers," as well as the "advice of fiscal agents in New York, or some other center, should also be sought," he said.[16] Indeed, the idea of a public-private partnership does not begin to capture the modernization of municipal debt; the citation practices and revolving door of personnel make it hard to figure out where "the public" ended and where "the private" started. The coronation of bankers and credit analysts as experts, and the reliance of city technocrats on their advice, furthered the centrality of creditors to the remaking of the built environment.

Modernization, Reconversion

There were important local inflections of debt modernization. The San Francisco Charter of 1932 modernized management of the purse, providing the controller's office with "sweeping powers over all public agencies." So long as the controller held the support of four of the eleven members of the Board of Supervisors, he could not be removed. This meant that controllers did "not serve at the pleasure of the mayor and they are not reachable by the ballot; in reality, they have life tenure."[17] From an administrative standpoint, the job was meticulous. It fell to the controller to manage records of all city financial transactions. His task was to determine the cost of city infrastructure and to develop and deploy systems to manage the collection and disbursement of money. The charter also gave the controller "wide power to control the execution of the budget." But no one person could possibly manage the transactions, departmental accounts, and revenue estimates of such a dynamic entity. The office had multiple divisions and a growing technocratic workforce that handled revenue flows and payrolls, managed bond interest and redemption payments, audited the transactions of the city's utility projects, and advised on legal matters. None of this technical work would have proceeded without the secretarial unit that functioned "as a central stenographic pool for the entire Controller's office."[18]

Through bondholder protective committees and reporting on the latest default and fiscal troubles of borrowers, creditors had demonstrated that missing a principal or interest payment would not soon be forgotten. Within the controller's office, technocrats in the Division of Accounts and Statistics developed a dry system of accounting to make sure this did not happen. Staying in the good graces of bondholders meant sticking to a manual, double-entry system of crediting and debiting payments, closing accrual accounts at the end of the fiscal year and beginning anew on July 1. The controller's office kept card records "in visible index (multiple-ring) binders," separating debt incurred directly by the city from that of so-called public service enterprises (a general name for a group of enterprises—the Hetch Hetchy water system, Municipal Railway, airport—that provided a utility or service to the public and the city). Along with the 10⅜" × 4⅝" cards were paper schedules, "deposit slips for money received from the sale of bonds," and other technical ephemera.[19] One can imagine an infinite pile of paperwork.

With diminished revenues, tax delinquency, and calls for relief expenditures, the Depression accelerated the learning curve of public finance. "Whatever our titles may be, auditor, controller, commissioner of finance," controller Harold J. Boyd contended, finance officers had to be more than "mere keepers of the books." By working with "warm hearts but cool heads," they could check aspiring politicians and help their city finance the demands for public health, education, and recreation.[20] Through MFOA, Frederick L. Bird, director of municipal service with Dun & Bradstreet, exposed municipal technocrats to "the science of municipal administration." According to Bird, lenders had to be confident that a city was governed by exacting standards; its protocols for managing statistics, budgets, audits, and statutes must be of the highest caliber.[21] Bird spoke of ratios, proportions, and trends. What was the "size" of debt-service charges? What was the annual rate of debt reduction? What was the "probable trend of taxable valuation"? What were the "possibilities for developing special sources of revenue"? And what was "the margin for increasing taxes without overburdening the taxpayer"?[22] Cities could modernize debt administration by applying scientific standards. Still, "behind these technical appurtenances of administration are people," Bird declared. It fell to the finance officer to purge those sectors where "boss rule lingers, fat contracts still go to political favorites, hack politicians continue to encumber the payrolls, and the haphazard efforts of novices in administration have not given way to the planning of technicians."[23] The lesson was clear: when it came to municipal debt, nontechnocratic input from too many different sectors was a problem. Corruption and patronage politics had to be purged and democratic decision-making greatly circumscribed.

By the time he took over as San Francisco's controller in 1946, Harry Ross was tasked with managing the science of municipal finance, on one hand, and the social and political implications of shifting demographics, the costs of infrastructural wear and tear, and the expectations cultivated by the New Deal state, on the other. The task, in other words, was to manage the social needs and political pressures that shaped and were shaped by shifting revenues, expenditures, taxes, and debt.[24]

Throughout the late nineteenth and early twentieth centuries, San Francisco's racial axis was defined along white/Asian lines. This changed with the arrival and settlement of African Americans. What was the second Great Migration of African Americans for the urban North was San Francisco's first. If the 1941 edition of *Negro Motorist Green Book* is any indication, San Francisco's hotels, restaurants, barbershops, and service stations for black travelers paled in comparison to those in Chicago and Detroit. Black migrants might grab a drink at Jack's Tavern at 1931 Sutter Street, head to one of three beauty parlors on Sutter or Fillmore Street, and pick up a few items from Riggan's drug store at 2600 Sutter Street, but it took a great migration for a social milieu and a segregated commercial landscape to flourish. In search of wartime employment,

TABLE 1.1 San Francisco's population, 1940–1990

Year	Total population	White population	Black population	Asian* population
1940	634,536	602,701	4,846	22,843
1950	775,357	693,169	43,419	30,238
1960	740,316	604,097	74,771	45,899
1970	715,674	511,186	96,078	70,401
1980	678,974	395,081	86,414	94,526
1990	723,959	387,783	79,039	139,187

*People of Chinese and Japanese descent.

Source: Fredrick M. Wirt, *Power in the City: Decision Making in San Francisco* (Berkeley: University of California Press, 1974), 33; US Bureau of the Census, *United States Census of Population*, 1970–1990 (Washington DC: Government Printing Office, various years).

African Americans arrived from rural Louisiana, Oklahoma, and Texas. The number of African Americans in San Francisco rose dramatically from around 4,800 in 1940 to some 32,000 in 1945. Meanwhile, the proportion of residents of Chinese and Japanese descent rose only slightly, and San Francisco remained overwhelmingly white. By 1945, the city's population reached 827,400, an increase of 30 percent over a five-year period (table 1.1).[25] Black arrivals and Chinatown residents would no longer tolerate being banished to dilapidated housing or having their children confined to underfunded schools and neglected parks. White settlers likewise demanded the infrastructural provisions of a broader social wage. This meant borrowing, which in an overwhelmingly white city had so far meant borrowing for a white public. In the face of demographic transformations, would infrastructural investment continue to occur along segregated lines, or would other neighborhoods and communities be deemed worthy of debt?

San Francisco streets took a pounding from foot and military traffic during the Second World War.[26] Slums and blighted housing had grown worse.[27] Parks and recreational areas were few and far between. The Bay Shore Freeway, cutting through the Father Crowley playground on Seventh and Harrison Streets, would soon make things even worse. Residents of all age groups from the South of Market and Mission neighborhoods would no longer be able to play baseball or handball. Eliminating the park was "enough to get a woman down," explained Miss Car-michael, who lived near Third Street. "Except for Crowley there is absolutely no place for grammar kids to play, and I mean absolutely none. The children major in dodging trucks." Even a playground under the "dark and dreary" Bay Bridge ramp was "better than nothing."[28]

The city's public schools were also in need of major investment. At Lawton Elementary, first graders attended a congested, twenty-foot "draughty corridor" that hardly passed for a classroom. It wasn't just that Franklin School on Eighth Street near Bryant was old; the building was "flanked by truck depots out of which vehicles shuttle[d] all day long," making the end of a school day perilous. The Bret Harte School on Third Street and Key Avenue was over capacity; its second graders moved between "flimsy portable structures" and "a small, steeply-slopped" poor excuse for a playground. First graders elsewhere were forced to "tramp the streets" in what was effectively one of the city's "many walking classrooms." When it rained, students were "herded" into the Sunnydale public-housing project. Some buildings were unsalvageable and others in need of upgrades, ensuring that parents moving to the "fast-growing" Sunset neighborhood would demand new schools. The commitment to an "educational birthright," as the superintendent of schools put it, necessitated that San Francisco borrow for its children.[29]

Ross's predecessor as controller, Harold J. Boyd, had comprehended a straightforward struggle between the propertied few and the impoverished masses. "As the demands from the many" for more increased, "the demand for reduction in governmental costs—from the relatively few who make the major direct contribution to those costs—grows louder," Boyd explained in 1939. Wedged "between these two contending forces," finance officers had to determine how to borrow to furnish infrastructure while keeping taxes low enough to stave off tax revolts.[30] The New Deal state fragmented this class struggle. Calls for tightening the governmental belt were met by a louder demand for expenditures for public works. By the 1940s, and especially after World War II, the "many" had developed a "newfound rights consciousness," one historian wrote.[31] Those rights extended well beyond those of housing, social security, and employment to include the right to recreational space, quality streets, and convenient transportation. Although he was ostensibly tasked with managing revenues and expenditures, the actual challenge before Ross, then, was to manage the manifold requests from newly empowered interest groups. From developers came requests to use municipal debt to subsidize a speculative building boom. Organized labor sought to channel municipal borrowing power into a full-fledged public works program. Liberal reformers demanded a response to the human emergencies of slum housing, while others pushed for the desegregation of public housing, parks, and schools. Confronted with

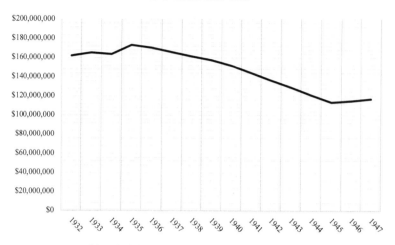

FIGURE 1.1 Total bonded debt of San Francisco, 1932–1947. "Total bonded debt" includes general purpose and so-called public service enterprise debt, with the latter forming an outsized portion of the total debt during these years.

Source: Annual reports of the controller of the City and County of San Francisco (San Francisco: Office of the Controller, 1933–1947).

cascading demands, finance officers were advised to insulate municipal debt from the constant "disconcerting pressures and distractions that are bound to arise," as Frederick L. Bird put it.[32]

Slum clearance, downtown redevelopment, public parks, and schools were costly. More to the point, San Francisco could not borrow for whatever, whenever. Municipal finance officers had to work around the city's debt limit and acceptable tax rates. They relied on local entities to circumvent the first institutional constraint. They turned to different kinds of debt instruments to navigate the second constraint, a sociopolitical one.

The Charter of 1932 had mandated that bonded indebtedness could not exceed 12 percent of assessed valuation of property. With that amount at $1,281,812,029 as of June 30, 1947, finance officers had to amalgamate existing debt with proposed issues to fit near, but not too close, to the limit of $153,817,443.[33]

In a roundabout way, federal and state legislation also allowed cities to execute redevelopment projects in ways that insulated debt ceilings. The federal Housing Act of 1937 had given birth to municipal public-housing authorities, and the Housing Act of 1949 amplified their financial powers. When the San Francisco Housing Authority (SFHA) issued municipal bonds and notes, these debts neither required voter approval nor counted against the city's debt ceiling. At the state level, the California Community Redevelopment Act of 1945 enabled the creation of redevelopment agencies. An "instrumentality" of California that worked "on behalf of and under the policy direction" of the city, the San Francisco Redevelopment Agency (SFRA) was established in 1948.[34] Like the SFHA, the SFRA possessed the power to issue tax-exempt bonds and notes without voter approval. And because the SFRA's indebtedness also did not count against city debt limits, the agency could raze slums while keeping the city below its 12 percent indebtedness threshold.[35]

When it did not rely on other debt-issuing entities, San Francisco wielded its own borrowing power, using two debt instruments. General obligation bonds rested on the sovereign ability of the issuer to levy and collect property taxes to service debt. Because these bonds pushed up the city tax rate, they also mandated voter approval and counted toward the debt ceiling. San Franciscans would have to be convinced that infrastructural projects were worth an uptick in the property tax rate. Municipal finance officers could also issue revenue bonds backed by fares, fees, and user charges. Whereas a two-thirds majority was required to pass a general obligation bond measure, a simple majority was all that was needed to approve a revenue bond measure. The choice between the two debt instruments was very much political, as one might provoke a property tax revolt and the other might mean higher user charges for airports, Municipal Railway service, and the like. Both debt instruments could be used to revamp the built environment, and both could undermine social stability. Moreover, finance officers had to balance between onerous voter thresholds and a higher cost to borrow. As a relative newcomer to the bond scene, revenue bonds often came with higher interest rates.[36] Of the more than $16.2 million in annual "grand total" interest and redemption payments required for fiscal year 1948–49, close to $11 million in payments were tied to revenue or public service enterprise debt.[37]

The first real test to sell San Franciscans on debt came in November 1944. For the Citizens' Committee for Sewer Bonds (CCSB), the case for passing a $12 million sewer bond measure revolved around the trinity of capacity, age, and development. When pouring rains hit the cracked pavement, the streams flowed into sewers much too small to handle runoff storm waters. San Franciscans quickly found themselves ankle-deep in the sewage that swamped their homes and businesses. With the war winding down, the CCSB claimed that sewer construction work would help absorb returning wartime veterans and protect the bay and ocean coastlines from pollution. Replacing main sewer lines, some of which were "worn out after sixty years of service," was also a sound economic investment, as annual maintenance costs were running as high as $350,000. Applying the logic of development to waste management, the CCSB described the extension of a vast network of pipes, chambers, and manholes to accommodate and stimulate the "early development of vacant areas within the city." Sewers, the logic went, made for newly improved neighborhoods, and improved neighborhoods meant increased taxes that would ultimately help the city pay for the sewer system. In the burgeoning Sunset and Richmond neighborhoods, borrowed funds were critical to building an enlarged treatment plant. Debt would also be used to purchase land for a much-needed treatment plant in the North Beach neighborhood. New pipes would run underneath properties in the Haight-Ashbury, Castro, and Mission District neighborhoods. The sewer improvement program would also address the drainage areas just north of Golden Gate Park, and the downtown financial district would see all sewers enlarged. Even if other neighborhoods did not directly benefit from the infrastructural investment, an improved system of "sewers and sewage disposal," the CCSB explained, was "as essential to a city as plumbing is to a home."[38]

The CCSB was important not only for what it explained but also for who did the explaining. It was one of the many ad hoc assemblages that would appear each June and November to persuade the public. Along with chair Jerd F. Sullivan Jr., a vice president with Crocker First National Bank, was Parker Maddux, chair of the CCSB's finance committee and president of the San Francisco Bank.[39] Providing a long list of endorsements from individual power brokers and prominent medical doctors was a discernable tactic. So too was securing the support from such prominent bond financiers as Charles R. Blyth of the investment bank Blyth & Co. If the presence of Sullivan and Maddux was indicative of the nesting of financiers in city government, the list of endorsements betrayed the outlines of a postwar progrowth coalition of real estate groups, organized labor, merchants, neighborhood groups, and civic organizations.

The sewer bonds brought elected officials, city technocrats, taxpayers, and bond financiers together. As the measure explained, the cost of the sewage system was "too great to be paid out of the ordinary annual income and revenue."[40] Issuing debt through the municipal bond market allowed borrowers to secure huge chunks of funds, while spreading out principal and interest payments over an extended period. Instead of tapping the city treasury in one fell swoop, the Board of Supervisors would levy and collect taxes each year until the bonds were paid off. As a fixed expenditure, the job of city finance officers was to align the temporality of tax collections with the annual principal and semiannual interest payments to bondholders.

The November 1944 election was, in a way, an anticlimax of a lengthy process that required technical surveys of the sewage network, evaluations of dollars and cents, hearings before the Board of Supervisors, and certified approvals by numerous city clerks. The bond measure itself was two-dimensional. By the time voters stamped a big "X," or pulled a lever over the word "Yes" or "No," the measure had been seen, truncated, debated, and authorized by a host of elected and appointed officials. The measure passed with overwhelming support.[41] By March 1945, the city's director of public works gave the green light to a storm sewer project just south of Golden Gate Park.[42]

Having sold the public on debt, the city moved to sell the bond to investors. Bond sales occurred on a prearranged weekday date, and at a precise moment that accommodated different time zones. At 10 a.m. on Monday, January 7, 1946, San Francisco would award the bonds to whoever would charge the lowest net interest.[43] At base, a notice of sale was an advertisement; it reflected the borrower's attempt to recruit the savings of investors. But notices of sale also underscore the central concerns of bondholders. Indeed, bondholders, who lost mightily during the 1930s, had to be sure that defaults and delinquencies were unlikely.[44] They did so by sizing up the strength and legitimacy of the administrative functions of the city. Many cities issued general obligation bonds that were backed by the full faith and credit of the issuer to repay; the relative strength of administrative capacities became a way to differentiate among issuers who made similar promises. There was a double meaning behind the specification that the Board of Supervisors "had the power and [was] obligated" to levy taxes on most property "without limitation of rate or amount." The terms were directed as much to the voters who were now on the hook as it was to prospective buyers, who could be confident that they would be paid, come rain, hail, sleet, or snow. That the bond attorneys at Orrick, Dahlquist, Neff, Brown, & Herrington offered their legal stamp of approval was a further sign of legitimacy. One of their own had signed off.

Lenders were also concerned with guarantees, or ways of off-loading their holdings. The ability to collect tax-exempt interest income from municipal bonds at a time of high federal marginal tax rates was the primary attraction. But taxation was political, and politics could undermine this prime feature. The notice of sale thus specified that if, "prior to the delivery of the bonds," the income from debt became subject to federal taxation, the bidder could "be relieved of his obligation under the contract to purchase the bond." Finally, lenders cared about democracy less as an idea and more for how it protected or jeopardized their holdings. An increase in general obligation debt might place undue stress on property taxes and, in the process, impinge on creditor claims. Hence the notice of sale specified that the sewer bonds had been approved by two-thirds of all voters. This threshold, designed to protect property holders from debt voted on by non–property holders, not only amplified the veto power of a minority over a majority but also became a way of protecting creditor claims from extravagant borrowing. In an early sign of their upcoming dominance of the municipal bond market, by charging a remarkably low rate of 0.5557 percent, Bank of America, NT&SA (BOA) won the bonds.[45]

The successful vote for, and sale of, the sewer bond gave the city more confidence in returning to voters with more "progress" bonds. In November 1947, Harry Ross explained how six proposals would affect the city tax rate. On Election Day San Franciscans had before them detailed projections of interest costs, principal payments, and how both would hit their pockets.[46] The high turnout and election results demonstrated overwhelming support. More than 181,000 voters agreed to take on $20 million to rehabilitate the motor coaches, tracks, modern streetcars, garages, and electrical systems of the Municipal Railway system. Close to 174,000 agreed to incur a $2.2 million debt to complete the city's purchase of the Market Street Railway Company. Nearly 181,600 said "yes" to a $22.85 million bond to improve, widen, extend, and enlarge surface streets, embankments, and viaducts. Some 162,800 welcomed the idea of borrowing $5 million to pay for public parking lots and garages, among other street parking facilities. More than 178,000 agreed to take on another $25 million of Hetch Hetchy water bonds to finance a pipeline connecting two portals across the San Joaquin Valley. Finally, some 176,100 voters endorsed a $12 million municipal bond to improve existing parks and playgrounds and to facilitate the acquisition of lands needed for "gymnasiums, swimming pools, [and] athletic grandstands," among other recreational facilities.[47]

It was not uncommon for the registrar of voters to publish arguments in support of or against bond referenda, supplementing dry cost-benefit analyses with appeals from business groups, organized labor, liberal reformers, and others. These arguments serve as an index of power: a way of exploring the relative prestige of some groups and evidence of electoral coalitions. Take, for instance, the June 1948 $2.8 million bond measure for juvenile court and detention facilities. Bond issues pertaining to public education and health gave married white women a voice within a technocratic realm dominated by white men. With more than a few "Mrs." names listed among bond supporters, the New Juvenile Home Campaign Committee argued for replacing the detention home at 150

Millions of Men are Marching Home!

MARCHING HOME to what?

1. Poverty and Leaf-Raking?

OR

2. Permanent, Productive Jobs In Private Industry?

There is only one answer. We have not won the war with weapons unless we can perpetuate the peace with WORK.

Jobs! Jobs! Jobs! Jobs!

The expansion of San Francisco Airport will provide permanent jobs in private industry for thousands of men and women — and a payroll of more than fifty millions of dollars annually!

Vote YES on No. 1 and No. 2

FIGURE 1.2 "Millions of Men Are Marching Home! . . . Vote Yes on No. 1 and No. 2" (November 6, 1945). To vote against airport bonds was to endorse poverty and menial employment for returning World War II veterans.

Source: Folder "Elections.1945," San Francisco Ephemera Collection, San Francisco History Center, San Francisco Public Library.

FIGURE 1.3 "These Are Typical Permanent Airport Jobs in Private Industry . . . Vote Yes on No. 1 and No. 2" (November 6, 1945). Airport bonds promised to create jobs.

Source: Folder "Elections.1945," San Francisco Ephemera Collection, San Francisco History Center, San Francisco Public Library.

★ ★ ★ ★ ★

FOR A CITY REBORN

Vote YES on Progress Bonds

(Propositions 1 thru 7)

★ ★ ★ ★ ★

YOUR CITY IS A LIVING THING

A healthy, growing city, like a healthy, growing human body, thrives in proportion to the efficiency of its circulatory system. A city's congested streets is like a human body's hardened arteries. A city's jammed transit system is like a human body's clogged bloodstream. No city can thrive on a sick circulatory system.

Likewise, no city can grow beyond its water supply and its other essential utilities. Nor can a city become culturally great, nor sound in its moral fibre, nor confident of the future of its youth if it is deficient in its recreational facilities.

GROWTH REQUIRES PLANNING

Those who are planning the future of San Francisco recognize these fundamental facts. Already, three vitally important steps have been taken toward consummation of San Francisco's Master Plan. These were (1) airport expansion (2) increased sewerage facilities, and (3) railway consolidation.

Now, the time is at hand to take the next six progressive steps to meet the insistent demands of an ever-expanding population. These involve six bond proposals and one enabling charter amendment.

These are not all-time solutions of the problem of shaping a master design for pleasant living; but they are all basic and essential steps toward that goal. Their fulfillment will bring us that much nearer to our ultimate objective. And that is a reborn city which will tolerate no shackles on its faith in its future greatness.

HOW THESE STEPS WERE PLANNED

The transit, traffic and thoroughfare phases of the problem represent the combined thinking of all city departments concerned, as expressed through the Administrative Transportation Planning Council, have been approved by an expert committee of private citizens and have been ordered submitted to the people by the Mayor and the Board of Supervisors.

These phases comprise a closely-knit and dove-tailed program, fitted together by unanimous agreement of these experts and they include the best and most workable features of the many plans previously submitted through official agencies.

The prime purpose of this program is to modernize the city's circulatory system, thus preventing harmful decentralization with consequent adverse effects on property values and public convenience. The prime purpose is to provide means and space to move people faster, more safely and more comfortably.

FIGURE 1.4 "For A City Reborn . . . Vote Yes on Progress Bonds" (November 4, 1947). Debt was presented as key to the revival of San Francisco.

Source: Folder "Elections.1947," San Francisco Ephemera Collection, San Francisco History Center, San Francisco Public Library.

Otis Street, a facility built in 1915 that was "ANTIQUATED." Worse, the "crowded rooms, lack of provision for educational work," and the inability to execute the "proper segregation of youth as to sex," made it difficult "to provide [the city] modern methods of solving its youth problems."[48] Postwar white women often aggressively defended white homes and neighborhoods, but they also tended to vote to protect public health and children.[49]

It was one thing to convince San Franciscans to approve bond issues. The demand to finance so many new and neglected projects was great, and the ubiquitous pressure to keep taxes and fees low also mandated that finance officers borrow as cheaply as possible. They needed interest rates on municipal debt to diverge absolutely from historic patterns. When one financier with the investment bank Halsey, Stuart & Co. commented in November 1944 that interest rates for state and municipal governments were "the lowest in modern financial history," finance officers had reason to pay attention. Whereas the average yield on twenty-year bonds was 4.15 percent between 1922 and 1931, in the first nine months of 1944, the average was 1.65 percent. That is, municipal borrowers in 1944 could borrow the same amount for 60 percent of the cost five years earlier.[50] By the spring of 1946, more than a few American cities could issue a twenty-year bond at less than 1 percent.

What determined interest rates, and why were they so low? One banker linked the ability of cities to sell bonds at low interest rates to macroeconomic policy. Cities could not affect interest rates, removed as they were from gold flows, the expansion and restriction of bank credit, and legal limitations on reserve requirements and mediums of investment, all of which shaped "competition to invest," banker Roger W. Valentine explained. For Valentine, the interest rate charged on municipal bonds was a partial reflection of the global political economy of credit. According to Roland Robinson, an authoritative source on capital markets and municipal bond financing, the yields on state and local government debt "were unusually sensitive to Federal Reserve credit policy." That is, if money was "scarce," the Fed purchased large amounts of bonds from sellers who then deposited "Fed payments in their banks . . . thus expanding available capital for loans, payments, and cash." If the Fed believed there was too much money in circulation, it sold bonds, "absorbing the money from the buyers and removing it from their commercial bank accounts and the economy." Through its credit policy the Fed managed the overall money supply in ways that could boost or deflate the municipal bond market in particular and long-term capital markets more generally. To ask an economist or a bond financier, interest rates were low because of a unique global moment in monetary policy, tax policy, supply, and demand.[51]

Harry Ross possessed a number of techniques to manage the city's debt load. Turning to the municipal market, though, necessitated a very different tool kit. Ross and his fellow finance officers had to respond to the structural relationship between borrowers and lenders, managing, as it were, the city's credit profile. Once technocrats had lodged their ability to manage distributionary struggles in the municipal bond market, they needed to learn how that market worked. Casting the infrastructural fate and social welfare of urban residents into the market, finance officers parlayed with credit appraisers, raters, bankers, and bond attorneys at the conferences and in the publications of the MFOA. Those became critical sites where they learned the tools of the trade and much more.

Conditions, Parables, and Norms

Federal tax policy and the relatively small number of investors served as key pillars of the municipal bond market. Municipal borrowers depended on the desire of wealthy individuals and select institutional investors to shield their capital from taxation. Following the passage of Sixteenth Amendment in 1913, wealthy individuals became major purchasers of municipal bonds.[52] When the federal government opted to make incomes from its obligations taxable in 1941, it effectively gave states and their political subdivisions a virtual monopoly on tax exemption. The appetite of wealthy Americans for municipal bonds grew all the more voracious. We might say that municipal bonds were the midcentury version of today's offshore tax havens. The market among individual buyers was relatively small. Indeed, the number of people wealthy enough to loan huge chunks of funds for a significant stretch of time, and who preferred the guarantees offered by state and local governments over higher-yielding corporate bonds and stocks, was limited. Wealth inequality and the cultural predilections of individual investors "intent on capital preservation" made for a relatively small group of potential individual bond buyers.[53]

Because of the small pool of lenders, the slightest of changes was magnified. Between 1945 and 1956, state and local governments invested in themselves, but as bond buyers they were relatively minor players in the market. The same was true for fraternal societies, mutual savings banks, and life insurance companies.[54] City finance officers paid attention when, in August 1947, one Chase Manhattan banker noted that commercial banks, subject to a combined 38 percent normal and surtax on corporations and "taxed at the full corporate rate on net marginal investment income," were becoming "important buyers" of municipal bonds. Whereas commercial banks acquired 18.5 percent of state and local government debt in 1948, by 1950 the percentage had risen to 57.8 percent.[55]

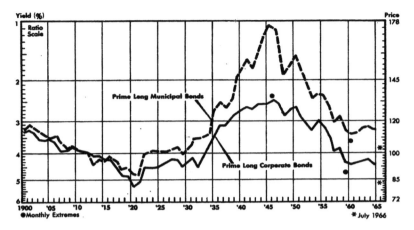

FIGURE 1.5 Comparative yields on "prime" municipal and corporate bonds, 1900–1965.

Source: Joint Economic Committee, Subcommittee on Economic Progress, "State and Local Public Facility Needs and Financing: Volume II," 89th Cong., 2nd sess., December 1966, 280.

Thus, for cities looking to borrow, everything—the streets in disrepair, schools for baby boomers, water treatment plants, and garbage disposal sites—was tied to the investment decisions of small and powerful lenders alike. Those decisions were deeply conditioned by federal tax policy. The macroeconomic conditions of the municipal bond market were well "beyond the control of municipal officials."[56]

Municipal technocrats had to abide by the social norms of lenders. Finance officers were advised to outsource the drafting of bond ordinances, resolutions, and financial advertisements to only the most reputable bond attorneys. What amounted to a hierarchy of municipal bond attorneys broke along regional lines. In New York City, for instance, the firm Wood, King, and Dawson served "as bond counsel for many of the outstanding governmental units in the United States."[57] In California, Orrick, Dahlquist, Herrington & Sutcliffe (ODHS) was one of two nationally recognized legal experts in general obligation bonds. When one member of the San Francisco Board of Supervisors asked why the city paid ODHS when it could secure an opinion from the city attorney for free, a financier with Blyth & Co. explained that the opinion from reputable attorneys was "essential to attract good competitive bidding. We wouldn't touch the bonds without a well-recognized firm's opinion."[58] David Ellinwood, manager of the Municipal Department of Moody's Investors' Service, added that municipal bonds "accompanied by what we call a 'local' opinion" came with a "higher interest cost . . . than a bond of the same city which carries a 'marketable' opinion."[59] What a city paid in higher fees, the reasoning went, it gained in lowered borrowing costs.

The structural position of bond attorneys was peculiar. On the one hand, when municipal bond attorneys delivered speeches at MFOA conferences, they told public finance officers that attorneys helped buttress the legal underpinnings of revenue bonds, perhaps minimizing the risk to holders and lowering the cost to borrow.[60] On the other hand, bond attorneys also used MFOA to pass along ideas about the proper relationship between the state and the private sector. Their close social and ideological proximity to creditors was illuminated by lawyer David M. Wood, who during the 1940s had led the charge against federal regulation of the municipal bond market.[61] In August 1950, he put a spin on the dangers of the federal government, dramatizing the dual eclipse of municipal autonomy and augmentation of federal financial power with a modified parable of the Garden of Eden.

Early commercial towns were the wellspring of the modern city, marked by freedom, liberty, and autonomy. But the 1930s and the Great Depression brought dangerous temptations. The lush green pastures of freedom gave way to unemployment. Property values collapsed. Municipal bonds went into default. Fearful of tax revolts and at their debt limits, cities could not borrow to resolve unemployment through public works projects. The federal government slithered its way into the garden to offer grants and loans, willing also to purchase the bonds of cities at lower interest rates. Soon, emergency relief turned into full-fledged dependency. Whether "oblivious of the fact, or ignoring it," municipal officials "were surrendering, piecemeal, the autonomy of their respective municipalities." Too many cities had been ejected from the garden into the cold world of dependency.[62] In this parable of debt and governance, dependence on the federal government was dangerous, while dependence on the bond market, credit appraisers, bankers, and fickle investors was virtuous. The story spoke to the ways in which advice could masquerade as ideology. Indeed, at the heart of technical advice about debt were moral arguments about governance, democracy, responsibility, and integrity.

City finance officers needed to know how to capture the attention of bond buyers. Although David Ellinwood of Moody's had limited "practical experience as a public official," with some "misgivings" he advised finance officers on how to structure a bond sale. Treating the municipal bond market as a thing that could be managed, where "favorable conditions" could be identified and acted upon, he outlined the "three simple rules" for finance officers. For starters, achieving the lowest possible interest rate was predicated on parlaying with "several reputable investment bankers." Finance officers should "obtain their opinions" regarding the price outlook for municipal bonds and "ask them" about upcoming large municipal bond issues. Doing these things might obviate extreme competition for limited funds. Not only were municipal technocrats encouraged to listen to the advice of raters, they were also told that they were lost without the opinions of bond financiers.[63] What had been a suggestion during the Great Depression had become a foundational norm.

Ellinwood felt he knew bond buyers enough to highlight their likes and dislikes. Taking their feelings into account was the second rule. During the late 1930s, some bankers punished cities for refinancing debt at lower rates.[64] In August 1947, Ellinwood carried this advice further, saying investors "do not like callable bonds." If, in the event of low interest rates, borrowers sought to redeem and refinance before a bond reached maturity, Ellinwood suggested borrowers provide "added compensation," perhaps "a premium equal to one year's interest." That is, cities were expected to compensate bondholders for pursuing the best interest of taxpayers. Ellinwood also noted that "most investors dislike annual interest payments," preferring semiannual ones. Because bondholders "frown upon the delays in collection and possible costs to them where bonds and interest are payable only at some remote point," borrowers should minimize this "inconvenience." They should allow bondholders to collect principal and interest payments at the borrower's treasurer's office, to be sure, but also at one of the "large money centers" in "New York or Chicago."

For voters, municipal bonds were mere instruments to unlock funds for schools and the like. But for investors, bonds were commodities, so as with any other commodity, finance officers had to make their "merchandise as attractive . . . as possible."[65] One banker avowed, "Good publicity can pay good dividends and adverse publicity can be quite costly."[66] Advertising was necessary to convince lenders that San Francisco's bonds, for instance, were better than Detroit's. David Ellinwood likened bonds to shirts: just as shoppers were unwilling to pay the "same price for a shirt of unknown brand though perhaps it had the same thread count," investors would not purchase unfamiliar bonds "except at a substantially lower price." The lower the price paid for a bond, the higher the yield, which meant higher interest charges for borrowers. It was analogous to a merchant selling you an off-brand shirt but charging a higher sales tax because of the discounted price. Even if the underlying economic conditions of a city were equal to those of its better-known counterparts, investors preferred familiar bonds "over those of a community about which they know little or nothing." More than objective conditions separated one bond from another, and a name brand item was made through a bondholder's access to information about the bonds for sale. If this made little economic sense, Ellinwood maintained that it was simply "human nature to be suspicious when essential financial information is not available, and suspicion breeds caution and even avoidance."[67]

That Ellinwood spoke with such confidence was ironic. Bond financiers and credit analysts had quickly learned to project expertise that the 1930s demonstrated they lacked. That city finance officers listened attentively underscored the allure of a shared technocratic discourse and the pressures to borrow cheaply to deliver on the infrastructural rights postwar Americans demanded. The promise of low interest rates was the carrot, but the stick was there.

Moody's analysts could reasonably assert that they knew the likes and wants of investors largely because the bond ratings they produced became commonsensical. Abstraction was at the heart of it all, on two interrelated levels. Finance officers, city planners, and elected officials transformed the actual city into numbers, images, and projections, leaving a mountain of municipal documents. Rating agencies relied on these documents to transform cities into commensurable commodities to which investors turned to extract capital. Indeed, these municipal documents were as much about offering an internal blueprint for reimagining and financing the built environment as they were about performing creditworthiness. At another level, raters standardized the thousands of issuers of municipal debt. Letter grades made the city legible to investors, enhanced the fungibility of bonds issued for sale, and enabled bankers to purchase bonds and resell them to investors who never set foot in the issuing community.

To do the work of abstraction, Moody's analysts leveraged the past and fused it to a present assessment of the future quality of a bond. By providing historic data on instances of default, Moody's encouraged its subscribers to consider the role of history in differentiating between two bonds with the same rating. But *which history* was most pertinent? It was odd indeed when Moody's included 1932 data about tonnage shipments in and out of San Francisco and detailed the 1939 appraised value of city-owned and operated utilities in its 1955 manual. That year Moody's spoke of the city's "splendid railway facilities" and described an industrial landscape dotted by thriving "printing and publishing, sugar and refining, slaughtering and meat packing, foundry and machine shops." It alerted investors to the firms specializing in "lumber, metal products, clothing, leather, furniture, food preparations, chemicals, building materials."[68] But this was an older history of the city.

If an abstraction "exists in the world at all," writes historian William Cronon, "it does so only as a multitude of real things" and through "their even more multitudinous relationships to each other."[69] San Francisco's "Aa" rating was at once the aggregation of things—ports, industrial plants, railway facilities—and a representation of the flow of information from city finance officers to credit analysts.[70] The problem, however, was that some of the information on which Moody's relied was like milk: it went bad quickly. But Moody's still kept the carton in the refrigerator, behind fresher ingredients.

The threat of stale information could be minimized. When credit analysts insisted that sharing certain kinds of information was good for a municipal borrower, the advice served to enlist municipal finance officers in the business success of bond rating agencies. Some finance officers seemed to believe that the quality of an annual report was "measured in terms of bulk," and they sent to Moody's "a listing of every birth and death in the community, every item on the police blotter and a verbatim reproduction of the town treasurer's cash journal, but contain no other financial crumbs." David Ellinwood insisted this was the wrong way to preempt the innumerable "questionnaires coming to you from investors and their representatives."[71] Instead, he said, municipal technocrats should display financial information in ways that mirrored private corporations. The neat, symmetrical display of balance sheets, revenues, and expenditures was familiar to the buyers of corporate stock and should be emulated, another appraiser remarked.[72]

Credit appraisers outlined the "moral responsibility" of cities to the wider financial community. Making timely interest payments was not enough. Bondholders had a right to know the size of a city's debt and whether its budget was balanced. To contend otherwise was "deplorable; equally, it is shortsighted," Ellinwood declared. By wrapping a moral right to know in the appeal of low interest rates, credit analysts were able to enlist city technocrats in facilitating the business of collecting, reproducing, and analyzing "financial information from cities all over the country."[73] In the moment, rating agencies were able to profit from selling that information to subscribers. In the long run, the voluntary submission of information extended the gaze of capitalist surveillance.

The rationale behind selecting the City Bank of New York as San Francisco's fiscal agent was to make life more convenient for bondholders. The consequences were more profound. For its service, San Francisco compensated the bank to the tune of more than $5,900 in 1946–47.[74] Much to the chagrin of local financiers seeking to build out the Wall Street of the West, the advice constituted a feedback loop. When San Francisco took the advice of using a New York firm, it helped to strengthen New York City's position as the finance capital of the world.

Charter requirements were also signals to lenders. As one senior accountant observed, the architects of the 1932 charter made "it easy for bond dealers to gauge the community's credit standing."[75] Indeed, not long after its implementation, the Anglo California National Bank published a detailed profile on San Francisco's credit. The charter created a "strongly centralized government" and endowed the controller's office with "complete supervision and control over" expenditures. Of great concern to bondholders, charter reform had strengthened the efficient, unencumbered ability of technocrats to collect taxes, and the "penalties for delinquencies [were] severe."[76] The forensic analysis of bond financiers was made easier by the city's modern representation of information. The annual report was as much an internal fiscal reckoning for San Franciscans as it was a conduit of information for lenders. Within these reports, the neat, orderly projection of bond interest and principal requirements well into the future could suggest sound debt administration, or otherwise.[77] The mandated issuance of quarterly and annual reports offered "in intimate detail all of the factors that are of interest to dealers in municipal securities." It is no wonder Harry Ross's "mailing list for these reports looks like the subscription index for the *Wall Street Journal*."[78]

Despite, or perhaps because of, the advice secured through MFOA, there emerged a striking disconnect between how lenders and finance officers thought the municipal bond market worked. Lenders understood it as being powered by social connections. As the technocrats par excellence of the postwar city, city finance officers exuded a deep confidence in their abilities to manage supply and demand. San Francisco senior accountant Joseph P. Crosson encouraged other municipal technocrats to believe there existed an appropriate time to strike. With patience and perception, "the law of supply and demand will be on your side when your obligations are offered for public sale." As they watched the market, the San Francisco Board of Supervisors distributed the "notice of sale to bond dealers throughout the nation." Alerting bankers to the infrastructural purposes of and interest rate limitations on the bonds, notices of sale could be extensive. Indeed, "the last San Francisco bond offering contained eight letter sized pages of printed information to prospective bidders."[79]

Through time management and temporal tinkering, San Francisco finance officers hoped to minimize tax burdens and elevate the city's credit standing. Timing was everything, both because the city had to deploy borrowing power when demand was high and because it allowed finance officers to better manage expenditures. Some projects did not require the money all at once, and so selling bonds "only when the money is needed [had] a decided effect upon savings in interest." Adjusting the life of some bonds to mature in ten years, others in fifteen years, and still others in twenty-five years did two things. It could ease the "tax burden for debt servicing in any one year." It could also preempt bondholders' fears that too much debt would come due in a single year beyond what San Francisco could handle.[80]

The upshot of this exchange was mixed. On the one hand, by parlaying with the makers of the bond market, municipal finance officers sharpened their professional identity. They became better attuned to the needs of investors, and, by deepening their social ties with the makers of the market, hoped to secure the lowest possible interest rates. On the other hand, MFOA provided the occasion to hear from people who spoke of the dangers of federal dependence and the merits of the market, who insisted that finance officers prioritize the interests of creditors, and who warned of the dangers of popular pressure. New Deal banking reforms gave bankers a seat at the table to finance the infrastructural needs of the state. Their allies came with them. Together, they advised finance officers on more than just how debt should be used and how the city was viewed. This proximity made cities subject to the moral strictures and the gaze and oversight of lenders.

Astonishingly, cities came to rely on a set of actors who failed considerably during the 1930s, who were marginal within their own firms, who labored in inefficient and wasteful spaces, and who were understaffed and overworked. It was almost as if bond financiers maintained their reputation as experts and wielded subtle power despite themselves. The ability of San Francisco to meet its many infrastructural demands hinged on a market that had to be recalibrated, a project that took shape in cramped offices, through social connections, and through a shared culture of racism, elitism, and patriarchy. We might call it a fraternity.

2. Fraternity

Beneath the city streets, airports, and schools financed through debt was a whole world that has largely remained hidden. It was a world very much conditioned by New Deal banking reform. Through the Banking Act of 1933, bankers in general, and commercial banks in particular, were permitted to remain critical intermediaries between large pools of investment capital and state and local government borrowers.

Bank of America, NT&SA (BOA) and its bond financiers were exemplary. Located in the heart of San Francisco's financial district, BOA's municipal bond department barely survived the depression-era years of lean offerings and diminished returns. Wartime capital controls delayed the realization of a paradigm that had only begun to emerge during the 1920s: financing the infrastructural needs of the state could yield great profits.[1] Much of this project was executed by Alan K. Browne, who had cut his teeth with the bank during the Great Depression and had found during his World War II service that writing army regulations, "work simplification methods," and "organizational charts" for the execution of "operating procedures" left him well prepared to modernize BOA's business of buying and selling debt. In 1946 he became an assistant vice president, and in 1955 he was named head of the Municipal Bond Section.[2] By 1971 he could boast having helped raise more than $10 billion for BOA's clients.[3] At the end of his career, Browne was appropriately regarded as "Mr. Municipal Bond."[4]

Across the globe borrowers were hungry for funds. The World Bank used debt to rebuild western Europe and stimulate development in the Global South.[5] The United States issued debt to manage its territorial and insular possessions. Through the Public Housing Administration, the federal government coordinated and supervised massive bond sales.[6] State treasurers traveled east on a "bond sale mission."[7] And cities issued bonds to deliver on the infrastructural promises to residents and neighborhoods deemed worthy of debt. Municipal debt was a small but critical niche of the bond market that Alan K. Browne sought to dominate.

As it turns out, the question of how bankers bought and sold municipal debt is a lot more complicated than textbook explanations would have it.

For starters, bankers had a lot of structural advantages. The war economy tested the limits of aging, outdated infrastructure, increasing demand for new fixtures. Low interest rates could lure more and more municipal borrowers, which the professional organizations of city finance officers encouraged. Last, high federal marginal tax rates made tax-exempt municipal debt attractive to the wealthy individuals and institutional investors whom bankers served. Bankers' successes, though, were made by much more than needs, business advice, interest payments, and tax rates. The postwar world of debt was one in which financiers ritualized their upper-class aspirations, expressed ideas of mastery and uplift, and advised one another on what to demand from their secretaries and how to get it. As a package, their business aspirations, systems used to assess a city's credit profile, and expressions of white male bonding helped power mid-twentieth century infrastructure. Put simply, the ability to remake the built environment was entangled with the business, politics, sociality, and culture of debt.

The Business of Debt

The rise of Bank of America as a force in the municipal bond business shaped and was shaped by postwar commercial, agricultural, and industrial growth in California.[8] In what might be called the "California strategy," BOA precipitated the economic and demographic booms by hitching its wagon to underwriting and investing in the debt of California and all of its political subdivisions. Relative to the municipal bond departments of Chase National Bank, National City Bank, Bankers Trust Company, and Harris Trust & Savings Bank, "none can compare in their respective States with our activity in the California municipal bond market," Browne boasted in July 1947.[9] "We should be second to none" in the market for California municipal debt, and loss of market share, he insisted a few months later, "*should not be tolerated.*"[10]

Before Browne and company could march into the postwar moment they had to scrub the spillovers from the 1930s. In March 1944 the Municipal Bond Department created a "trading account" by moving $5.5 million in bonds from an older "investment account." The point was "to take advantage of the tax value under existing Internal Revenue regulation" by carrying over "low cost bonds acquired over a period of many years, through takeover and during periods of high interest rates." These were bonds in "odd amounts," long-term bonds whose maturity schedules did not match the rhythms of commercial lending, and the bonds of "small names," or borrowers whose credit profiles were relatively unknown. After slotting the older bonds into the new trading account, the

TABLE 2.1 California municipal bonds underwritten by Bank of America, 1941–1947

Year	Number of issues	Par value	BOA liability (par value)	Amount purchased for investment
1941	119	$98,555,731	$2,922,300	$551,000
1942	33	$20,174,136	$3,202,333	$537,000
1943	14	$25,301,000	$3,661,666	————
1944	23	$58,122,000	$1,465,000	$130,000
1945	88	$104,700,000	$38,704,500	$25,358,000
1946	329	$192,342,250	$35,371,827	$42,098,200
1947 (5 mo.)	139	$87,197,100	$5,836,402	$8,907,000
Total	**745**	**$586,392,218**	**$91,164,030**	**$77,581,200**

Note: Some displayed totals do not match column totals due to rounding error.

Source: Alan K. Browne, Memorandum to R. A. Kent, "Underwriting of New Municipal Bond Issues," July 1, 1947, carton 3, Alan K. Browne Papers (BANC MSS 91/6), Bancroft Library, University of California, Berkeley, n.p.

bank then sold off the debts, "providing a continuous source of profits." The profits could have been greater still, Browne observed, but cleansing the portfolio provided something of a clean break before the bank took on the debts of the future.[11]

The early postwar signs were promising. In 1946, for instance, BOA helped underwrite 329 new issues of California municipal bonds, adding $42,098,200 to its investment account (table 2.1). The Investment Bankers Association of America anticipated that although municipal bonds were not used to finance single-family homes, the forthcoming "vigorous revival of the housing boom" among the age-25-to-34 cohort would compel cities and suburbs to borrow in order to finance parks, streets, and roads. In short, bankers could profit from "a vast increase in the debt of State and local governments."[12]

Predictive trends were useful, but it took work to push the municipal bond division to the center of BOA's lending activities. Because upper management was not fully aware of the promise of municipal debt, Browne felt he had to explain what he and his colleagues did. His superiors would only know how the municipal bond division created value for the bank and its stockholders if they fully understood the "mechanics of underwriting," he wrote in July 1947. Along with profits, municipal debt yielded "collateral benefits." When a bank underwrote a bond offering,

TABLE 2.2 Out-of-state municipal bonds underwritten by Bank of America, 1941–1947

Year	Number of issues	Par value	BOA liability (par value)	Amount purchased for investment
1941	4	$120,097,000	$4,212,000	$1,964,000
1942	4	$87,090,500	$575,000	————
1943	6	$20,851,000	$2,151,666	$2,396,000
1944	12	$75,577,000	$840,000	$91,000
1945	5	$86,205,000	$2,837,000	————
1946	22	$102,781,800	$5,522,000	$2,975,000
1947 (5 mo.)	16	$565,327,000	$18,650,000	$10,842,000
Total	**69**	**$1,057,929,300**	**$34,787,666**	**$18,268,000**

Source: Alan K. Browne, Memorandum to R. A. Kent, "Underwriting of New Municipal Bond Issues," July 1, 1947, carton 3, Alan K. Browne Papers (BANC MSS 91/6), Bancroft Library, University of California, Berkeley, n.p.

it agreed to lend funds. The hope was that the borrower would then deposit those funds with the underwriting bank. Holding the deposits of nation-states had long been a crucial source of liquidity and capital. Securing municipal deposits—funds that the bank had mobilized in the first place—was no different. Purchasing the bonds of a city, suburb, or state also affirmed "the Bank's interest in local civic affairs" and accrued "local and national publicity." To be regarded as a good corporate citizen might even convince city finance officers to turn to the bank as a financial adviser.[13] All of this doubled back. Parlaying with technocrats would allow the bank to update the manifold credit profiles of municipal borrowers, "improve public relations," and better respond to the needs of institutional investors.[14]

Without a substantive commitment to administrative reform, though, BOA had been coming up short. The bank did "not always produce the winning bid," wrote Browne. "In fact, we frequently are in second or third place, or possibly lower." An expanded workforce was needed to handle California and to help the bank step up its purchase of out-of-state debt. Indeed, in 1946, BOA underwrote just twenty-two issues of new out-of-state municipals and purchased just $2,975,000 of them for its investment account (table 2.2). "With the exception of the head of the trading section," Browne lamented, "there are no other individuals in the trading section capable or qualified to direct or even assist in this phase of our work." Out-of-state debt was too profitable an area for BOA to remain geographically provincial.[15]

A bond symbolized a borrower's long-term commitment to its citizenry. A borrower was essentially making a twenty- to thirty-year investment in the social welfare of its residents. Having borrowed at a fixed interest rate, city technocrats like Harry D. Ross could project the costs of debt over an extended period of time. These time horizons did not match those of commercial bankers. During the prime of the 1920s, long-term municipal bonds might yield investors 4 percent or more. But between January 1, 1934, and January 1, 1939, the average yield on municipal bonds of the twenty largest cities fell from 5.48 to 2.77 percent.[16] Surveying the field of new offerings in 1945, Browne no doubt saw yields hovering just above 1 percent. Interest rates and yields, two sides of the same coin reflecting the perspectives of borrowers and buyers, respectively, were fluid. It was bad business for bankers to hold a lower-yielding, long-term bond that did not match prevailing rates. Bankers would still accumulate tax-exempt interest income on these bonds, but they missed the opportunity to purchase newer, higher-yielding ones. Moreover, commercial bankers had to be mindful of customers' shifting loan demands. "Loans not only bear a higher rate of return" but are also "important to customer relationships and are often determinate of a bank's ability to attract deposits—the life blood of the business," as one student of the market explained.[17] For these reasons, Alan K. Browne insisted on remaining "active in the bank range of maturities (1 to 10 years)." He continued, "Not more than 25% of the bonds in the Trading Account will mature beyond 5 years. . . . Bonds due in less than 1 year should be avoided except on basis of cash purchase" and sold "so that cash sale of newly acquired inventory will not show a basis loss."[18] In the memorandums and thick reports of municipal bond dealers, schools were coded as commodities, and commodities were slotted into trading accounts and segregated into one- to four-year and five- to ten-year brackets. The social welfare of Americans had become further intertwined with tax advantages, commercial lending demands, and anticipatory yields.

The temporal norms governing BOA's purchase of municipal debt perhaps gives the impression of a profession marked by administrative symmetry and orderly transactions. But there was something magical about attempts to resell debt. To facilitate that process, bankers used the *Blue List*, "a daily record of the inventory of securities *being offered for sale.*"[19] Transparency was not a virtue for the Municipal Bond Department, which sought constantly to "create an illusion of activity." Browne explained, "Tired offerings, i.e., over 10 days old . . . will be withdrawn for a rest. . . . If a large block is available, caution should be shown in disclosing the entire amount."[20] The bank's disclosures were shaped by their desire to attract buyers and project an image of success. Indeed, the *Blue List* must be read not as a guide to actual sales but as a strategic medium through which bankers burnished claims to dominance.

Although BOA was involved in underwriting many bond issues, it rarely did so alone. By the early twentieth century, underwriting syndicates had become the primary means by which financial institutions mobilized investment capital in large sums. Syndicates allowed banks to act collectively and lend to borrowers, all while minimizing the liabilities of individual firms. As they were cooperative, yet hierarchical arrangements, membership in syndicates was contingent upon access to capital, relative prestige, and friendships.[21] Under Browne, BOA sought to lift hierarchy to new heights.

The increase in the number of municipal bond offerings and the uptick in the dollar amount incentivized bankers to forge more underwriting syndicates. BOA's collaboration with Blyth & Co.; R.H. Moulton; and Heller, Bruce Co. in April 1947 to underwrite a $560,000 bond offering for Modesto, California, recalled a time when commercial and investment banks partnered to distribute relatively small liabilities.[22] The emerging trend was evident in February 1948, when a group that included Bank of America, Chase National Bank, Bankers Trust Company, and National City Bank submitted the winning bid to underwrite $22 million in San Francisco debt. Another group headed by Blyth & Co. underwrote $3 million in debt for San Francisco's street improvement program and an older $2 million bond issue to aid the city's airport.[23] By the spring of 1951, San Francisco was dependent on bankers' organizing connections. Without syndicates it would prove difficult to sell a $10 million offering.[24]

Browne saw the position of the syndicate manager, and the kinds of power it afforded, as key to Bank of America's rise. As early as July 1947, Browne was willing to coordinate the various liabilities that participants were willing to take on; redistribute among other syndicate members; and, if necessary, either have the BOA assume "the amount not underwritten" or decide that the syndicate "does not bid." But rank was the precondition. "The Bank will manage all accounts," he said. It would "always be a major," its financial commitment "never less than that of any other member" of a syndicate. The bank might relinquish its position in the local New York City and Chicago press, but it would, by and large, "always appear first in any advertising" of the municipal bonds for sale.[25]

Following "many months of collaboration with attorneys and accountants," in November 1952, Browne circulated a sample syndicate agreement among the nation's bond dealers. The agreement made clear that to join a BOA-managed syndicate was to relinquish decision-making to a manager with barely checked power and authority. BOA would act on behalf of the "Syndicate without limitation by any particular power." Past participants in BOA-managed syndicates might use that experience as a guide, but BOA would "not be obligated to follow any particular or specific practice." Members could opine on the maximum price to bid and could drop out if they pleased. However, the manager possessed "full authority" to determine the terms of the bid and the choice of bond counsel. Moreover, BOA maintained that it was under no obligation, whether because of loyalty or past success, to reassemble a syndicate "with the same membership, or with relative participations." The manager would approve the incurrence of expenses or liabilities among members, and members had to submit to the manager "a copy of their firm's latest audited financial statement."[26] Outrage ensued: some bankers thought syndicate governance transferred "excessive authority" to the manager. The requirement to submit financial statements to their "competitors" was self-defeating. "'Alarms and excursions' were sounded" over what appeared an imposition of the cold, bureaucratic contract upon an informal, gentlemanly culture. All of the rules and procedures seemed an affront to "the municipal fraternity."[27]

In a sense, the process of rule among bond financiers mirrored the outlines of urban governance articulated by creditors. The management of debt, whether in terms of a debt ceiling or distributing liabilities, was to be handled by a select few. The circumscription of democratic input was a structuring principle. The quid pro quo of boss rule and the bankers' informal gentlemanly culture were to be phased out, replaced by streamlined administration. Just as some bankers sought greater control over their friendly rivals by dictating procedures and demanding information, bond financiers aimed to slowly tighten their grip over municipal borrowers.

Lenders encouraged city finance officers to see municipal debt as a commodity that needed to capture the attention of a limited pool of buyers. But bankers saw it differently: with thousands of borrowers, from cities to authorities to agencies, how should they decide which bonds—all tax-exempt, many backed by the power to tax—to purchase?

Bankers analyzed and compared "the credit status of the issuing body" with those of "similar bonds," Browne explained. They then positioned a bond issue amid the macroeconomy (the volume of new issues against the demand) of the municipal bond market to determine "the relative value of the bonds being sold." Notwithstanding "any peculiarities connected with the sale," bankers furthered the abstraction of a city, town, and authority. If the credit status was similar enough, San Francisco could be substituted for Los Angeles.[28]

Bank of America's bond financiers were collectively evaluating the credit profiles of municipal borrowers and profiting from differences, blemishes, and similarities. In this they were joined by bond rating agencies, which have been described as "masters of capital."[29] But their mastery was narrow and, ironically, amplified less by the market than by the federal government. Skepticism toward Moody's Investors Service and Standard & Poor's ran deep and wide. Like bankers, rating analysts had emerged from the 1930s with a disgraceful record.[30] Some bankers acknowledged the value of these firms in assessing the chances of a default but saw ratings mostly as useful for starting conversations with institutional investors.[31] Others acknowledged the "tremendous task" the firms performed but concluded that ratings were more useful to smaller financial institutions and individuals than to larger commercial banks and well-established investment houses.[32] What gave bond ratings real force was not only that they became a common standard for lenders and city officials; by the late 1930s, federal regulators also came to rely on credit ratings to judge the quality and safety of bonds held by major commercial lenders.[33]

At no point did Moody's and Standard & Poor's single-handedly determine municipal creditworthiness. Bank of America's municipal bond financiers consulted two distinct spectrums: the first for California "names," the other for out-of-state "names." "There will be no restriction as to rating on California municipal bonds," Browne declared. Yet all California names were not equal. So-called second-grade credits and prime names were the benchmarks of the California spectrum. It might be said that they thought about bonds like cars. Like older models with a ton of mileage, bonds in small par value amounts with long maturities were "second-grade." These debts might be purchased on behalf of "small dealers."[34] By contrast, bond financiers took other commercial banks, investment banks, and insurance companies, as well as the managers of public funds and investment counselors, to the grand showroom. "Names in particular to keep on top of," Browne explained, included "State of Californias, East Bays, Golden Gates . . . S.F.'s, L.A.'s, San Diegos, Long Beaches, Oaklands . . . Santa Monicas, Pasadenas."[35] In this showroom, the bonds of the state and some of its cities, suburbs, authorities, and districts became commensurate, top-of-the-line models, but with enough differences among them to appeal to different bond buyers.

Evaluating the credit profiles of out-of-state borrowers was more complex. Bankers might look out for "general market names."[36] Ratings could be useful. Indeed, non-California names "must be rated 'Baa' or better by Moody." But Browne encouraged his colleagues to value their own judgments over those of Moody's when it came to some highly rated names.

"Marginal out-of-State credits rated 'A' by Moody . . . such as New Yorks, Philadelphias, Detroits, Bostons, Louisianas, Chicagos including Park and Sanitary Districts, Cook Countys, and Clevelands will be kept to a minimum."[37] Browne didn't explain what made these names marginal, but his statement does show that creditors used various criteria to determine municipal creditworthiness. It also suggests how bond financiers instrumentalized criteria to buy the debt of some cities while avoiding the debt of others. Bankers could further constrict the pool of lenders for governments they deemed unfamiliar, poorly rated, or marginal.

Once bankers set up a spectrum of borrowers, the question was how to monitor changes to a name; in other words, how to animate spectrums of municipal creditworthiness. Because cities were affected by economic downturns, worsening slums, greater demands from the polity, and business slowdowns, decisions that shaped revenues and expenditures could affect the value of a name. So "to anticipate 'weak spots' in our holdings," Browne thought it wise to collect historical statistics and the most up-to-date information on government borrowers whose "credit picture" was constantly changing.[38]

Part of what made municipal debt such a peculiar commodity was its dynamism. And decisions by an electorate could catalyze its volatility or stability. Democracy was paradoxical for bankers. Through their approval, voters might expand the opportunities for bankers to purchase the bonds of a particular city. And voters themselves could raise the ranking of their own city depending on how they voted. Yet the power to vote might also infringe on revenue sources for existing bondholders. Because democratic input on bond measures had been circumscribed to a mere "yes" or "no" at only two points per year, the lead-up to bond referenda gave bankers a chance to mobilize against any democratic infringement.

Bankers might draw on welfare proposals to adjust their categorizations of good and marginal debt. In October 1949, Alan K. Browne turned to the *Daily Bond Buyer* (*DBB*) to assuage concerns over California's Proposition 2, which sought to devolve to counties the administration of aid to the aged and blind. Browne predicted the move would make aid costlier. Moreover, the administrative costs were "yet to be felt." Browne had to walk a tightrope: even as he warned against welfare provisions, he worked to enhance confidence in California municipals. Browne pointed to prevailing yields, which suggested "an investor can feel that his holdings of California municipal bonds have not suffered credit-wise." Being a bondholder meant contending with democracy, and California was "not expected to be conservative in all of its actions." Nevertheless, he maintained that "California has always seen fit to defeat movements which would harm its credit." If bondholders found yields and precedent unconvincing, Browne pointed to the "unlimited financial support" of those working to defeat the proposition: "Current betting odds favor the defeat of Proposition 2."[39]

The bankers who underwrote debt were the same people with opinions about revenues and expenditures. The people who advised finance officers how to enhance their city's credit profile were the same people with opinions about the appropriate scope of the welfare state. The people who developed hierarchical valuation systems were the same people with concerns about how democracy might undercut their investments. New Deal banking reform thus did more than allow bond financiers to underwrite the infrastructural needs of the American state. It also permitted bankers to bring their overlapping identities and ideas to bear on how a borrower should behave.

The problem for Alan K. Browne was that no one seemed to care about what municipal bond bankers were doing. The copious reports and visions of bureaucratic reorganization produced little or "no acknowledgement."[40] Indeed, the grand aspirations clashed with the brutally slow realities of administrative reform, the silence from upper management, and the relatively marginal status of municipal bond financiers at Bank of America.[41] These weren't abstract processes or unknowable figures. Including Browne, in 1953 BOA had twelve municipal bond financiers: Lawrence H. Prager, William S. Durrant, and J. Alcock were in charge of the trading section; James Reed, Herman J. Metz, A. E. Stone Jr., F. McSorley, and Harry P. Bolton directed the underwriting section; Alan V. Bartlett, Walter J. Gudat, and Paul H. Prescott managed the statistical section; and there was bond cashier Frank J. Kennedy.[42] There were four new hires that year, most "relatively young and inexperienced" and facing an "unprecedented volume of new financing."[43]

Browne's appeal for more personnel had been granted, but the second-floor office of 300 Montgomery Street had what R. A. Kent, a vice president in BOA's investment division, called a "space problem." The entrance lobby was spacious, but click-clacking from the adjacent Telegraph Department produced a "noisy background and an untidy vista for visitors to the Bond Investment Department." Visitors would be greeted by the "incumbent" secretary, likely a white woman charged also with "answering telephones . . . [and] miscellaneous typing duties," but she had to share the desk with "certain staff members." Municipal bond bankers had to negotiate with corporate bond financiers over access to the only conference room, or else use Alan K. Browne's office, which could accommodate "only a few." The conference room ironically lacked a conference table, was cluttered with "statistical reference books," and was poorly ventilated and small.

By November 1953, bankers within the municipal, corporate, and railroad divisions shared just two turret board desks, three adding machines, seven calculating machines, two teletypes, twenty-six five-drawer legal files, thirty-nine four-drawer legal files, and a small number of bookcases and library shelves. Sometimes this equipment was used primarily to organize space. File cabinets "to a large extent serve[d] as a dividing line between the Trust Department and Bond Investment Department and as a barricade adjacent to the Telegraph Department."

The rational, bureaucratic ideals of the midcentury corporation suffered. "The general floor plan by Divisions," Kent noted, "has been obliterated out of necessity." Likewise, neat, symmetrical organizational charts of administrative authority did not reflect reality. New personnel sat "wherever there were empty desks or some space to fit additional desks." It was common for corporate bond financiers to sit with the municipal bond financiers. The result was chaos, with bankers trying to decide which bonds to bid on and at what price in separate offices, or amid secretarial phone calls, queries from visitors, and the sounds of telegraphs.

For R. A. Kent, the unglamorous work environment went beyond the lack of comforts to dint the social and economic capital of the bank. The arrangement of the workplace, he said, "does not give the impression of a well planned, well coordinated department." Who would submit to being managed in a syndicate by a firm whose reference materials were randomly placed atop "window ledges"? Moreover, the "confidential and fiduciary nature of much of the work of the Department is seriously harmed by the overall problem of space."

To some extent these complaints were performative: they allowed bankers to call for more personnel, new office space, and more capital. However, the descriptions also reveal that bankers profited *in spite of* inefficiency, poor supervision, paltry on-the-job training, and burdensome labor within a cacophonous "overcrowded and jumbled department."[44] That cities depended on these lenders underscores how surveillance and waste, banker weakness, and technocratic faith in manageable markets went hand in hand. Ultimately, bankers wielded power less because of their rational business practices and more because of the reliance of cities on their services.

Social Ties

The memos, reports, sample contractual agreements, and surveys are not only the material culture of finance capitalism; they also offer insight into how bankers related to one another. Trade organizations such as the Investment Bankers Association of America helped soothe disputes, refine technical knowledge, and assist municipal bond financiers statewide to brief others on cities' financing needs.[45] The *DBB* told bankers about themselves and sometimes published obituaries of members of the fraternity.[46] It also explained prevailing norms. Take, for instance, the Bank of America's underwriting survey, which the *DBB* regarded as quite possibly "the most penetrating analysis of municipal bond underwriting and sales procedures ever undertaken." In January 1958, the cadre of municipal bond bankers at San Francisco's BOA office began circulating a lengthy questionnaire among their peers nationwide.[47] By April of that year, BOA had received more than sixty pages of answers and comments, with "more than 300 detailed replies" from bankers in "25 States and 39 different cities." All told, the survey detailed the opinions "on almost every conceivable aspect of municipal bond financing," proclaimed the *DBB*.[48]

To say that bankers could not live with or without underwriting syndicates is also to say that, despite their grievances, they were deeply committed to the fraternity. A few respondents were frustrated that "too many members contribute little or nothing to particular deals." The result was smaller earnings "for those who generally do a good job." Conversely, some complained that "smaller members have little or no voice in pricing bonds." Some were generally satisfied with their participation in syndicates, "except with Bank of America." Others found that "95% of the time Bank of America syndicates are intelligently managed." The "trend toward manager fees on competitive sales," combined with the "dictatorial approach of some managers" made syndicate participation maddening. Nevertheless, by enabling "competitors to work together," as one banker remarked, syndicates remained "the best method so far worked out to handle a big issue," according to another. The organizational structure and sociality among participants permitted banks with less capital to buy large bond issues, divide the risk among participants— "there's safety in numbers"—all while deepening "knowledge" of municipal debt "through discussion." Profits were the greatest benefit of all, of course. For bankers attuned to the infrastructural purpose behind a municipal bond offering, syndicates were "the only mechanism . . . to build schools and municipal improvements, and to facilitate United States' civic progress to a firm America for the future."

The responses from the nation's bankers provide a window into their likes and dislikes, what they thought they were doing, and what it meant. Municipal bond financiers agreed that advertising was integral to reselling bonds, but advertisements provoked something of a cultural war. There was some agreement on the hierarchy of advertising mediums.

Among the useless were *Barron's*, the *Commercial & Financial Chronicle*, *Boston Herald*, *Investment Dealers' Digest*, *Philadelphia Inquirer*, and *Washington News*. They did not say why, but respondents either skipped these venues entirely or posted ads in them purely "as a matter of record." They preferred the *Blue List*, *Daily Bond Buyer*, and *Wall Street Journal* as the cream of the crop.

The respondents debated whether to adopt new approaches to advertising the reselling of municipal debt. Some bankers were skeptical that new issue advertisements had any effect. If they did, it was only to a "small degree," one remarked. Another financier avowed that new issue ads helped "build up [the] standing of [the] firm," but only, another countered, if the firm still held those bonds: "[In] many cases bonds all sold before advertisement appear[ed], causing embarrassment." Some viewed the use of vignettes in new issue advertisements as essential: scenes that captured rapid transit systems in motion, construction workers installing massive flood control structures below ground, doctors walking through upgraded hospitals, architects examining scaled models of new urban layouts, and teachers prepping for the day's lessons told a story of how buying and selling debt helped revamp the nation's built environment.[49] Proponents of the advertisements clashed with bankers who argued that the most effective way to resell bonds was the old-fashioned way: through dealer contacts and phone calls.

A few respondents declared they either did not need or did not like new issue ads that used scenes to exemplify a bond's purpose. "For the most part," a banker noted, the ads were "pretty silly; in some cases verging on the emetic." Another claimed to be "violently opposed" to such ads. The difference of opinion hinged on a reading of the people to whom bankers resold debt. "The principal purpose of a municipal advertisement is to enlighten the professionals," said one respondent. Another said, "These men have no emotions and no imagination; therefore pictures of little cuties going to school"—rather than bland "tombstone" ads, which contain minimal artwork, if any—"are downright silly on the financial pages." Bankers, this respondent contended, were confusing the purpose of reselling debt with trying to "popularize municipal bonds with the common people (a tough job)."[50]

Bond clubs strengthened the ties within the fraternity. From San Francisco to New York, Chicago to Philadelphia, and Milwaukee to Denver, bond clubs served as a pivotal local organizational link in a national network of bond financiers.[51] These nodes helped turn individual bond financiers into a cohesive group: bondmen.[52] As bankers struggled to secure buy-in from their bosses, bond clubs allowed them to teach, listen to, and recruit one another. The national linkage of bond clubs offered occasions for municipal bondmen to learn about investment opportunities, hear from municipal finance officers about debt administration, and learn with whom they should partner to finance the nation's municipal infrastructure.[53] The San Francisco Bond Club (SFBC) provides a particularly apt example of how bankers strengthened the social ties and institutional connections integral to the buying and selling of debt.[54]

Organized in 1930, the SFBC grew out of a merger between the Investment Banker's Club and the San Francisco Bond Sales Managers Club. As the SFBC later noted, these earlier associations aimed to promote "fraternity" among securities dealers in the San Francisco Bay Area and "the prominent financial men who visited."[55] In this way the SFBC was distinct from its more specialized cousin, the San Francisco Municipal Bond Club, though membership often did overlap.[56] To some extent, the SFBC's explicit emphasis on socializing harkened back to late nineteenth-century elite urban men's clubs.[57] However, while bond clubs fused a similar elitist impulse to the boosterism of local chambers of commerce and the jovial, familial atmosphere of service clubs, SFBC membership was explicitly tied to debt finance.[58] So long as the applicant was engaged in "the underwriting, trading and distributing" of debt, it mattered little whether he worked at an investment banking house or in the bond department of a commercial bank.[59]

The SFBC's declaration that membership was open to "any man" was redundant since anyone in finance was almost inevitably male and white.[60] Yet there were subtle changes coming. The postwar entry of white women into the financial sector broke along class lines. A few white women worked as executives or municipal bond statisticians, among other specialties. Excluded from white men's bond clubs, they formed their own.[61] In most instances, however, white women worked as secretaries, and here, too, they formed professional organizations.[62] Bond clubs consolidated whiteness along elite, gendered lines. Moreover, white women's differential status as municipal bond statisticians, on the one hand, and as secretaries, on the other, helped reproduce a gendered racial identity that also afforded distinct class privileges. It was how elite white women learned about investment opportunities and broadened employment opportunities for other elites, while secretaries worked toward professionalization and better compensation.[63]

As with the bonds they bought and sold, debt was a central technique of white upper-class mobility. SFBC members paid initiation fees, semiannual dues, and assessments.[64] While some bondmen undoubtedly drew on their own capital for these fees, they also cashed in on their banking ties. With the cost of club memberships "*very* high," Alan K.

Browne later recalled, a new admit "would get an interest-free loan to pay his initiation fee," after which he would "pay off the loan in due course."[65]

The rules governing SFBC membership helped further its national reach. Applicants had to be "personally known by a majority of the directors." By setting a maximum of twelve active members from a single firm, the SFBC created more slots for bankers from many different financial institutions. By and large, membership was contingent on working near the San Francisco financial district and residing in the Bay Area.[66] That the SFBC allowed a handful of nonresident members was an important qualification: it elevated the San Francisco financial district as a center of gravity while also enabling bankers to orbit in and beyond the city. The SFBC listed as nonresident members Francis B. Bowen of the Development Bank for the Government of Puerto Rico, Warren Ruxton of the First Boston Corporation, Houston Hill Jr. of the New York Hanseatal Corporation, and Theodore L. Haff Jr. of Smith, Barney & Co.[67] Nonresident bankers, Browne noted, allowed San Francisco bankers to deepen their connections with Wall Street.[68] Their membership might even aid Bank of America's attempt to purchase and monitor the credit profiles of out-of-state "names."

The SFBC carved out up to fifteen slots for "honorary" members, men who "achieved distinction or made an outstanding contribution" to investment or commercial banking, corporate and municipal law, financial advertising and writing, investment account management, or counseling.[69] Many of these men presided over large amounts of capital.[70] The membership class enabled bondmen to channel the millions and billions of dollars held by commercial and investment banks and institutional and individual investors into tax-exempt debt. Thus it was hardly a coincidence that Bartlett T. Grimes of the Fireman's Fund American Insurance Companies joined the SFBC.[71] In 1955 the Fireman's Fund held $150,000 in San Francisco school bonds.[72] A year later it added $50,000 in San Francisco sewer bonds to its portfolio.[73] Surely honorary members Arno A. Rayner of the Industrial Indemnity Company and Robert H. Lautz of the New York Life Insurance Company similarly recognized the bevy of dividends they received from joining the SFBC.[74]

Though they lacked direct access to capital, both as invited guests and as honorary members, attorneys sharpened the ideological positions of bondmen and assisted municipal bond transactions. Bondmen were not antistatists. With the state as the backbone of the municipal bond business (tax exemption, progressive income tax rates, infrastructural needs, war financing), how could they be? Still, lawyers massaged banker fears of federal financial and regulatory powers.[75] A municipal bond transaction necessitated a stamp of approval from a bond attorney to confirm that bonds were legally issued. With only a "few nationally-recognized law

TABLE 2.3 Banking and SFBC membership

Firm	Employees with SFBC membership
Dean Witter & Co.	18
Blyth & Co.	12
Schwabacher & Co.	11
Bank of America, NT & SA	9
J. Barth & Co.	9
Merrill Lynch, Pierce, Fenner & Beane	7
Stone & Youngberg	6
Glore, Forgan & Co.	5
Weeden & Co.	5
First Boston Corporation	4
Salomon Bros. & Hutzler	4
Hannaford & Talbot	3

Note: Many members of the San Francisco Bond Club (SFBC) also worked for firms that participated in underwriting syndicates managed by BOA. Here is shown a sample of firms with at least three employees who held some type of SFBC membership (active, associate, honorary, nonresident, or lifelong) between 1947 and 1965.

Source: "Banks and Investment Dealers Associated with Us in Joint Accounts Managed by Us," in Alan K. Browne, Memorandum to Mr. R. A. Kent, "Underwriting of New Municipal Bond Issues," July 1, 1947, carton 3, no folder, Alan K. Browne Papers (BANC MSS 91/6), Bancroft Library, University of California, Berkeley, 1–2; "San Francisco Bond Club," December 1965, carton 4, loose material, Alan K. Browne Papers (BANC MSS 91/6), Bancroft Library, University of California, Berkeley, 18–26.

firms" that specialized in "municipal law," Alan K. Browne recalled, the firm Orrick, Dahlquist, Herrington & Sutcliffe was essential to the business.[76] An honorary member of the SFBC, attorney George Herrington might simultaneously play the role of bond counsel for Bank of America, function as in-house legal specialist for the SFBC and its municipal bond-men, and be the person whom city officials paid before issuing a bond.[77]

Ultimately, SFBC membership and participation in underwriting syndicates reinforced each other. Between 1941 and 1947, for instance, more than ninety commercial and investment banks formed joint accounts in underwriting syndicates managed by Bank of America. In addition, eighteen of these commercial and investment banking firms had employees who, by 1965, had become members of the SFBC (table 2.3).[78] The overlap strengthened the social ties among bondmen and forged the personal and institutional connections necessary to respond to and capitalize on the needs of municipal borrowers around the country.

White Male Bonding

SFBC bondmen swore that the material in their annual lampoon, the *San Francisco Tapeworm*, was published strictly "for the amusement of Club members."[79] However, the *Tapeworm*'s headlines, editorials, illustrations, advice columns, letters to the editor, photographs, and classified advertisements were not merely externalities, cultural overflows, or aberrations from the "real" workings of the municipal bond market. Bondmen refined their technical knowledge of the business through "jokelore."[80] If white male bonding was essential to the functioning of underwriting syndicates and jokelore was a means of building trust, then the rituals enacted through the *Tapeworm* helped bankers affirm their identity and remake their end of the municipal bond market.

The SFBC began publishing the newspaper-style lampoon "through the courtesy and co-operation of the *San Francisco Examiner*" in 1929–1930.[81] Specializing in wordplay and double entendres, the *Tapeworm* resembled the Bond Club of New York's publication the *Bawl Street Journal* and the Municipal Bond Club of New York's *Daily Bond Crier* (clearly a play on the *Daily Bond Buyer*).[82] These lampoons were steeped in a local flavor, but they also satirized bankers from out of town. "A Founder of the San Francisco Bond Club was summarily expelled from membership," reported the 1955 edition of the *Tapeworm*, "for submitting some humorous material to the BAWL STREET JOURNAL."[83]

At times, bondmen poked fun at their banks and themselves in these publications. The historic Kidder, Peabody & Co. became "A NON-PROFIT ORGANIZATION (We Did Not Plan It That Way)."[84] The *Tapeworm* portrayed a congressional hearing to which Alan K. Browne of Bank of America and Lester Empey of Wells Fargo Bank were called "because they [were] the weighty men in the banking business," a reference to their body mass. In keeping with his propensity to file copious reports, Browne "read a short statement of 150 pages on the relation of inflation to the expansion of credit." When asked how to keep inflation down, Browne responded, "Probably cutting out the fifth martini at dinner."[85]

Most jokes, however, were not self-referential. Bankers ridiculed women, people of color, the poor, and the rich. The jokes overlapped. What appeared to be a joke about class was also about whiteness; whiteness was also about patriarchy. In joking, bondmen unintentionally revealed how much financing sewers, managing syndicates, and rationalizing bond departments depended on the homosocial bonds and the racist assumptions of elite white men. Whiteness takes on particular forms of privilege, exclusion, and status property depending on class position. Wages are never distributed equally, and classes have distinct practices, rituals, and aspirations. Moreover, the elite class position into which bondmen were born, and furthered as financial intermediaries, meant that their identities conferred access to a distinct set of political economic benefits unavailable to middle- and working-class white Americans. In short, the relative class privileges of whiteness matter.

After twenty-five years as a member, Alan Browne was elected president of the San Francisco Bond Club in 1955. His tenure, the *Tapeworm* declared, would herald a transition "from Lunys to Munys": from the reign of lunatics who "dragged our once sedate and sober bond club down through the depths of degradation" to that of Mr. Municipal Bond, whose management skills could establish "order out of chaos." Browne's election also marked the move "from Sportin Blood to Blue Blood."[86] "Blue Blood" gestured toward Browne's class background as one of the Sons of the American Revolution and a child of wealth.[87] It also underscored his plan for those who were not born of privilege. As president, Browne would ensure that "Bond Club membership include[d] privileges at . . . [the] Pacific Union Club . . . [and] Bohemian Club," among other elite spaces in the Bay Area.[88] This was an odd promise to make. After all, some SFBC members were already members of these Gilded Age bastions of class power.[89] Perhaps irony was the point. The preoccupation with lineage was more explicit. Calling on all graduating college seniors, the *Tapeworm* posted a job advertisement to work at Shuman, Agnew & Co., but only if applicants supplied a photograph and description of their "Genealogical Background."[90]

At the same time that bondmen emphasized the importance of strengthening ties with bond buyers, they joked about ripping them off. In a "Dear Abby" column, "ALMOST BROKE" wrote in need of advice for dealing with his longtime securities dealer. "All the bonds they have sold me are in default. . . . Their representative is rude and doesn't bathe." He asked, was it time to change dealers? Abby preached unquestioned loyalty. Besides, given his pseudonym, she concluded, "You haven't much farther to go anyway."[91] If bond investors were to look, they'd find a section in the *Tapeworm* just for them: "An Informative Column of Riddles and Sorcery for Suckers."[92] "Don't Make Mistakes," the investment counseling firm Leppo Dorking & Sherman cautioned bond buyers. "We Make Them For You . . . We are Specialists."[93]

Bondmen drew on a durable racist trope to clarify how they profited from reselling debt. Historian Philip Deloria has noted how playing

Indian was a way for white American men throughout the twentieth century to naturalize conquest, dispossession, and national identity.[94] Thus,
C. F. Childs & Co. used the image of a Native American man adorned in
a feathered war bonnet to underscore the firm's historic role as creditor
to the state. The firm said of its "founder," "Him Scalp First Customer
We Keep Up Good Work."[95] Whether through mock advice columns or
violent imagery, bondmen saw ripping customers off as integral to their
success. The joke was in poor taste, but they weren't lying. Whether
through colonial dispossession or selling overvalued bonds to customers at greatly increased prices, scalping was key to longevity.

Bondmen talked about the bonds they financed in San Francisco differently than they talked about bonds financing a sewer system for the
Chumash Indians in Moorpark, California. In one *Tapeworm* editorial,
bondmen depicted the Chumash as so "primitive" that "they probably
spelled the name of their city backward." Their waste management solutions were described as terribly simple: the Chumash simply moved "the
Tee Pee" whenever bodily waste "became heel high;" only when "space
diminished some" and stumbling "drunks" found themselves knee-deep
in waste did the limits of a makeshift bathroom become apparent. As the
Tapeworm argued, it was not so much "the coming of the white man"
that uplifted Chumash Indians. Rather, by advising city finance officers
and mobilizing investment capital, white *bondmen* helped Moorpark finance its water and sewage system and helped transform the community
into "one of California's great cities." With the system almost complete,
bondmen anticipated that the "rallying cry" of the Chumash Indians,
"No more Pee Pee in the Tee Pee," was on the horizon.[96]

In some sense, this jokelore put a modern twist on notions of primitive accumulation, casting Indians as permanent relics within a modern
world. In this view they were, and would always remain, in need of modern sanitary systems. Hence, their presence in a municipality made that
borrower an indefinite means of capital accumulation.[97] Funding sewers
for profit was what bondmen did. When they financed sewers for Indians,
however, they saw the task as one of racist uplift for a people unable to
help themselves. Bondmen played off the technical terms of municipal
bond finance to argue that debt in general, and bond financing in particular, served a most valuable civic duty: it was what allowed California,
its cities, and its suburbs to leave the primitive world of Indians behind
to join the modern world.[98]

While they waited for new office space and furniture, bondmen taught
one another how to organize office space and manage the mountain of
paperwork that underlay municipal bond transactions. Spatial problems
provided occasions to joke about sex and objectify their secretaries.[99] In

one cartoon, bankers at "Chash" Manhattan Bank's government bond department, having searched for a file through cabinets and drawers, eagerly decided there was only one more place to look, as they eyed a buxom secretary (figure 2.2).[100] Another cartoon implied that bondmen had their secretaries organize the listing of bond prices, answer phone calls, and reconfigure office furniture for sex (figure 2.3).[101] Hence, charts of rising bond prices, pencils used to edit reports, telephones to dial

FIGURE 2.1 "$100,000,002 State of California Bonds," *San Francisco Tapeworm* 1, no. 26 (May 21, 1960).

FIGURE 2.2 "Chash Manhattan Bank," *San Francisco Tapeworm* 1, no. 27 (May 5, 1956). The name is a wordplay on "Chase Manhattan."

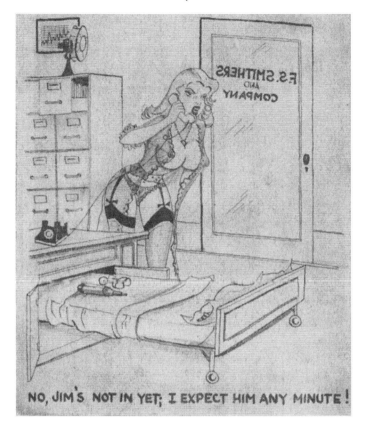

FIGURE 2.3 "F. S. Smithers and Company," *San Francisco Tapeworm* 1, no. 26 (May 21, 1960).

customers, and fans to cool down poorly ventilated rooms were more than artifacts of buying, selling, and distributing securities. For bond-men, these objects were interchangeable with objectified secretaries, to be displayed, handled, probed, and turned on.

When they did not depict pornographic scenes, they treated the female body as interchangeable with the bonds they bought and sold. Thomas M. Hess of J. Barth & Co. published an advertisement in the *San Francisco Tapeworm* seeking buyers of a "SECRETARY. BLONDE." For Hess, secretar-ies were like investment securities: they bestowed upon the holder the rights of temporary or long-term ownership. Hess insisted that despite her being used, not only was his secretary in "Excel. Cond.," but as an interest-bearing security, she came with "Two sets" of undergarments.[102] Fellow bond financier Collins L. Macrae of Wulff, Hansen & Co. wanted to buy a diversified batch of securities. Like an investor who opted for

San Francisco and Detroit municipal bonds, Macrae was in search of "MODELS" of "All types, sizes and ages." Thus, his colleague's listing was somewhat provincial. "Non-Caucasian" models, Macrae specified, were also "acceptable."[103]

Relegated to the secretarial tasks of typing, mailing, and answering phone calls, most white women in bond finance were poorly compensated.[104] In the "Letter to the Editor" section of the *Tapeworm*, one secretary inquired about writing for the lampoon: "Us girls can always use a little extra dough." Indeed, "the wage they pay in banks is pretty low, and it helps a lot if we can pick up a buck or two here or there."[105] Winning the annual "*Tapeworm* Beauty Contest" would not generate any extra cash, though. With over six hundred contestants competing for Miss Tapeworm of 1952, the lampoon spelled out the winning criterion. All a contestant had to do was "stretch a tape." Usually bondmen specialized in pricing bonds trading at, above, or below par. This time they stretched the "tape" to measure the breast, waist, and hip sizes of contestants. Instead of a par value of $1,000, at "38″ 24″ 36″," Miss "Desire de Boys" was priced at "an even par." She soon clarified her knowledge of financial markets in a supposed interview. Alcohol revealed her hidden understanding of the municipal bond business: while intoxicated, she declared, "I like it Bonded. I'm in control longer." Instead of a cash prize, Miss de Boys earned the chance to serve bondmen coffee and breakfast at their annual spring outing.[106]

In his *Tapeworm* advice column, "Count Farco" reasoned that secretaries had little to complain about. Whereas a bondman's wife was stuck "with the brats at home," secretaries had it made. "Where else can you find the necessary capital" to afford you a "mink coat, the jaguar and that apartment atop Nob Hill"? Of course, given the prospect of mergers and acquisitions, there was always the threat that "the girl in the next office will take over." He suggested some ways for secretaries to both protect and supplement their meager incomes, such as displaying their bodies. "There is no need . . . to wear constricting garments." All that was necessary was a "peek-a-boo blouse or skin tight sweater and skirt." Intelligence should be expressed through bodily fluency in "bending over gracefully in front of a file cabinet" to pick reports off the floor. Secretaries who failed to "show good judgment" would find themselves banished "to the file room—for filing purposes only." Both to protect the coveted secretarial position and to chart a path of upward mobility, Count Farco concluded that secretaries should remember that a specific wardrobe and bodily movements were "certain to get a raise out of him."[107]

The financial jokelore and technical terms amounted to a broader pedagogy of bond finance. Together, both discourses formed a common

knowledge base. By developing trust through racism, elite white supremacy, rip-offs, and misogyny, bondmen furthered their ability to act
collectively to stitch together the municipal bond market. In this inefficient, wasteful, discordant, and deeply patriarchal work environment,
bondmen might marry their secretaries or have affairs, and certainly
fantasized about sleeping with them. Bondmen imposed certain sexist
behaviors on their secretaries, and, just as important, on themselves.
In this way the avowedly satirical *Tapeworm* supplemented business reforms and administrative reports detailing profit, loss, and interest income. As a bundle, it was how municipal bondmen remained "Abreast
of the Market."[108]

3. Playground

During the 1950s, boosters and municipal officials in cities around the country adapted older urban forms and supported new sectors and industries to achieve economic growth. Out of the "Arsenal of Democracy" came a sprawling automotive complex in Detroit. Warplanes soon gave way to domestic airplane production in Los Angeles and San Diego. To different degrees, other Sun Belt cities pursued growth through defense, aerospace, and extractive industries and hoped perennial "recreation, a consumption-based lifestyle, [and] low-density development" would attract the *right* settlers. Other areas and regions of the United States were devastated by capital flight and plant closures.[1] To avoid a similar fate, San Francisco's boosters, city officials, and municipal technocrats sought to refashion urban space to meet the needs of an expanding financial service sector and the consumer demands of the white middle class. In so doing, they hoped to augment San Francisco's stature within the Bay Area, extend regional prominence along the West Coast, and elevate the city's position in the national urban hierarchy.

As the city fastened economic growth to finance, insurance, and real estate (FIRE), those sectors sought to use debt to further San Francisco's position as the Wall Street of the West. Office building construction and the uptick in white-collar workers betrayed a broader shift away from manufacturing and toward high-end services. Between 1960 and 1970, twenty-four office buildings of thirteen to fifty-two stories were constructed in the heart of San Francisco's financial district.[2] As early as 1963, the San Francisco Department of City Planning observed the increasing importance of FIRE, which included "banks and banking services, insurance carriers and agencies, investment and security houses, finance agencies, real estate and its allied services." These activities were part of "the only category in which employment in the city ha[d] increased at a greater rate than the metropolitan areas as a whole."[3] As manufacturing employment decreased by thirteen thousand workers between 1960 and 1970, employment in the FIRE sector increased by eighteen thousand workers. In that sector, 4 percent worked in sales; 12.4 percent were professional and technical employees; 19.7 percent worked as managers, officers, and/or proprietors; and over 63 percent worked as clerks.[4] The financial sector was investing in its own spatial future to deal with office clutter and lack of personnel, among other problems about which bankers like Alan K. Browne and R. A. Kent complained.

The Department of City Planning and the City Planning Commission formed the two administrative nodes within an urban planning network that rested on close cooperation with such groups as the San Francisco Chamber of Commerce, the Building Owners and Managers Association, and the San Francisco Real Estate Board.[5] Through joint publications, urban planners not only became enmeshed in a broader constellation of public-private relations but also, through maps, blueprints, and other static renderings, produced visions of a renewed city that would confirm "*San Francisco's function as a regional or continental Administrative and Financial center.*"[6] Invested in this spatial vision, bankers, real estate developers, and insurance brokers hoped to use municipal debt to clear blighted downtown property, facilitate the transportation of white workers, and enable smooth travel for suburbanites, visiting businessmen, and tourists.

The New Deal remade the racial state into a racial *welfare state* that afforded more benefits, protections, and access points to white Americans than to nonwhites. Bond referenda extended white rights into the realm of consumption. The revamping of San Francisco's arts and entertainment offerings, as well as attempts to attract white suburbanites through convenient public transportation and parking, betrayed the belief that achieving economic growth was predicated on attracting and capturing the consumer dollars of white people. Even once-stigmatized neighborhoods could become a key means of economic growth. With the white subject taken as a norm, Chinatown became an asset to the city largely because it afforded white San Franciscans, suburbanites, and tourists a novel chance to consume.[7] Infrastructure was thus not only a means of achieving economic growth by accommodating the white consumer, tourist, and executive; it also symbolized an investment in middle-class whiteness per se. From public parks and museums to roads and parking garages, infrastructure was an expression of white rights, of the expectation of an expansive public. Offering a San Francisco twist to the Keynesian city, streets, parks, and museums were repurposed in service of "state-backed, debt-financed consumption."[8] Just as federally guaranteed mortgages propelled white middle-class suburbanization, municipal debt made possible the well-paved streets, downtown parking garages, new sports arenas, and rehabilitated art spaces for the white middle- and upper-class urbanite. White construction workers in segregated building trades enjoyed the spoils by literally building the consumer playground and upgrading crumbling cultural landmarks.

By the late 1950s, then, San Francisco's municipal officials confronted two questions. The first was how to meet the demands of organized labor, business elites, and liberal reformers in ways that also maintained the city's strong reputation among bankers, appraisers, bondholders and bond buyers. What was built, who was employed to do so, who would have access and on what terms, and whether municipal debt was used to aid private development or the public well-being came to reflect unequal responses to the demands of these empowered interest groups; whether San Francisco maintained its "Aa" bond rating and remained creditworthy was contingent on how creditors evaluated the city's response to those demands. The second question was this: Which infrastructure projects could also lead to economic growth, a prerequisite for maintaining—and, better still, enhancing—the city's credit profile? The city answered both questions by developing infrastructure tied to financial services, investing in its cultural landmarks, and building out the consumer playground, furthering an infrastructural investment in whiteness along distinct class lines.

Nesting

San Francisco's bond referenda were the culmination of struggles and alliances between institutional forces that relied on the ballot to secure public funds. With expenditures, fares, and tax burdens at stake, successful bond proposals hinged on the ability of organized labor, city employees, business groups, and clean-government and liberal reformers to mobilize constituencies. The "Statements before Voters," that lengthy, biannual document that explained the purpose of a bond measure, also contained the dim traces of alliances between different groups, perhaps even the occasional dissenting opinion. The document, along with a relatively large voter turnout, might give the impression that the referendum was an open space for organized interests to advance their projects.[9]

There is another way to look at the referendum: as an artifact of the circumscription of democracy. Many decisions had already been made before the San Francisco Labor Council mobilized union members or the Municipal Improvement League rallied city employees. Even the Municipal Conference, which organized retailers and real estate groups around downtown redevelopment, held a subsidiary position to bond financiers. When Mayor George Christopher announced new bond proposals in 1958, he issued threats and demanded the Board of Supervisors do whatever it took to advance a progrowth agenda. Supervisors, meanwhile, explained to city departments why some bond issues but not others were granted, and authorized the allocation of bond funds.[10] However, when it came to debt administration—deciding on the dollar amount, whether the city lent its credit to other borrowing entities, whether and how the city secured expert opinion—many of the conversations, decisions, and practices had been restricted to participation by a few. Indeed, it was not the mayor's office but the city controller, not businessmen in general but municipal bondmen in particular, who shaped debt administration.[11]

The *San Francisco Chronicle*'s Art Hoppe commented with slight hyperbole that he who was appointed controller was the "most powerful man in City Hall." Seeking out this obscure figure, Hoppe followed "a devious, unmarked trail . . . to a small, sparsely furnished office tucked away in the far southeast corner of City Hall." There, Hoppe found "a small, rotund, balding man" behind a desk, smoking a cigar. "This is Harry Ross," the man who controlled the city simply because "he knows where the money is." Hoppe used colorful metaphors to explain what Ross did. Municipal finance was a "weird maze." City money was tucked away in "various little squirrel holes." Ross was responsible for keeping "the governmental machinery fed." He was successful because he was "like a veteran shell-game proprietor." In the obscure world of municipal finance, Ross managed city expenditures, soundly administered debt, and played confidence games with the best of them. The "experts," Hoppe concluded, "agree Mr. Ross' fiscal policies have saved the city millions of dollars."[12]

Knowledge of municipal finance only went so far as the close proximity between municipal technocrats and lenders. Together, controller Harry Ross and the city's leading municipal bondmen devised a way to insulate the debt ceiling. Through use of a nonprofit corporation, the *Chronicle* explained, "the city lends its credit to private business to build garages and stadiums and other facilities to which it eventually gains title."[13]

The San Francisco Parking Authority (SFPA) provides a particularly apt example of both the social connections on which infrastructural investment rested and the new liabilities that emerged as a result. In April 1958, the SFPA approved construction of a 1,450-car garage beneath Civic Center Plaza. As a relatively unfamiliar borrowing entity, the SFPA would find it difficult to sell the bonds without paying exceptionally high interest rates. But the SFPA could only charge so much for parking before drivers looked elsewhere. A negotiated bond sale offered investment banks Hannaford & Talbot and Taylor & Co. the chance not only to purchase the $4.5 million bond but also to extract additional guarantees. The SFPA would have to generate $325,000 annually in revenues to pay bondholders. It could rely on $36,000 from the state of California, which rented out the bottom floor. However, in case parking revenues did not cover the rest, "the city [would] underwrite any deficits that may occur in the first

10 years of operation."[14] The city might insulate taxpayers in the present, but future San Franciscans might be liable for a project they had never voted on. In effect, the debt arrangement gave all San Franciscans skin in the game of building parking for consumption and developing retail near parking garages.

Years later the *San Francisco Bay Guardian* identified the economic winners. Well-connected attorneys like Al Monaco, who helped establish the Fifth and Mission garage, were among them, collecting "fees ranging up to $100,000." As garage bondholders, insurance companies earned tax-exempt interest income—more than $83,000 and $326,900 annually on the Ellis-O'Farrell and Golden Gateway garages, for example. Wrote one journalist, "To guarantee this annual income, they write penalty clauses into the contracts which discourage early repayment, which keeps the profits away from the public till the last bond is paid off 30 to 40 years later." Local banks did not complain about this arrangement. Indeed, they held and invested some $6 million in idle trust funds.[15]

The SFPA spoke to a deeper structural relationship. The emphasis on appointments and expertise created space for bondmen to become further nested in urban governance. First established in 1947 by Mayor Roger Lapham, the Bond Screening Committee (BSC) was a further instance of how bankers became deeply involved in steering the course of postwar redevelopment and how lenders were at the table in ways other power blocs, much less everyday voters, were not.[16]

Shortly after he assumed office as mayor of San Francisco in 1956, George Christopher "corralled a herd of business and financial counselors" to serve on the BSC. That committee, the *Chronicle* remarked, had "quasi-official standing," advising on "which municipal bond issues to submit to the voters, for what amount of money, and when." Christopher selected attorney Lloyd Dinkelspiel, accountant John F. Forbes, and George Johns of the San Francisco Labor Council as members. Walter A. Hass Sr. of the famed Levi Strauss & Co., Cyril Magnin of Joseph Magnin stores, Otis R. Johnson of Union Lumber Co., and automobile dealer Albert E. Schlesinger stood on behalf of merchants. But most appointees came from the fast-expanding FIRE sectors in general, and the world of bond finance in particular. The BSC strengthened city officials' ties with commercial bankers from Bank of America and Wells Fargo and with investment bankers from W. P. Fuller Co., Blyth & Co., and Dean Witter & Co. Jerd F. Sullivan Jr., president of the Crocker First National Bank, was chair of the BSC.[17] If the Municipal Finance Officers' Association offered a national exchange of ideas between technocrats and lenders, the BSC was the local counterpart. What's more, the people on whom cities relied to underwrite debt were some of the same people nested in urban government through various committees and commissions, and in advisory roles.

What power did the BSC have, how was it wielded, and who checked it? What did it mean for lenders to be nested in the management of San Francisco's debt? The particular powers flowed from their stature as prominent businessmen and bond market experts. On the one hand, the BSC could not unilaterally dictate bond measures. The Board of Supervisors could ignore the committee's advice, which was "not legally necessary."[18] On the other hand, as experts, they could and did trim the dollar amounts of bond issues. Committee members weighed what the market could digest against the infrastructural demands.[19] The BSC's power stemmed from the belief that the opinions of experts enhanced municipal creditworthiness, thus strengthening the confidence of a bond buyer. Because the members "represent[ed] the business community," having their approval was "comforting."[20]

The BSC wielded a sort of extralegal power—clout that made elected officials responsive to their concerns. It was only partially true that the Board of Supervisors had "the final say on what measures will appear on the ballot."[21] In early February 1958, for instance, the BSC "demanded answers" clarifying the costs and legal questions pertaining to a few bond proposals.[22] The BSC later "angrily refused to take action" on four bond proposals totaling $13.6 million. Although the BSC refused to "pass on" to the Board of Supervisors its endorsement of referenda that would refurbish the city's Civic Auditorium and Palace of the Fine Arts, it offered its "blessings" on two bond issues totaling nearly $25 million.[23] Chairman Jerd F. Sullivan Jr. was exasperated after hearing presentations from health director Ellis Sox and Ronald H. Born, director of public welfare, about the need to build five new health centers and construct a new Public Welfare Department building. Claiming that the two plans signaled the absence of "an overall-all plan," Sullivan and the BSC "revolted," refusing to endorse the $3.4 million and $3.3 million proposals.[24]

By securing the "usually high-priced advice" of experts for "free," San Francisco technocrats might improve the city's credit standing and lower the cost to borrow.[25] But nothing was free. In effect, their appointments permitted bondmen to monitor their internal valuation systems of creditworthiness, updating which issuers were quality "names" and which were marginal. San Francisco received advice, and, in exchange, bankers secured advance notice of potential bonds well before voters showed up at the polls. What's more, legitimizing different kinds of financial offerings was an expression of local power. As one journalist explained, by weighing heavily bond issues that favored a particular vision of economic growth, the BSC denied "the rest of the city of bonds for a decent Muni railroad, more park and open space, more recreation facilities, [and] a modern capital improvement program." To "cut or veto bonds that more directly benefit the residents" was to insist that downtown development, and its immediate stakeholders, held top priority over ordinary San Franciscans.[26] Not only were social services and basic infrastructure tied to the market but through appointive committees such as the BSC, hospitals, recreational issues, and public health took less priority.

Municipal officials turned to bondmen to mobilize opinion and explain how large-scale projects might be financed. To secure an endorsement from prominent financier Charles Blyth was seen as pivotal.[27] In 1953, Supervisor Marvin E. Lewis conveyed his "sincere appreciation and gratitude" to Blyth for arranging a luncheon with the "publishers of the leading newspapers." For Lewis, the conversation resulted in supportive editorials, which, in turn, influenced the formation of the Bay Area Rapid Transit Commission (BARTC).[28] When rapid transit plans stalled, one supporter of the venture encouraged Mayor Christopher to put the question before "our own Charles Blyth."[29] Not long afterward, Christopher was "happy to report" a meeting with Blyth and other bankers "whose financial acumen can be of value to San Francisco."[30]

Through the Blyth-Zellerbach (B-Z) Committee, by 1956 Charles Blyth and industrialist J. D. Zellerbach had organized business executives from various corporations and sectors behind urban renewal.[31] When Blyth died in August 1959, fellow bond financier Roy Schurtleff took his place on the B-Z Committee.[32] Municipal bond financiers got something more than fulfillment of their civic responsibilities to the city in which they worked or lived. They got a professional advantage.

Once they went down the path of indebtedness, municipal finance officers had to determine how to enhance the value of their bonds. Bond financiers became authoritative figures; their access to capital, presumed knowledge, and capacity to secure expert opinion were needed to convince bond buyers. The financial adviser, the engineer, and the attorney, were also seen as possessing the requisite technical knowledge to enhance the value of municipal debt. That was why the governor appointed Alan K. Browne and Arthur J. Dolan Jr., of Bank of America and Blyth & Co., respectively, to BARTC.[33] There, these men commissioned reports that bundled ideas about space, growth, and finance. In 1953 BARTC selected the New York engineering firm Parsons, Brinckerhoff, Hall, and Macdonald, which paired existing data on how and where people moved with anticipations of future travel patterns. A year later BARTC contracted with the Stanford Research Institute to explore how to finance the transit system.[34] Municipal bond consultant and underwriting investment bank Stone & Youngberg was hired to determine the tax rates needed to cover principal

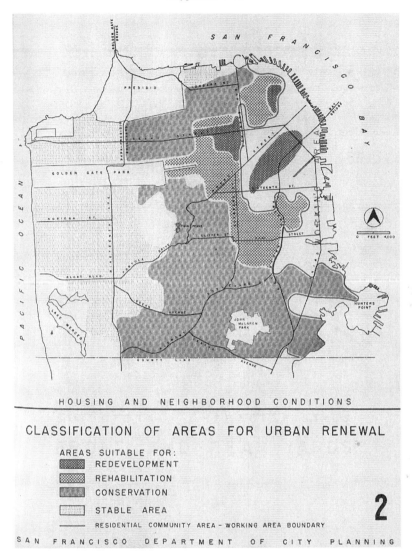

FIGURE 3.1 San Francisco Department of City Planning, "Classification of Areas for Urban Renewal" (September 1955). The classification schema informed the preservation or demolition of existing buildings, communities, and social ties.

and interest payments on bonds and how the financing plan would affect other municipal borrowers throughout the Bay Area.[35] As financial consultant, Smith, Barney & Co. used the Stone & Youngberg report to anticipate the future assessed valuation of Bay Area property and detail the dollar amount of bonds needed to cover the cost of construction.[36]

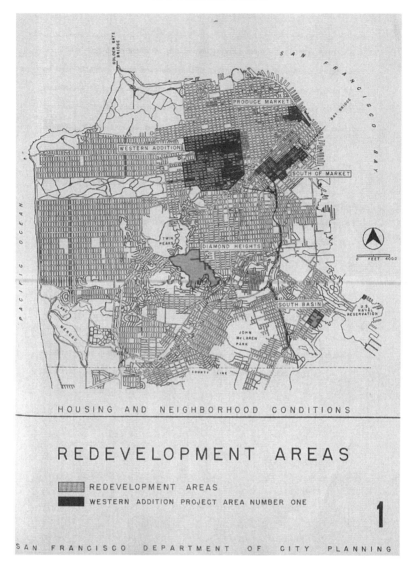

HOUSING AND NEIGHBORHOOD CONDITIONS

REDEVELOPMENT AREAS

REDEVELOPMENT AREAS
WESTERN ADDITION PROJECT AREA NUMBER ONE

1

SAN FRANCISCO DEPARTMENT OF CITY PLANNING

FIGURE 3.2 San Francisco Department of City Planning, "Redevelopment Areas" (September 1955), showing concurrent redevelopment projects.

Within the insulated world of debt, the relations among technocrats, bankers, and consultants formed a feedback loop through which estimates were built atop estimates to justify a particular vision that placed San Francisco as the economic and cultural hub of the Bay Area.

When elected officials and technocrats assumed that the expert opinions of lenders might broaden the market for their bonds and lower the cost to borrow, this was less because of their technical prowess and more because these were the men who organized other bankers to buy the bond issues they helped originate. In this way, the November 1956 airport bond was telling. Not content with stitching together the municipal bond market—indeed, recognizing the link between that process and local bond measures—Alan K. Browne served as chairman of the blandly named City-Wide Committee for the Airport Bonds.[37]

The referendum was an artifact of technocratic decisions and expert screenings. The belief that debt administration should be insulated from popular pressure and the idea that enhancing the value of debt commodities was predicated on parlaying with bondmen had morphed into a structural arrangement. Even if individual bankers on the BSC opposed a specific bond issue, as bondmen they had the chance to buy, hold, or resell the bonds they helped shaped. It was by wearing multiple hats that bondmen expanded their interests. They could screen, monitor, and organize syndicates in ways that promised them vital infrastructure and tax-exempt interest income. Likewise, serving as experts and lenders also allowed them to call for limits to other expenditures. They helped steer San Francisco out of its problems, in part by deepening an infrastructural investment in middle-class whiteness.

Investment

San Francisco faced two problems. The first was particular to the city, and the second was of concern to cities nationwide. As urban planners explained in March 1950, the city was "land hungry."[38] At less than 50 square miles, San Francisco had considerably less land available than there was in, say, Los Angeles, Detroit, or Oakland. The famed seven hills of San Francisco made for gorgeous topography and spectacular views, but they hamstrung development. Suburban subdivision within city limits was untenable. Indeed, "there was little vacant land upon which new structures could be placed."[39]

The postwar period saw the continued trend of industrial dispersal beyond San Francisco city limits, and throughout the East Bay and Contra Costa counties.[40] The migration of some administrative and insurance offices from downtown to the Southern Peninsula raised the haunting question of whether this dispersal was a harbinger of things to come.[41] Relatedly, although San Francisco would remain an overwhelmingly white city, from 1950 to 1960, the percentage of white San Franciscans declined (from 89.4 to 81.6 percent).[42] Retail decentralization followed on the heels of white middle-class suburbanization. For Paul Opperman, director of the Department of City Planning, both phenomena threatened the "the traditional supremacy of downtown San Francisco." With downtown property accounting for 21 percent of the city's taxable real estate, "downtown is San Francisco, and its fate is the fate of San Francisco."[43] Reports from the city's Federal Reserve district bank spoke to declining store sales.[44] The opening of Macy's in the Westlake shopping center in Daly City, just beyond the boundaries of San Francisco in San Mateo County, appeared the death knell.[45]

Land concerns and fears of all that suburbanization represented placed greater pressures on city officials to reclaim land and tear down slums. The San Francisco Redevelopment Agency, as we have seen, helped the city protect its debt ceiling. But it was also tasked with stimulating housing, consumption, and new work opportunities for the white middle and upper classes. During the 1950s and the first half of the 1960s, the SFRA engaged concurrent urban renewal projects in the Western Addition, Diamond Heights, and Commission District neighborhoods.[46] The specter of white flight was the subtext; each project featured sketches of detached single-family homes and apartments whose views might keep white tenants from leaving the city.[47] Just a few feet from planned high-rise developments were theaters, restaurants, art galleries, and outdoor cafes.[48] Embedded in so many city planning documents was a hope that white middle-class professionals would stay in the city, drawn to the proximity to work, the gorgeous views, the consumer playground, and the parks, recreational space, and restfulness that matched those of the suburbs.[49]

Whether residents fled or remained, they would have a new playground and cultural landmarks for their enjoyment. White-collar workers traveling between their homes and work downtown would be accommodated. A metropolitan rapid transit system and improvements to the Municipal Railway might reduce bottlenecks into and traffic congestion in the city. Major surface streets took on new importance as feeders to the Southern, Mission, and Crosstown Freeways.[50] New parking garages and on-street parking could aid in boosting retail sales.[51]

From the Golden Gate Bridge to Fisherman's Wharf, San Francisco had no shortage of structures, buildings, and landscapes of cultural significance. Yet the M. H. de Young Museum, the Steinhart Aquarium, and the Palace of Fine Arts cried out for rehabilitation. Take, for example, the de Young. During the 1950s its education department had seen an uptick in annual attendance, and the Van Gogh exhibition of 1958–59 was a smashing success. But patrons who attended weekly lectures or gallery tours moved through "makeshift" facilities. For years, museum staff requested "the replacement of the condemned warehouse by an education department wing with a proper auditorium, painting amphitheater, children's classroom, [and] teaching gallery," but to no avail.[32] Funds from a $3.6 million bond proposal might do the trick. Expanding boating facilities by adding some 220 yacht berths near the Gas House Cove would surely benefit those fond of sailing the Bay. By the late 1950s, San Francisco had added baseball's New York Giants to the fold, but accommodating them required borrowing $5 million to build a stadium. Finally, a $2.3 million bond would help the city purchase property and build a park near the Ferry Building.[53]

Stimulating local tourism was of little value if the means of traveling in and out of the city were faulty. In November 1956, supporters of a $25 million bond measure encouraged San Franciscans to take on debt to finance the upkeep and expansion of the airport. With American cities entering the "Jet Age," failure to approve the measure would not only damage the city's reputation but also preempt the chance to capitalize on "the travel dollar, . . . an increasingly important factor in our economy." Bond failure would also threaten the willingness of private business operators at the airport to expand their payrolls and push levels of employment well beyond the "more than 11,000 persons . . . privately employed" there.[54]

San Francisco's infrastructural investment in middle-class whiteness was grounded in its working-class companion, the segregated building trades. Discriminatory unions not only limited job opportunities for black craftsmen but also prevented, as one scholar has written, black workers "from acquiring new construction industry knowledge." While some black craftsmen found work through the Cement Masons Local 580 and Laborers Local 261, many more were slotted into low-level jobs. The International Longshoremen's and Warehousemen's Union hesitated to take on the Building Trades Council, and the city rarely interfered. In San Francisco during the 1950s and early 1960s, skilled construction jobs were for white men, and the city's building trade unions worked to keep it that way.[55]

Municipal debt proved key to what was effectively a cross-class, intraracial compact. White workers built the playground for the white middle class. And well before white consumers attended Giants Stadium, before white workers even began constructing it, wealthy white bondholders collected tax-exempt interest income on it. The rise and fall of this compact deserves as much, if not more, attention as the now-familiar arc of the postwar progrowth coalition.

San Francisco's infrastructural investment in whiteness rested on selling the public on debt. Whereas liberal reformers insisted on the "birthright" of San Francisco children to secure passage of public-school bonds, members of the progrowth coalition emphasized civic beauty, revenues, and collective uplift. Sometimes San Franciscans rejected such arguments, as in November 1953 and November 1958 when they turned down six out of six bond measures. Although it is tempting to treat these rejections as a function of the recessions of 1953 and 1958, there is little evidence for that idea. At most, the *San Francisco Chronicle* noted that some voters engaged a form of pocketbook politics, supporting self-liquidating state bond issues, while rejecting local issues that would push up their tax rates.[56]

City officials and the press most often attributed failure to poor leadership, procedural hiccups, and high voter thresholds. In November 1953, for instance, Supervisor Edward T. Mancuso attributed failure to a "lack of leadership" from Mayor Elmer E. Robison.[57] Robinson countered by suggesting that future bond issues should not appear during off-year elections.[58] Robinson was not alone in underscoring the procedural flaws. In a letter to the *San Francisco Chronicle*, John H. Mahler of San Francisco observed that "the publicity given these bond issues was hardly aggressive." The placement of favorable articles "on the back pages of the daily newspapers" was not a recipe for success.[59] Similarly, after the rejections of November 1958, others underscored "cumbersome" ballot procedures.[60] The *Chronicle* thought it better "to group together bonds for necessities and present them at one election and to group together bonds for desirable, new, imaginative projects and present them at a different election."[61] Elected officials and ad hoc committees, the *Chronicle* contended, might do a better job vigorously defending the importance of bond issues. Stanley Scott asked, "Why do we require a 2-to-1 majority before our local bond issues can pass, when State bond issues need only a simple majority?"[62] As we will see, the two-thirds majority would continue to prove the bane of select bond referenda. In the meantime, bond boosters and the press refined their salesmanship.

The press helped mold opinion by underscoring the benefits and costs of building the consumer playground. But the process of selling a bond to the public could be sloppy. In February 1958, the *San Francisco Chronicle* highlighted just how unprepared the Board of Supervisors was in deciding whether to put a bond measure for the Palace of Fine Arts before voters. How was the board supposed to act when "no one had ever made a thorough study of the cost of reconstructing the Palace of Fine Arts"?[63] Newspapers also suggested how the public should vote, and why. For the *Chronicle*'s Mel Wax, failure to pass a multimillion-dollar bond to build a new wing of the de Young Museum meant the owner of "a fabulous $5 million collection of Oriental Art" might take "one of the greatest private hoards of Oriental art in the world" to another city.[64] In some cases, the *Chronicle* assumed a strong editorial stance, as when it urged its readers to make "a sound investment in civic beauty" by approving debt for the Palace of Fine Arts.[65] Similarly, passing a bond for the Civic Auditorium, currently in such "poor condition to attract and accommodate conventions," the *Chronicle* explained, would "produce substantial revenue" from visitors.[66]

The Citizens' Committee for the Palace of Fine Arts, a group consisting of San Francisco's Labor Council, Council of District Merchants Association, and Junior Chamber of Commerce, as well as the Golden Gate Restaurant Association, explained that there was something in the bond measure for everyone. San Francisco would bolster its image by investing in "one of the most classically beautiful buildings built during the 20th century." Turning the Palace into a "year-round" convention center would provide construction work and also guarantee "San Francisco of an increasing number of convention visitors who spend, according to official estimates, $35.00 per capita per day."[67]

Selling San Franciscans on debt often meant insisting that a deracialized subject would benefit from universally cherished values. Engineer and BARTC member John C. Beckett spoke of the needs of "the American people." Above all else, Americans valued their "freedom to travel at any time and place, and with great speed." And while the car was useful in this respect, the effect was "congestion, irritation, and frustration."[68] "It is plain," Becket concluded, that if this trend were to continue, "the greatest advantage of the automobile, freedom to move as one pleases, will be lost."[69]

Such statements resonated with San Franciscans. In an April 1957 letter to the Mayor, Alvin Guthertz of San Francisco maintained that the fate of the city lay "in having unhampered freedom of movement."[70] San Francisco resident Milton Raash agreed that, given the expected population growth in the peninsula, rapid transit was essential. Without it, "I'm afraid it will be impossible to get to and from the city."[71] Douglas Hayward went further. The thought of having to "struggle in choking traffic" was enough to make one "consider a move away from the city."[72] As a frequent commuter to the East Bay, Marjorie Kelley argued that congestion was "endangering the future of our city." Writing to Mayor Christopher, she declared, "We need Rapid Transit!"[73] Warren Northwood wondered, "Will we strangle in a mass of confusion while other Bay Area cities enjoy freedom of movement and adequate transportation"?[74]

Not everyone accepted the assertion that bond measures would lift all boats. James Hurst, chairman of the Citizens Committee for Tax Economy, consulted a different calculus to determine the city's spending priorities. He outlined a nascent taxpayer critique of debt finance that would become full blown in the years ahead. A vital project was

TABLE 3.1 Results of San Francisco bond referenda, 1952–1959

Proposition	Purpose	Outcome
11/4/1952: Prop. E	Municipal Railway (MUNI) bonds, $6,620,000	Failed
11/4/1952: Prop. H	Firehouse bonds, $4,750,000	Passed
11/3/1953: Prop. A	MUNI improvement bonds, $2,749,000	Failed
11/3/1953: Prop. B	MUNI rehabilitation bonds, $3,871,000	Failed
11/3/1953: Prop. D	Warehouse and voting machine bonds, $495,000	Failed
11/3/1953: Prop. E	Library bonds, $1,894,950	Failed
11/3/1953: Prop. F	Exhibit hall bonds, $3,275,000	Failed
11/3/1953: Prop. G	Recreation bonds, $4,400,000	Failed
6/8/1954: Prop. F	Sewer bonds, $12,645,000	Failed
11/2/1954: Prop. A	Exhibit hall bonds, $3,275,000	Failed
11/2/1954: Prop. B	Recreation center bonds, $5,000,000	Passed
11/2/1954: Prop. C	San Francisco Hospital bonds, $5,830,000	Passed
11/2/1954: Prop. D	Laguna Home and Hospital bonds, $5,475,000	Passed
11/8/1955: Prop. A	Power bonds, Hetch Hetchy water bonds, $54,000,000	Passed
11/8/1955: Prop. B	Courthouse bonds, $13,000,000	Failed
11/8/1955: Prop. C	Playgrounds and recreation center bonds, $7,000,000	Passed
11/8/1955: Prop. D	Off-street parking bonds, $11,000,000	Failed
6/5/1956: Prop. A	Hall of Justice bonds, $19,475,000	Passed
11/6/1956: Prop. A	School bonds, $27,000,000	Passed
11/6/1956: Prop. B	Airport bonds, $25,000,000	Passed
11/5/1957: Prop. A	Courthouse and alterations of City Hall bonds, $22,150,000	Failed
6/3/1958: Prop. B	Recreation and park bonds (Steinhart Aquarium), $1,575,000	Passed
11/4/1958: Prop. A	Courthouse and alterations of City Hall Bonds, $22,150,000	Failed
11/4/1958: Prop. B	Palace of Fine Arts bonds, $3,600,000	Failed
11/4/1958: Prop. C	Ferry Park bonds, $2,785,000	Failed
11/4/1958: Prop. D	Civic Center Auditorium bonds, $7,225,000	Failed
11/4/1958: Prop. E	Department of Electricity maintenance yard bonds, $1,500,000	Failed
11/4/1958: Prop. F	Department of Public Works maintenance yard bonds, $1,300,000	Failed

TABLE 3.1 (*continued*)

Proposition	Purpose	Outcome
11/3/1959: Prop. A	Civic Center Auditorium improvement bonds, $7,575,000	Passed
11/3/1959: Prop. B	Ferry Park bonds, $2,970,000	Failed
11/3/1959: Prop. C	Palace of Fine Arts bonds, $1,800,000	Passed

Note: This list does not include bond issues that dealt with procedural norms governing the issuance of debt. And, by definition, it does not include issues that did not require voter approval.

Source: San Francisco Public Library Ballot Proposition Database.

subjective, so Hurst asked, what was the city giving up in order to finance its cultural landmarks? Public transportation to the Palace of Fine Arts was "not convenient." The measure begged the question, who had access to the space? Weren't the Opera House, Cow Palace, Brooks Hall, and Civic Auditorium enough? Hurst insisted borrowing "for necessary buildings, transit, sewers, redevelopment, etc., must come first" before expanding the playground for elites.[75]

With each bond referendum came the questions of which projects were worthy of debt and which neighborhoods and communities would have access to infrastructure projects. The new Ferry Building Park, claimed Harold L. Zellerbach, chairman of the Citizens Committee for Ferry Building Park (CFBP), would transform "three blocks of blighted, run-down, dilapidated, one- and two-story structures that add nothing to the city's economic worth." In its place, cochairman Alan K. Browne averred, would come "green trees and lawns, fountain, open space, and breathtaking vistas of downtown and the Bay." Since the project met the approval of "virtually every civic, industrial, fraternal, labor, and business group," Zellerbach encouraged the public to approve the measure. Between the lines, however, were differential benefits. Even the CFBP made clear that the park was for people working and living downtown. Surely $2.7 million, not to mention the interest payments on the bond, was a lot to invest in a single park.[76] Its backers asked San Franciscans to take on debt in ways that delivered a windfall to property owners in the area If public transportation was as poor as city planners maintained, why should residents of the outer Sunset and the southeast neighborhood of Bayview pay for a park far from where they lived? These questions presaged revolts over unequal benefits, burdens, and input over how the city should develop.

Will They Sell?

Revamping the city's cultural landmarks would require more than just convincing the electorate to take on debt. It would necessitate navigating a dramatic shift in the balance of power between municipal borrowers and creditors. Whereas issuers of long-term, highly rated municipal bonds borrowed at 1 percent in 1946, many of those same borrowers might expect to pay 3½ percent in 1957. Always a controversial federal subsidy, tax exemption had survived in part because municipal officials, in tandem with lenders, had persuasively claimed that it allowed cities to improve infrastructure at lower rates and, consequently, limited municipal reliance on state and federal governments. Through this "indirect" subsidy, the federal government reluctantly relinquished potential tax revenue. But the arrangement only made sense if the cost to borrow was low. By the late 1950s, it was becoming increasingly clear that creditors were the real beneficiaries of tax exemption.[77]

High interest rates jeopardized the infrastructural investment in whiteness, economic growth, and delivering on the white expansive notion of the public. Indeed, November 1956 made clear the difference between approving bonds and selling debt. A $27 million public-school bond could boast overwhelming support from organized labor, real estate and retailers, the local chambers of commerce, and organized parents and teachers. Airport bonds could secure endorsements from the city's major business groups. Both issues could pass by a wide margin, and still remain on the shelf.[78] Like voters nationwide who authorized more than $2 billion to resolve "the scarcity of schoolrooms, the jams on highways and bridges, the shortage of sewers," San Franciscans approved the bonds before them. The real question was, as the San Francisco Chronicle's Sylvia Porter presciently asked, "Will they sell?"

Rising costs betrayed the ways in which dependence on financial markets could undermine electoral decisions. Voters agreed to tax themselves and pay user charges and fares, but state and local governments would "find it brutally tough" to borrow. Municipal technocrats worked to finance vital projects and services through the municipal bond market, "and in this market," wrote Porter, "the pressure has been relentless." She predicted bonds would be held off the market until rates fell. And if San Francisco held its nose and decided to borrow, it would be "compelled to pay the highest interest rates in more than a quarter-century." Doing so would "add millions of dollars to the already heavy tax load they impose on us." It was ironic that when voters finally agreed to go into debt "the money markets 'dictate' the projects be put off," Porter concluded.[79]

The Municipal Finance Officers' Association (MFOA) continued to serve as a forum on the pedagogy of bond finance. In February 1957 Wade S. Smith, director of municipal research at Dun & Bradstreet, summarized two interrelated problems. All too often some cities "with the highest credit" had been unable to sell their bonds except "at interest costs greater than at any time since the depression." Those "with less attractive credit standing" often failed to receive a single bid. The outcomes differed, but both scenarios owed to the "tightening money supply and higher interest costs."[80] To be among the well-regarded "names" and boast an "Aa" rating from Moody's could not insulate San Francisco from the disruptions of high interest rates. As the cost to borrow escalated, the timely submission of fiscal details to information brokers and securing the advice of credit appraisers assumed greater importance.

Through trade organizations such as the MFOA, San Francisco's technocrats learned of the importance of anticipatory work. They were told of their moral responsibility to circulate information to firms. Credit rating agencies and trade papers then made a business out of selling that information to creditors. As we have seen, firms like Moody's collapsed information into a letter grade and sold ratings to subscribers. In this, credit rating agencies were joined by the *Daily Bond Buyer* (*DBB*). As it was "the trade paper of the municipal bond fraternity," explained one bond rater, "you will certainly not get the best results if you fail to advertise" there.[81]

San Francisco's finance officers had long relied on the *DBB* to reach bondmen, institutional investors, and wealthy individuals.[82] By the 1950s, however, the *DBB* helped San Francisco build its consumer playground by providing a catalog of bonds in stock or soon to hit the market. When the *DBB* announced publication of San Francisco's annual capital improvement report in February 1958, it not only highlighted a five-year debt program but also alerted investors to the possibility that close to $220 million, from both "bond issues that are already approved" and "future bond issues," might be coming their way.[83] If voters approved, more highly rated and well-regarded "names" tied to renovating the city's aquarium and Ferry Building Park would hit the market.[84]

The *DBB* offered financiers, bond buyers, and bondholders a view onto municipal finance, helping creditors keep tabs on good "names," supplement what a rating could not fully capture, and identify investment opportunities through a borrower's fiscal problems. By lending large sums to municipal borrowers, bondholders developed a stake in how the municipality was managed. The question was how the holders of city debt could monitor the strength, robustness, and diversity of revenue sources, and whether demands for infrastructure and services impinged on their hierarchical claims to interest and principal payments. Whether through direct correspondence with municipal technocrats or scouring the many city reports, the *DBB* offered bondholders and buyers a window into city management.[85]

By announcing the publication of San Francisco's annual report, for instance, the *DBB* alerted investors to how they might track changes to the city's credit profile.[86] Through the *DBB*, San Francisco broadcasted vital information that might convince investors that the city's airport was thriving. "Passenger traffic soared to new highs during 1959," rising by 13.4 percent from 1958, the *DBB* reported. "Revenue from airport terminal concessions has increased by 5½ per cent per passenger in two years, resulting in $250,000 more revenue from this source than in 1956–57."[87] Revenue flows and passenger traffic became ways of measuring the strength of San Francisco revenue bonds.

San Francisco might have broadened the market, but if revenue targets fell below expectations, or if expenses grew beyond acceptable limits, the submission of information gave bondholders the leverage to extract concessions and raise doubts about the strength of a "name." The arrangement worked out if the city borrowed cheaply, but it also extended the scrutinous gaze of lenders, backed by moral strictures and penalties.

In the late 1950s, at least, delays, budget shortfalls, and revenue gaps weren't necessarily a problem. What might be regarded as budgetary woes could even provide an opportunity for buyers in search of high quality "names." Given the thousands of bonds being authorized, floated, bought, and sold, it was curious that the *DBB* focused on the pyramiding costs of bringing the baseball Giants to the city. When San Franciscans approved the $5 million bond in 1954 to finance a portion of the new stadium they became responsible for at least $397,000 in annual payments for fifteen years. Bondholders would be paid from "property taxes, unless surplus stadium revenue was available." By March 1958, however, it was increasingly clear that the total costs exceeded the $10 million price tag. The city bond measure provided enough money to purchase the land, while leaving little to cover the $4.4 million needed for access roads and ancillary sewer and water lines. Municipal technocrats might borrow from Peter to pay Paul, drawing from "various street and sewer funds" to make up the difference.[88] From the vantage point of investors, though, the city's decision to delay street work and its freeway improvement program to plug shortfalls for the stadium might mean more bonds to buy.

Rule of Experts

Shortly after World War II, the leading credit rating analysts, bondmen, and bond attorneys used technocratic professional organizations to insist on the moral responsibility of city officials to circulate information. Lodged between volunteerism and coercion, San Francisco's technocrats turned to information brokers because they concluded that doing so was essential to capturing the attention of investors and borrowing cheaply. They had also been urged to insulate much of the world of municipal debt from democratic input. It was not merely that lenders became nested in urban government, giving them greater say over the polity. It was also that in pursuit of a Keynesian city, San Francisco came to rely on a set of actors with very different interests. Where San Francisco and its municipal siblings sought to borrow cheaply, lenders sought higher interest payments. When different groups called for different spending priorities, lenders might call for limits on expenditures, while steering development in ways that privileged certain sectors of the economy.

A parasite is perhaps what lenders became, but the process of latching onto the body was contingent on the confluence of borrowing needs and the search for tax havens; on a mix of volunteerism, technocratic faith, and coercion. San Francisco may have been infected, but this is no more than a metaphor; it does not account for how the shift in urban governance occurred. It was through advice from raters, dependence on bondmen to underwrite debt, the nesting of bondmen in urban government, the submission of fiscal details to information brokers, and the commitment to investing in whiteness that asymmetrical dependence was made. It would take the fiscal crisis of the state for the consequences to become full blown. Before the late 1960s, however, the use of municipal debt powered the making of white residential space, an expanded financial district, the profitability of public housing, and accumulation through dispossession.

PART II

The Paradox of Debt

4. Shelter

In late September 1958, Joseph L. Alioto, chairman of the San Francisco Redevelopment Agency (SFRA), advertised the sale of $11 million in short-term notes to finance urban renewal in the Western Addition neighborhood. Interested parties were offered a number of details, including how to submit bids, when the notes matured, and where note holders could go to collect principal and interest payments. The notice clarified that the debt was a "special obligation" of the SFRA but was also "secured by a requisition agreement" between the agency and the federal government. Should prospective lenders have any concerns, the legal opinions of bond attorneys Orrick, Dahlquist, Herrington & Sutcliffe, would be "furnished" to underscore their "validity."[1] As the principal player in buying, holding, and selling California municipal debt, Bank of America, NT&SA submitted the winning bid in late October.[2] Although the notes were issued by an unfamiliar borrower, the layers of federal guarantees and protections gave bankers all the confidence they needed.

Two years later the San Francisco Housing Authority (SFHA) made a similar appeal. Standing among a number of other housing authorities from around the country, the SFHA hoped bidders would purchase notes in the amount of $7 million "being issued to aid in financing its low-rent housing program." It was the authority's eighty-fourth offering. The SFHA likewise used its contract with the federal government to affirm the safety of investment. With the federal government having agreed to "make an advance loan" to the SFHA before the notes matured, holders were virtually guaranteed timely payment of principal and interest. But whereas lenders to the redevelopment agency had to wait a year to retrieve their principal, the SFHA's offering matured in just four months' time. The shortened maturity schedule virtually guaranteed the SFHA would be back to borrow again.[3]

Bond financiers situated themselves as critical intermediaries between large pools of capital and the many borrowing entities working to expand urban housing. Whereas the kinds of city debt thus far explored rested on San Francisco's pledge to deliver principal and interest payments, the debts issued by the city's municipal siblings offered that and a federal pledge. Together, bankers and public authorities and agencies had begun to address the problem of shelter through the expansion of rental housing, but not without shielding capital from federal taxation and kicking back rents to lenders.

The fraught racial politics surrounding urban renewal and public housing were conditioned by the terms of municipal debt. Financial relationships were both powered by and predicated on a racial contract. Equipped with borrowed funds, the SFRA's technocrats executed all of the things for which the agency is known. It carried out eminent domain, facilitated "Negro removal," acquired and cleared land, helped make white middle- and upper-class space by selling land to developers of high-rise luxury apartments and commercial office buildings, used the proceeds of land sales to pay off federal loans, and, amid any number of delays in site clearance and reselling that land, received rental revenue from black tenants while subsidizing garbage collections.[4] Meanwhile, since lenders had first claims on revenues, black and brown public-housing tenants ranked much lower in budgetary priorities and, as interest rates rose, would see a decline in investment in the places they called home.

Focusing on the overlapping forms of shelter, as that which protected capital and which renters called home, brings into view the battle between capital segments, or what I call "little c," "middle c," and "big c." In the first category fell the city's slumlords, absentee owners, and small-property owners. Middle c included developers who speculated in blighted rental property and used federally guaranteed mortgages to build rental housing and single-family homes for middle-class white people. Finally, big c included the bondmen working for commercial and investment banks and the kinds of institutional investors who could simultaneously lend millions of dollars to borrowers around the country and wait years for a return of their principal. Although each segment was offered a range of government guarantees, by the mid-1950s the state effectively privileged the continued accumulation strategies of real estate developers, bond financiers, and insurance companies over little c. Black middle-class professionals and public-housing tenants, renters of Japanese descent, residents of Chinatown, and white white-collar professionals, among others, experienced the consequences of this struggle, though here, too, the burdens were not felt equally. Just as the infrastructural investment in whiteness was an important engine of midcentury racial capitalism, the battles between little, middle, and big c over the provision of shelter proved yet another avenue for racial capital accumulation.

Little *c*, Big *c*

The politics of housing in San Francisco shaped and was shaped by legal decisions and public policies at the state and federal levels. The US Supreme Court in *Shelly v. Kramer* (1948) outlawed racially restrictive covenants on neighborhood residency. Not long afterward, middle-class residents of Chinese and Japanese descent found housing in the Sunset and Richmond districts. The blockbusting techniques of real estate agents gave middle-class African Americans the chance to purchase older housing in the Oceanview-Ingleside neighborhood.[5] Although the SFHA had deployed a "neighborhood pattern policy" to racially segregate the city's public housing, the California courts found that approach unconstitutional in 1954's *Banks v. SFHA*.[6] Racial and ethnic minorities could officially live in any of San Francisco's public-housing projects. By the late 1950s, the previously all-white Valencia Gardens project in the Mission District became home to Latinos, Asian immigrants, and Asian Americans. The North Beach project also came to house various racial and ethnic groups and, by the late 1960s, large numbers of Chinese immigrants.[7] The breakdown of de jure segregation at the state and local levels intersected with the federal government's revamped attempt to fund public housing. Both dynamics infringed on the accumulation strategies of local absentee owners and landlords.

In this city of renters, where a small few owned large tracts of land, absentee owners, slumlords, and minor property owners barely got by.[8] A long-standing way to make it, though, was by capitalizing off the overall housing shortage within a racially discriminatory market. Even when black professionals found rental housing, they often paid a premium for it.[9] Meanwhile, landlords like Benjamin Fireman—who had, as the *Sun Reporter* remarked, "a suitable name for the fire traps which housed his tenants"—depended on racial segregation "to wax fat off the poor."[10]

Take, for instance, conditions in the Western Addition–Fillmore neighborhood. San Francisco's African American population rose from fewer than five thousand in 1940 to more than forty-three thousand by 1950; many of them had settled in this area.[11] Drawing on various surveys, census data, and assessor records, in October 1952 the SFRA concluded, "Approximately 815 persons own 730 parcels of real property in the project area. Of these owners about 317 also reside in the area."[12] Burdened by second and third mortgages, many of these owners barely avoided bankruptcy. They did so by subdividing properties to maximize rental income. Black families sardined into attic apartments lived above "noisy, dirty, and in some cases noxious" commercial and industrial businesses "which range[d] from printing plants to automotive repair shops and from bars to cleaning establishments." Japanese renters might live next to "junk filled empty store fronts" or "long unused lots."[13] In Chinatown, residents similarly paid relatively high rents to live in properties without electricity or running water.[14]

We have seen how, in a city with limited landmass and where the specter of white flight loomed large, the pressures to destroy slums and repurpose land was high indeed. But how to rehouse poor racial and ethnic minorities within a racially discriminatory housing market? If public housing was the answer, how to work around the high price of land, federal price limits, and vigorous local opposition to new public housing? Municipal debt served as the balm, but its use infringed on the profits of slumlords. Indeed, the further embrace of debt signaled a privileging of big *c* institutional capital over and above the extractive pursuits of little *c* slumlords.

As the *Wall Street Journal* observed in June 1951, it was the "unique feature of unconditional government backing" that made so-called new housing authority bonds "an entirely new factor in the tax-exempt securities field."[15] Bondholders were creditors, but who among them laid first claim to principal, interest, and, in the event of a default, the project itself? Moody's Investors Service explained the hierarchy: while the federal government ranked first in collecting interest payments on previously issued loans and securing title to housing projects, private investors had first dibs on collecting principal.[16] Moody's declared that what mattered most was the "unconditional obligation" of the federal government to deliver payments to bondholders. To this was added "the pledge of the new operating income of the housing project."[17] New housing authority bonds furthered the abstraction of the city, laundering tax-exempt income of its connections to specific public-housing projects. Bond financiers collapsed the particularity of a housing authority into a homogenized security. They purchased debt with the assumption that, regardless of who lived in the projects, what really mattered was the federal pledge. The investors who purchased public-housing debt from underwriters were so far removed—spatially and temporally—from the initial transaction that they engaged not with the racial politics of a housing authority but with the Public Housing Administration (PHA), which provided them with guaranteed income. In one instance, the SFHA offered for sale $12 million in new bonds, which they awarded to Blyth & Co., the low bidder. While the firm worked to resell the bonds, the SFHA used the funds to repay moneys advanced by the federal government, refinance debt on older projects, and "cover the construction costs" of new projects.[18]

TABLE 4.1 Sample of American Employers' Insurance Company holdings of new housing authority bonds, 1956

Housing authority	Par value	Yield	Maturity
Detroit, MI	$195,000	2.38%	1977
Little Rock, AR	$55,000	2.13%	1973
San Francisco, CA	$300,000	2.38%	1966

Source: United Statistical Associates, Municipal Holdings of Insurance Companies (1956), 98, 48, 464.

Through guarantees to bondholders, the state nipped the profit margins of those who made a living on slum housing and expanded the channels of investment for institutional investors.

The bonds created a hierarchy not only among lenders but also between lenders and public-housing tenants. In effect, income was earmarked first for payments to bondholders and secondarily, if at all, for project operations. As the national orchestrator of new housing authority bond offerings, the PHA consolidated and offered a large block of public-housing debt. Bankers sliced the bonds into various groups with differing maturity schedules and yields. It was through this process of differentiation that SFHA bonds found their way to investors' portfolios.

It is difficult to determine the names of the individual buyers of public-housing debt, as they are protected by fiduciaries. It is slightly easier to identify institutional investors who were publicly traded and who produced annual reports and other documents to proclaim the success of assets and assuage concerns over liabilities. This performance gave rise to other firms that analyzed these statements. During the 1950s the United Statistical Associates identified countless insurance company holdings of school bonds, debts tied to airport expansion, water improvements, hospitals, and parking garages. It is thus unsurprising that insurance companies were also major holders of new housing authority bonds (tables 4.1–4.3).[19]

Insurance companies agreed to lend housing authorities huge chunks of funds, securing differential interest payments over time. Some holders of SFHA bonds also invested in other housing authority bonds. Other firms sold off SFHA bonds in search of higher yields. For instance, in 1955–1956 the American Re-Insurance Company liquidated $32,000 in SFHA bonds bearing 2.13 percent.[20] By the end of 1956, American Re-Insurance held $201,000 in new housing authority bonds for Lanett, Alabama; $168,000 in new housing authority bonds for Blytheville, Alabama; and

TABLE 4.2 Sample of Continental Casualty Company holdings of new housing authority Bonds, 1956

Housing authority	Par value	Yield	Maturity
Camden, NJ	$400,000	2.38%	1980–1984
Chicago, IL	$500,000	2.38%	1980–1984
Cleveland, OH	$170,000	2.25%	1980–1982
Detroit, MI	$400,000	2.38%	1980–1984
San Francisco, CA	$880,000	2.25%	1970–1978

Source: United Statistical Associates, Municipal Holdings of Insurance Companies (1956), 98, 235, 464, 567, 689.

TABLE 4.3 Sample of American Mutual Liability Insurance Company holdings of new housing authority bonds, 1956

Housing authority	Par value	Yield	Maturity
Daytona Beach, FL	$50,000	2.13%	1986
Little Rock, AR	$400,000	2.13%	1983, 1986–1987
San Francisco, CA	$100,000	2.13%	1979–1980

Source: United Statistical Associates, Municipal Holdings of Insurance Companies (1956), 98, 48, 146.

$500,000 in bonds issued by the Miami Housing Authority, all with a relatively high yield of 2.63 percent.[21] Other investors paired their holdings of SFHA bonds with those offering much higher yields. While the Standard Accident Insurance Company of Detroit collected 2.13 percent on a $177,000 investment in SFHA bonds, it also lent $100,000 to the Boston Housing Authority in return for 2.9 percent tax-exempt income.[22]

Holding public-housing debt was a temporal bet: to what extent would today's investment decisions be insulated from future inflation? Some companies made good bets. The Farmers Insurance Exchange of Los Angeles held $786,000 in SFHA bonds due to mature between 1957 and 1966.[23] Similarly, the Zurich General Accident and Liability Company held $100,000 in SFHA bonds set to mature in 1962.[24] Most companies, however, took on twenty-five- to thirty-year obligations whose maturity dates fell roughly between 1970 and 1987. There were all kinds of reasons for these temporal preferences, ranging from statutory limits on investments, to the synchronization of interest and principal payments with obligations to policyholders, to limits on capital. Some of these later maturation dates made for sour investments. Given the relatively shallow secondary market for municipal bonds, it is likely that the holder of a SFHA bond in 1955 was the holder twenty years later. If the Ohio Farmers Indemnity Company, which in 1958 held $140,000 in SFHA bonds, remained the holder in 1974–1975 when those bonds matured, or the Michigan Millers Mutual Insurance Company still collected 2.38 percent in tax-exempt income on its $58,000 investment until 1973, these and other long-term bondholders experienced the wrath of inflation and were paid in cheaper dollars.[25]

The established history of the postwar American city has held that the public-private practice of redlining repelled institutional capital, such that slumlords, petty capitalists, and loan sharks dominated inner cities. According to one account, it was not until the Housing and Urban Development Act of 1968 that the state used "its power and resources to protect the investment of private capital in the inner city."[26] But if we move the focus from one financial instrument—the mortgage—to another—new housing authority bonds—we find millions of dollars invested in the inner city throughout the 1950s.

As early as 1940, SFHA officials recognized their weakness when negotiating with slumlords. The ability of slumlords to command a higher price per square foot than what the federal government was willing to pay had two consequences. First, it led to delays in building badly needed public housing and, as a result, to capital extraction through poorly kept, crowded subdivided properties in the Western Addition, Hayes Valley, and North Beach neighborhoods. Second, the inflated acquisition costs forced the SFHA to build public housing "in outlying areas where land is available at low prices."[27]

By locating public housing in redlined areas and issuing tax-exempt, federally guaranteed debt, the SFHA inadvertently monetized the city's most devalued lands in new ways. Suddenly, redlined neighborhoods, once defined by racial threats, slum dwellings, and "unpleasant odors" from nearby stockyards and packing plants, were outlets for institutional capital.[28] Indeed, what is most striking is that every public-housing project built during the 1950s and early 1960s was located in a redlined or "no-lined" neighborhood (figure 4.1).[29] Price limits, not to mention opposition from white homeowners, kept public housing out of San Francisco's more valued neighborhoods. As a result, debt-financed projects in redlined neighborhoods yielded capital to insurance companies around the country.

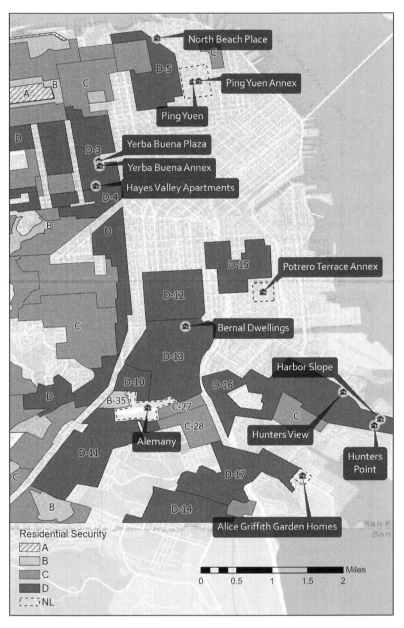

North Beach Place

D-5

Ping Yuen Annex

Ping Yuen

Yerba Buena Plaza

D-3

Yerba Buena Annex

Hayes Valley Apartments

D-4

D-15

Potrero Terrace Annex

D-12

Bernal Dwellings

D-13

Harbor Slope

D-10

D-16

B-35

C-27

C-28

Hunters View

Alemany

D-11

Hunters Point

C

D-17

B

D-14

Alice Griffith Garden Homes

Residential Security

A
B
C
D
NL

Miles
0   0.5   1   1.5   2

FIGURE 4.1 San Francisco's permanent public-housing projects. Map by Parmanand Sinha.

Source: San Francisco Housing Authority, *Twenty-Sixth Annual Report* (1963–64); 1937 Home Owners Loan Corporation residential survey map of San Francisco, RG195, HOLC, location 450, 68:6:2/box 147, National Archives II.

If in 1944 federal public-housing commissioner Nathan Straus assumed that "capital in almost unlimited amounts" would be "available at low interest rates for public housing," something had gone wrong fifteen years later.[30] When nineteen housing authorities issued $104 million worth of bonds in May 1959, the average cost to borrow was 3.78 percent.[31] The PHA responded by postponing the sale of long-term debt, and, when cash was needed, it encouraged the issuance of short-term notes.[32] Public-housing authorities were dependent on the same market that threatened to upend San Francisco's infrastructural investment in whiteness.

During the 1950s and early 1960s, federal regulations hamstrung many of the ambitions of commercial bankers. They were "thwarted" in their attempt to expand loans and prohibited from offering enticing interest rates to attract new deposits. Middle-class white Americans also increasingly put their savings into financial institutions and investments "beyond the purview of commercial banks." Bondmen, meanwhile, struggled in a glutted market. Thus, along with mergers, suburban branch-bank expansion, and innovations in consumer credit, public-housing notes were a welcome addition.[33] Bank of America (BOA) had been "a prime dealer in temporary loan notes of Local Housing Authorities, Redevelopment Agencies," declared bond financier Alan K. Browne.[34] Indeed, BOA lent funds on a short-term basis to the SFHA throughout the 1940s.[35] The bank remained committed to the short-term debt instruments in large part because of what the notes offered: injections of liquidity and greater cash flow at a time of increased consumer loan demands. And with the SFHA promising, as it did in February 1960, to repay $7 million in just four months' time, public-housing debt provided interest and a shortened time horizon between one investment and the next.[36]

Bondmen treated urban renewal and public-housing short-term debt as largely commensurate. They benefited, however, from one crucial difference: whereas notes for urban renewal projects came with interest rate ceilings, public-housing notes did not.[37] Bankers could not impose unlimited net interest costs upon borrowers; they had to work "within the limits imposed by the notice of sale," Browne explained.[38] Nevertheless, they profited from the proliferation of short-term debt without interest caps and ceilings. Rather than fund the construction, upkeep, maintenance, and beautification of crumbling housing projects, bankers used the absence of interest rate restrictions on short-term public-housing debt to capture income. While public-housing authorities were bled dry, BOA increased its holdings of PHA notes from $165 to $270 million between December 31, 1964, and September 15, 1965.[39]

While the SFHA complained of rising administrative costs and operational deficits, it had little to say about its fixed liabilities—which were assets for bondholders. Between 1951 and 1965 the SFHA had issued $53.8 million in new bonds and retired a little more than $9.4 million, for a total long-term debt outstanding just above $44.4 million. At $4 million, the SFHA's short-term indebtedness appeared relatively small. However, the cycle of borrowing and repaying funds quickly by borrowing again implied that the SFHA's short-term debts could change from month to month. By its very nature the organization's annual report could capture only a momentary glimpse of this shapeshifter.[40]

The debtor-creditor arrangement did more for institutional capital than for the tenants who lived in the housing it funded. That one side looked to borrow at low interest rates and the other side sought higher interest payments was par for the course. What made the public-housing arrangement unique was that the layers of guarantees, protections, and hierarchy of claims betrayed in a most glaring way the divergent interests of borrowers and bondmen, tenants and creditors. In a sense, the program became a laboratory for the profitability of poverty and how short-term debt could mollify the cost-profit squeeze of bondmen.

And Guarantees for All

By the late 1950s, urban planners had produced a mountain of documents alleging the threat of blight in the city. In response, the San Francisco Board of Supervisors authorized urban renewal in three areas.[41] The Western Addition A-1 project was bounded by Post Street to the north, Eddy Street to the south, and Franklin and Broderick Streets to the east and west, respectively. All told, approximately twenty-eight blocks of central city land fell within its boundaries. The Diamond Heights project was defined by Portola Drive and Clipper Street to the north, O'Shaughnessy Boulevard to the west, and a number of loosely winding streets to the south and east. Finally, the Ferry Building and downtown anchored the Golden Gateway, a seventeen-block project just northwest of the Ferry Building and bounded by Embarcadero, Market, Sacramento, Battery, Front, and Broadway.[42]

Local action, though, was not enough. It took the support of financiers, manufacturers, and real estate developers, as well as a novel financial tool, to get these projects off the ground. The SFRA did not have the power to levy property taxes. How else could the agency raise the working capital needed to purchase land and acquire rights of way, among other costs? The SFRA could either wait for direct federal loans or borrow through the municipal bond market. The agency, like other redevelopment agencies, issued so-called preliminary loan notes. These were tax-exempt, short-term debt instruments that typically matured in one year.[43] As the Housing and Home Finance Agency (HHFA) clarified in 1959, "most of the funds contracted to be loaned" for urban renewal projects "are not actually disbursed." Redevelopment agencies instead used their contract with the federal government "as security to borrow private funds at more favorable rates of interest."[44] Before the notes matured, the federal government agreed to lend funds to the SFRA. Those federal loan payments were "irrevocably pledged first" to delivering principal and tax-exempt interest income to note holders. Upon the SFRA selling or leasing reclaimed land, it used the proceeds to repay the federal government.[45] Here was a complex process of lending across levels of government, between agencies and financiers, and whereby land became further embedded in the real estate and municipal bond markets. By 1961, more than $820 million of the $1 billion borrowed through the federal guarantee of urban renewal debt was outstanding.[46] With short-term debt at the center of a web of reimbursements, 1958 "set records for virtually every category of urban renewal activity," the HHFA gleefully announced.[47]

Much like the public-housing authority, the SFRA used state power in ways that ultimately privileged the accumulation strategies of big *c* over the needs of small-property owners. The part played by real estate speculators and developers, however, made all the difference. Urban renewal offered middle *c* a chance to build housing for the kinds of white people deemed essential to the city's survival.

The SFRA employed a disparaging discourse ultimately meant to minimize the claims of property holders. The existing homes in the Diamond Heights area were not only old but were also owned by "more than 500 widely scattered individuals" who fueled the trend of "sporadic sales of small parcels" that "left the area divided among several hundred different owners." "Scattered" was code for small, petty property owners, many of whom did not hold "clear title to their property."[48] Neither the "obsolete" distribution of fruits and vegetables nor the recalcitrant produce merchants had a place within the new Golden Gateway.[49] Blight was a capacious concept; it could be used to denigrate black neighborhoods and to minimize the rights afforded to white property owners, too. The words "scattered," "obsolescence," and "blight" were part of a broader discourse mobilized by champions of redevelopment to facilitate removal.

By law, the SFRA was required to pay fair market value for blighted property. As a "public agency" it saw no contradiction between advancing the "interests of the general public" through redevelopment and protecting ownership "rights as well."[50] Nevertheless, the SFRA used its own land valuation and appraisals to pay as little as possible. Appearing before the Board of Supervisors, Morely Goldberg, the SFRA's attorney, spelled out the negotiating process. Property owners had between thirty and ninety days to negotiate "the price for each parcel" with either the city's real estate department or "an authorized independent appraiser." The SFRA promised to be fair, but "if the property owner objects," Goldberg declared, "the entire property will have to be taken over through eminent domain."[51] Seeking to motivate merchants and property owners within the area just north of the Ferry Building to sell, in February 1960 the agency promised to pay *fair value at once* for the property as it is now used." As an added perk, the SFRA would reimburse moving costs and made available its technical staff to help with the move.[52] But by May 1962, the SFRA lamented it had no choice but to execute "eviction proceedings" to advance the Golden Gateway project.[53] If the carrot of fair market value was insufficient, the SFRA used the stick of eminent domain.

But what could be done when real estate speculators used inside information to complicate the process? As a member of the Board of Supervisors between 1941 and 1953, Chester MacPhee had a hand in designating the Western Addition for redevelopment. He was also a stockholder and director of Del-Camp Investment Corporation, which went on to acquire more than forty properties in the Western Addition.[54] Del-Camp drew on insider knowledge, personal connections, and state guarantees to speculate in rental properties, all of which inflated prices for them. Indeed, this problem was so great that in 1960 the comptroller general of the United States ruminated on the techniques of an unnamed San Francisco corporation that had captured "illegal income."

The unnamed corporation took advantage of black Americans' maddening search for housing and the city's desperate attempt at land reclamation. A year after its founding in 1954, the corporation had acquired seventeen properties in the Western Addition and increased its real estate holdings in adjacent areas. It raised rents in some properties, "unlawfully converted" other buildings, and took both actions in still others. In one instance, the firm subdivided a three-story, two-family Victorian home into sixteen smaller units and a three-room apartment. Although city inspectors found the building to be "substandard and . . . subject to condemnation," they were astonished to find that the corporation had more than tripled its annual rental income.

Whereas small-scale absentee owners and slumlords hoped that rental income would keep them ahead of mortgage payments, the ultimate objective for this corporation was reselling property to an eager redevelopment agency. Along with the president of a local savings and loan association, the partners, employees, and "relatives of a partner in the brokerage firm" purchased stock in the corporation. Using a loan from perhaps the same savings and loan association, the corporation acquired property and

FIGURE 4.2 *The Way It Used to Be—Western Addition A-1*, undated.

Source: Box 4, "Buildings by Name of Owner/Developer," folder "A-1 Unidentified," San Francisco Redevelopment Agency Records (SFH 371), San Francisco History Center, San Francisco Public Library.

waited for the SFRA to come knocking. By providing income statements that projected an increase in rental income, the corporation could also supply inflated mortgage appraisals. When the SFRA attempted to purchase these seventeen properties in 1958, it could offer no more than the federally approved price of $341,750. The corporation demanded $500,000. It took until the end of 1959 for the agency to acquire the property, paying thousands of dollars more than its own appraised value. Stockholders received dividends and nonshareholders realized long-term capital gains.[55]

The campaign in the Western Addition clarifies three distinct features of urban racial capitalism at midcentury. The first pertains to the differential benefits of ownership. Absentee owners might have neglected their property or subdivided it beyond recognition, but they were still owners;

they would be paid fair market value, even if the SFRA used the stick of eminent domain. The second is that although there were guarantees for all owners of property, the state privileged some segments of capital over others. Despite paying fair market value, the SFRA still elevated the profits of the FIRE sector over and above these small-scale owners and slumlords. Finally, displacement was not the product of individual choices but occurred through expensive relationships and costly arrangements between the state and private sector. Seeking economic growth through the tactics of land reclamation and property acquisition, the SFRA used borrowed funds from Bank of America to purchase inflated property from real estate speculators to then displace African American renters.

Reclamation

It took the prescient eye to see matters of dollars and cents in the fenced-off lots and building materials scattered atop dirt mounds. Yet James Baldwin, the famed novelist and social critic, made clear the connections between land and capital, money and race. Standing in the heart of the Western Addition's urban renewal project area, in the spring of 1963 Baldwin observed all of this had "something to do with money." The land had been "reclaimed for money," which meant "Negroes have to go."[56] From the peddlers of short-term debt to the compensated slumlords, from the developers using FHA-guaranteed mortgages to the insurance companies and institutional investors who purchased those mortgages, urban renewal in the Western Addition symbolized the profitability of black and brown dispossession and the investment in whiteness.

Before the US Commission on Civil Rights (CCR), and in the press, redevelopment officials were called on to answer three questions about displaced people. Who were they? Where did they go? Why was it so difficult to rehouse them in safe and decent living quarters? All dislocated families of "moderate or low income" faced the problems of limited land, low vacancies, and high rents. What made white moderate- and low-income renters different from "minorities," however, was that the latter were "in an unfavorable position in the housing market because there [was] so very little housing open to them."[57] This was a euphemism for racism; an anemic way of directing attention toward unidentifiable actors and away from real estate agents, banks, and homeowners; a lame telling of opening and closings, without identifying who closed what doors and how; spider webs without spiders. To paraphrase one historian, all moderate- and low-income San Franciscans had a land and rent problem, but minorities of various class standings had that and a racism problem, too.[58]

Urban technocrats often transformed the actual people dispossessed of their homes and communities into mere numbers and percentages. The names, not to mention the friendships, businesses, and weekly rituals, were given short shrift, their stories turned into proportions and ratios. Indeed, the cold calculus of counting heads matched the banality of debt offerings and sales. Justin Herman had just assumed the job of chairman of the SFRA when he was called before the CCR in January 1960. He noted that upon beginning "relocation activity" in January 1958, some 1,800 families and 1,900 individuals lived in the project boundaries of the Western Addition. He neither specified what counted as a family nor indicated how many people those families comprised. "Of this number," though, 80 percent were nonwhite and 20 percent were white.[59]

There were others who emphasized that not all nonwhites were minorities in the same way. Frank Quinn, executive director of the Council for Civic Unity, clarified that nonwhites included African Americans, "Japanese and others."[60] Tarea Pittman, acting secretary of the West Coast branch of the National Association for the Advancement of Colored People (NAACP), insisted that urban renewal campaigns were "displacing a majority of non-Caucasian families and in most cases a majority of these non-Caucasian families [were] Negroes."[61] Finally, the city's main African American newspaper, the *Sun Reporter*, specified that of the eight thousand individuals displaced, "40% are Negroes and 20% Japanese. About 90% were tenants, renting their overcrowded, crummy flats from prosperous landlords."[62]

Black people have always been much more than statistics, and the Western Addition–Fillmore neighborhood was much more than segmented parcels. Black residents participated in a thriving street culture. Willie Brown, later the city's first African American mayor, arrived in 1951. He and other black San Franciscans "would get dressed to kill. You saw great peacocks. Stacey Adams shoes with the white strings showing that [they] had been cleaned up with Clorox." Black folks were helping to develop a segregated enclave economy. By the start of World War II, Jack's Tavern, "the first club in the Fillmore to be managed by and cater to African Americans," was joined by other clubs such as the New Orleans Swing Club and Elsie's Breakfast Nook. Black San Franciscans in their finest garb might hope to catch Count Basie, Billie Holliday, and Sarah Vaughn and the Bop City's Celebrity Night. In 1942 black entrepreneurs such as Wesley Johnson Sr. purchased property in the Fillmore, using the first floor to house the Texas Playhouse/Club Flamingo and the second for the Hotel Texas. During the late 1940s the Primalon Ballroom at 1223 Fillmore Street made profit out of segregation: the club only booked African American performers.[63] The area was the "cultural hub for

San Francisco's Black population," journalist Wade Woods recalled, and "money was circulating in the Fillmore" throughout the 1950s.[64]

Urban renewal would eventually dismantle this enclave economy, but in the interim, black entrepreneurs collected segregated profits. Julian Richardson, cofounder of Marcus Books, worked with other black merchants to form the Committee for Community Solidarity (CCS). Each month the members agreed to spend a certain amount at a specific black business. The CCS also published a directory of black-owned businesses throughout the city. The illicit economy was the second means by which profits were gleaned. Much to the chagrin of the African American *Sun Reporter* newspaper, prostitution, gambling houses, and a thriving narcotics trade smeared the Fillmore. It was not uncommon for operators of reputable black business to invest their profits in the gambling activities of the Three Leaf Clover Club at 1841 Post Street.[65]

Ultimately, "Negro removal" became the dominant way to summarize the relationship between demographics, place, and time; the teleological end point that flattened all that a black presence had once represented into a story of loss and elimination. But there was life in the midst of urban renewal. In July 1960, one writer for the *Sun Reporter* described the scene as cranes stood tall on the streets of Post and Eddy. The "bulldozers roared and ripped away, pouring clouds of powder onto the houses still occupied and driving their tenants daffy with the noise." The sounds of crashing debris and shattered glass, the vibrations of jack hammers drilling into concrete in random spurts, and the soot stains on the exteriors of closed windows created "a depressing atmosphere for the housewives who have had to live in it all day, and for the children who have come home to it every day after school." By the time the SFRA worked to rehouse eligible families in public housing, "the projects were filled."[66] Justin Herman noted that displaced residents settled "in the immediate area adjacent to the project area." Basically, "these families have moved from blighted area to blighted area."[67] Frank Quinn offered other ways to account for the movements of the displaced. Upticks in illegally converted apartments and in elementary school enrollments among children using the same address indicated that the displaced were "doubling up" in the kinds of subdivided units the SFRA sought to demolish. As Quinn cleverly put it, "We are razing slums and raising slums—'razing' in the sense of cutting them down, and 'raising' in the sense of creating new ones."[68]

By the early 1960s, "separate but equal" and racist restrictive covenants had been undermined by the courts. Land reclamation and housing developments for idealized white residents would thus have to occur through other means. The remaking of exclusionary white middle- and upper-class space in particular, and of a housing market stratified by class and race more generally, occurred not through laws but through rental scales and income brackets, not through explicit denigration of black residents but through purportedly color-blind idealizations backed by layers of government guarantees. It was illegal to exclude black Americans from the Diamond Heights area. It was perfectly legal, however, for Justin Herman to pledge his support for moderately priced housing that would also keep social undesirables and "welfare recipients" out of there.[69] Similarly, in the midst of acquiring land, demolishing substandard buildings, and removing African American and Japanese renters from the Western Addition, the SFRA announced its land sale program for the area. Developers would have the chance to build "apartments to serve the needs of moderate- and middle-income families, as well as families of high income."[70]

The mechanics of exclusion were not lost on some. With rents set between $125 and $270 per month, many of the proposed apartments in the Western Addition were for people who made more than $10,000 annually—the city's "upper one-third income group," as the *Sun Reporter* explained. Rents would be "set so high that none of the relocated people" could realistically return. Although city planners often spoke in color-blind language, it had "become quite obvious" that redevelopment meant "the conversion of a predominantly colored area into an all-white residential neighborhood." What began as a way to clear slums and poor living conditions had become a means of displacing "lower income groups and colored people."[71] Even if developers and property managers did not discriminate, black incomes were still stunted by racial exclusion and exploitation in labor and housing markets. For the NAACP's Tarea Pittman, this reality meant "the average Negro family [would] be precluded from occupying" planned housing developments throughout the city.[72] (In its final projection of the Golden Gateway, the SFRA confirmed that more than 90 percent of the apartments there would rent for between $110 and $290).[73]

As they provided shelter to the city's white middle class, developers protected their capital by drawing on federally guaranteed mortgages. On June 18, 1962, the SFRA was proud to announce the FHA's commitment of $20 million for construction of more than 790 apartments in the Golden Gateway, "the largest FHA mortgage ever issued in the west." As when insurance companies purchased public-housing debt, the purchase of this FHA mortgage by John Hancock Life Insurance represented an "unmistakable note of confidence," the SFRA concluded.[74] Some developers, such as Ring Bros., drew on conventional mortgages to build the 396-unit Diamond Heights Village and 265-unit Gold Mine Hill. Other developers in Diamond Heights, though, drew on a number of FHA-guaranteed mortgage instruments to produce a landscape of apartments, cooperative units, duplex, and single-family homes.[75] Whereas some portions of the middle *c* capital segment speculated in blighted property, others got in the business of real estate development. Government guarantees undergirded both acts.

Historian N. D. B. Connolly has shown how landlords and real estate developers relied on FHA mortgage insurance to build and profit from rental housing for black people in midcentury south Florida.[76] In San Francisco, federal mortgage insurance was key to constructing high-rise luxury apartments in spaces cleared of black and brown people. The Cathedral Hill Corporation secured FHA section 220 mortgages (the mortgage instrument especially designed to insure developments in urban renewal areas) to finance the twelve-story Cathedral Hill West and twenty-five-story Cathedral Hill East towers. The insured mortgages permitted the developers to construct a mix of studios and one-, two-, and three-bedroom rental apartments. Some five hundred feet from the Cathedral Hill East tower, another developer drew on FHA section 213 mortgage insurance (designed to stimulate cooperative housing) to construct the nineteen-story luxury Carillon Tower.[77] What the racial welfare state had done for developers of suburbia, it was beginning to do for developers of urban high-rise apartments. All told, the racial welfare state unlocked "the rent on whiteness, the profit on whiteness, the residuals on whiteness, the returns on whiteness," in the words of one philosopher.[78]

Although these kinds of housing developments paid dividends to developers and financiers, they also exacerbated older housing problems. In 1962, the National Association of Real Estate Boards (NAREB) produced something of a report card on urban renewal in San Francisco. The "residential and commercial core" of the new Western Addition, the Golden Gateway's "curtainwalled complex of offices and apartments," and the all-encompassing development of Diamond Heights evidenced the "great rebirth" of the city. However, the NAREB was concerned that the urban renewal program had "been too heavily weighted in favor of luxury apartments." Without setting aside "land in renewal areas at prices which will enable construction" of apartments renting for much less, San Francisco would become "a community of the rich and the poor."[79]

Strikingly, solutions to the recurring problem of high rents often fell back on the timeless mechanism of black expendability. Hunters Point, the southeastern neighborhood redlined due to a longer and deeper history of toxic and hazardous land uses, concomitantly became the site for public-housing projects in which black people lived, as well as a tax shelter for public-housing bondholders. The area had been monetized, but some thought it was perhaps time to reclaim the land for other purposes. Indeed, for some municipal officials, the 137 acres that encompassed the neighborhood, its proximity to the waterfront, and its equable climate made Hunters Point an ideal space for white middle-income housing. From one technocrat to another, Justin Herman wrote to the man in charge of managing the city's credit profile, Harry D. Ross, with a plan. Herman suggested that the 117 acres that housed the Ridge Point temporary housing project "be sold for private ownership of housing . . . for families of moderate income."[80] In December 1965, the Board of Supervisors considered how reclamation could benefit white people squeezed by high-priced rentals. Touting the antidote of whiteness, the Board of Supervisors hoped that renewal might "attract additional white people to Hunters Point and abolish the ghetto atmosphere."[81] We will soon see just how dramatically the urban uprisings in this southeastern neighborhood changed the city's plans, while also heightening the importance of dealing with the ghetto.

Compared to New York City or Chicago, San Francisco's public-housing stock was virtually nonexistent. Nevertheless, by 1958 the SFHA had become the city's largest landlord, in charge of some 4,250 units in fourteen permanent low-rent projects.[82] Through debt, the San Francisco Housing Authority came to house poor residents while providing safe investment outlets for bondholders. This arrangement also allowed the SFHA to infringe on the territory of little c, fostering new avenues of accumulation for insurance companies in ways that undermined the profits of slumlords.

The *Banks v. Housing Authority of San Francisco* decision of 1954 gave African Americans access to all of the city's public-housing projects. And by 1960, African Americans occupied more than half of the total number of project units. A similar trend could be found in Chicago, Los Angeles, and New York.[83] In what might be described as the tipping-point effect, "once nonwhite tenants in a predominantly white project exceed between about 25 to 35 percent of the total, whites tend to reject the project so that it will go all-nonwhite under certain conditions," one historian observed.[84] By 1960 integration was won, but the prize for poor black and brown folks was confinement to fast-deteriorating structures scattered throughout the city. And as public-housing projects were stigmatized and black mothers were dismissed as pathologically inept and exemplary of the undeserving poor, bondholders collected interest payments. The deterioration of public-housing projects was taken as proof of the failures of socially oriented public policies rather than as a consequence of a structural arrangement that, from the beginning, privileged the claims of bondholders.

Most historians who note the ways in which urban renewal displaced scores of African Americans fail to explain why it happened. They reflexively treat "Negro removal" as a product of individual or structural racism. At best, they hint at some connection to markets. The imperatives of the bond market helped to make middle- and upper-income housing in San Francisco racially exclusionary. That is, the postwar expressions of gentrification were intimately tied to the relationships, dependencies, and terms of municipal debt. The pressures to make sure that new housing, commercial development, and amenities for white consumers would generate revenues sufficient to pay creditors led to a privileging of those tenants who were deemed least "risky"—in other words, white and relatively high income. As interest rates soared, there became even greater pressure on the SFRA and the city more generally to privilege the kinds of racially segregated and higher-income communities that would entice real estate developers. James Baldwin was right that "Negro removal" had something to do with money, and that "something" was tied to the use of debt to realize the economic value of whiteness.

5. Crunch

On May 22, 1964, President Lyndon B. Johnson outlined his vision of a Great Society. At once aspirational and reflective, the vision of "abundance and liberty for all" was also a commentary on just how good the postwar years had been to the white middle class. Their opportunities for education, leisure, and commerce were abundant; safety and a renewed relationship to nature became a deliverable social right.[1] Billions of dollars in municipal debt, much of it issued at relatively low interest rates, fueled the affluence. In the twenty years after World War II, total indebtedness of state and local governments rose from $16.5 billion to approximately $99 billion. The reliance of borrowers on municipal debt also showed no signs of subsiding. Nearly $122.8 billion in total municipal bonds were sold between 1946 and 1965, $48.7 billion (40 percent) of which was sold between 1961 and 1965 alone (figure 5.1).[2]

In San Francisco, millions in what might be called baby-boomer bonds were used to build and restore public schools. Debt-financed parks, recreational centers, and cultural landmarks offered spaces for white youngsters, visitors, and patrons to play. Refurbished streets, parking garages, and public transportation helped bolster consumption and employment in financial services. Concerns over juvenile delinquency fed into new court and detention facilities. The city's slum clearance program helped turn portions of the city into white space. From rehabilitated cultural landmarks and shopping facilities flowed increased revenues into municipal coffers. Investment in the streets, pipes, and tunnels—the quotidian infrastructure on which basic services and growth through finance and consumption relied—minimized expenditures that might otherwise go toward maintaining worn-out infrastructure. And where debt did not directly boost municipal revenues or reduce expenditures, such as through baby-boomer bonds, debt improved the life chances for white children who attended revamped public schools, and, through investment in fashionable cast-iron street lamps, contributed to the image of San Francisco as safe, clean, and modern.

By March 1965, President Johnson pivoted to discuss the poor, the elderly, and those "discriminated against." Too many lived in dilapidated

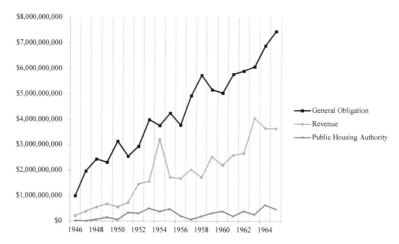

FIGURE 5.1 New issues of state and local long-term municipal debt in the United States, 1946–1965.

Source: Joint Economic Committee, Subcommittee on Economic Progress, "State and Local Public Facility Needs and Financing: Volume II," 89th Cong., 2nd sess., December 1966, 106.

homes without adequate plumbing. He drew attention to the millions of Americans who learned inside decaying school buildings, which only increased the chances of "dropouts, delinquency, and social disorganization."[3] Johnson could have been talking about the disparity between any American city and suburb, but there were profound inequalities within cities, too. By the mid-1960s one San Francisco official could truthfully declare, "We have a black ghetto, we have a Spanish surname ghetto, [and] we have a Chinese ghetto."[4]

Through matching grants, Johnson maintained, the federal government could serve as a catalyst and lever. Cities could pair their borrowing powers with federal financial power to provide quality schools for millions of additional children, welfare and health centers, transportation facilities, refurbished water and sewage systems, and greater access to airports, museums, libraries, parks, and playgrounds.[5] All of this would prove expensive for cities. In December 1967, Congress estimated that by 1975 state and local governments would need $328 billion to meet capital requirements; close to 50 percent of those requirements would be financed through the municipal bond market.[6] In short, the combination of federal financial support and the local commitment to the Great Society's infrastructural promises would foment "concomitant expansions in municipal debt."[7]

Johnson made his appeal just as the rhythms of the domestic and global economy began to go off beat. The Vietnam War and the Great Society disrupted economic expansion and the white middle-class expectation of unending prosperity. Military infrastructure and the war were expensive, with direct costs increasing from $5 billion in 1965 to a remarkable $33 billion in 1968. The finances of the Great Society presumed noninflationary growth. The rising balance-of-payments deficit and beginnings of an inflationary cycle were additional signs of a domestic economy in distress. The federal government was also adding to the deficit through a dramatic increase in welfare spending, which between 1963 and 1967 climbed from $14.5 billion to $35 billion.[8] The credit crunch of 1966 quickly dashed the Great Society's infrastructural agenda and the opportunity to remedy many of the inequities produced in the immediate postwar years. As interest rates rose, and the duress of municipal borrowers intensified, the relationship between borrowers and lenders revealed itself for what it always had been: an unequal power dynamic that only appeared symbiotic because of the confluence of postwar needs. Attempts by borrowers to maneuver around the rising cost to borrow enabled bankers to relieve their own cost-profit squeeze.

Defense, Offense

With the federal government in their sights, municipal bondmen threw stones from afar while also capitalizing on the commitment of the racial welfare state to deliver white rights through government guarantees. Bondmen had no problem with the debts issued by public redevelopment agencies and housing authorities and backed by federal pledges. However, they opposed direct, low-interest loans at fixed rates, which matured well into the future. This threat proved especially palpable when, in the late 1950s, and in the context of rising interest rates on municipal debt, some municipal borrowers gladly locked in with the federal government at 3 percent interest for fifty-five years—circumventing the municipal bond market and the creditors who made a living off of dependence.[9]

Financiers, along with bond attorneys, credit appraisers, and other members of the municipal fraternity, harangued against the dangers of federal control. As Gordon L. Calvert, municipal director and assistant general counsel of the Investment Bankers Association of America, explained, "our system of government is based on the belief that the Federal Government should not take over functions of private business." Direct federal loans not only eroded this principle, but also fomented "a dependence on the Federal Government . . . which effects a gradual erosion of the responsibility of the local government."[10] The US Chamber of

Commerce likewise decried the ways in which "low cost loans and long maturities" from the federal government might "undermine the principle of local responsibility."[11]

Even as they spoke in moral terms, bond financiers and their allies made clear the material stakes of amplified federal financial power. Direct, low-cost loans would "merely substitute Federal financing for private financing," the *Daily Bond Buyer* (*DBB*) summarized.[12] Bankers could count on friends in high places to make a similar point. Albert M. Cole, administrator of the Housing and Home Finance Agency, explained that the interest rate on federal loans to local governments must not be "substantially below that now prevailing or likely to prevail in the private municipal bond market for a sizable portion of municipal bonds." Supplanting private for federal funds was, he concluded, "undesirable."[13]

Bankers' fears were not entirely overblown, especially as the volume of federal programs swelled during the 1960s. The dramatic uptick in federal grant-in-aid programs—from $1.8 to $30.3 billion between 1948 and 1972—was facilitated by federal liaison offices in cities around the country.[14] The broader change within fiscal federalism was matched by proposals to provide financial alternatives to state and municipal borrowers. In February 1960, the *DBB* alerted readers to the polemics of Texas congressman Wright Patman, who felt that "a great many banks" were "not adequately serving the needs of the local people." He declared, "A good argument could be made" that "the Federal Government should adopt some other kind of arrangement to provide a market for bonds issued by the States and the cities."[15] Patman was one of a few congressmen to underscore the inequality—and dangers—of borrower's dependence on the municipal bond market. That "interest rates have been going higher and higher on exempt municipal bonds, which are just as good as taxable Federal bonds," he averred, did "not make sense." Patman, drawing on his New Deal roots, called for another Reconstruction Finance Corporation (RFC), which helped refinance borrowers in default and "bailed out the great State of Arkansas . . . and then other States and counties." The RFC's refinancing operations "permitted people to vote bonds, to build schoolhouses and roads" and provided cities with "a ready market for their bonds at low rates of interest."[16] The *DBB* grew nervous when Patman proposed alternatives to the punitive criteria of raters and bankers.[17]

The insecurities were on display when bondmen met at San Francisco's Fairmont Hotel in October 1966. Many federal financing programs were an "unnecessary duplication," the *DBB* summarized. Investment banker Alvin V. Shoemaker insisted that even if they opposed the Great Society, bankers should "become more fully aware of the possibilities and opportunities inherent in these programs." With their structural position on the line, it was essential to further situate themselves as critical intermediaries and profit from the plethora of debt instruments. The assessment of the problem—"Federal Aid Surpasses Volume of Tax-Free Municipal Financing," read the *DBB*'s headline—and the recommendation of critiquing federal power without relinquishing potential profits landed Shoemaker a "standing vote of applause" from "an audience of more than 300 people."[18]

Bondmen stayed abreast of the threats and opportunities by working closely with the *DBB*, which, "in cooperation with the Investment Bankers Association" (IBA), published a list of grants and loans approved by federal agencies. The goal was to ensure "that private financing of the balances of the project—if there be such—may be worked out by IBA members."[19] From the vantage of bondmen, the seemingly excessive expansion of federal financial power made this a big "if." They paid attention when, in December 1964, soon-to-be vice president Hubert H. Humphrey proposed "the establishment of a kind of domestic 'World Bank' to help finance the costs of rehabilitation of depressed areas." And they felt reassured when Humphrey insisted that the War on Poverty might be financed "through private channels." They seemed to dodge another bullet when Humphrey proposed more federal guarantees "to stimulate the investment of private funds into those areas of the economy that need help."[20] Bankers might disdain social welfare, joke about ripping off poor customers, and support a quasi-domestic World Bank, but only if, as with the World Bank's reliance on Wall Street, financing the War on Poverty occurred through them.[21]

Creditors had a heightened stake in the infrastructural provisions of the Great Society. Credit appraisers would be called on to rate the bonds of ever more borrowers. Bondmen would be called on to underwrite decaying school buildings, streets, and parks. Tax-exempt income, resale profits, and subscription fees were on the line.

Financing affluence and poverty had made for lush times for bondmen, none more so than the financiers at San Francisco's Bank of America, NT&SA (BOA). When the San Francisco Bond Club named Alan K. Browne Investment Banker of the Year in June 1958, it signaled BOA's dominance in the municipal bond business.[22] By the late 1950s, investment bank Halsey, Stuart & Co. had become BOA's biggest rival. Halsey, Stuart & Co. underwrote 41 general obligation and revenue bonds totaling $131.6 million during the second quarter of 1957. On its heels, BOA "led the field in the volume of municipal issues managed during the third quarter" of 1958, underwriting 23 issues totaling $162 million.[23] In 1960

California and its political subdivisions issued 462 general obligation bonds at a par value of $815.3 million. Having refined their approach to syndicate governance, BOA-managed syndicates underwrote 64 percent (295) of these issues at a par value of over $693 million.[24] BOA's financing of urban renewal and public-housing debt matched its buying and selling of municipal bonds issued throughout the state. BOA's California strategy was paying dividends.

Their successes perhaps compelled BOA's top brass to finally respond to the years of requests for administrative and spatial reforms. In early 1964 the Bond Investment Securities Division (BISD) was formed, placing investment securities activities under one roof and under the direction of Alan K. Browne. The division was no longer relegated to the cramped second-floor office; the new ninth-floor office offered better views and accommodated the dramatic increase in staff. The professional, clerical, and training personnel at BISD in 1966 had doubled in the past three years, to 248 people, with 80 percent of the growth in clerical services. A BISD document insisted the new personnel "was necessary because without assistance from computers a great deal of manual handling of positions and transfer of securities has been required." Some administrative procedures changed, but the reliance on poorly compensated, gendered clerical labor remained the same: the increased labor costs would be held in check through reliance on "more lower cost clerical staff to manage the increase in volume."[25]

In August 1965, *Finance* magazine profiled BISD's leading bondmen. When he was not skiing or playing tennis, Theodore A. Griffinger coordinated the operations of the investment banking administration. Under him sat William E. Ashley and Lawrence H. Prager. Ashley was in charge of the government bond dealer department, which did "between $100 and $200 million in these securities a day." Prager, meanwhile, presided over the municipal bond dealer department, which did "one of the largest trading volumes in the secondary market of any dealer in the nation." Thirty-six-year-old Leland S. Prussia administered the investment portfolio, "getting a broad picture of how the bank manages its resources." Prussia detailed how to identify the "bellows" of a bank's liquidity. Greater demand for consumer loans necessitated that the bank "sell off securities." Changes in public deposits also affected the bank's liquidity and, in turn, its capacity to purchase debt. Prussia and his assistants offered BISD the inside scoop on the overall state of BOA's capital; they helped bondmen position the credit analysis of "more than 10,000 authorized issuing agencies in the state" in relation to the "bank's liquidity position." Armed with information about "the taxing powers" of a borrower, BISD could decide which debts to purchase, at what price, and in what amount.

It would be easy to envision thousands of bonds moving from issuer to underwriter to the ultimate investor across city and state lines as dematerialized financial instruments in some abstract space. But municipal bonds were tangible commodities. Henry C. Ehlen, who administered BOA's deliveries and accounting administration section, coordinated the movement of these things. "Tickets giving all the necessary information on a transaction are written on the ninth floor and sent to the large vault room in the basement for processing," *Finance* clarified. The elevator opened into a space that was "windowless except for a wide expanse of bullet proof glass across the front." With $750 million of bonds in a vault, the room had "three gun slots through the glass, happily never used yet." The staff worked busily processing orders in this fortified space. It took anywhere between thirty and ninety days to deliver bonds. Depending on the final destination and size of the city, the deliveries and accounting section might use Brink's air courier service or "insured, registered mail."[26]

By the mid-1960s, BOA's approach to syndicate governance was tried and tested. The bank gave emerging firms and well-established institutions a chance to join so long as they did not "dilute the strength of the account." BOA reviewed past results in order to "emasculate or eliminate non-producers." Bondmen played the role of the ultimate Bond man— that is, James: BOA stayed abreast of its competitors through reviews of the "reasons that brought about their winning bids" and through ".007 efforts." They would covertly emulate the operations of their competitors and, through "use of mirrors," reflect that image to convince their "competitors' partners" to join BOA-managed syndicates instead.[27]

Through social ties forged inside of bond clubs and the lampoons of high finance, bondmen had stitched together a national market. By April 1965, BOA claimed its syndicates often contained "between 250 and 400 members."[28] Elsewhere bondmen replicated BOA's approach to statewide dominance, to the detriment of BOA. Texas banking firms managed syndicates that underwrote expanded transportation networks, new stadiums, and upgraded schools in the fast-growing cities of Dallas and Houston.[29] BOA's insistence that it bid only as managers, and the "historical commitments of major underwriters," meant that it was "unable to form strong accounts to bid for nationally known credits" in Minnesota, Missouri, and Texas.[30] Alan K. Browne hoped to penetrate other parts of the country by using BISD's expense accounts to cover "club dues . . . professional organizations and . . . orientation trips to California and the IBA Convention in Florida."[31]

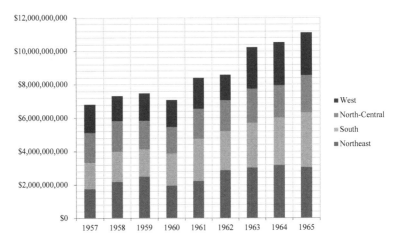

FIGURE 5.2 New issues of municipal bonds by region, 1957–1965.

Source: Joint Economic Committee, Subcommittee on Economic Progress, "State and Local Public Facility Needs and Financing: Volume II," 89th Cong., 2nd sess., December 1966, 147.

The bond financing of California and the Sun Belt was at once exceptional and ordinary. On the one hand, California was in the middle of a long economic boom. The southern part of the Golden State formed a crucial node of the postwar military-industrial complex and, as such, was transformed by new defense-related industries. Aircraft production and electronics gave rise to a well-compensated, white technical and scientific labor force. These workers had the disposable incomes to take trips to Disneyland and the credit standing to purchase amenities for their new suburban homes. Just as auto manufacturing gave rise to a host of ancillary services, California's defense industry contributed greatly to the growth of retail, tourism, and other sectors.[32] In the Bay Area, the FIRE sector and high-end services generally made for white, white-collar workers who were able to attend baseball games and shop at Saks Fifth Avenue.

Outside of California, as well as within it, the tremendous growth of suburban subdivisions around cities like Phoenix also meant bonds galore.[33] On the other hand, older cities and communities throughout the Northeast and Midwest looked to use debt to maintain or upgrade aging infrastructure. In both the old and new "belts," the demands from Americans for improved public schools, parks, and water systems amounted to a relatively even distribution of new municipal bond issues (figure 5.2). There were critical regional differences, but bondholding opportunities were truly national in scope. Cities experiencing economic growth and those in decline generated profits for bondholders just the same; precisely because of decline, there were perhaps more profits to be had on debt issued by communities outside of the Sun Belt.

The administrative reforms, syndicate partnerships, clubs, and trade forums and organizations allowed these bankers to take advantage of a remarkable shift in the balance of power between municipal borrowers and creditors. In 1966, the after-tax interest income derived from BISD investments in taxable and tax-exempt securities totaled $78 million, $44 million of which came from tax-exempt investments. This was $28 million more than in 1963. Browne and his staff touted the "efficiency of the changes in management policies," but the uptick in interest income yields on tax-exempt investments from 2.09 percent to 2.70 percent was largely due to "the general rise in interest rates in the U.S. during the period."[34]

The credit crunch of 1966 was a major inflection point in the upward drift. Interest rates on US Treasury bills rose above the interest rate ceilings set by Regulation Q, a New Deal check on irresponsible lending. Capital shifted into higher-yielding investments. Banks were left with fewer funds on which to lend. Structural limits on capital precipitated a battle royal among corporations, small businesses, suburban consumers, and municipal borrowers.[35] When San Francisco, its municipal siblings, and borrowers throughout the country turned to the municipal bond market throughout 1966, the cost to borrow was exceptionally high. At 3.92 percent, the Bond Buyer's June yield index was "the highest since November of 1934."[36] By 1968 the average cost to borrow hovered above 4.5 percent.[37] As one municipal bond analyst put it, "The 1.50 percent bonds of the 1940's and the 2.50 percent bonds of the 1950's are being replaced by today's 4.50's and 5's."[38] Put simply, the era of borrowing at low rates, such that it had been, was over.

End of the Old, Birth of the New

The credit crunch of 1966 sharpened the fundamental differences between municipal borrowers and creditors. The same market that provided relatively low-cost funds and stability of investment was beginning to force borrowers and lenders to retrench. Borrowers delayed debt sales for schools and issued short-term debt at high interest rates. Bankers faced their own cost squeeze. They might cut overhead costs, sell off long-term debt, embrace short-term securities, and reduce clerical personnel. Both borrowers and bankers had a cost problem, but, dependent as they were on their creditors, borrowers had far less room to maneuver. What's more, their recalibrations offered bankers a way out of their own problems.

In July 1966, Paul Heffernan, the relatively new managing editor of the *DBB* castigated the federal government for rising short-term interest rates but celebrated those rising rates as an investment opportunity.[39] In what was a case of the "left hand not knowing what the right hand was doing," the Federal Reserve and the Federal National Mortgage Association set off a "rate war." The "officially-contrived—although unintended—confusion" triggered a battle among commercial banks, savings and loan associations, and federal agencies to woo investors by offering ever higher yields on short-term debts.[40] The following month, the *DBB* explained that high rates "are an unavoidable consequence of the times. And the times are 'good times.'"[41] Without question, the *DBB* editorialized, the municipal bond market was "writhing in fatigue and apprehension." However, this "distress" would be a minor footnote, and "the way the ball was kept bouncing [would] be remembered." The credit crunch was an important way "of separating the men from the boys."[42] Through this market moralization—good and bad times, tests and vigilance, men and boys—the *DBB* made clear a fundamental insight. Both borrowers and lenders had to navigate the credit crunch. However, with high yields as the flip side of high borrowing costs, a borrower's squeeze was a banker's gain.

When San Francisco successfully sold a bond, the cost to borrow a similar amount for similar purposes became more expensive. When San Francisco sold its 1960 Series A sewer bonds in the amount of $3,250,000 on March 1, 1962, the bonds came with interest rates between 2¼ and 3 percent. By contrast, the 1964 Series B sewer bonds sold in the amount of $2.5 million on November 1, 1966, came with interest rates between 4 and 6 percent.[43] At 3.01 percent, moreover, San Francisco's net interest cost on the 1966 bonds was markedly higher than the 2.84 percent of 1958, but a bargain compared to 1967's 4 percent.[44] Expenditures for interest payments registered at $3.75 million in 1965–66, rising to roughly $5.3 million in 1967–68.[45] San Franciscans were on the hook not only for city bonds but for other debt as well. In late August 1966, the Bay Area Rapid Transit District (BARTD) board set a tax rate of 41.7¢, up 10.9¢ over the previous year. "All but five cents of the levy goes to service the interest on the $250 million in bonds" sold to investors, the *Daily Bond Buyer* remarked.[46]

The correlation between high rates on long-term bonds and the hesitancy of bond buyers to hold long-term debt in an inflationary setting underlay San Francisco's embrace of short-term debt. Municipal borrowers still issued long-term debt: in 1965–66 San Francisco's outstanding long-term debt was $201.2 million, and it rose to $259.6 million in 1967–68.[47] But the uptick in short-term debt was far more dramatic. Over those same years, short-term debt outstanding jumped from $23.5 million to

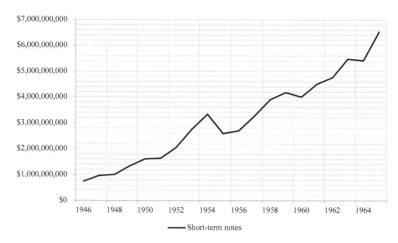

FIGURE 5.3 New issues of state and local short-term debt in the United States, 1946–1965.

Source. Joint Economic Committee, Subcommittee on Economic Progress, "State and Local Public Facility Needs and Financing: Volume II," 89th Cong., 2nd sess., December 1966, 106.

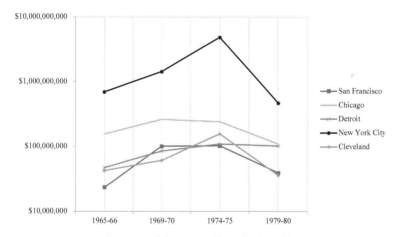

FIGURE 5.4 Gross short-term debt outstanding of select cities.

Source: US Bureau of the Census, "City Government Finances," 1965–66, 1969–70, 1974–75, and 1979–80, https://www2.census.gov/govs/pubs/city_govt_fin/.

$66.4 million.[48] Other cities also increasingly accepted the trade-off between borrowing at relatively low rates at greater frequency and issuing long-term debt at higher rates that might incite tax revolts. The trade-off came with consequences. For borrowers, the turn to short-term debt conditioned the horizons of city officials, truncating the ability to cater to different constituencies to achieve long-term projects. Short-term politics had to comport with what inflation did, and it pressed officials to abide by an accelerated clock. Borrowers now had to contend with bond buyers' shortened extractive time frame, which was at odds with long-term investment in social welfare.

In a sense, San Francisco emulated the borrowing activities of housing authorities and redevelopment agencies that had used short-term debt just to get by. The architects of the public housing–urban renewal programs maintained that coordinated sales, government guarantees, and tax exemption were enough to keep interest rates low, and lowering the cost to borrow would reduce dependence on federal direct loans. Two offerings in the summer of 1966 symbolize the ways in which dependence on the private bond market played into the hands of debt peddlers.

The August 1966 $240 million sale of public-housing notes was routine. So too was the search by the San Francisco Housing Authority (SFHA) for $1.3 million in funds. The notice of sale told potential buyers that the housing authority "will retire its maturing Temporary Notes, if any, and will repay" the federal government "all moneys already advanced to it with accrued interest." Here was an implicit hierarchy of claims on the principal. "With the remainder," public-housing authorities promised to "meet the cost of construction of its projects."[49] Borrowing might enable construction, but only after lenders redeemed their original investments.

Given the caps on monthly rents, it was unsurprising that the SFHA's operating expenses outpaced rental increases. But the gap was dramatic. While maintenance costs rose around 13 percent between 1963 and 1966, rental income rose just 3 percent. The "wanton destruction of buildings" necessitated hiring glaziers to recut and replace broken windows. The SFHA blamed window breakers without entertaining how inflation, dependence on an extractive market, and the prioritization of lenders over tenants also contributed to escalating maintenance costs.[50] The macroeconomic world of interest rates might have been beyond the scope of their critiques, but when tenants launched rent strikes over broken elevators and unlit stairwells, they were also protesting an arrangement of government guarantees and skewed priorities.[51]

That summer the Urban Renewal Administration (URA) and redevelopment agencies around the country were also in crisis mode. Facing record-breaking interest rates, URA chief financial officer Max Lipowitz felt the program was on a never-ending roller coaster. Interest payments were the loops that left some redevelopment agencies hanging on for dear life. "Lord only knows where it's going to end."[52] On the eve of an August 1966 offering, federal technocrats expressed a "hope to do something better percentagewise" than the previous month, but with interest rates "still on the rise, the outlook is uncertain," they said.[53]

In consortium with redevelopment agencies from Wichita, Kansas; Boston; and Philadelphia, the San Francisco Redevelopment Agency (SFRA) looked to sell notes that matured on March 10, 1967. The SFRA was ambitious, offering a total of some $23.6 million in notes for its Diamond Heights and Golden Gateway projects, as well as for the second phase of urban renewal in the Western Addition (A-2).[54] What made the Western Addition offering different was the attendant interest rate limitation. Whereas the SFRA could pay no more than 4⅛ percent on Diamond Heights and Golden Gateway notes, it could pay a maximum of 4⅜ percent to prospective lenders. That the SFRA was able to sell just "a sizable part of the scheduled financing" suggests that some chunk of debt went unsold.[55] What is clear is that when Wells Fargo purchased notes, it unlocked funds to execute the A-2 project.[56]

The significance was twofold. First, the results signaled a temporal disjuncture. The SFRA had originally entered into a federal contract for Diamond Heights and Golden Gateway during a moment of low interest rates. By 1966, the SFRA worked within older limits that were designed to keep debt-service payments low but that financiers could circumvent by purchasing other, higher-yielding debt. The ordinary note sale also betrayed the power differentials between technocrats who believed they could manage the market and buyers who could capitalize off the structural dependence of redevelopment agencies on their services. That federal technocrats encouraged redevelopment agencies "to get out and . . . induce your local bank" to help pick up the slack anticipated from the lack of interest among regular "big-bank customers" not only signaled the borrowing crisis; it also underscored how borrowers had only defensive solutions that ultimately rested on wooing the capital of lenders, large or small.[57]

The constraints on the SFRA also speak to a much larger story. Across the nation and across a variety of municipal borrowers, the cost to borrow severely upended infrastructure projects. Redevelopment agencies scaled down the dollar amounts of preliminary loan note offerings, willing to settle for less working capital at lower interest rates, but aware they would soon return to the bond market. Seeking $2.3 million through improvement bonds, officials in Anaheim, California, rejected bids charging between 4.27 and 4.39 percent. Because of interest rate ceilings, Tulsa,

Oklahoma, auditor William F. Lambert failed to receive bids for two various-purpose bond issues. Even rolling short-term debt into long-term bonds was increasingly difficult. After rejecting bids to finance Cleveland public schools, the school district's clerk-treasurer was left scrambling to retire $6.3 million worth of short-term notes and anticipated having to issue $8.7 million in bond anticipation notes, still another variety of short-term debt that treated the actual long-term needs of schoolchildren in makeshift fashion. When Boston issued $5 million in notes due to mature in just two months' time, it was forced to accept an astonishing 4.49 percent interest rate from the National Shawmut Bank of Boston. In Baltimore, technocrats looking to finance public-school construction and improvements did not receive a single bid for a $31.8 million offering. The interest rate limitation of 4.5 percent was too low for creditors, who could secure that much for lending far less at much shorter intervals. All of this was during the summer and fall of 1966, though the long-term consequences stretched well beyond.[58]

With the Great Society, the federal government had taken crucial steps toward addressing the racial inequality of affluence. Local governments, school districts, and redevelopment agencies looked to meet the feds halfway. But because social welfare was linked to the municipal bond market, the ability to deliver on infrastructural promises was greatly undermined. Sky-high interest rates made borrowing untenable. The twenty-year era of relatively cheap money was over. Black mothers and fathers, who themselves had attended underfunded schools or played among the debris, now had to send their children to public schools with frayed electrical wires and watch them grow up in concrete jungles.

Bondmen working for San Francisco's Bank of America and New York City's First National City Bank had risen above their competitors. National rivals, the two firms partnered to profit from rising rates. In June 1966, First National and BOA, "jointly and individually," won $16.7 million of the urban renewal notes, which allowed the firms to secure remarkably high-yielding investments.[59] In July of the same year, the two purchased $2.1 million in public-housing notes issued by the housing authority of East Baton Rouge, Louisiana, at 4.08 percent, and $1.7 million in notes issued by the North Little Rock, Arkansas, housing authority at 4.09 percent.[60] Laundered of its connections to specific projects, and collapsed into commensurate commodities backed by government guarantees, debt delivered astonishing yields. In one of its many advertisements that summer, the BOA asked, "IS TODAY THE DAY for short term profit?" As financiers who "make and maintain markets" in foreign debt and preliminary loan notes, among other "short term securities," the bank's traders looked to turn record interest rates on short-term

IS TODAY THE DAY for short term profit? One phone call to any trader in our government trading room will tell you ... and you can put your money on his information! Our traders have covered the money market from one end of the country to the other by the time you call. They'll have the market strategy, sharply competitive pricing and a larger choice of availabilities in the hard-to-get maturities at the tips of their fingers ... Reliable but creative service is something you can count on ... and a larger selection of profit making opportunities is something you can bank on ... Today may be the day ... call one of our government traders and see ...

We make and maintain markets in Federal Funds, U.S. Treasury Obligations, Banker's Acceptances, Public Housing Notes, Temporary Loan Notes, Warrants and other short term securities. For information on tax exempt securities contact our Municipal Bond Department.

BANK INVESTMENT SECURITIES DIVISION

Bank of America NT&SA

SAN FRANCISCO · LOS ANGELES · NEW YORK CORRESPONDENT

San Francisco, call: W. E. Ashley — (415) 622-2634 • Los Angeles, call: H. Cardin — (213) 683-3318 • New York, call: C. E. Pierson—(212) 425-6770

FIGURE 5.5 BISD, "IS TODAY THE DAY for short term profit?" Investors could rely on BOA to profit from various short-term debts.

debt into "profit making opportunities" (figure 5.5).[61] Oddly enough, the financing of public housing and urban renewal helped such commercial banks as BOA, First National City Bank, and Continental Illinois National Bank & Trust Co. finance the appliances, durable goods, and many other features of the postwar consumer's republic. One division of a commercial bank contributed to the capital on which another relied to place credit cards in the hands of middle-class whites.[62]

Underwriting banks risked holding bonds whose market price could change or distributing bonds that investors might not want. That is, they risked a diminishing difference between the purchase price and re-sale price, known as the "spread." Bankers hoped for a gross return that would more than cover the costs of distribution, financial advisory ser-vices, and overhead expenses.[63] By the mid-1960s, however, underwriters confronted a clear and demonstrative trend: the spread was in decline. In 1958 a borrower who issued a $250,000 to $500,000 municipal bond paid between $4,800 and $8,600 to investment bankers for their under-writing services. By 1965 that price ranged between $3,000 and $5,900, a decline of 30 to 40 percent.[64] By the mid-1960s the "profit squeeze" had become "one of the most vexing and most discussed problems facing municipal bond underwriters and dealers."[65] It was particularly acute for investment banks. At its annual convention in December 1964, the Investment Bankers Association of America "warned" of "the declining part that investment bankers are playing in the capital market," the *DBB* reported. One New York bond financier urged investment bankers "to move into the short-term investment field." Doing so would help bank-ers "stay the decline."[66]

Bondmen discussed how the credit crunch affected their business practices. "It has been a difficult year in 1966 for those of us engaged in Municipal Finance," Alan K. Browne declared. Voters continued to ap-prove new bond issues, which increased the volume of new long-term debt. But long-term bonds at fixed interest rates seemed to be falling out of favor with investors. "The reservoir of authorized but unsold bond is-sues continues at a record level," Browne said. Municipal finance officers often waited to strike at the right time, issuing bonds only when funds were needed and when rates were low. Now, however, large chunks of funds were needed for infrastructure but interest rates appeared bound-less. What's more, matching grants, a key mechanism of the Great Society, "continue[d] to spur debt incurrence." The problem for bankers was not so much mobilizing enough savings to supply large sums to borrowers, but managing "the costs of doing business," and struggling through diminished "residual profits" in the context of increasing sup-plies of "attractive" municipal debt.[67]

Municipal bondmen proposed a range of solutions to their cost prob-lems. By eliminating manual planning and reporting on departmental budgets, Lloyd Hatchers of White, Weld & Co. anticipated that computers might allow for "greater cost control."[68] For Anthony E. Tomasic, sole proprietor of Pittsburgh's Thomas & Co., machines were too costly. He viewed the telephone as "the cheapest for a small house" to use in doing business, and he planned to rely even more on his longtime "head bookkeeper" to maintain records.[69] Thomas L. Ray, vice president of the Mercantile Trust Co.'s bond department, responded by sometimes dropping out of syndicates, in part because of the problem of supply: "When you're bidding with many different managers on a given day and lots of bonds selling . . . you as an underwriter in four or five different accounts could get hit with all of them." The Mercantile Trust Co. also "eliminated" lengthy and incredibly detailed tombstone advertisements, embracing instead "quarter-page ads."[70] Alan K. Browne outlined a series of solutions for large and small bond departments. For those facing a "cost-profit squeeze," Browne suggested that managers reconsider whether branch offices were "necessary and desirable." They should embrace communications equipment to "help cut overhead." They might reduce subscriptions to financial advisory services and publications.[71] By July 1967, BISD embraced retrenchment, imposing reductions "in paper flow" and its "clerical force," and eliminating "non-essential functions" and "duplicating and overlapping activities."[72] In bankers' retrenchment, white female secretarial labor bore the brunt of the cost-profit squeeze.

Sizing up the bond business, the *DBB* concluded that the credit crunch would "probably accelerate the structural changes" already underway. The paper anticipated "split-ups" of the very syndicates and partnerships bankers had worked so hard to establish. The world of finance could expect "shotgun" unions of desperate firms. When the *DBB* predicted "spinoffs of personnel," it spoke to the musical chairs of high finance. If bankers were let go, they might quickly find work with another firm— unless more than a few "undiversified firms" closed their doors.[73]

Tracing the holdings of state and local debt by the hundred largest banks in the country, the *DBB*'s Mary R. Ciarlo observed a slight sell-off. As of September 30, 1966, those holdings aggregated $18,266,968,000, a decrease of close to $296 million (1.59 percent) compared to the previous year.[74] The drop-off confirmed the *DBB*'s observation that the "agony in which the municipal market is now caught" was largely due to the momentary exodus of "the biggest buyers" of municipal bonds. Indeed, commercial banks had "checked out overnight without leaving a forwarding address."[75] Even if they returned, the question was, for how long? As we will see, whereas in 1966 the commercial banker's solution was largely one of internal retrenchment, by the 1970s, many reputable commercial banks would say goodbye.

In California, at least, borrowers could still count on local underwriters to lend. Between September 30, 1965, and the same date a year later, syndicates headed by California banks won 484 bond issues valued at over $1.6 billion. Smaller investment banks might have been reeling, and some of the largest banks opted to sell off their long-term holdings, but California banks underwrote 85 percent "of the total number of state and municipal [bonds]."[76] The sales were driven in no small part by Bank of America's BISD, which remained the top player in the municipal bond market.[77] As of September 30, 1966, BOA held more than $1.8 billion in municipal debt, an investment class that made up 10.2 percent of BOA's total assets. With just above $1 billion in municipal debt holdings, the First National City Bank and Chase Manhattan Bank NA, both of New York, ranked second and third.[78]

The good times continued to roll. In early September 1966, for instance, the Municipal Bond Club of Chicago hosted its thirtieth annual Field Day at the Drake Hotel and Elmhurst Country Club. Bankers from San Francisco, Detroit, Kansas City, Dallas, Puerto Rico, Seattle, New York City, and Los Angeles attended, deepening their social ties over cock-tails, food, tennis, softball, golf, and horseshoe pitching. Along with the profits they took home from friendly competition, Leonard W. Witkowski of Chicago's Drexel Harriman Ripley "took home an Oldsmobile station wagon as a raffle prize," while Gus T. Drabik of A. G. Becker & Co. in Chicago left with a Zenith color television set.[79]

Bondmen faced a cost-profit squeeze, and the casualties of the busi-ness might worsen. Nevertheless, federal solutions to inflation might only stimulate their prospects. In July 1966, investment bank Halsey, Stuart & Co. noted that an increase in federal income taxes "to ward off further inflationary pressures" would spark even greater demand for municipal bonds. "Tax increases make tax-exemption more valuable," the *DBB* wrote. Even if borrowers delayed or canceled offerings, or scaled back the infrastructural promises of the Great Society, the structural de-pendence of cities on the bond market ensured sunny days ahead for bondmen. Cities and suburbs still had to finance schools, roads, and sanitation and water systems. City officials who saw sports stadiums as a way to achieve growth incurred still more debt. "The bond houses," in sum, "see little chance of a decline in the volume of tax-exempt financ-ing," the *DBB* succinctly concluded.[80]

The credit crunch did more than upend the infrastructural provisions of the Great Society. It revealed that a borrower's duress was a finan-cier's bonanza. Moral parables of the good times of a credit crunch be-trayed that higher interest charges went hand in glove with higher yields. The structural dependence of cities on financiers, established through New Deal banking reform and built up over the postwar years, allowed bondmen to relieve their own cost-profit squeeze by tightening the constraints on borrowers. Municipal governments would return repeatedly to an extractive market, a sometimes monthly cycle that also shortened political horizons for borrowers. Instead of a long-term commitment to the citizenry, short-term debt signified an ascendant concern among governments with paying the next bill; making sure creditors got paid on time, without necessarily making enduring improvements to the social welfare of residents. Throwing rocks at the federal government, bond financiers sought to protect their position and were assured by governing officials who reasoned that bankers had an important part to play in dealing with underdevelopment around the country. As the rising cost to borrow was reflected in increased city taxes and public transit fares, and as the racial injustices of infrastructural inequality continued to go unaddressed, the question of whether to approve a bond issue became much more than that. It stood as a referendum on the postwar debt compact itself.

6. Revolt

On July 13, 1966, the *Daily Bond Buyer* (*DBB*) updated its catalog of highly rated San Francisco bonds. The paper noted that bond supporters had "cleared an important hurdle" when some of "the most powerful businessmen and bankers" sitting on the Bond Screening Committee endorsed the measures. The *DBB*'s explication of the bonds' purpose, of whether still more bond issues related to transportation and the airport would soon appear, and of whether federal funds would be available to supplement local revenue sources was consistent with the well-established coding of social needs into dollars and cents, bondholder protections, and intergovernmental support.[1] But as the summer turned to fall, it became increasingly clear that this bond drive was different. Just a few days before San Franciscans went to the polls in November 1966, the *DBB* reported, "Mayor Shelley has been told that there is growing opposition [to the bonds] in this city's Negro community."[2]

The go-to paper for bond financiers, bondholders, and bond buyers had begun monitoring black political revolts. Where activist groups pushed for civil rights, the *DBB* considered how boycotts and affirmative action infringed on revenues, disrupted potential bond offerings, and challenged local governance in ways that threatened the safety of municipal debt.[3] Thus the fairly standard *DBB* entry above, made possible through ongoing correspondence between the paper and municipal technocrats, not only signified the refusal of black San Franciscans to acquiesce to the city's debt program but also symbolized a critical change in how lenders were relating to cities.

For nearly twenty years the insulation of municipal debt from day-to-day politics, the routine assemblage of a progrowth coalition of powerful interest groups, and run-of-the-mill arguments had swayed enough voters to incur debt for transportation, recreation, entertainment, schools, and countless other infrastructural projects. At most, San Franciscans could vote on certain kinds of municipal bond issues that had been screened by municipal technocrats, bankers, and other leading businessmen. The endorsement of business groups and labor proved crucial to the success rate of bond referenda. San Franciscans were repeatedly sold a similar package of arguments: Approving a public-school bond would allow the city to invest in the general welfare of all its children. Voter approval was necessary to help develop the city's economy and vitalize the cityscape. Debt-financed streets, parking facilities, and public transportation would resolve untenable congestion. Rehabilitating the city's cultural landmarks would accommodate and entice more visitors to spend throughout the rest of San Francisco. Street lighting and improvements to the city's jails would make the city safer.

By the mid-1960s, the tried-and-tested approach to municipal debt was beginning to unravel. Rank-and-file workers, along with white middle-class residents—two of the beneficiaries of the infrastructural investment in whiteness, and dependable voting blocs—were beginning to challenge the inequality of debt. The *San Francisco Bay Guardian* helped nourish a current of left-wing populism, demanding that debt be issued for the long-term interests of all San Franciscans, not just developers or bankers. Finally, as Frederick M. Wirt observed, the unraveling was also due in no small part to the emergence of new political actors "with new definitions of policy objectives and priorities." Whatever consensus existed among financiers, merchants, real estate, labor, and city technocrats was thoroughly fragmented by the city's racial and ethnic minorities in general, and black political agitation in particular. The 1960s marked a political arrival not because minorities were new to the city "but because, in a fashion not known before, they [were] moving to participate in the urban decisions" shaping public investment.

Between 1958 and 1964, San Franciscans passed 83 percent of the twenty-four bond issues on the ballot. By contrast, voters approved just 39 percent of the twenty-three bond measures between 1965 and 1971.[4] The city's housing authority and redevelopment agency continued to issue debt without voter approval, but when San Franciscans were offered the chance to say "yes" or "no" and decide whether to service debt into the future, they increasingly refused what bond promoters were selling.

The Bay Area Labor Council's deeper engagement with the inequality of debt, black boycotts of bond referenda, years of systemic neglect that gave rise to civil violence, and legal injunctions had something in common: these were revolts against the downstream effects of a postwar debt arrangement. The white workers, middle-class white women, black San Franciscans, and residents of Chinatown behind these revolts did not resist the structural relationship between borrowers and lenders, because that arrangement was largely concealed. These revolters hit on relationships between social classes and processes of wealth inequality, but this was popcorn politics, not a social movement. Yet when San Franciscans critiqued disproportionate spending priorities, the lack of democratic input, and the infrastructure-for-all arguments, they inserted themselves into the technocratic sphere of determining how debt should be used. Lenders folded these revolts into their broader concerns about investing in cities. The revolt that mattered most was the one inside the creditors' imaginations.

Minorities on the Rise

There were three different expressions of minority political power that targeted San Francisco's racial infrastructural inequality. The first was the *civil violence*—call it a riot, rebellion, or insurrection—that broke out in September 1966.[5] Other minority residents pursued *legal challenges* to the destruction of, and unequal investment in, their neighborhoods. Drawing from a long tradition of *boycotts*, black San Franciscans refused to support the city's bond priorities without getting jobs and better services in return. Although the participants in each action differed, these expressions of minority political power were more than demands for equal infrastructural investment. They asserted their place within a social contract that, for much of the postwar period, was a racial contract between the city and its white residents.

As early as December 1965, Justin Herman of the San Francisco Redevelopment Agency and Eneas J. Kane of the city's Housing Authority wrote urgently to federal housing officials. The redlined Hunters Point neighborhood contained all the signs of dissension, and federal support was essential to "avoid a situation such as that which caused the outbreak in the Watts area of Los Angeles."[6]

The initial spark soon came about. On September 27, 1966, a white police officer in Hunters Point confronted several black teens who he claimed had been joyriding in a stolen vehicle. While two kids got away from the encounter, sixteen-year-old Matthew Johnson did not. He was shot and killed. Then as now, there were different versions of the story. According to police, Johnson was killed after the officer fired a few warning shots. However, at least one witness indicated that the "three shots were fired at the kid, not in the air."[7] Another observer was concerned with what happened afterward, asserting, "An SS man attached to the San Francisco Police Department murdered a Negro child and let him lie face down in a hot, dirty, vacant lot for about an hour."[8]

The next day the headlines were as one might expect: "Riots in S.F.— Guard Called," "Looting and Arson Erupt," "Mayor Declares Emergency." For those insulated from Hunters Point; for those who had not heard the thump of airborne bricks hitting the ground, the shattering of glass bottles and broken windows, the *San Francisco Chronicle* described the scene of "racial violence," though one that was thankfully not "another Watts." That the paper situated "several hundred youths" within a "poverty-stricken neighborhood" was more than set design. It suggested that the murder of Matthew Johnson was the final straw in years of infrastructural neglect.[9]

Nearly everyone could agree that among the city's many "danger spots," and as one of the "city's poorest and most segregated neighborhoods," Hunters Point suffered from many layers of structural racism.[10] But the riot quickly spread to other neighborhoods. Black youths "were seen walking down Fillmore near Ellis street shortly before midnight with new television sets." The windows of Fran's Apparel Shop at 1513 Fillmore Street were smashed, though resident John Hunter insisted that this was the work of a "white kid who used a hatchet."[11]

Urban tactical militarism was the immediate response. When the San Francisco Police Department enforced a six-day evening curfew in Hunters Point and the Fillmore-Western Addition, violators were arrested and black folks who worked overnight shifts had to adapt to the martial landscape.[12] Armed with "M-1 rifles and bayonets," between 1,200 and 2,000 California National Guardsmen patrolled Hunters Point and the Fillmore District.[13] Some troops walked, while others rode "shotgun aboard fire trucks," ostensibly to protect firefighters extinguishing the raging flames.[14] Violent policemen riddled the Bayview Community Center with bullets.[15] By October 1, half of the remaining National Guardsmen were reassigned to Candlestick Park, the city's prized and costly debt-financed sports arena.[16] Intrastate coordination, occupation and patrol, violence, and the protection of property stood at the center of a "riot blueprint," a protocol "used 10 times since Watts."[17]

White elected officials responded via backroom dealings with reputable African American leaders. Through Mayor Jack Shelley's Ad Hoc Committee on the Disturbances, black political elites recommended the city launch a robust employment program.[18] In the city's main African American newspaper, contributors insisted black people be afforded "permanent jobs at the prevailing rates of pay." Those with "arrest records" should be given employment opportunities. Job training programs were necessary to increase the skills of black workers with distended ties to the labor market.[19] San Francisco's black leadership class attempted to channel political unrest into a deeper engagement with city government, calling for a local commitment to enhanced work opportunities that matched the programs and impulses of the War on Poverty.

Whether through direct participation in the riots, negotiations with city government, or supportive editorials in the black press, black folks made it clear that infrastructural neglect, underinvestment, and unemployment would no longer be tolerated. Indeed, the riot was the flash point of a black revolt against decades of political, social, and economic isolation.

The structural inequities that conditioned the uprisings in Hunters Point could be found in other parts of the city, too. In late 1966, journalist S. C. Pelletiere chronicled the extreme and somewhat peculiar inequality in Chinatown. According to James Chinn, an Urban League worker at Chinatown's Adult Opportunity Center, the federal Manpower Development and Training Act (MDTA) had barely been put to use in the neighborhood: just ten people had been trained in janitorial and clerical skills. And while the Office of Economic Opportunity made available some $1 million for programs ranging from English language and tutoring services to social casework, for Chinn, only increased MDTA appropriations would help remedy the racial income gap. Like the exclusion of black workers from construction workers' unions, the supposed "gentleman's agreement against Chinese applie[d] to practically all crafts," Pelletiere explained. Across a variety of industries, trades, and sectors, Pelletiere observed, "The average Caucasian worker makes more in fringe benefits than a Chinese draws in salary."

As that racial income gap widened, the emphasis on economic growth through racialized consumption meant greater prosperity for entrepreneurs of Chinese descent. "Many Chinese have left the ghetto for the Richmond and Sunset districts without incident," wrote Pelletiere.[20] White people were still the majority in those neighborhoods, but a sizeable number of non–African American minorities had settled there throughout the 1960s.[21] Just as black landlords sometimes exploited black tenants, racial inequality was reinforced through *intra*racial class relations among Chinese residents of San Francisco. Chinatown's small shops were considered "prime real estate renting as high as $600 a month." These shops were also "indigenously owned." A merchant might have "to pay a wealthy Chinese landlord $15,000 for the privilege of renting," a massive overhead expense. Pelletiere wrote, "This forces down wages, introducing the issue of Chinese exploiting Chinese," or conflicts between owners and tenants, tenants and workers.[22] Ironically, Chinatown was integral to San Francisco's consumer playground, but it lacked parks and playgrounds for its residents. The dearth of recreational space for schoolchildren, or for elderly residents seeking fresh air, was the flip side of the infrastructural investment in whiteness.

If riots were one flash point of a broader revolt against systematic neglect, another was legal recourse. With the help of the San Francisco Neighborhood Legal Assistance Foundation, in late August 1969 George

Woo, a self-described "poor" resident of Chinatown, attempted to torpedo a $9.9 million bond measure. Compared to the rest of the city, in Chinatown there were 4.5 times more people for each acre of recreational land. Woo asserted that between 1961 and 1969, the Recreation and Parks Commission had "allocated to Chinatown an average of 10 cents per person for park and recreation purposes while allocating to the city at large an average of 67 cents per person." Having been "deprived of equal benefit," Woo was unconvinced by claims of the bond measure's citywide benefit. More debt for parks and recreation would further the pattern of disproportionate investment.[23] Woo drew attention to how public space had come to mean white space, while Chinatown residents were enlisted to pay for soccer fields elsewhere or to rehabilitate Golden Gate Park, one of the city's "most famous attractions."[24] The United San Francisco Freedom Movement, meanwhile, organized against another round of dispossession and reclamation in the Western Addition. Foregrounding community self-determination, black organizers like Hannibal Williams and Mary Rodgers formed the Western Addition Community Organization to propose alternative visions of renewal and, through legal action, to delay and disrupt the SFRA's Western Addition A-2 campaign.[25]

The rise of black political power, and the ability of black San Franciscans to disrupt the city's debt program, were most evident in the November 1966 bond election. There were essentially two related but distinct strands of what we might call "black bond politics." The first was a sort of patronage politics articulated by the black leadership class. The second was an argument against taxation without representation, a critique of spending priorities and of conscription into a debt arrangement that offered black folks very little. Both spoke to how debt was used, but whereas advocates of the former argument concluded that political appointments were a fair exchange for bond support, those who articulated the latter position would only be content through the reconfiguration of the redistributive burdens of public finance.

The *Sun Reporter* found its editorial voice when it came to debt. Throughout the 1950s, the paper had endorsed bonds for parks and recreation, the Steinhart Aquarium, the Palace of Fine Arts, and, in a rare substantive editorial, the chance to revamp the de Young Museum.[26] It was not as if black San Franciscans did not enjoy arts and entertainment, or as if nonwhites were racially excluded from the city's public playground. By definition, de facto segregation meant there was no law that excluded Chinese residents from public parks in Russian Hill; no law to prevent nonwhites from driving downtown to shop on resurfaced streets. Indeed, one of the more complex aspects of the postwar history of racial inequality in America is how, in the absence of explicitly racist rules and laws, resources still flowed along white middle- and upper-class lines; how public infrastructure and services, and with it, access to social protections, benefits, and upward mobility, were distributed in unequal ways.

In the lead-up to November's bond referenda the *Sun Reporter* evaluated and revolted against business as usual. Since the end of World War II, it wrote, "the Negro voters of San Francisco have given above a 90 per cent Yes vote in support of all local bond issues."[27] Things were different in 1966. The San Francisco branch of the NAACP would support the bond measures, but only on one major condition: the city had to appoint a "Negro" to the Public Utilities Commission, the political body in charge of construction, maintenance, and operation of the city's MUNI railway, water system, and airport. Speaking on behalf of "the Negro community," Arthur Lathan and Clifton A. Jeffers promised "that unless such an appointment [was] made, [they would] work to defeat" the bond measures.[28] And since that appointment had not materialized, "No" was the *Sun Reporter*'s official recommendation.[29]

The attempt to leverage this record of voter support to demand a voice in municipal governance drew from a longer tradition in which black men and women parlayed with the white elected and appointed officials to secure services and infrastructure for black neighborhoods.[30] The tactic was also informed by a sober assessment of how power worked in San Francisco. Behind assertions that Mayor Shelley was "spineless," or that the "Downtown Association and the business community of San Francisco continually exert pressure on the Mayor's office to deny Negroes the opportunity to serve on the Public Utilities Commission" was a prescient diagnosis of the relationship between city government and business elites. With business groups pushing from one side, the *Sun Reporter* sought to cohere and mobilize African Americans into a formidable group that would not only vote against airport and MUNI bonds in November 1966 but also urge "No" "on all future bond issues until members of racial minorities" were appointed to boards and commissions.[31]

Yet the *Sun Reporter* was also a business. It welcomed financial support, even from supporters of the issues it opposed. Recognizing the growing importance of the black bond vote, the ad hoc group San Franciscans United for Yes on "A" and "B" posted full-page advertisements just days before the referenda. The group included many prominent black voices. Reflecting the usual approach to selling the public on debt, moreover, the ad hoc group implored readers to support issues that meant "Jobs . . . Jobs . . . Jobs . . . ."[32]

Black employment was clearly important. But one of the end-around solutions to the more encompassing package of demands in general, and to black agitation against unequal investment and tax burdens in particular, was to promise more jobs without specifying the terms of employment in and across sectors. Why pay "taxes" and "higher prices" for the expansion of MUNI service that, despite offering a stop in the Fillmore, expanded routes to "downtown . . . jobs we cannot get?" queried Lee Brown in a letter to the *Sun Reporter*. "All that we are good for, all that we are wanted for, all that we are used for," Brown continued, "is to provide the yes votes to cut our own throats." That is, black San Franciscans voted for bond measures that were essential to the infrastructural investment in whiteness and expanding the financial sector, two vectors of the local political economy that made little room for them. If the black press and church spoke out against the MUNI bonds, the city's African American residents would "show the special interests that we are through being used, through being made their tool."[33]

For the *Sun Reporter*, municipal debt had become just the latest terrain of struggle within the broader black freedom movement. Years of support for city bonds and requests for greater political representation fell on deaf ears. It was now up to black folks to engage in some form of civil disobedience. Saying they had "no representation on the San Francisco Public Utilities Commission or the Bay Area Rapid Transit District," black San Franciscans revolted against more expenditures.[34] For some, this refusal was analogous to the "don't buy where you can't work" campaigns, part of a broader repertoire of "techniques which civil rights groups [had] found advantageous."[35] All told, the *Sun Reporter* put its own spin on "no taxation without representation" and expanded the parameters of the black freedom movement. If that movement was, in its most radical formulation, about extending the privileges and protections of civil and political rights and ending economic oppression, the *Sun Reporter* intimated that these tenets were bound up with the burdens of taxation, the expropriation of revenues, the inequality of debt, and the governing structure over which these matters were decided.

After the MUNI and airport bond issues failed in November 1966, the *Daily Bond Buyer* (*DBB*) characterized San Francisco voters as "economy-minded." Although prone to deracialize racially inflected matters of debt, this time the *DBB* made special note of the opposition from civil rights organizations and demands from "Negro leaders."[36] And indeed, some black leaders expressed a growing confidence in their ability to shape the outcome of bond elections. "We think we kept the Negro vote from going higher," explained *Sun Reporter* owner Dr. Carlton Goodlett. Goodlett hoped the expression of black bond politics would "be a national trend wherever we face an unfriendly administration," a tactic the *San Francisco Chronicle* correctly identified as perhaps "another weapon in the Negro revolution."[37] Black San Franciscans were revolting against a municipal debt arrangement that for twenty years had relied on black support and their tax dollars, while buttressing a local economy in which they were either excluded or relegated to the back offices. They had no way of checking the issuance of debts by the San Francisco Redevelopment Agency, debts that helped to facilitate Negro removal. However, when offered a chance to approve bonds that would extend service to the places from which they were removed, black San Franciscans revolted against claims of infrastructure for all.

Left-Wing Populism

The exercise of minority political power had an important but little-recognized left-wing counterpart. In San Francisco some people registered municipal bonds for what they were: a redistributionary claim of a few on the many. In this light, the question of whether to approve debt was itself a referendum on a redistributionary struggle between those who could shield capital through tax havens, and those who paid escalating property and sales taxes. It was one of the rare moments in mid-twentieth-century political discourse in which the problem of wealth inequality and the special benefits afforded to the upper class was made explicit.[38]

The "City and County Propositions," a document that identified electoral candidates and charter amendments and explained the fine details of bond referenda, became a forum through which some of the middle-class beneficiaries of the infrastructural investment in whiteness revolted against technocratic claims and neat projections. The $96.5 million Municipal Transit System bond issue of November 1966 and the $98 million airport bond of November 1967 prove illustrative.

In the spring of 1966, James K. Carr, general manager of the San Francisco Public Utilities Commission, explained the benefits of the $96.5 million MUNI bond. It would help realize a "high-speed network" of rail systems and bus lines that would connect the southern and western residential sections of the city to downtown. Select routes would also directly connect to the Bay Area Rapid Transit (BART), a three-county public transit system. Borrowing to expand MUNI, then, was pitched as a way to shorten the travel time between work and home for residents of San Francisco and facilitate the movement of travelers between the city and other parts of the Bay Area.[39]

The claims of freedom of mobility had convinced San Franciscans enough to carry the BART bond election in November 1962. When they

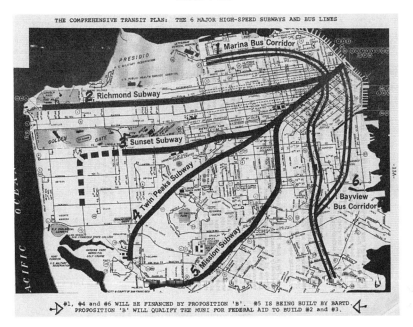

FIGURE 6.1 High-speed subway and bus lines to be financed by Proposition B, 1966.

Source: Proposition B: "The Comprehensive Transit Plan" (November 1966), folder "Elections. November 1966," San Francisco Ephemera Collection, San Francisco History Center, San Francisco Public Library.

said "yes" to the $792 million bond, they agreed to service debt well into the future.[40] Just four years later, more than a few voters expressed remorse. Marguerite Warren, secretary of the Committee to Inform Taxpayers, was unfazed by maps detailing expanded MUNI routes. The spatial renderings and cost analysis seemed too similar to that which already burdened her pocketbook. She asked, why pass the bonds and push up tax rates when "you now pay 41.7 [cents] for BART"? Thomas Dillon, chairman of the Home Owners and Tenants Protective Committee, contended San Franciscans had delivered "a blank check for a Billion Dollars of Tax Money" when they approved the BART bond. "We are paying dearly for our mistake. Don't make the same mistake twice."[41]

The cost estimates of municipal technocrats were almost entirely based on the assumption that the recent past could be used to anticipate the future. When in the mid-1950s the circuit of consultants, municipal finance officers, and bondmen asserted that BART bonds could be sold at interest rates between 2 and 2.5 percent, they assumed that such terms conformed to the average interest rates and maturities "prevailing in recent years" on municipal debt.[42] They assumed that past performance could be modeled and extrapolated to predict future interest charges. But at an interest rate of 4.4 percent, the sale of BART bonds in October 1967 made clear the impossibility of neat projections.[43] It was for good reason, then, that many San Franciscans were increasingly skeptical of claims that higher airport revenues were inevitable or that airport revenue bonds would not increase taxes. For Thomas Dillon, the bonds were a "Vicious Booby Trap"; airport earnings would not "magically" jump from $4.9 million to $20 million. "And remember," he said, "if this reckless gamble misfires," much like the BART system, "your taxes will skyrocket to absorb this whopping debt."[44]

Dillon used the airport bond measure to explain the often hidden mechanisms that produced wealth inequality in the United States. Being fixed in place, rental properties were different from mobile financial instruments like bonds, but how owners used these distinct assets to offload their tax burdens was the connective thread. Rental property owners, with whom most San Franciscans were familiar in this city of renters, passed along increased property taxes to their tenants in the form of higher rents. Similarly, wealthy individuals shielded themselves from high federal income taxes by purchasing municipal debt. As a result, the racial welfare state had to make up for the attendant loss in revenues. While everyday San Franciscans paid federal income taxes, "wealthy citizens [could] evade paying a single dollar . . . through their purchase of these city bonds," Thomas Dillon argued.[45] Indeed, the bonds were "a 100% Free Hideout for tax dodging wealthy individuals and firms."[46]

Just as the *Sun Reporter*'s editorial staff began urging a deeper engagement with bond politics, other forums emerged to challenge the interpretive hegemony of the progrowth coalition. Founded in 1966, the *San Francisco Bay Guardian (SFBG)* quickly became a progressive alternative to the *San Francisco Chronicle* and *Examiner*. Of the many notable features of the *SFBG*'s coverage, the first was its translation of the social and economic costs of municipal debt. The second was its articulation of a left-wing vision of how debt should be used.

The *SFBG* was neither antidebt nor prodebt; it endorsed some bond issues and opposed others. Thus, the *SFBG* was able to translate the otherwise difficult-to-read, technocratic explanations of how much San Franciscans would pay in total costs. In June 1968, the *SFBG* supported a measure to transform Market Street from its present "dirty, ugly" condition: "The real cost would be $33.3 million, if one is so uncharitable as to include the hidden cost of $8.8 million in interest charges." By explicating the purpose of the issue and pointing the reader to "hidden" interest payments, the *SFBG* helped readers decide whether the bond measure was in "the long-range best interest of the city."[47]

It was no small thing for the *SFBG* to emphasize the long run. As we have seen, San Francisco's increased embrace of short-term debt abbreviated the political horizons of municipal officials and truncated the long-term obligations to its citizenry. Indeed, if debt is a social relation extended through time, as one scholar has observed, the embrace of short-term debt during a moment of escalating interest rates abridged the city's obligation to residents, while cyclically extending its obligations to creditors.[48] The *SFBG* acknowledged that the cost was undoubtedly high but that over the long run, improvements to Market Street might support greater accessibility for pedestrians, prevent slips and falls, and enhance physical safety.

As older arguments for debt began to unravel, bond referenda provided the *SFBG* the opportunity to articulate a new vision of the social compact between the city and debt servicers. The paper supported issues for which there was "something for everybody, in every section of the city."[49] Not all neighborhoods had to benefit from a bond in order for it to receive the *SFBG*'s endorsement, but the paper found unacceptable those issues that only enhanced the property values of private interests.[50] In a sense, its editors and columnists recognized the ways in which states shape markets. This allowed the paper to critique a process whereby certain developments were "subsidized by public financing amounting to millions of dollars in tax exempt bonds."[51] For the *SFBG*, the problem was not debt per se, but how debt for the consumer playground crowded out other priorities such as schools, housing, and transportation that truly benefited all San Franciscans.[52]

As important as the paper was in nourishing a left-wing analysis of debt, that analysis also spoke to the outsized power of bond financers, bond buyers, and bondholders. The *SFBG* critiqued the inequality and corruption of tax assessments and exposed millions in back taxes owed by "as many as 500 big companies."[53] However, by endorsing certain long-term, infrastructure-for-all bond measures, the *SFBG* revolted against prevailing local spending priorities but did not challenge the dependencies of cities on debt and the bond market for basic infrastructure and social welfare.

The truism that debt haunts future generations has been used by deficit hawks to rail against the expansion of social welfare. But there is another way to look at the axiom. That voters invoked Bay Area Rapid Transit when deciding on different transit systems spoke to how past borrowing decisions weighed on the present. It affirmed how BART and other projects were seen as albatrosses that exacerbated unequal tax burdens and the inequality of political power. It made clear that once the system was set up, those benefiting from it were not the ones who paid for its mistakes.

Beset by a multitude of problems, poor budgeting, rising labor costs, and the Vietnam War, BART's cushion for inflation and contingency expenses was slowly melting away. By 1966, BARTD needed an additional $150 million to finance the escalating costs of materials, equipment, and labor.[54] The BARTD board responded with the idea of selling revenue bonds; bondholders would be paid through a sales tax imposed uniformly throughout the three counties. Although the initial legislation gave the district the power to issue all kinds of debt instruments, the board of directors needed Governor Ronald Reagan to approve the issuance of the bonds.[55]

Formed in late 1968, Bay Area Citizens to Save BART (BACSB) was outraged by the thought of being taxed, again, by an unelected board of directors. Mrs. Elmer A. Weden Jr. observed that the sales tax had "one feature which appeal[ed] to BART directors" but was at odds with the desires of most people: the directors "would not have to ask the people for permission to levy this tax on them." Weden was outraged that she and so many others might be forced by a group that was "in no way elected by or responsible to the people" to pay a sales tax. How to justify this power of mere "political appointees"?[56] As fellow traveler Robert Tideman noted, for California to permit a "non-elected board" to levy such a tax was "to take a very long and backward step indeed."[57] Weden and Tideman framed their critiques in terms of democratic power. If the BARTD board and its allies wished to levy a sales tax, BACSB insisted that this power be checked by "a vote of the people."[58]

It was suggestive when BACSB proclaimed to have the support of the central labor councils of San Francisco, Alameda, and Contra Costa Counties, with their "more than 190,000 members." This appeared to signal a slight crack in the progrowth coalition. By all means "get on with the business of completing BART construction," declared one labor official. But to do so through the sales tax "would only lead us to believe that the Directors of BART are attempting to provide a tax shelter" for the owners of "large tracts of unimproved property in direct proximity to BART transportation lines."[59] Robert Tideman asked whether it was BART's purpose "to serve as an engine for the enrichment of a few at the expense of the many." If so, then a sales tax levied atop the general property tax to cover bonded indebtedness was surely appropriate. But make no mistake about it, he declared, the sale tax "hits the poor, penalizes trade, and is regressive."[60] That is, it compounded the vulnerabilities of the poor, working class, and middle class by taking a greater percentage of their incomes.

These critiques ultimately went unaddressed. On April 3, 1969, a *New York Times* reporter observed the excitement of the young and old "as a binocular-shaped, 10,000-ton section of steel and concrete was lowered into a trench at the bottom of the bay." While some let their minds float with the thought of trains moving swiftly underwater, others focused on Governor Reagan's endorsement of a 5½-cent sales tax to resolve BART's financing woes. The sales tax would be in place "long enough" to generate $150 million, thus allowing the board of directors to sell its revenue bonds.[61] It was the first of many repeated regressive bailouts.[62]

Taken together, the critiques by poor residents of Chinese descent against the disproportionate allocation of funds, arguments coming out of the black press against taxation without representation, and discussions of how debt shifted the tax burden onto poor, working-class, and middle-class San Franciscans, represented a dramatic rebuke of the city's municipal debt program. During this momentary breach, a moment of political agitation and mobilization for greater democratic input, those who benefited little from the postwar debt arrangement, as well as some of those served by new, refurbished infrastructure, revolted.

And yet, at each point the revolters pushed against a hollow point, one that had been long screened and that did not expose the heart of an unequal relationship between borrowers and creditors. The revolt left untouched how riots, injunctions, and boycotts were folded into interest rate penalties. Precisely because the world of debt was largely hidden from view, these revolters could not see how lenders watched in horror from afar at the revolting, blighted, ungovernable, and blackened city.

The Revolting City

The urban riots of the 1960s were major ruptures in postwar America. When we think of the riots as triggering a shift from the fleeting War on Poverty to the indefinite War on Crime, as compelling the federal government to extend thirty-year home mortgages to low-income black women, or as expanding black radical freedom dreams, we can see that the long, hot summers fostered a significant sociopolitical transformation of the American city.[63] The economic fallout of the riots was equally consequential. As the *Wall Street Journal* explained not long after the assassination of Martin Luther King Jr., "ghetto-area businessmen in a number of major cities . . . [were] finding themselves frozen out of fire and casualty insurance by mass cancelations of policies, higher rates and refusals to renew protection." Without insurance, the inability to secure a mortgage or borrow money for inventory threatened long-term business prospects.[64] The riots generated another equally powerful temporal phenomenon: the acceleration of a speculative insistence on short-term extraction, of short-term debt as a shortcut to tax-exempt interest income.

Bond financiers had turned municipal debt into commodities that could be differentiated by the reputation of the borrowing "name" involved. But the urban riots raised new problems. On August 13, 1967, the *New York Times* asked, "Will the Riots Hurt Municipal Bond Sales?" It was a complex question that raised others. Was it time—the distance between the event itself and the moment of purchase—that influenced the decision to buy or avoid debt? If the impact of riots on bankers was diminished sales, could rioting cities expect an even higher cost to borrow? Finally, since riots represented both an immediate and a long-term threat to city property and expenditures, they potentially impinged on long-term debt holdings. How, then, would riots affect the market for short-term debt?

"I won't buy any bonds of a city that's had a riot," one institutional investor declared in August 1967, close to a year after the uprising in San Francisco, but less than a week after riots in Milwaukee. With the Wisconsin event still "fresh in his mind," this investor rejected Milwaukee's bonds, but not San Francisco's.[65] This curious discrimination worked in the banker's favor. Indeed, bondmen did not avoid but made a market in riot-torn cities. On March 5, 1968, for instance, bondmen linked a day's decline in municipal bond prices to "the possibility of urban riots this summer." Bankers were speculating in the futures market in riots. They could drum up support for short-term debt among investors looking for tax-exempt returns but weary of tying up their capital for long stretches in a city like Detroit or Newark.[66] But this distinction was artificial. Within the changing evaluations of municipal creditworthiness, all cities were vulnerable to riots. Riots became a way to buttress the allure of short-term debt, which, uncoincidentally, helped bondmen navigate their own cost-profit squeeze.

The riots triggered a broader discussion among lenders about the turmoil of the city. Lagging economic growth, obsolete industrial plants, tax revolts, and demands for governmental services were made worse by the "exodus of the middle class," and rising expenditures too "often pumped into problems that appear to be intractable," explained one student of bond finance.[67] For Robert C. Riehle, vice president of Moody's Investors Service, "few, if any, of the nation's older and larger cities have been without problems." Despite, or perhaps because of, urban renewal, urban cores were still marked by "blight."[68] Thomas Morris, a vice president of

United California Bank of Los Angeles, explained that large cities bred all kinds of problems. "Transportation becomes strained," creating lags in the movement of goods and personnel essential to local and national commerce. Perhaps worse was the magnetic effect of large cities, which "draws the drifter, the criminal, the prostitute, and the beggars." While Riehle told a declensionist narrative whereby older cities lost the battle to blight, Morris maintained that in their very essence, large cities were uncontrollable. Urban life and blight had "become almost synonymous," and newer cities were not insulated.[69]

Some of the same people and firms who had advised municipal technocrats immediately following the war still did so. Only this time, in the context of the urban uprisings, their moral parables of responsibility morphed into ideological rebukes. When Dun & Bradstreet's Frederick L. Bird had encouraged municipal finance officers to insulate debt policy years earlier, he had in mind speculators who would use borrowed funds to aid pet projects. By the late 1960s, however, credit analysts identified other so-called pressure groups seeking to despoil sound fiscal governance for their own selfish ends.

Having "succumb[ed] to the pressures of special interests and minority groups," Moody's insisted too many municipal finance officers were losing their grip on sound debt management.[70] In light of the expressions of minority political power, there was a certain truth to the claim. But what analysts really meant was that racial and ethnic minorities were using their political power to challenge demonstrably unequal urban fiscal priorities, to revolt against the prevailing debt arrangement that delivered the spoils to bondholders. Indeed, if anyone was a special interest group who used public funds to augment their own interests, it was lenders. But that was not how they saw it. Instead, they came to believe the city was losing its way.

The attempt to pin the troubles of American cities on labor and racial and ethnic minorities would become full blown in the 1970s. In many ways, though, Moody's vice president Riehle replayed an older argument about black people and municipal fiscal extravagance. During the late nineteenth and early twentieth centuries, sellers of financial information occasionally hinted that elite white governance was a precondition for lending to a municipality. Within that framework, all black people plundered private property and mismanaged public finances. Poor whites were only slightly redeemable because they were white, but they could not and should not govern. Only white men of property could govern honestly, shield their governments from despoliation, and manage fiscal affairs.[71] Riehle stripped away these explicitly racist representations. For him, suburbanization was detrimental not merely because of what it did to a city's tax base but also because of whom the city lost. The flight of "the young, vibrant middle-income group" was lamentable because older cities could not escape "the influx of others, who through no fault of their own possess modest skills and limited earning capacity."[72] Suburbanization implied "the potential loss of an electorate with a desire for efficient, conservative, sophisticated government" would be filled, presumably, by racial and ethnic minorities who would vote for inefficient, fiscally liberal, primitive government.[73]

Municipal bond raters most often spoke in a deracialized discourse of technocratic aggregations and euphemisms. When Standard & Poor's Brenton Harries acknowledged that the rating agency considered race "only from the economic standpoint," he was really commenting on the ways in which federal policy privileged white suburbs over blackened cities, the imbricated forms of employment discrimination and exclusion against racial and ethnic minorities, and how the mobilization of "non-whites" against these forms of oppression would affect municipal coffers.[74] Robert C. Riehle saw a tension between the pursuit of "lofty ideals" and constraints on expenditures. While he called it an accepted "obligation of the society in which we live" to provide for "the unfortunate, the ill and oppressed," too much generosity meant it was only a matter of time before "the welfare load or burden on major cities" became too much to shoulder, ultimately "transferred to the Federal government."[75] These analysts did not miss the structural factors that underlay the problems of the city. However, perhaps because of the immediate gains of the civil rights revolution, and the mutually constitutive eclipse of "race" as a category of analysis and the rise of color-blind euphemisms in public policy discussions, they flattened the structural story into a deracialized one about class and social inequality.

In their accounts, revenues and expenditures must always guide and circumscribe the relationship between the state and its citizenry. And if municipal technocrats and elected officials chose to abide by a different moral calculus, the municipal bond market would react. As Riehle put it, the "threat" of borrowers having to pay a higher interest rate and being penalized "for fiscal excesses" served as "an incentive for a community to keep its financial house in order."[76] Brave and wise was the city that took on the challenge of arresting minority political power, sticking instead to "acceptable" investments.

For city officials around the country the question was how, if at all, would suburbanization, revolts, and other forces become constitutive of bond ratings. Complaints about the bond rating system more generally prompted congressional hearings and a flowering of studies during the late 1960s and early 1970s.[77] Some of the leading credit analysts criticized their former employers and went on to establish their own models. For instance, W. H. Tyler & Co., whose founder, Walter H. Tyler, had worked for Standard & Poor's, urged a move away from "value judgments." His model of bond rating included a number of factors such as the "non-white population" within a category of a borrower's "intangibles," which could have positive or negative valence.[78] These were alternative ways to measure creditworthiness, but the social values of creditors were largely the same; the quantitative approach still made borrowers commensurate yet different, coding social welfare in terms of yields, bond prices, and ratings.

It was in this context that the Investment Bankers Association of America named Thomas Morris the winner of its annual essay competition for his work outlining the limits of the existing bond rating system and sketching an aspirational model.[79] In December 1966, the *DBB* reprinted the entire text. While municipal bond ratings "form the common language of dealers, investors and issuers," Morris argued for the need to substitute "subjective . . . opinions" for "logically assembled" statistics in economic models that could "predict" optimal and disconcerting changes to the credit base of states, cities, and special districts. Morris proceeded from the assumption that the world could be neatly divided into discreet categories ("legal," "economic," "political," and "social"). Analysts might determine which variables should be included within each of those categories. The economic and social, for instance, included such factors as kinds of industry and value of real property. "Of at least equal importance" were a community's "people—their education, age, race, earnings, debt paying habits." All the variables should be weighted so as to calculate a "numerical rating" somewhere between 60 and 119, offering far greater precision than the letter grades of Moody's and Standard & Poor's and the vague descriptions—"Better Medium Grade"—of Dun & Bradstreet.[80]

Morris framed his project as different from Moody's and Standard & Poor's, but he relied on many of the same metrics and assumptions. Borrowers whose median family income fell above $6,788 earned 1 point, while those with a median family income between $3,400 and $4,500 were given −1 point. That poor cities would be penalized was to be expected. The real question was why raters had the power to do so in the first place. Borrowers with "unlimited" tax limits were neutral (neither plus nor minus). Those with limits on the kinds of property that underlay debt-service payments might be docked −1 or −2 points. This reflected the bondholders' view that any restrictions on the ability of cities to levy and collect taxes, especially property taxes, would weaken the marketability of general obligation bonds. Morris's model not only recalled the ideas embedded in older forensic profiles of borrowers but also foreshadowed why lenders found property tax revolts so disturbing.

Prevailing and aspirational models made explicit that evaluations of municipal creditworthiness were more than mere reflections of racial inequality; they actively constructed it. When Morris identified the percentage of nonwhites as a critical variable, he showed how creditors put a seemingly objective gloss on a highly racist and subjective process:

> This factor is included in the realization that accusations of being anti-Negro might be forthcoming. But the facts are irrefutable—the Negro community in metropolitan areas has a lower income, higher crime rate, higher birth rate, higher percentage of welfare cases, higher unemployment rate, and a lower educational level. These conditions are unfortunate and hopefully will improve, but they lead to increased debt while not contributing significantly to a community's ability to pay, and thus are deleterious factors.

"Nonwhites" did not really mean nonwhites but served as a euphemism for "Negro." Like Moody's Robert C. Riehle, Thomas Morris echoed theories of social pathology to present urban African Americans as moochers who inexplicably continued to have children who would only exacerbate the unemployment and welfare problems of blighted, crime-ridden, inefficient cities. For Morris, there were no class differences; all black people within cities everywhere were drains on municipal funds. Thus, black people and the conditions they allegedly produced were "deleterious factors." Borrowers would not gain points from having a population that was less than 15 percent African Americans, but penalties would be imposed as that percentage rose above 15 percent, with a point docked for every additional 10 percent.[81] Although the Morris model was aspirational, it contained many of the ideas and assumptions that had long been incorporated into evaluations of municipal creditworthiness. Notions of racial governance were integral to the rubrics and moral strictures of lenders. Morris was just the most explicit when it came to black people.

When they discussed the ills of the city, bankers and credit analysts did not focus squarely on quantitative metrics. Rather, they commented on the violation of the postwar racial contract. Instead of borrowing responsibly for Keynesian growth fueled by and for white middle- and upper-class Americans, cities were increasingly borrowing to meet the demands of minorities, or, perhaps worse, offering them a seat at the table of urban governance in ways that upended sound debt management. If the credit crunch exposed the fundamental divisions between municipal borrowers and creditors, the political revolts laid bare the ideological inclinations of lenders, who then penalized borrowers for violating the racial contract.

The mid-1960s tightened the tension over what cities were: for residents, they were places of residence, work, and leisure; for bondholders, they were a means of capital accumulation. City officials faced calls for greater democratic accountability from below in ways that might also make lenders wary. How should they respond to black political demands that, if neglected, might torpedo bond issues, while also acknowledging that bond raters might penalize the creation of greater room for black political input? San Francisco's governing officials were between a rock and a hard place. Declining urban services and infrastructure, civil violence, and bond revolts undermined the safety of investing in the city. But if pumping expenditures into seemingly obstinate urban problems was seen as shortsighted at best, how else could they prevent "another Watts," or, for that matter, another Hunters Point? And how could they do all of this while keeping taxes low?

7. Failure

San Francisco had momentarily escaped association with the riots and thus avoided the costs of a downgrade and a blighted borrowing reputation. Yet the idea that some investors might refuse to buy the bonds of rioting cities, or the suggestion that bankers could secure slightly higher interest rates by speculating in riot futures, gave a greater sense of urgency to addressing spatial and racial inequality. Between 1968 and 1971, the deepening of racialized poverty, infrastructural neglect, and the fear that both would give rise to riots compelled municipal officials to propose bonds specifically designed for the Hunters Point neighborhood. Long forsaken, the neighborhood and its residents now occupied center stage. But this reliance on debt collided with opposition to higher taxes, growing antipathy toward city government, and, for some, aversion to borrowing for black futures.

When an exceptionally large number of San Franciscans went to the polls on November 5, 1968, Proposition A, a measure for parks and recreation, fell 3,170 votes shy of passing.[1] The following year, labor, ethnic groups, religious organizations, and countless other civic organizations pledged their support for a $5 million public-school bond. It failed.[2] So did a June 1970 public-school bond measure. All the while, voters approved bonds for other, more expensive projects. How can we make sense, then, of the uneven results? Of selective failure? There are numerous ways to narrate failure, but the most interesting story is what these rejections symbolized.

For starters, the rejections point to the catch-22 in which municipal officials were ensnared, a vexing dilemma rooted in the complexities of the urban fiscal crisis. The urban crisis was as much about riots, urban decay, and inner-city poverty as it was about escalating tax rates, regressive taxation, increased expenditures, and higher interest costs on debt.[3] Riots, urban blight, and racial inequality raised the cost of municipal borrowing. The only way to lower it was to address the underlying structural causes, which would be paid for by selling bonds. But to sell more bonds, especially during a time of escalating interest rates and market volatility, meant adding to the burdens of city taxpayers.

It is tempting to treat the failures of the late 1960s and early 1970s as a product of escalating interest rates on municipal debt. And, indeed, rates were sky-high. Prime municipal borrowers experienced the peaks and valleys of borrowing costs, and for twenty years, the most highly rated among them had paid as low as 1 percent interest in 1946 and as high as 3.2 percent in 1966. On May 14, 1970, the Bond Buyer Index reached "the highest level in the 75-year history." "AAA"-rated school district bonds yielded 6.50 percent, while one university issued its "A"-rated revenue bond at a whopping 8.43 percent.[4] Just a few days before San Franciscans decided on the city's public-school bond measure, the Dow Jones municipal bond yield stood at 7.06 percent, a level not seen in over forty years.[5] The average yield on California municipal bonds also "soared to a record high" of 7 percent.[6] If the question of the late 1950s was whether city-approved bonds would sell, by the late 1960s and early 1970s, the question was how to borrow without provoking a tax revolt that might threaten urban stability and political regimes.

Yet the ways in which different San Franciscans comprehended the burdens of debt reveals a great deal about the city's changing racial and class politics. San Francisco is often characterized as one of America's most liberal cities, but the word "liberal" is often misconstrued. The characterization glosses over different visions of urban liberalism. It does not recognize the trick of color-blind liberalism, "a distinctively white (not colorless)" ideology that facilitates white racial advantage not through individual efforts but through the "work" that whiteness does in society.[7] It also obscures the battles between those people committed to color-blind liberalism and others who insisted on a very different lexicon and approach to politics. The bond measures of the late 1960s and early 1970s reveal something far messier than the "liberal" characterization. Advocates of color-blind liberalism defended the boundaries of acceptable political discourse against African Americans who described the city as antiblack and looked to leverage and confront white supremacy to secure new schools and parks for their children. Color-blind liberals also faced off against racists, who, according to San Francisco's image of itself, were thought not to reside in the "City That Knows How." Ultimately, bond failures did not only signify a disinterest in investing in black futures. These failures also signaled a broader retreat from the short-lived promises of the Great Society and the fleeting commitment to tackling the racial inequalities inscribed over the postwar period.

"No Sandboxes, No Swings"

Hunters Point: No other neighborhood better demonstrated the paradox of racial inequality in a sea of affluence. Here, the hillside apartments offered panoramic views. Looking in one direction, public-housing tenants could recall busy wartime scenes at the US naval base and see the mighty Bay Bridge stretching from San Francisco's financial district to Oakland. Elsewhere, these views would command a fortune. But Hunters Point was "a special kind of ghetto."[8]

Like so many other neighborhoods to which African Americans had been relegated, Hunters Point became an object of study in the late 1960s. Arthur E. Hippler, a self-described white "liberal-activist graduate student," had his long-standing interest in black pathology rekindled by Daniel Patrick Moynihan's report, *The Negro Family: The Case for National Action*. Hippler saw Hunters Point as the ideal ethnographic location for examining the origins of black matrifocal households, where the "same pathology [was] reproduced in each generation" and "self-hate and self-denigration" governed black men. After four months of field research and psychological tests in 1966–67, Hippler concluded that black people in the area were either "essentially passive" or engaged in misdirected activities that only confirmed their "internalized fear of whites." His book *Hunter's Point: A Black Ghetto* is an amalgam of dubious social science, Freudian assumptions, and a handful of interviews that became foundational to the ghetto studies literature.[9]

The book and municipal officials alike endorsed black pathology and treated the ghetto as a single stigmatized category. Differences and distinctions within it disappeared. Most everyone saw Hunters Point as a ghetto, though they could not agree on exactly where it was.[10] One city agency used a single census tract as the basis for its own redevelopment plans. Another city department included a portion of public-housing projects along with rental and single-family properties in the adjacent Bayview neighborhood in its application for federal aid.[11] For many, the presence of a public-housing project defined the area; everything else faded into insignificance. Although Hippler interviewed a handful of families who, by his own admission, were "*not* typical of San Francisco blacks—perhaps not even of all Hunter's Point residents," he treated two distinct neighborhoods, Hunters Point and Bayview, as a single area.[12] Despite the fact that "there [were] many residences which [were] in very good repair and which appear[ed] to be [in] good standing condition," the stain of public-housing projects and the territorial concentration of poor black people were sufficient for Hippler and others to collapse Bayview and Hunters Point into a single, blemished place.[13]

But even public housing in Hunters Point was not a single thing. There were two basic kinds.[14] Made of "lathe and plasterboard," the "temporary" projects contained eight two-bedroom apartments within "long, barracks-type structures." Meanwhile, 1,400 families lived in the "permanent" projects, built of relatively superior construction materials in the same architectural style.[15] Although the San Francisco Housing Authority originally planned to demolish these temporary units in 1949, the lack of rental housing within the reach of tenants forced it to extend the life of these increasingly deteriorating units.[16] And the projects continued to shelter capital.

Shortly after the assassination of Martin Luther King Jr., and as a "swift follow-up" to the Kerner Commission analysis of the long hot summers of 1967, the San Francisco Conference on Religion, Race and Social Concerns published an exhaustive study of racial inequality in the city. Produced *"for* white people *from* white people," the conference implored the city's religious institutions to help redress police violence, unemployment, inequitable living conditions, and the disparity in social services. The quickness with which the tome was produced reflected fears that San Francisco had not responded to the structural forces that produced urban uprisings. Because Hunters Point was the epicenter of the riots of September 1966, the conference paid special attention to the demographic profile of the area, finding that Bayview–Hunters Point's population was relatively young and poor: 47.2 percent of the population was under the age of eighteen, and 32 percent of families earned less than $4,000 annually. One in four people were deemed unskilled; one in fifty were identified as professional or technical workers. The high school graduation rate was abysmal, and some 30 percent of residents had not finished grammar school.[17]

The steady march of industry out of San Francisco and the racial discrimination that structured employment in the high-end service sector virtually guaranteed that black residents of Hunters Point would have to travel far for work. Yet the public transportation system made this difficult. The Bay Area Rapid Transit system bypassed Hunters Point entirely. Further, black residents claimed that MUNI drivers circumvented the neighborhood's bus stops. One researcher concluded that it took an hour and a half to travel from Hunters Point to the major manufacturing centers in Fremont, San Leandro, and Hayward. And that was if nothing went wrong. The everyday rhythms of black life in isolated, underfunded neighborhoods could and did make Hunters Point residents late for work. Black residents helped service debt for the MUNI system, but it did them little good. Between the spatially selective routes and the whims of bus operators, the city's public transportation system made travel to the major manufacturing centers in Alameda County "so long that it exclude[d] workers from making the trip for all practical purposes."[18]

In addition, public recreational space was hard to come by. City planners observed that whereas 14.5 percent of all city acreage was devoted to recreational use, only 3.5 percent of the total acreage in Bayview–Hunters Point was available for similar purposes. Instead, land held "auto junk

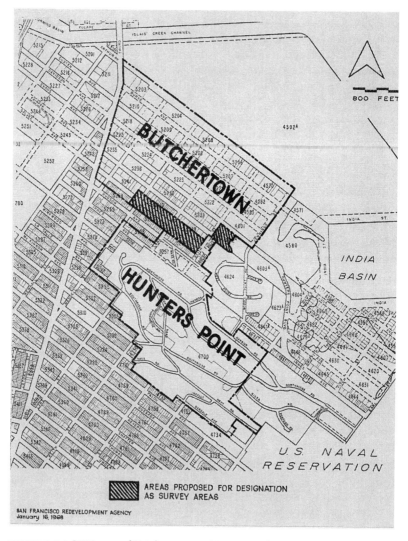

FIGURE 7.1 SFRA map of Butchertown and Hunters Point, January 16, 1968.

Source: Box 9, folder "HUD, Hunters Point, 1968–1969," Joseph L. Alioto Papers, 1958–1977 (SFH 5), San Francisco History Center, San Francisco Public Library.

yards, garbage and trash dumps, malodorous meat processing plants." Still lingering were the "abandoned and rotting industrial buildings of firms that [had] moved away from the decaying district."[19] Indeed, there were "no places in Hunter's Point that [could] conceivably be thought of as entertainment centers."[20]

Fueled by federal support, San Francisco's municipal officials, city planners, and finance officers attempted to radically transform the southeast section of the city. The Board of Supervisors designated Hunters Point a renewal site in December 1963.[21] Soon afterward, the San Francisco Redevelopment Agency (SFRA) secured a $14 million federal grant to initiate the adjacent Butchertown industrial redevelopment project.[22] That project would not revive the glue plants or fertilizer processors of the late nineteenth century, but importing tons of soil to compress the marshy, polluted, and sinking grounds might strengthen the bearing capacity for new industrial activities and expand opportunities for blue-collar workers.[23]

Proposition A, a $6.4 million bond measure, was part of this attempt to invest in Hunters Point. The proceeds from the November 1968 measure would fund two new recreation and park areas, an enclosed swimming pool, and illuminated walkways throughout the 133-acre Hunters Point redevelopment area.[24] A significant portion of the proceeds would go toward the city's mandatory contribution to the project. Citizens for Proposition A (CPA) was one of the many ad hoc bond committees formed and disassembled over the postwar period. Cochaired by telephone executive Sydney G. Worthington and the Board of Supervisors' only African American member, Terry A. Francois, the CPA explained to voters that every dollar the city spent was matched by two federal dollars. That is, if voters approved the debt, the city's $3.85 million contribution would be matched by a $7.7 million federal grant.

The CPA hoped that the faces of black and brown children would convince San Franciscans to support the bond. Yolanda Westry, an African American girl from Hunters Point, was used to anchor the bond drive. In something of a cause celebre, the seven-year-old could be seen on bumper stickers or flyers sitting in her school uniform atop the mayor's limousine. Yolanda was among countless children who played "on steep, rocky hill sides . . . in the streets between cars," not too far from "junk yards and trash dumps." Photographs of third graders inside a dilapidated elementary school, optimistic children playing on cracked pavement, and an introspective black boy sitting atop the dirt hills that formed his playground were among the many images in newspaper-style articles, posters, and pamphlets circulated to rally support for the bond issue.[25]

Yes
on
A
Please

For her—
For our city, for ourselves.
Bayview-Hunters Point Park Bonds
604 Mission St., Room 500
San Francisco, Calif. 94105
Tel. 421-8412

FIGURE 7.2 "Yes on A Please." Yolanda Westry's appeal to voters.

Source: Folder "Vertical File (VF): S.F. Elections. November 1968. Propositions," San Francisco Ephemera Collection, San Francisco History Center, San Francisco Public Library.

Prop. A was at once a dramatic departure from the usual approach to bond finance and consistent with years of selective investment. For starters, the early twentieth-century pattern of borrowing for specific neighborhoods had long been replaced by packages that, in theory, promised to invest funds in multiple neighborhoods or in projects that served a large share of San Franciscans. But those bonds had in fact been used for specific neighborhoods, privileged sectors and activities, and largely for the white middle class. Indeed, the riots had undermined the fiction of race-neutral infrastructural investments. Prop. A, a bond issue that would create construction jobs, accelerate the redevelopment of southeast San Francisco, deliver playgrounds to the children of black workers, and address blight and decay brought together an eclectic mix of supporters. The core organizers of the campaign included Democrats and Republicans, members of the International Longshoremen's and Warehousemen's Union, black activists, and directors of some major corporate and banking firms.[26] The CPA counted the Chamber of Commerce, the Down Town Association, and the San Francisco Labor Council among its backers.[27] The progrowth coalition's support was matched by a ringing endorsement from the Federation of Public Employees and the San

Photo by Ben Spicer

CAN'T WE GIVE HIM A DECENT PLAYGROUND?

FIGURE 7.3 "There's so much in our city." San Francisco was a playground, but for whom?

Source: Folder "Vertical File (VF): S.F. Elections, November 1968, Propositions," San Francisco Ephemera Collection, San Francisco History Center, San Francisco Public Library.

Francisco Council of District Merchants.[28] Fresh off of boycotting some of the city's other bond priorities, the black press endorsed Prop. A.[29]

Endorsements were matched by daily outreach. Staffers met with parents, teachers, and black parishioners.[30] They circulated tailored letters to cement support from rank-and-file union members and black folks. Whereas the "Labor Letter" emphasized taxpayer savings and job growth, the "Black Letter" wrapped its appeal in the garb of black nationalism. Prop. A, this letter stated, "is one issue that really has soul! . . . Our brothers and sisters in Bayview-Hunters Point, and their children, are counting on you!"[31]

Pathology and white liberal guilt were instrumentalized to sell the public on tackling racial inequality. For some, passing the bonds was one step toward remedying urban decay, crime, delinquency, and the many other "pathological" problems affecting the area.[32] But perhaps more interesting than these standard descriptions of the urban crisis was what supporters thought about the people they sought to convince. It was clear that the "bonds benefit Black people," campaign manager Thomas N. Saunders stated. Although "we may never get the support of the vote 'no' red neck," he continued, "we should be able to appeal to the conscience of decent, white middle-class voters."[33]

Other supporters went to great lengths to insist that the bonds were not charity. They refuted the claim that black people did not pay taxes and the popular assumption that only white homeowners and corporations could rightly call themselves taxpayers. Indeed, African Americans in Hunters Point had paid sales taxes on goods and property taxes through rents, effectively servicing debt tied to street lighting fixtures, public recreational facilities, and public schools.[34] "Since 1951" thus became a rallying cry: black people had paid taxes but had not "received a just share for their money in the way of parks" and recreational facilities in seventeen years.[35]

If ghetto pathology and taxpayer arguments were insufficient, supporters invoked fears of another riot. "We are very fortunate," commented Police Chief Thomas J. Cahill, that there was still time to resolve the "serious racial tension in San Francisco." Nevertheless, he argued, "we cannot delay in taking this very important step."[36] According to Jerry Flam of the SFRA, failure of the bond measure might intensify the "racial and social problems which have wracked the city in the past months." Flam maintained that black folks might interpret failure "as a strictly anti-Negro vote," and that might mean "our famed, liberal city could join Detroit and Newark as urban battlefields."[37] Embedded in these claims was the concern that violence might place San Francisco under the probing gaze of already suspicious lenders. With blighted bonds came higher interest charges. Better for San Franciscans to pony up now before another riot surely exacerbated taxpayer burdens.

The failure of the bond measure prompted detailed breakdowns of voting patterns, voter thresholds, and campaign financing. Thomas M. Saunders explained, "We did well in Black and "upper class" neighborhoods." Despite expanded outreach in the Sunset, however, opposition from voters there as well as from the Mission and Richmond districts proved decisive in the bond's failure.[38] Some blamed the arduous two-thirds voter threshold.[39] Whereas a simple majority was needed to approve California general obligation bonds, those of its cities, counties, and school districts required the approval of a two-thirds majority.[40] Others complained about the lack of campaign contributions. Cocktail parties that had offered contributors the chance to parlay with Mayor Alioto had hardly paid off.[41] While Bank of America, Bechtel, Pacific Telephone, and the Construction and General Laborers Union, Local No. 261, donated between $500 and $667, most contributions came closer to the pathetic $5 offered by Alan Jacobs, director of the Department of City Planning.[42] In the succinct words of one campaigner, "I have never seen a campaign so rich in lip service and poor in funds."[43]

And yet the two-thirds threshold did not prevent the passage of many bond measures during the 1950s and early 1960s. Nor had the tax revolts thrashed all of November's bond measures. The fact that more than 71 percent of voters approved a $61 million bond for the Port of San Francisco necessitated "some soul searching." As the editors of the *Argonaut* asked, "Why would a strictly business or commercial issue pass so easily, and a human need, so desperately required, fail? Particularly when the port debt would be 10 times as great as the other?"[44] Only some debt burdens were acceptable. "We failed because we called upon the voter to do something for someone else and that someone was Black," Saunders declared.[45]

Dilemmas

From Boston to Charlotte, throughout California and elsewhere, by the late 1960s access to equitable public education, and the battles over integration, busing, and resources were at a fever pitch.[46] Within this context, a public-school bond measure for Hunters Point and, later, for San Francisco's public schools, sparked fierce battles over whether and how white supremacy continued to steer infrastructural investment, and it triggered attempts by different segments of the city to protect and expand the boundaries of acceptable political discourse.

Those looking to expedite industrial redevelopment through the Butchertown project, expand new housing opportunities for low-income

African Americans, and tackle the markings of infrastructural inequality were undeterred by Proposition A's failure. They returned in November 1969 with Proposition B, a $5 million bond that would modernize elementary schools and build two new ones in Hunters Point.[47] As one supporter explained, the measure was "the only bond issue with a 'Black' label on it." It thus attracted opposition and could be the catalyst for "bitter reaction from the Black community."[48] The measure did fail, and it triggered a subtle change in the tactics used to convince San Franciscans to take on public-school debt. Backers of a June 1970 $45 million public-school bond measure retreated to well-worn universal claims and threats that appeared color-blind but were always racially tinged. That measure incorporated the $5 million bond for Hunters Point that had been defeated seven months prior. In effect, the architects of the measure wanted it both ways: they hoped that collapsing the particular into the whole would help the most neglected part of the city, without also explicitly engaging discussions of structural racism.

The June issue also failed, though its significance is not reducible to the outcome. Indeed, the November 1969 and June 1970 measures provoked a range of political positions, some of which were consistent with San Francisco's political culture of color-blind liberalism, and others of which pushed at the acceptable boundaries of political discourse from different directions. Of course, there were white liberals who sought to appeal to the best intentions of all without reference to race. They were joined by racial pragmatists who thought it necessary to leverage white supremacy to secure approval; racists who might still vote for the bonds to keep the city from implementing a busing program; black property owners who voted against bonds for black children out of fear that they would be displaced; elite white property owners who collapsed particular needs into more general population trends; and, finally, indignant racists who fused a critique of local government to anti-black narratives of criminal pathology and portraits of the underserving black poor.

The Proposition B bond drive prompted a tense debate over how to best frame the measure. At the core were questions fundamental to the city's image of itself. To what extent should white supremacy be leveraged to deliver capital improvements to segregated, long-neglected black schools? How could supporters reconcile an explicit engagement with their own, and the general public's, racism and color-blind politics?

One side might be called the racial pragmatists, who confronted the realities of white supremacy in a city that proclaimed the absence of racism. As one columnist explained, rising birth rates in Hunters Point and the attendant increase in school enrollments meant "those old wartime crackerbox schools won't hold all those kids no matter how you shoe-horn them in." On the eve of the election, he warned, "It's build or bus, buster. Take your choice."[49] As historian Mark Brilliant has shown, there was perhaps nothing more threatening to many white and Chinese parents than the school board busing their children. Supporters of Prop. B hoped that this opposition, and the dramatic claims from groups such as Parents and Taxpayers that busing was "nothing but legal kidnapping," would be enough to sell voters on debt.[50]

Citizens for Proposition B (CPB) maintained that immediate construction was "insurance against the need for busing Hunters Point students to other schools."[51] Their October 1969 news release added, "The children of Hunters Point don't want to be bussed to other schools far from their homes." But without the bond, busing was inevitable.[52] For racial pragmatists, including many black parents, activists, and community leaders, this strategy had political utility. One observer poignantly noted that if reference to busing helped deliver new public schools to black children, "they would like to have it mentioned."[53] Their pragmatism was indicative of a broader approach to desegregating public schools not for the sake of brushing elbows with white children but so that black children could benefit from the public investment in white children.[54] Black parents sought to use the state's infrastructural investment in whiteness to secure dividends for their own kids.

On the other side, part caricature and part real, there stood the city's overt racists, the "bigots who don't give a damn about better schools for black kids." It was precisely because of their racism that they might approve Prop. B. To them, debt and taxes were better than seeing black children "scattered to our neighborhoods," as journalist Guy Wright observed.[55] There were differences between the racists and racial pragmatists, but both effectively acknowledged that white supremacy was a potent force in the city.

Racial pragmatists differed from white liberals. On behalf of the Human Rights Commission of San Francisco (HRCSF), Gail Roberts wrote with indignation to the San Francisco Unified School District (SFUSD). The HRCSF, she declared, had long supported "quality integrated education for all of the City's pupils." And while its members were "aware of the urgency of building new schools," they despised "an appeal which is basically white racism." Roberts demanded "public repudiation of any racist intent" insinuated in campaign ephemera.[56] Similarly, Mrs. Friedman, president of the League of Women Voters of San Francisco, demanded an immediate disavowal of CPB campaign strategy. It was unacceptable for CPB to issue "a threat to white parents that unless these schools are built, little black children will be bussed into white schools." She claimed the way to convince voters was to "appeal to the best instincts of our fellow citizens." CPB, in other words, should emphasize the need for "equality of opportunity in education."[57]

In a sense, the HRCSF and the League of Women Voters sought to close the window forced open by the racists, racial pragmatists, and black residents who rejected the color-blind approach to urban politics. Feeling the heat, the SFUSD's associate superintendent called on campaigners to strike "reference" to busing "from any of the literature."[58] CPB exchanged busing for a dry cost-benefit analysis and moral suasion.[59] The irony was not lost on journalist Guy Wright, who observed that the bonds might fail because "white do-gooders" remained committed to appealing "only to the pure in heart."[60] By avoiding direct confrontation with antiblackness and the ways in which whiteness structured public investment, "well-intentioned" white liberals might contribute to "what the City's real racial bigots desire—defeat of all measures which benefit the City's minority groups."[61]

Not all black San Franciscans supported the Hunters Point bond. Some opposed Proposition B because it threatened their property rights. Of the $5 million in bond proceeds, the SFRA planned to use $110,000 to purchase four acres of land at Hudson Avenue and Keith Street for a new $2 million elementary school.[62] However, the SFRA had to first demolish homes and a newly built church along Hudson Avenue.[63] As the owner of two of these homes—"three years old, newly painted and hardly bulldozer material"—African American Irene Parker was outraged.[64] "Not one of us," Parker declared, "were told there were plans for schools and a park where our homes and church stand."[65]

On October 26, 1969, the Bayview-Butchertown Property Owners League (BBPOL) met at the Galilee Baptist Church. Parker, Wallace Murphy, and other league members were forced to decide between protecting their property and communal spaces of worship on the one hand, and new and refurbished public schools for the black youngsters of Hunters Point on the other.[66] That black middle-class renters were expendable had been one of the lessons observed by the *Sun Reporter* years earlier. But the SFRA's plan highlighted something else. Not all property owners were the same, and property ownership did not insulate black people from dispossession.

These property owners formed the Hunters Point Citizens Committee against Proposition B. The group contended that just as elderly residents had been "ousted" for public-housing developments elsewhere, under the pretense of new elementary schools, Prop. B would lead to their own displacement.[67] They also took issue with the damaging spatial assumptions upon which the bond drive rested. Although the ghetto might be employed as a discursive trope to secure public support for debt, that same use enabled the city to erase black property ownership. By saturating the public with images of run-down bungalows, descriptions of sleaze, and editorials on the hazards of public housing, black property owners observed that Bayview was "lumped together with Hunters Point as part of San Francisco's black belt," as one journalist summarized. For Parker, the bond drive denied the existence of an integrated neighborhood of private-property-owning citizens committed to the upkeep of their community; a racially diverse, well-maintained area was erased through the daily photographs of dilapidation in the newspapers.[68]

These were not members of the black bourgeoisie interested solely in protecting their class interests. There was something far messier: a blend of property rights arguments, a belief that claims of racial integration might shield the neighborhood from destruction, and echoes of what the political scientist Michael Dawson has described as "linked fate."[69] Parker and others also meshed a critique of infrastructural neglect with black nationalism to convey a communal concern for black San Franciscans. As Murphy explained, the BBPOL was neither "opposed to redevelopment in Hunters Point" nor "trying to alienate ourselves from our brethren."[70] Forced into a corner, they were being made to choose. For twenty years, during a moment of low interest rates the city had borrowed in pursuit of economic growth through white infrastructural advantage. After black folks revolted, the SFRA's response was to target and displace black property owners to relieve the powder keg of racial inequality.

The Butchertown redevelopment project ignited a similar conflict among black San Franciscans. With twenty-nine of forty-three original wrecking yards slated for eviction, the only option for many of these black operators was to relocate to undesirable, low-valued land. For the *Sun Reporter*'s Emory Curtis, land value and prices were racially inflected. The city, he declared, would not dare relocate light industry to the white, upper-class neighborhood of Pacific Heights. Practically speaking, it would have been impossible to do so, but Curtis highlighted the ways in which "City Hall" continued to reserve light and heavy industry and the attendant environmental hazards for black neighborhoods. Meetings before the Board of Supervisors turned into clashes between Bayview's African American property owners, intent on keeping industry out, and other black folks dependent on "scrap-yards" for their livelihoods.[71] In sum, the city did more than attempt to negate black ownership, congregation, and business. It manufactured class conflict.

For Emory Curtis, these squabbles were symptomatic of an urban political economy that disadvantaged black workers. He observed the consequences of what city planners, developers, and financiers had put in motion years earlier. Predicated in part on the expansion of the FIRE sector and high-end services generally, San Francisco's political economy locked black people "out of the growth areas of economic development." Promises from the chamber of commerce to place black folks in entry-level positions in the private sector, or the pledge from municipal officials to expand public-sector employment, could not offset the trend toward black people "steadily losing their position in the job market," he reasoned. Without more industrial work, African Americans would find themselves evicted from the city itself.

Curtis had a plan for this, a vision of industrial economic development that took cues from the Butchertown redevelopment project. Following World War II, suburban governments pitched the industrial park as providing enough land for sprawling one-story modern plants.[72] San Francisco did not have the space to emulate these suburban strategies, but in the late 1960s, the SFRA proposed the India Basin Industrial Park as "providing job opportunities for unemployed and underemployed residents of the Bayview-Hunters Point community." Upon reclaiming vacant lots, "unimproved" streets, and wrecking yards, the SFRA imagined significantly more acres for industrial use. While the acreage for auto wrecking and salvage activities would go from twenty-five acres to zero, the India Basin Industrial Park would devote more land to the meat industry (from sixteen to twenty-three acres) and to industry in general (from nineteen to fifty-two acres). Finally, the SFRA imagined some eighteen acres devoted to a freeway.[73] Land was fixed, but it could be reconfigured for political and economic objectives. The extension of the Bayshore Freeway might have connected to the Southern Crossing Bridge, a plan "that ha[d] been talked about for at least 20 years," Curtis noted. The Southern Crossing would connect Butchertown to the East Bay and its diverse economic activities. According to Curtis, this "would make the Butchertown area a focal point" of industrial development. Butchertown could then provide "immediate access" to ocean and railroad shipping, freeway access, and "easy access to the San Francisco and Oakland airports." Curtis insisted the Southern Crossing was a boost to industries, offering "access to customers, goods and materials. Additionally, this new bridge would be of prime benefit to the port developments in that area: more jobs that we would have a fair shake at getting." Even if "land costs and city taxes" restrained industrial development in Butchertown, the Southern Crossing would make it "easier for Bayview-Hunters Point residents to reach the industrial areas of East Oakland and Southern Alameda county."

As in his analysis of class conflict and the disproportionate protections afforded white upper-class neighborhoods, Curtis identified the

racial and class interests that aligned to obstruct this vision of industrial economic development. "For the umpteenth time," the Board of
Supervisors delayed the construction of the Southern Crossing, a move
Curtis believed was designed to give the Bay Area Rapid Transit District
(BARTD) "a chance to capture a major share of the cross-bay commuter
traffic." BARTD, which ran into severe financial difficulties well before
the transit system was up and running, was locked in a battle for commuters, especially white ones. There was some truth to Curtis's claim
that the Board of Supervisors' delay "was a blatant play for the votes of
the whites who see San Francisco as their toy and playground." But it
was also true that without hitting its annual target for passengers and
generating sufficient fares, BARTD would have to seek another bailout.
The funds needed to pay revenue bondholders had to come from somewhere. Curtis also pointed to the strange bedfellows working against the
Southern Crossing. In advance of the June 1972 multicounty referenda
to construct the bridge, Curtis maintained that "the downtown interests, conservationist, liberal whites, et al have joined forces to delay the
Southern Crossing. They'll even get some of our leaders to buy their line
that BART comes first and our interests come second."[74]

Like the bond measures for Hunters Point parks and schools, the
Southern Crossing proposal suffered overwhelming defeat ("no": 384,245;
"yes": 114,132).[75] And as with the selectivity of bond rejections, this failure
foreclosed a vision of black industrial futures. San Francisco city planners often spoke of the "inevitable" extension of the financial district and
industrial activity as obsolete, rhetoric that treated urban redevelopment
as a natural process, shaped by demographics and market forces. But in-
evitability and obsolescence were political claims. The visions proffered
by people like Curtis were not old, but they existed alongside attempts
to expand high-end services. Moreover, Curtis articulated a spatial vision that clashed with the city's highway and freeway revolts. Indeed,
which vision was progressive and which was conservative is not so easy to
parse.[76] Nevertheless, just as the Great Society's attempt to leverage federal grants and the bond market came too late, the SFRA's belated commitment to the industrial development of Butchertown was no match
for the alliances between the FIRE sector, conservationists, BARTD, and
white liberals.

By June 1970 the cost of public-school debt was now seen as too much
to bear. And indeed, the burden of rising borrowing costs was palpable. When controller Nathan B. Cooper (who succeeded Harry D. Ross)
offered the usual technocratic details behind the $45 million school
bond, he actually made clear that lenders were the real beneficiaries of

the federal tax-exempt subsidy. Assuming a particular maturity on the bonds, and with actual principal and estimated interest charges in hand, Cooper concluded that if authorized, city taxpayers would be on the hook for nineteen annual payments of $3.6 million to bondholders. Interest morphed the $45 million public-school bond into a $68.4 million expenditure that would deliver more than $23 million in tax-exempt interest income to bondholders.[77] To prevent an upswing in the property tax rate, technocrats made a remarkable recommendation: the public-school bond might be considered part of the "City Capital Improvement Program," a program "Financed by Sales Tax Revenues."[78] Looking to reconcile the tension between racial inequality and escalating tax burdens—the two sides of the urban fiscal crisis—they proposed regressive taxation as a compromise.[79]

The anticipated burden of public-school debt fed into the concerns of elite white homeowners. For some of the more vocal opponents, the June 1970 bond measure betrayed a Board of Education that was violating property rights, engaging in fiscal chicanery, and burdening San Franciscans with extravagant projects. Take, for instance, the Marina Civic Improvement & Property Owners Association and the West of Twin Peaks Central Council, which represented an even larger collective of homeowner and improvement clubs in white, upper-class neighborhoods—a cluster of "island suburbs."[80] The umbrella organization translated the sentiments put forward by the Balboa Terrace Homes Association, St. Francis Homes Association, Lakeshore Acres Improvement Club, Merced Manor Property Owners Association, and Monterey Heights Homes Association, among other property associations, into a cogent argument against public-school bonds.[81]

These elite property owners couched their opposition to public-school bonds in terms of fiscal responsibility and expropriation. The Board of Education not only failed to explain how funds would be spent but also furtively nestled a $5 million expenditure for Hunters Point elementary schools in the June 1970 bond measure. Why, the group contended, was this expense included if "the voters turned [it] down last November"?[82] The Board of Education, they claimed, owned too much public land and property and was hungry for more. Indeed, the board had a hand in displacing Mrs. P. Da Prato of 631 Park Way, Mr. and Mrs. Gualtiero Mazzei of 64 Pomona Street, absentee owner Elisabeth Lazzareschi of 1611 LaSalle Street, and the many tenants living on the land selected for the Bayview elementary school.[83] Speaking to a citywide audience, many of whom were sensitive to removal, dispossession, and displacement, these property owners claimed, "The Board of Education is still condemning

people's homes up to this very moment . . . you could be next!" Elite homeowners called on San Franciscans to resoundingly vote "no."[84]

We have seen how the rising cost to borrow and the attendant hike in
the tax rate shaped powerful progressive critiques of debt as bonanzas for
wealthy tax dodgers. But there were other tax revolts brewing in the city.
Jeffrey J. Drapel, who lived not too far from a nearby BART train station,
articulated a racist and reactionary brand not unlike that seen in the postwar South or, for that matter, in the East Bay. Seen in one light, Drapel
and his Committee for Safe and Decent Schools (CSDS) might be taken
as representative of a broader democratic neighborhood movement. He
and others demanded a move away from the at-large system of elect-
ing the Board of Supervisors and toward district-based elections.[85] CSDS
secured more than 58,000 signatures toward this end.[86] Seen in another
light, Drapel was part of a broader conservative reaction to the demands
and gains of the civil rights revolution and the exercise of minority political power. Bond financiers and many white middle-class homeowners
secured distinct wages of whiteness depending on the kinds of assets
they owned. They did, however, share a virulent opposition to the exercise of state power by working-class black people, and a disgust toward
a liberal state that conceded to black and minority political economic
demands. "Never in history of this beautiful city," a CSDS newsletter declared, "have the citizens been more abused, taxed, pushed around and
ruthlessly exploited." City government, Drapel claimed, was under the
sway of "liberal demagogues" who held too much power. A district-based
election system and the rejection of "anything that will cost money," he
reasoned, were the antidotes.[87]

Drapel differed from the elite property owners, however, in one important respect: he registered high borrowing costs and high taxes in
the most racist of terms. He was representative of the racists of which
racial pragmatists spoke. Through his discussion of black power, riots,
and crime, Drapel tapped into a current of white racism that developed
alongside the black freedom movement.

Using infrastructure, curriculum reform, and the riots as his touch-
stone, Drapel made his case against the $45 million public-school bond.
Although the bond was for all of the city's public schools, the inclusion
of the $5 million expenditure for Hunters Point blackened (so to speak)
the entire package. Drapel urged San Franciscans to vote against the
measure, not merely because of the fiscal weight of debt but because "we
can't afford to build modern buildings to be destroyed by militants." He
found the inclusion of Eldridge Cleaver's *Soul on Ice* and Leroi Jones's
Dutchman and the Slave in a high school curriculum on black studies to

be disreputable. Why should taxpayers, he asked, pay for new schools in which "children from poverty pockets" were taught "robbery, hold-ups and other crimes"?[88] Whereas some supporters recalled the riots to persuade the public to vote for the bonds, Drapel used them to make the opposite point: even if lenders penalized the city for its deepening urban crisis, bad behavior should not be rewarded. In his view, investing in radicalized black children would only lead to the destruction of the facilities for which reputable San Franciscans paid.

On June 2, 1970, San Franciscans had before them potent arguments about municipal extravagance, the excesses of liberal governance, teach-ers on strike, black radicalism, and allusions to busing. Some opponents framed the public-school measure as yielding to dangerous, illiterate, criminal black children. Others underscored the fiscal, seemingly color-blind argument that a massive bond measure at a time of overall declin-ing birthrates was unnecessary.

The November 1969 and June 1970 public-school bond rejections had proved a microcosm of statewide and national trends. Whereas California led the way in borrowing for public schools in the late 1950s, the tide receded dramatically by the late 1960s. During the 1968–69 ac-ademic year, 191 school districts in the state held 227 bond elections, of which 146 (64.3 percent) failed. Californians rejected the prospect of taking on more than $862 million in debt for public schools.[89] Of the $1 billion in bond proposals submitted to state and local voters across the country in June 1970, voters rejected 68.7 percent—more than $693 million. The degree of defeat was up sharply from the previous year, when voters had turned down 39 percent ($309,526,283) of the $788 million submitted for approval.[90] The attempts to remedy one side of the urban fiscal crisis collided with the other side. It is fair to say, then, that while municipal officials played critical roles in carrying out retrenchment, the retreat from an investment in social welfare was also realized through the actions of voters.

"The taxpayers' revolt," proclaimed one observer in November 1969, "has become a reality for San Francisco."[91] That year San Franciscans rejected not only Hunters Point elementary school bonds but also two bond referenda tied to park facilities and general capital improve-ments.[92] As one commentator put it, "all issues involving a substantial expenditure of city funds were clobbered."[93] But, like the waves of the San Francisco Bay, the tax revolt advanced, receded, and splashed un-evenly. San Franciscans selectively rejected public investment. Put simply, they refused "to finance better urban services and protection for their most disadvantaged citizens, the segment that would benefit most from improvement in rundown schools, bad lighting, poor fire safeguards, crowded courtrooms, and skimpy recreation," in the sharp words of one scholar.[94]

Clouded

It was easier to tinker with voter thresholds than it was to redress both the illicit infrastructural investment in whiteness and the rendering of black neighborhoods as unworthy of debt. By November 1969, the American Civil Liberties Union of Northern California contended that the two-thirds rule was a clear violation of the "one-man, one-vote" mandate.[95] In June 1970, the California Supreme Court agreed, ruling that future municipal bond issues needed only a simple majority to pass. In a provocative ruling, the court dismissed claims that the threshold preempted the "immediate financial catastrophe and ultimate collapse" of municipal governments. The predictions of "the crushing burdens of debt foolishly incurred by reckless or malevolent popular majorities" in fact obscured how the two-thirds rule gave greater voter power to "no" voters, effectively denying "yes" voters an equal say.[96] These doomsday scenarios were the language of bondholders. The California Supreme Court was not persuaded.

Yet with an appeal expected, a cloud still hung over California's municipal borrowers. In late July 1970, two major bond attorney firms, Orrick, Herrington, Rowley & Sutcliffe of San Francisco and O'Melveny & Myers of Los Angeles, questioned the ruling. "In actual practice," the *Daily Bond Buyer* (*DBB*) remarked, "approval by either of the firms is essential before local government agencies can place their bonds on the market."[97] Without the backing of the municipal fraternity, future bond issues were dubious. As George Herrington explained, "no bond holder will take the risk."[98]

The court's decision also "clouded the legality of local bond elections." With an appeal headed to the US Supreme Court, Assemblyman John Knox of Contra Costa County presented a bill to affirm the California Supreme Court's ruling. He contended that borrowers could not wait either for the appeal to be heard or for a final decision. It was "impossible for cities, counties and school districts to sell their bonds when approved by a simple majority."[99] Legal limbo threatened to upend the construction of hospitals, schools, parks, and street lighting, among other infrastructural fixtures.

With the hope that they could secure a simple majority, supporters returned in November 1970 with Proposition B, a $5.5 million bond to remedy the run-down, overcrowded schools in Hunters Point. They made the usual argument about savings for the city, minimal increases in the city's tax rate, and the costs of delay. They framed the issue in terms of equality of "modern educational opportunities" for all.[100] The endorsement of the San Francisco Labor Council was about as familiar as Jeffrey J. Drapel's racist, antipoor harangues against debt.

By the late 1960s, writes one historian, "welfare had become firmly lodged in the California tax debate, not as a symbol of shared wealth assisting the needy, but as the embodiment of wasting taxpayer money."[101] Waste and extravagance were just as often racialized concepts backed by decontextualized numbers. It was true that San Francisco's welfare expenditures rose from $61 million in 1965–66 to $83.8 million in 1967–68.[102] What people did with these facts and figures, though, was another matter. Drapel folded a racist critique of welfare into his opposition to the November 1970 bond measure. If black children "need more classrooms," he declared, the Board of Education should simply "close all cafeterias and convert them into classrooms." Time had run out for an unelected Board of Education that found "money for busing the children to various locations, not for the sake of education, but for pleasing political pressure groups." He coupled his rants against black radicals with a disdain for free lunch programs and welfare expenditures. Black children should be given "some education instead of free hot dogs." With a city full of residents "on welfare," Drapel urged San Franciscans to "quit being Santa Clause [sic]—charity starts at home."[103]

If bond results can be read as an index of support for the city's spending priorities, then pollution control bonds mattered more than bonds for public education. Despite its being far costlier than the Hunters Point bond measure, more than 78 percent of San Franciscans approved a $65 million bond for pollution control, compared to 63 percent who voted for the $5 million Hunters Point school bond. Given the California Supreme Court ruling, that 63 percent might be enough to fix decrepit schools. The *San Francisco Chronicle* urged patience. It "won't mean a thing until the Supreme Court of the United States settles the question of requiring two-thirds approval." As city engineers expedited pollution control by extending a sewer outfall into the bay, the paper predicted, "It appears that little will be done until the two-thirds question is settled." New construction and modernization of the Hunters Point schools would have to wait.[104] Finally, in June 1971 the US Supreme Court affirmed the two-thirds rule. Chief Justice Warren Berger avowed, "There is nothing in the language of the Constitution . . . that requires that a majority always prevail," a sentiment the *Wall Street Journal* took as "a harbinger of a new 'strict constructionist' philosophy" of the court.[105] "Seldom," the *Oakland Post* editorialized, had a Supreme

Court "decision zeroed in more directly upon the affairs of our local Bay communities."[106]

The legal rulings betrayed something else. They made explicit what had been hinted at in the financial press, through the social dynamics of the municipal fraternity, and through exchanges between finance officers and lenders. The legal challenge to the two-thirds threshold revealed that even when the courts decided one way, lenders could still lock borrowers out. Legal opinion mattered, but it was that of the bond attorney that was especially important. The social norms of the municipal fraternity—reliance on the opinions of reputable bond attorneys—took precedence.

When the weakened progrowth coalition, municipal technocrats, and elected officials sought to navigate the catch-22 of the urban crisis, San Franciscans of various stripes weren't having it. In a roundabout way, Drapel and others got their wish. From riots to taxation, busing to safety, the range of arguments used by supporters of bonds for Hunters Point signaled their commitment to fix the blight, decay, and racial inequality of the area, and an awareness of the threat of racial inequality to the city's credit standing. But despite the broad range of support from merchants, athletes, labor, and civic groups, bonds for playgrounds and street lighting in Hunters Point failed. A once-surefire issue, the prospect of bonds for the city's public schools was now blackened and rejected. Technocrats, redevelopment agencies, realtors, and bankers had made racial inequality by steering public funds and deciding who and what was worthy of debt. Between 1968 and 1971 the combination of voting thresholds, rising interest rates, escalating tax burdens, and racism intersected to push large swaths of San Franciscans to reinforce that inequality.

Ultimately, the response to the various failures was to further insulate bond finance from popular input and democratic oversight. Just after the war, San Francisco finance officers turned to nonprofits, housing authorities, and redevelopment agencies to help expand the consumer playground and housing opportunities. City controllers, accountants, and other municipal finance officers saw these authorities, agencies, and districts as essential to protecting the city's debt limit. This overall pattern continued. As the *DBB* explained in August 1972, negotiated sales between bankers and "new debt creating agencies that have been spawned in an attempt by municipalities to market obligations outside of their legal debt ceilings" were soaring.[107] These debt-creating entities also continued to serve as important vehicles for countering voter opposition.

Unbound by voter approval, the San Francisco Redevelopment Agency issued lease-revenue bonds to build and lease an elementary school to the city. Circumventing the two-thirds requirement on general obligation bonds issued by the city allowed black children to attend the two-acre George Washington Carver elementary school on Oakdale Avenue.[108] On the other hand, in response to general obligation bond failures, the SFRA issued bonds that were far costlier.[109] If, as we saw in chapter 6, many San Franciscans broke through the insulation of bond finance from popular input, it was quickly patched up by dislodging bond finance even further from democratic oversight and pushing urban infrastructure into a more expensive bracket of debt.

Still, the question remained: Would taxpayers be on the hook for covering the costs of something they had never approved? How could a public school generate revenues needed to make rental payments and pay bondholders tax-exempt interest income? Commenting on the proliferation of these kinds of "innovation gimmicks in municipal finance," the *DBB* saw the maneuver as a "borrowing front." In the end, it was the "parent government" that made lease-rental payments to the SFRA; a mere "borrowing dodge" that allowed municipal officials to "avoid expending the same money as interest and principal debt payments that might crowd or violate a constitutional debt limit," or the wishes of voters.[110] And in the end, lease-revenue bonds, short-term notes, and the proliferation of other species of tax-exempt instruments added to the already outsized power of creditors.

PART III
Supremacy

8. Eclipse

On August 7, 1974, San Francisco mayor Joseph Alioto told Congress "a story of horror." The memories "of getting bond issues out and not receiving a single bid" were still fresh, and repeated rejections had become uncomfortably familiar. But to successfully sell the public on debt only to have major financial institutions look askance was, for Alioto, unprecedented. This undercut the ability to deliver social provisions and made the task of governance more difficult. It was frightening "when you cannot borrow the money to build your hospitals." Fears of rising crime intensified when the city could not finance its police stations. Ever more youngsters were confined to underfunded public schools and deteriorating parks. The smell of putrid waste overflowed from neglected sewer systems. The Environmental Protection Agency responded to public concerns over environmental degradation, but if bankers did not underwrite pollution control bonds, San Francisco could not tackle "the very expensive demands of ecology."[1] Canceled offerings, collapsed sales, and banker disinterest—in short, the borrowing fates of public-housing authorities, redevelopment agencies, and cities around the country—were now San Francisco's.[2]

The horror was made worse by the economic crisis of the 1970s. The Federal Reserve's attempt to contain short-term credit expansion by raising the overall cost to borrow heightened the battle over credit. "Indeed, accessibility to the money and capital market for all but the largest and most creditworthy has been impaired."[3] With corporations, small businesses, cities, and suburban consumers competing for funds, and inflation raging "at a much-too-rapid pace," Moody's anticipated "further upward pressure on interest rates."[4] Retail and wholesale prices surged in 1974, and by the end of that year the country experienced double-digit inflation. Unemployment reached a postwar high of 8.5 percent soon afterward. The real gross national product slowly recovered, and the unemployment rate fell over the course of the decade, but for nearly ten years, double-digit inflation battered the economy.[5]

Although high borrowing costs were nothing new for municipalities, inflation produced a cascading effect. When San Francisco could not borrow, "vitally needed public facilities [did] not get built." This delayed construction. With labor costs going up, inflation pushed up the eventual cost of projects as well.[6] We have seen how bond rating analysts identified disproportionate expenditures as a strike against cities. When inflation increased sanitation and welfare costs, cities shuddered at the widening budgetary gaps.[7] The rising cost of fuel, building materials, and labor "translate[d] into one single phenomenon. City expenditure demands [were] vastly outstripping the revenue availability to city governments."[8]

When bankers did not bid, San Francisco was "not without recourses to do something about it," as Alioto explained. He "called the large banks in the area and reminded them of how much we had on deposit from our city retirement funds," suggesting "very kindly" that $56 million might be moved elsewhere. Holding public deposits over their heads, Alioto told bankers "that there had better the hell be a bid" when the bonds were reoffered for sale. There was. However, the mayor acknowledged that the old forms of economic power were beginning to crumble. San Francisco might threaten to shift funds, but "we no longer can use even that type of economic clout," Alioto said.[9] The older relationships between bondmen and city government, and expectations of competitive bids, went unfulfilled. The kinds of incentives on which cities relied to entice potential underwriters were no longer attractive. San Francisco, like other borrowers, was dependent on actors who could pick and choose, who might jettison the bond market entirely. And when borrowers did successfully sell a bond, they paid exorbitant rates that some regarded as "outright robbery."[10]

The 1970s marked a major inflection point in the history of urban dependence on a punitive market. For nearly forty years, the lifeline extended through New Deal reforms had allowed commercial bankers to underwrite the infrastructural and social welfare needs of local government borrowers. Commercial banks picked up the slack when other institutional and individual investors pared down their purchases of municipal bonds. By the 1970s, however, dependence on commercial banks and a shrunken market proved devastating. Dependence was a structural problem—created by New Deal banking reforms, and reinforced through a technocratic faith among city finance officers in their abilities to manage markets and through the persuasive words of credit analysts who viewed federal dependence as far more dangerous than reliance on the bond market.

Yet this structural problem was overladen with and, to a large degree, subsumed by a very different issue. Dependence on reticent lenders was obscured by fears that the borrowing woes of New York City would trigger a full-scale financial contagion. Yet what happened was less a financial contagion than a simulation of a crisis on behalf of a political project. That political project was structural adjustment, an attempt to scale back some long-term obligations without adjusting others. With big-city borrowers identified as posing a systemic risk to the financial system as a whole, and certainly to other municipal borrowers, municipal officials and lenders debated whether New Deal–style intervention or financialization was the best path forward. They ultimately agreed on a new round of retrenchment for the most vulnerable and guarantees for investors.

Exodus

The exodus of commercial banks shocked the municipal bond market. During the 1960s, commercial banks translated increased deposits, growth in assets, and the pursuit of tax shelters into a remarkable appetite for municipal bonds. Roughly between 1960 and 1965, commercial banks allocated 20 percent of their earning assets to tax-exempt securities. Holding some $30 billion in state and local debt obligations, they surpassed individual investors by the end of 1965. As life insurance companies, mutual savings banks, pension funds, and credit unions fled the municipal bond market in 1967, the nation's municipalities depended even more on commercial banks to finance nearly $30 billion in capital requirements.[11] Indeed, between 1959 and 1969, commercial banks financed close to 70 percent of the growth in municipal debt, and by 1970, they held nearly half of all outstanding municipal securities.[12]

The most prescient warned against extreme dependence. As early as September 1966, one economist with Salomon Brothers & Hutzler explained, "There is no other institutional investor who can really replace the commercial bank in the municipal market." The withdrawal of commercial banks would "continue to cause congestion in this market, resulting in not only higher rates but postponements and cancellations of municipal financing."[13] Six years later, one Federal Reserve official commented that the "golden age" for borrowers was over. The need to meet contentious loan demands limited the funds available for commercial bank investment. Commercial banks were also realizing profits through other investment outlets "on a scale reducing the need for tax-exempt income."[14] While the New Deal had siloed capital and credit markets, restricting investment outlets for commercial banks, the walls began to slowly break down during the 1970s. As historian Kim Phillips-Fein has shown, commercial banks increasingly found the returns on real estate investment trusts and income from international banking far more attractive than fixed interest payments on long-term municipal debt. Throughout the 1970s capital and credit began to move more freely.[15]

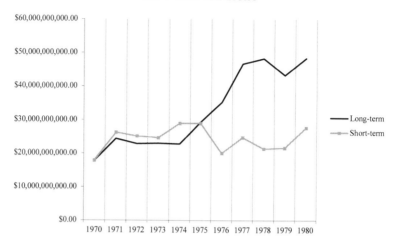

FIGURE 8.1 State and local short-term and long-term borrowing in the United States, 1970–1980.

Source: Joint Economic Committee, "Chaos in the Municipal Bond Market," 97th Cong., 1st sess., September 28, 1981, 72.

Although individuals stepped up their purchase of municipal bonds, they could not match the distribution networks, social ties, and institutional capital of commercial banks.[16]

There were profits to be had for those who remained. From so-called moral obligation bonds to debt issued to rehabilitate property in older, formerly redlined neighborhoods, the municipal bond market had become a deep and wide "galaxy" of new and repurposed debt instruments.[17] By the late 1960s, borrowers from around the country had learned from the South, issuing so-called industrial development bonds to aid the capital investment of private companies in their cities, counties, and towns.[18] Exceptions to the Tax Reform Act of 1969 allowed borrowers to continue this kind of financing for sports arenas and pollution control equipment.[19]

By the early 1970s, proposals to construct new large-scale public-housing projects were dead on arrival. Nevertheless, local housing authority notes still flooded the market. Bankers who purchased the tax-exempt notes did two things. First, they provided funds to housing authorities, funds that were then rerouted to the federal government to repay "all moneys already advanced to it with accrued interest. With the remainder it will meet the cost of construction of its projects." Second, as middlemen, bankers skimmed off the top.[20] Likewise, slum clearance had been discredited, but the short-term notes issued by redevelopment agencies might help commercial bankers out of liquidity problems. The instruments might also provide another medium for investors seeking a tax shelter without tying up their capital in potentially dangerous, rioting cities.[21] Finally, the more conservative investor interested in federally guaranteed tax-exempt interest payments for an extended period of time had a big batch of bonds to look forward to. The sixty-sixth sale of new housing authority bonds, in January 1971, "pushed the total value of bonds sold through this program past the $7 billion mark."[22] By then the federal government had come to embrace home ownership for low-income African Americans, but public housing still generated rents for investors.

The change in the dollar amount of short-term financing was equally shocking. Outstanding short-term debt rose from $11 billion to $18 billion between 1969 and 1974.[23] At more than $1.8 billion, the week of September 9, 1974, provided "the largest one week offering in the history of the short-term market."[24] The bonanza of short-term debt also presented "a historical buying opportunity" for financiers, explained the United Virginia Bank.[25] Bank of America anticipated "the massive reinvestment job that awaits portfolio managers when their safe-harbor short paper matures."[26] Although inflation intensified the profit squeeze for afflicted banks, liquid financial institutions in search of "tax-free income" would be "handsomely rewarded with yields over 6% on top quality bonds with five- or six-year maturities."[27] Bondholders enjoyed collecting high interest payments, but inflation could erode their wealth.[28] Prospective municipal bondholders could either demand higher yields on long-term debt to offset fears of being paid in cheaper dollars, or select from the expansive catalog of short-term debt.[29]

Commercial banks did not flee wholesale, but they dramatically reduced the amount of annual purchases. In 1971, they acquired $12.6 billion in municipal debt. Four years later the amount was $1.8 billion.[30] Whereas Bank of America held more than $2.5 billion in municipal debt on December 31, 1973, a year later, its holdings were a little over $1.9 billion.[31] Similarly, Citicorp liquidated $202 million in municipal securities in 1976.[32] To some extent this reduction was a matter of scale and capitalization. From the end of 1972 through 1974, commercial banks with more than $500 million in deposits trended toward liquidating their holdings. By contrast, banks with deposits of less than $100 million acquired $7.2 billion in municipal securities.[33] By the mid-1970s, municipal borrowers depended on capricious large commercial banks and on those with less capital.

The changing position of commercial banks influenced the stature of their bankers. For nearly forty years, Alan K. Browne had helped local borrowers deliver on the infrastructural promises expected of the racial welfare state. As commercial banks turned toward other investment outlets, his stature diminished. In 1971, Browne left BOA to join

Drexel Firestone as an investment banker in New York City.[34] Despite, or perhaps because of, his marginalization, Browne became the most astute observer of changes within the world of municipal debt.

The eclipse of the municipal fraternity reflected broader changes in the municipal bond market. Browne arrived at Drexel Firestone just in time for a merger, one of many sweeping the securities industry.[35] As the firm transitioned to its new corporate identity, Browne found his responsibilities to be "somewhat farcical." Working in the fixed income division, he said, "I find my knowledge and experience of little use."[36] Nationwide, the retirements of municipal bondmen signaled "an even greater erosion." Browne confided to an old friend in July 1973, "It looks as though we are a passing generation."[37] Watergate conspirator and one-time bond attorney John N. Mitchell lamented the eclipse. He confirmed that the postwar municipal bond business was, as one journalist put it, "a small, elite men's club." But, Mitchell insisted, "there has never been a finer group in any financial community."[38]

For Browne and others, the eclipse was punctuated by the emergence of a new culture of finance and a different political posture toward borrowers. Browne complained of the "new cult in the bond field" based in New York, which assumed "enormous risks, whip[ped] the bonds around, [and] move[d] on to the next deal."[39] It was a culture devoid of civic pride. Francis R. Schanck of Bacon, Whipple & Co. Investment Securities tellingly explained that no longer were "some of the 'good old boys' among our municipal friends" selected to prominent positions.[40] Browne and Schanck observed that other bankers, many of whom had not cut their teeth during the Great Depression and who were not interested in the fate of borrowing communities beyond matters of dollars and cents, were the new market and opinion makers.

Embedded in Browne's somewhat ego-driven critique of the new culture, social ties, and politics was a deeper concern with a shaky bond market. Cities didn't only face the problem of high borrowing costs, diminished investment demand, and a widening gap between revenues and expenditures. Layered atop these problems was the social perception of a financial contagion. Browne tried to use whatever influence he had to warn against the threat bad borrowers posed to even the most reputable. New York City defined the problem, but its problem was San Francisco's, and Detroit's, too.

Contagion

New York City was banished from the municipal bond market in the spring of 1975.[41] The combination of federal subsidies for white suburbanites, outmigration of manufacturing companies, and state constitutional restrictions on city taxes underlay what quickly became a moral parable about the failures of urban liberalism.[42] The urban fiscal crisis was often reduced to a story of bad behaviors and games of "I told you so." Alan K. Browne recalled that the founder of BOA, A. P. Giannini, once admonished him "to never commit bank funds for the purchase of New York City bonds." While working at BOA, Browne later decided to "give it a try" by forming underwriting syndicates with First National City Bank and Chase Manhattan Bank.[43] But soon after, he withdrew BOA "from underwriting and dealing in New York City paper and liquidated all investment holdings of New York City securities."[44] The Big Apple's practice of borrowing to cover deficits, relying on emergency loans, and forming new entities that effectively lent the city its credit by issuing moral obligation bonds made it, as Browne concluded, difficult to stay "abreast of the city's complicated finances."[45]

At first, the borrowing fate of issuers with similar municipal corporate titles was linked.[46] Indeed, it made little difference that a borrower possessed "an independent credit base." By the fall of 1975, "anything with the name 'New York' attached to it [was] suspect," Browne observed.[47] Lenders might penalize New York State when it effectively channeled revenue to its largest city. They might also penalize suburban issuers, who presumably had a stronger tax base. Browne spoke with one "prominent New York municipal bond broker" who was dismayed by the "creeping paralysis" on bonds issued by borrowers in New York's suburban counties.[48] The remark perhaps betrayed a change in the social value of suburbs relative to blighted cities. It might have betrayed an acknowledgment that despite the differences between city and suburb, the reliance on Albany for help linked the borrowing fates of the blighted and the idealized. Or it perhaps betrayed an attempt to profit off of subtle differences between "New Yorks." Either way, Browne anticipated slower bond sales, a glutted market for "New Yorks," and, with it, a reduction of funds for vital infrastructure.

Bankers were now essentially concerned with financial contagion. Once one set of bonds became risky, other bonds issued by the same or associated entities inherited the risk. But how far did guilt by association stretch? One journalist observed that investors were increasingly "beginning to avoid bonds and notes of many large cities like the plague."[49] From the vantage of investors, the search for capital accompanied the urgent "need to search out and discover other 'New Yorks,'" as one bond specialist commented.[50] The point was to avoid them.

The problem was that each lender had its own list of "problem borrowers."[51] Bankers and credit analysts speculated on which city would be next to fall. "At Least 8 Cities Besides New York City in Cash Bind," declared the *American Banker* in May 1975. For years, leading analysts from Standard & Poor's and Moody's Investors Service had advised municipal finance officers on how to maintain their credit profiles. Now, Standard & Poor's Brenton W. Harries told a gathering of securities analysts that his firm might suspend the ratings of other cities; others "suggested that Detroit and Philadelphia [were] high on the list."[52] Jackson Philips, senior vice president of Moody's, explained, "Everybody has their own list of cities they think must be in trouble." For banker Siesel E. Canaday of John Nuveen & Co., "The label 'big city' is a negative one. All the big cities get lumped in with New York in the minds of investors and brokers." Bruce Rockwell, a vice president of the First Michigan Corp. in Detroit agreed: "The paint brush is out. Many big cities have suffered considerably in investor confidence simply by being big cities."[53] Here was the capstone of the declensionist arguments lenders made in the 1960s. But how could a city avoid being labeled a problem borrower when multiple bankers and credit analysts made their own determinations that were hardly transparent? What were "big" cities to do in a climate in which they were penalized by virtue of demographic forces largely beyond their control?

The nationalization of New York City's ills threatened to taint San Francisco bonds. As Joseph Alioto explained, "If New York defaults, it's going to impair the credit ratings of almost every major city in the country."[54] Alan K. Browne agreed that the city was not immune. Although it was "conservative in incurring" debt, boasting "an outstanding record of fiscal conservatism" and sporting its "Aaa" rating as a badge of honor, no prophylactic "shielded" San Francisco from scrutiny.[55] If this was indeed a fiscal contagion, San Francisco was stuck in a hall of mirrors where it faced frightening reflections of itself and other borrowers.

There were different opinions on the relative vulnerability of San Francisco debt. Some considered it safe. Just a few years earlier, investors had rationalized buying its bonds but not those of other rioting cities. One journalist now added that San Francisco's charter buffered it from "New York-style budget juggling," like issuing short-term notes to cover budget deficits. Moody's likewise affirmed the city's "basic economic and budgetary strength."[56] With 25 percent "generally thought to be too high," as of 1970, less than 10 percent of the city's budget was devoted to debt-service payments.[57] Indeed, the ratio of debt-service expenditures to total city expenditures was relatively small. For 1974, for instance, total expenditures amounted to more than $640.7 million, only $20.5 million of which was for debt-service expenditures.[58] By 1974–75, San Francisco's short-term debt stood at $103.4 million, a drop in the bucket compared to New York City's $4.8 billion. With a little under $400 million in long-term debt outstanding, moreover, San Francisco was not nearly as burdened as the Big Apple, which had an unprecedented $9.9 billion.[59]

But these totals were somewhat deceptive. Other borrowers within the municipal boundaries had their own debts. "Bond interest and redemption payments will account for nearly half the budget for the Port of San Francisco," the *San Francisco Chronicle* reported in January 1978. The port had assumed older, more expensive state debts in 1969. Just the same, the fixed payments meant less flexibility for other commitments.[60] More to the point, the city was on the hook if other nonprofit authorities fell short. If the outsourcing of debtor power had helped cities insulate their debt ceilings, the maneuver also allowed for a sort of budgetary fiction. If revenues fell short, San Francisco—and its residents—would have to cover the debts of presumably separate and distinct borrowers.

The same indicators of fiscal health to which some pointed as evidence of San Francisco's immunity were used by others to cast doubt on its bonds. The genre of fiscal strain could help prove the point one way or another.[61] When researchers at the University of Chicago developed computerized "Fiscal Scores for U.S. Cities," they found that San Francisco's "fiscal strain" scores were "high," third only to those of New York City and Boston.[62]

But it was not really clear what investors were afraid of. Over the postwar period the risk of default had been slowly decoupled from municipal creditworthiness. The National League of Cities found fewer than fifty defaults on municipal bond issues in the twenty years since December 1947.[63] To be sure, a municipal default blemished a borrowing reputation, and, as such, was "a secretive matter. If it is reported, details are minimized," explained two analysts for Dun & Bradstreet. Of the known defaults, though, most occurred on toll facilities, irrigation districts, and other special-purpose revenue bonds, and were "relatively small in size and involved obscure, unknown issues." The odds of a default had greatly decreased, and in more than a few cases "there was no loss to the bondholder."[64] More importantly, the outsized leverage of bondholders and the punitive power of creditors meant that the threat of default had basically become nonexistent. But as the fear of a financial contagion swelled, the same markers of municipal creditworthiness were used either to affirm San Francisco's health or to lump the city with problem borrowers.

The contagion gave rise to a greater engagement with San Francisco's debt practices. From forensic profiles to legal challenges, from attempts to use referenda to demand greater democratic input over the issuance of debt to grassroots mobilization, San Franciscans—the true debtors who would pay for a tarnished borrowing reputation—saw the issue of contagion as especially pressing.

The San Francisco Civil Grand Jury (SFCGJ) revealed that attempts to build a consumer playground had become a serious liability. In 1975 the city's indebtedness totaled $673 million, an amount that masked debt's variety and forms of risk. General obligation bonds, while declining in relative terms, amounted to $179 million. So-called public service enterprise debt totaled $274 million. Nonprofit debt, a third class of tax-exempt municipal bonds invented by technocrats, lawyers, and bondmen, totaled $220 million. By the mid-1970s, nonprofit corporations issued these bonds to finance parking garages for the Yerba Buena Center, Civic Center, Japanese Cultural Center, and Golden Gateway complex. Among the corporations were the Municipal Railway Improvement Corporation, the San Francisco Airport Improvement Corporation, and San Francisco Stadium, Inc.[65]

This species of debt had become dangerous for three reasons. First, many of these nonprofit corporations might place taxpayers on the hook in the event of a shortfall.[66] San Francisco already used public funds to cover the debt-service payments of the Municipal Railway Corporation. Likewise, city taxpayers would pick up the tab if revenues from the Japanese Cultural Center garage were insufficient.[67] According to Madeline Nelson of the *San Francisco Bay Guardian* (*SFBG*), in 1972 city taxpayers paid "direct subsidies . . . of $29,710 for the Civic Center and $45,100 for the Western Addition" garage. The fact that the Western Addition garage had to be bailed out was terribly ironic. That neighborhood had been ravaged by urban renewal campaigns and reconfigured in the hope of attracting white middle-class residents. But despite the displacement of African Americans, the middle-class investment in whiteness had not materialized. Indeed, said Nelson, the Western Addition garage "loses money and can't even meet bond interest payments." She found that "the city has doled out $260,000 to subsidize this garage" between 1968 and 1972.[68] Municipal officials destroyed an entire neighborhood, paid speculators inflated prices for their property, and now required taxpayers, some of whom were surely among the displaced, to bail out a struggling garage.

A second problem was that debt service on these kinds of bonds was costlier. The SFCGJ's forensics report concluded that by 1980, principal and interest payments on nonprofit bonds would come close to surpassing that on general obligation debt. It was striking that interest paid in 1975–76 on nonprofit bonds was close to three times the principal amount borrowed (tables 8.1–8.3).[69]

TABLE 8.1 Interest and principal payments on San Francisco's general obligation bonds, 1975–1980 (in millions)

	1975–76	1976–77	1977–78	1978–79	1979–80
Interest	$8.7	$7.9	$7.0	$6.3	$5.6
Principal	$16.8	$16.3	$15.1	$14.8	$14.8
Total	**$25.5**	**$24.2**	**$22.1**	**$21.1**	**$20.4**

Source: William R. Shapiro, "Special Report on City Debt Management," ca. 1975–76, box 028, "Office of the Mayor San Francisco . . . Program & Budget Office 1976–77," folder "Bond Information," George Moscone Collection (MSS 328), University of the Pacific, 325–27.

TABLE 8.2 Interest and principal payments on San Francisco's public service enterprise bonds, 1975–1980 (in millions)

	1975–76	1976–77	1977–78	1978–79	1979–80
Interest	$12.3	$11.4	$10.5	$9.7	$8.9
Principal	$20.4	$19.6	$19.3	$17.7	$17.5
Total	**$32.7**	**$31.0**	**$29.8**	**$27.4**	**$26.4**

Source: William R. Shapiro, "Special Report on City Debt Management," ca. 1975–76, box 028, "Office of the Mayor San Francisco . . . Program & Budget Office 1976–77," folder "Bond Information," George Moscone Collection (MSS 328), University of the Pacific, 325–27.

TABLE 8.3 Interest and principal payments on San Francisco's nonprofit corporation bonds, 1975–1980 (in millions)

	1975–76	1976–77	1977–78	1978–79	1979–80
Interest	$15.2	$14.8	$14.4	$14.2	$13.9
Principal	$5.2	$5.7	$3.3	$4.6	$4.9
Total	**$20.4**	**$20.5**	**$17.7**	**$18.8**	**$18.8**

Source: William R. Shapiro, "Special Report on City Debt Management," ca. 1975–76, box 028, "Office of the Mayor San Francisco . . . Program & Budget Office 1976–77," folder "Bond Information," George Moscone Collection (MSS 328), University of the Pacific, 325–27.

Finally, although these debts were not legal obligations of the city, many conversations with "San Francisco investment bankers, bond traders, and municipal bond experts" revealed that the city could still be penalized in the event of a default. If the Board of Supervisors approved the decision of the nonprofit corporation's board of directors to issue the bonds, or if the mayor did "not veto" these approvals, the city would be linked "very closely to these bonds." Bankers explained that in the "thinking of investors," approval or the absence of a veto was taken as endorsement. One banker made the remarkable confession, "The city's credit or desirability as an investment vehicle may be linked . . . indirectly only by the thought processes of individual investors."[70]

It was one thing for ordinary San Franciscans to be conscripted into a debt arrangement. It was worse to be on the hook for debts that barely improved their well-being, as the *SFBG* routinely emphasized. From its inception in 1966, the paper quickly became one of the few local forums to articulate a left-wing critique of municipal debt. In the early 1970s the *SFBG* underscored two concerns. First, the problem with borrowing was not indebtedness per se but the discriminatory purposes for which the city borrowed. This perspective informed the paper's indictments of the underassessment of corporations and the "Manhattanization" of the city through high-rise developments for the benefit of downtown interests.[71] The second concern was the outsized power exercised by a handful of elites, thoroughly insulated from popular pressure and slanting public spending away from issues most affecting ordinary San Franciscans.

The *SFBG*'s John Mapel asked rhetorically why the city "pushed bonds that benefit big downtown business in San Francisco" instead of preserving open space, developing McLaren Park, or improving MUNI. Why did the city push bonds for the airport or its sports stadium instead of, as in the Progressive Era, issuing debt to "buy out [Pacific Gas and Electric] and bring the city's cheap Hetch Hetchy power to its own residents and businesses?" Mapel blamed the Bond Screening Committee (BSC) for distorting spending priorities. Since 1947, BSC members had previewed and shaped bond issues well in advance of referenda. Armed with information, bankers might anticipate bond offerings, and real estate developers might speculate in areas to be affected by planned infrastructure projects. Always a small, insulated contingent, by 1972 power in the committee had become even more concentrated. Perhaps in response to the 1960s spate of bond failures, Mapel observed the increasingly "authoritarian" decision-making power of just a select number of BSC members. Either that or, as committee member Arnold Archibald of the San Francisco Federal Savings and Loan Association explained, the BSC was "at loose ends for three or four years," lacking "the same depth of digging to it and really going to the heart of things." But if people on the committee were unsure if they were still members—"Nobody phones me anymore," one member said—then conservationists, minorities, neighborhood groups, basically "anybody outside of downtown San Francisco," had no representation at all. By and large, the BSC membership consisted of "an elite group of white, wealthy businessmen, half of whom live[d] outside the city." For Mapel, these were the men who "cut or vetoed bonds that more directly benefit the residents." These were the men who conscripted the public to cover "bond subsidies rolling on a one-way conveyor belt into downtown San Francisco."[72] The postwar debt regime had collapsed, but the BSC maintained its outsized power over who and what was worthy of debt.

Along with the *SFBG*, the referenda, courts, and grassroots mobilization became sites of democratic stirrings against the inequality of debt. Channeling fears of bankruptcy, the threat of public liability, and outrage over undemocratic, fiscal chicanery, in November 1976, supporters of Proposition P advocated voter approval before the issuance of lease-revenue bonds.[73] In 1977, San Franciscans brought suit against the undemocratic financial powers of the city's redevelopment agency.[74] The San Francisco Community Congress, a collection of neighborhood and community groups, not only rejected "class-biased" infrastructure projects and lambasted regressive taxation but also insisted that "membership on the Bond Screening Committee should be recast so that the general public is represented."[75]

If the late 1960s marked a momentary breach in the overall insulation of debt from popular pressure, fears of a financial contagion brought renewed attention to the relationship between debt, democracy, and inequality. However, in both the 1960s and the 1970s, the revolts, lawsuits, referenda, and bottom-up stirrings neither impinged on the structural relationship between borrowers and lenders nor intervened in the debate over how to solve the contagion. Indeed, the more interesting debate was not between local debt servicers and financiers but among financiers themselves, highlighting the eclipse of the old order and emergence of the new.

Therapy

Municipal bond financiers became divided over the question of federal intervention. For a time, bond financiers had no problem seeking bailouts for toxic debts. The *Wall Street Journal* opposed federal guarantees, but without them, it admitted "banks would be left holding the bag."[76] From his fortieth-floor office, in November 1975, Bank of America CEO and president A. W. Clausen initially began "with the basic premise that the survival of the fittest is the law of the land, or ought to be." But as he and fellow bond financiers discussed the consequences of a financial contagion, it became "clearer and clearer that federal assistance was the least onerous of all the alternatives."[77] Throughout the postwar period, lenders warned municipalities of the dangers of relying on the federal government for a handout. Now, hypocrites like Clausen thought this reliance was necessary for lenders' survival.

The more contentious question was how, if at all, the federal government should respond to the threats facing municipal *borrowers*. Hardly a New Dealer, Alan K. Browne urged President Gerald Ford and his closest confidants to embrace New Deal tools.[78] The mere suggestion had a "political aroma" about it, but why not, he wrote in October 1974, create a new Reconstruction Finance Corporation to purchase shaky municipal bonds and enable cities to refinance existing debt at lower interest rates?[79] To guard against "deceptive" underwriting practices, Browne even called for a strengthening of the Glass-Steagall Act's separation of commercial and investment banking.[80] It was "important that competition and the bottom line not be the criteria when it involves risking other peoples [*sic*] money."[81] Ironically, Browne here echoed the suggestions of people who had long been considered a thorn in the side of bondmen.[82]

When Browne acknowledged the stench of the idea, he also detected shifting political winds. By the mid-1970s, the idea of creating "100-percent guaranteed" municipal bonds through a federal insurance system, as one senator proposed, or through an extension of the federal government's sterling credit to municipal borrowers, had seen better days.[83] Even the National League of Cities worried that eliminating tax exemption via federally guaranteed bonds would place municipal debt in the same category as private bonds and push the cost to borrow even higher.[84] By framing one side of the borrowers problem as a lack of competition instead of, say, city dependence on financial markets and private creditors, other bond financiers were able to push for market liberalization. Put simply, claims of a financial contagion first subsumed the structural problem of dependence, and then offered a crucial venue for the advocates of financialization. City technocrats had been trained to view the municipal bond market as key to resolving local distributionary demands for improved public infrastructure. Instead of asking how the bond market might have exacerbated social conflicts, during the 1970s some bankers and their municipal friends doubled down, insisting that still more financial instruments and even less regulation of a largely unregulated municipal bond market were the antidote.

Some bankers intensified their opposition to Glass-Steagall. In the summer of 1972, BOA's Leland S. Prussia joined Amos T. Beason of Morgan Guaranty Trust Co., Hilliard Farber of Chase Manhattan Bank, and James W. Thompson of the North Carolina Bank, Charlotte, in forming the Association of Banks Underwriting and Distributing Public Securities. The purpose was "to broaden the participation of the commercial banks in the underwriting of tax-free obligations," the *DBB* explained. These bankers sought to underwrite revenue bonds, a class of securities from which they had been barred by legislation passed nearly forty years prior.[85] Commercial bankers had already enlisted municipal finance officers in this project. As the borrowing woes worsened, mayors such as Joseph Alioto endorsed the proposal, noting, "Anything at all that opens up the area of competition and that introduces a new element of competition would be a very desirable thing."[86] Though they failed in overturning this provision of Glass-Steagall, the fact that municipal officials embraced deregulation not only symbolized the postwar exchange of ideas between lenders and municipal technocrats but also spoke to the ironic coproduction of financialization.[87]

To hear the *DBB* explain it, the roots of the borrowers' problem was restrictive interest rate ceilings. States imposed those ceilings to protect taxpayers from paying exorbitant interest rates and to preempt municipalities from devoting a large share of expenditures to debt-service payments. However, in July 1974 the *DBB* maintained that those protections were the very reason why borrowers did not receive bids.[88] It claimed a state-mandated interest cap of 7 percent was why borrowers were left high and dry.[89] The answer to canceled offerings and zero bids, therefore, was to deregulate. The Bank of New York even went so far as to call for the "abolition of all rate restrictions on short-term borrowings," a suggestion "described as the most politically palatable package for solving the problem."[90]

The attempt to circumvent New Deal interventions went hand in hand with the eclipse of that generation of bondmen who experienced the ravages of the 1930s. Whereas the 1930s marked the "euthanasia" of the financier, as Keynes put it, and tremendous bondholder losses, by the 1970s a newer cohort of bankers and economists had become embedded in positions of federal power. Given new life through New Deal banking reform, enriched by the structural dependence of borrowers on their services, bond financiers now argued against federal refunding schemes. More than that, they saw in the debt crisis a chance to remake the posture of the welfare state.[91]

That project was big enough to include many groups, and bankers and sellers of financial information featured prominently. There were two

core economic features of structural adjustment. The first was retrenchment, or still greater cuts and reductions. However, only some things
were structurally adjusted; obligations to bondholders were not. Thus,
the second feature of structural adjustment was preservation or, at most,
adjustment of the time schedule of debt repayment without adjusting
the long-term commitment to bondholders. The political scope of structural adjustment entailed more than clamping down on expenditures
for social welfare; it demanded nothing short of reconfiguring the social
contract between the state and the citizenry. Bond financiers found common ground on three issues: Discipline was essential. Minorities, labor,
and the welfare state were to blame for the borrowing woes of cities. And
structural adjustment was the necessary corrective.

The emphasis on discipline was not new. During the 1930s, bankers
and municipal finance officers spoke of the need for cities to tighten
their belts and to reduce expenditures through severe cuts. Lenders ham-
mered home the same point throughout the postwar period. Hence, the
DBB's August 1974 editorial that "restraints are seldom pleasant, but it is
the duty of all levels of government to keep spending in line," was only
the most recent spin on a long-standing position.[92]

This position cut across generational lines and fed the emergence of
the New Right. When one banker explained that the debt crisis provided
"a real cleansing process," a reminder to "municipal governments that
they are subject to the discipline of the market, like corporations," he was
hardly alone.[93] Francis R. Schanck of Bacon, Whipple & Co. Investment
Securities reasoned that for defaulters especially, "the credit window has
to be slammed in their faces."[94] Investment banker Felix Rohatyn advocated state intervention and shock therapy through draconian cuts.[95] In
November 1975, Alan K. Browne encouraged Ronald Reagan to make use
of the debt crisis. Having launched an attack on social welfare as governor
of California, Reagan had his eyes set on the presidency.[96] Proposing dis-
ciplinary solutions to the debt crisis, Browne reasoned, would strengthen
Reagan's appeal among "conservatives" in "the populous states with serious financial problems." The threat of a "ripple effect" was real; "as night
follows day, there will be other defaults." Browne encouraged Reagan to
project a cogent understanding of municipal finance while also taking a
hard line against municipal "profligacy."[97]

Credit rating analysts and bankers offered a common narrative: Minorities and organized labor were to blame. Urban riots, the use of black voting power to disrupt bond referenda, and lawsuits launched by residents
of Chinese descent were indications that the city was not just blighted
but ungovernable. Browne thus found local governments' "indulgence
of minorities and labor unions" detestable.[98] For him, municipal acqui-

escence to greater housing, employment, educational, and workplace rights for people of color came at too great a financial cost. It was bad enough that cities were fighting against a financial contagion. The increased militancy of people of color would, the logic went, lead to bloated budgets and more borrowing for capital improvements. Their demands for greater public expenditures clashed mightily with the erosion of the city tax base and rising interest rates.

A once-crucial segment of the progrowth coalition, organized labor helped to secure passage of San Francisco bond issues. White workers literally constructed the various infrastructure projects on which the Keynesian city depended. But in the wake of labor strikes and vocal opposition to regressive modes of servicing debt, lenders came to view labor as a problem. Minorities and labor were drains on the city, and cities that succumbed to their demands deserved whatever penalties ensued.

Embedded in the claim of indulgence was a critique of the state. "The City," Browne declared, "stands for all that is wrong with the welfare state syndrome." Browne was referring to New York City, but he could have been talking about any and all cities. All levels of government had given into the demands of less reputable interest groups. Now, the city and the state searched for an "easy out" by appealing to the federal government for relief. But the federal government, Browne maintained, was perhaps the sickest patient of all. Too often it had "an unbalanced budget . . . [and] exceed[ed] its debt limit through . . . guaranteed debt." By guaranteeing the bonds of local housing authorities, for instance, the federal government "engage[d] in programs which [were] socially oriented but lack[ed] control."[99] For nearly thirty years, federal guarantees for bondholders did more than provide commercial banks with liquidity, profits, and dividends for shareholders: the federal government helped unlock banker prosperity. By the mid-1970s, however, Browne bit the hand that fed him, and he bit it hard.

Distinctively, structural adjustment targeted certain long-term obligations, while protecting bondholder interests. Banker Herman H. Kahn insisted that municipal bankruptcy would help restructure "extortionate" public-sector labor contracts and reconfigure short-term debts into long-term obligations.[100] Alan K. Browne urged the protection of "the little people who will be hurt—investors, taxpayers and those surviving on social services."[101] He did not say how this would happen. Nevertheless, he espoused "higher taxes," cuts to "civil service," the abandonment of debt-financed infrastructural projects, cutbacks in "wage and pension benefits," and a package of regressive fares, tolls, and fees.[102] Meanwhile, he recommended that bondholders form protective committees and plan for "inevitable" readjustments to extend short-term debt obligations well into the future. "This does not mean," Browne clarified, "loss of principal nor would it necessarily mean loss of interest."[103] Dealing with the problem of debt meant dealing with the problem of time. Bondholders would get theirs, albeit over an extended period. Other groups with whom the city had entered into a long-term compact would face cuts immediately. This consensus around discipline and blame made clear that the penalties for being "another New York" were high. The weaponization of a financial contagion pushed aspiring political candidates to restructure their long-term obligations to their constituents.

"The Message of New York Has Been Heard"

San Francisco's 1975 mayoral race occurred against the backdrop of the kinds of contentious political stirrings that made lenders wary. The supposed threats to sound debt administration—minorities, labor, tax revolts, democracy—appeared to be growing more intense. The spring of 1974 witnessed strikes by "the janitors, the hospital workers, the social and clerical workers. Many are black; most are women," one *SFBG* columnist observed. Bob Morgan, business manager of SEIU Local 66-a, explained what fueled the militancy of this "New Rank and File": "Parking tickets used to be $2, now they're $3." Inflation meant less meat for the same price. "Don't tell me I've got to get the same" pay, Morgan declared.[104] When public-sector workers struck repeatedly, they not only joined workers around the country but also confirmed banker suspicions that cities were inefficient.[105] When taxpayers rejected bond issues as part of a much larger tax revolt, bondholders might fear that the further deterioration of city services and infrastructure would eventually entail more expensive capital improvements.[106] When tenants battled against landlords, or when preservationists fought against advocates of high-rise developments, the lawsuits, injunctions, and ballot initiatives jeopardized the model of growth that earned the city high grades.[107] When the Zebra murders made headlines, bondholders worried that fears of crime might deter tourism, a central source of revenue for the city.[108] When San Franciscans insisted on democratic input on certain kinds of debt, they inflamed bondholder ambivalence about democracy. Lenders might grow more concerned about municipal governance when neighborhood groups fought and won against advocates of at-large elections for seats on the Board of Supervisors.[109] All of these dynamics could blight San Francisco debt and could also be used by lenders to exert greater control.

By October, George R. Moscone, Dianne Feinstein, and John Barbagelata had emerged as the leading mayoral candidates. Moscone was a

San Francisco native, former supervisor, and California Senate majority leader. Feinstein ran on downtown growth policies, while also promising "a major attack on violent crime."[110] Republican Barbagelata was "a slender, gray, bespectacled man, [who] comes across as nervous, driven and crochety."[111] A runoff election pitted Moscone, the prolabor liberal, against Barbagelata, the antiunion conservative.[112] By that point the Democratic Party had upended thirty years of Republican dominance in San Francisco. Nevertheless, the *Sun Reporter*, San Francisco's main African American newspaper, did not think Barbagelata a long shot. The recent election for Board of Supervisors, as well as the results of various propositions and bond referenda, suggested a "conservative philosophy" guiding white San Franciscans. Both Barbagelata and the new president of the Board of Supervisors, Quentin Kopp, "rode the crest of anti-busing sentiments" to newfound political fortunes. The "advancement by racial minorities" was seen as disturbing "sacred white majority prerogatives." A Barbagelata victory would merely prove the capstone of a "sustained conservative undercurrent."[113]

For all their differences, Barbagelata and Moscone promised to keep San Francisco from becoming another New York. They promised to be guardians of the purse. Barbagelata, explained one supervisor, was the "perfect guy to reap the revulsion to the New York syndrome." Indeed, one pro-Barbagelata campaign brochure declared, "New York is going bankrupt. It will happen to San Francisco unless spending is controlled."[114] Retrenchment was a bipartisan enactment, and two perceptive journalists noted that "Moscone on fiscal affairs and crime is not all that different from his conservative opponent."[115]

The *Sun Reporter*'s commentary proved an accurate read of the pulse of the electorate. In December, Moscone secured 101,000 votes, just 4,000 more than Barbagelata.[116]

He saw his narrow victory as confirmation that "San Franciscans have been frightened and justly so by the terrible experience of New York City." Moscone soon accelerated retrenchment. Budget cuts, spending controls, an independent budget commission, and increased policing were on the agenda.[117] San Franciscans, he promised, would bear witness to "the greatest sense of fiscal integrity they've ever seen."[118] Promising a "lean and hungry" administration, Moscone vowed to curb "profligate spending policies."[119] He insisted he was no "conductor of the gravy train."[120] He vowed to prove the compatibility between "liberal social policies and fiscal prudence."[121] Moscone's life was cut short far too soon (he was assassinated in 1978), but his brief tenure as mayor betrayed an emerging consensus among Democrats. In California and elsewhere, Democratic elected officials—black and white—governed on a position of severe restrictions on social welfare while pumping ever-increasing appropriations into policing.

The municipal budget, one historian has observed, was "the place where opposing visions of the city's future were contested, fought out, and finally decided."[122] Budgets could also reify or break with a city's existing strengths. George Moscone's 1976–77 budget provides a window onto the ways that San Francisco differentiated itself from other problem borrowers, and the clashing visions that ensued. Much like other newly minted West Coast mayors, Moscone's regime faced a vexing question.[123] How could he continue to finance infrastructure, service debt, and generate revenue in the midst of a taxpayers' revolt?

Moscone began from the premise that these were "difficult times" for San Francisco.[124] There was no "pot of gold, a secret cupboard, or some budget gimmick which 'makes it all work out.'"[125] His budget would attempt to stamp out the many kinds of "fiscal gimmickry which only delays our confrontation with reality."[126] The question was whether to employ the "meat axe" or a "sharper instrument."[127] Bankers and analysts who flagged undiversified revenue sources and select expenditures for specific interest groups profoundly conditioned the choice of instrument.

For starters, Moscone accelerated a new urban political economy predicated on select tax increases and greater reliance on regressive measures. "Our budget," he stated, would attempt to keep any increase in the property tax rate "to the barest minimum." He called for increasing the business license tax, parking lot tax, hotel room occupancy tax, and other "non-property tax revenue" methods.[128] Traffic fines and parking meters might also prove useful.[129] Then there was the question of expenditures. How, that is, could he maintain San Francisco's reputation as a safe consumer playground with tourist-friendly cultural landmarks? The district attorney's office could expand its staff. The city's Methadone Maintenance Program and General Hospital were also slated for slight increases. Moscone pledged "some small increases" for the Asian Art Museum and the Fine Art Museum of San Francisco. Small expenditures were pledged in support of the city's public libraries, recreational facilities, and parks.[130]

It spoke to the power of bondholders that Moscone's team could propose cuts without ever hinting at reductions in debt-service payments. Using the scalpel, the team cut at the city's public sector. In March 1976, Chief Budget Officer Rudy Nothenberg sent a warning to "All Department Heads." Moscone's budget intended to cover a $26.6 million deficit in part through "a *reduction in spending of 4%–5% from the previous*" fiscal year.[131] "The first jobs we will cut," Moscone added, were those "city funded positions which are currently frozen and vacant." Further "layoffs" were likely. The contraction of the public sector was a primary means by which San Franciscans would be "forced to live within our limited means."[132] Years of borrowing to further the infrastructural investment in whiteness had pushed the city's debt load to unacceptable heights. Facing that debt load, which African Americans had helped service, Moscone opted for cuts just when black folks were beginning to see gains in public-sector employment.

The Board of Supervisors found these reductions insufficient. As chairman of the Finance Committee, John Barbagelata worked with other supervisors to further emaciate the public sector. Some reductions were easier to deal with. The committee recommended eliminating seventy-three unfilled positions at the San Francisco Municipal Railway and cutting the wages of its platform employees. Expenditures for the Community Mental Health Services were reduced. Plans to fill vacant positions in the public library were shelved. And if the committee could not reduce an expenditure this time around, it flagged many social services as "in immediate need of drastic reforms."[133]

Other portions of the public sector were more difficult to contend with. Firefighters risked their lives, but seemingly only first responders who could claim to fight crime were safe. Hence, the Finance Committee called for defunding 82 of the 190 vacant positions within the fire department.[134] The stories of urban crime waves placed the Finance Committee in a bind. Barbagelata once regarded striking police officers as "hypocrites" who violated their oath to protect and serve.[135] On the other hand, the Board of Supervisors responded to growing concerns about theft and violence by standing "solidly behind the strengthening of the Police Department," Barbagelata remarked. The Finance Committee approved 175 new police vehicles but slashed $570,000 from the police department's Community Relations Program (CRP). The committee "decided to delete" seven of fifteen CRP officers. Barbagelata and his allies admired their own efforts. Their amendments to Moscone's proposed budget, they said, "represent the largest total reductions in the City's history, and have resulted in only a 1.97 percent increase from the current year's budget."[136]

Retrenchment was profoundly disruptive; it meant truncated artistic visions, greater strain between black folks and the police, untimely death, and continued suffering. Fiscal retrenchment could be costly to a new regime, so Moscone often pinned the blame on the Board of Supervisors.[137] For those subjected to cuts, however, the point of origin made little difference. Nor were select budget increases of much consolation. Frances Hicks, of the San Francisco Women Artists, was outraged by incisions made on the Art Commission.[138] On behalf of 500 artists,

Stefanie Steinberg likewise objected to the "enormous budget cut" to the city's art festival.[139] Alessandro Baccari, president of the San Francisco Council of District Merchants Association, sounded off against cuts to the district attorney's office.[140] With signatures from twenty-five police patrolmen, cadets, sergeants, and lieutenants, police officers Peter A. Balestreri and James P. Zerga denounced the budgetary assault on the SFPD's police cadet program.[141]

Others protested the disproportionate impact of retrenchment on the city's black, brown, poor, and working-class residents. To add more police vehicles while slashing an integral part of the CRP exacerbated the "potential fires" between the police and black residents, the *Sun Reporter* explained.[142] Roger Cornut, executive director of San Francisco Suicide Prevention Incorporated, said that reductions effectively pulled the pin from "a time bomb of major proportions."[143] To impose "massive cuts" during "a time of inflation and unemployment," explained one community advisory board, not only debilitated the "health and safety of . . . prisoners" but also harmed the lives of "poor and working people."[144] When the Board of Supervisors and the mayor finally passed a "bleeding budget," as the *San Francisco Chronicle* described it, they fulfilled the lenders' calls for fiscal discipline; shifted the blame onto minorities, poor people, and the public sector; and imposed yet another round of retrenchment.[145]

But beyond the cuts lay the other side of structural adjustment, or that which was hardly adjusted at all. Structural adjustment also meant fixed payments to lenders; the $15 million in principal and $10.5 million in interest payments on San Francisco's general obligation debt scheduled for 1978 were nonnegotiable. Debt payments were sacrosanct, not because keeping the promise to lenders was more honorable than serving the people, but because bondholder power was of greater concern to municipal officials than the outrage of ordinary residents. Fixed obligations to both lenders and social services were expensive, but only social welfare was coded as such. This coding was one way in which the city prioritized liberal property rights to creditors over social democratic rights to ordinary San Franciscans.

The *SFBG* began from the premise that the city "isn't broke," that there were plenty of places to turn for additional revenue without punishing poor and working-class people. Madeline Nelson suggested that municipal ownership of Pacific Gas & Electric would generate nearly $22 million annually. San Francisco might also flout the wishes of "large Eastern insurance companies" by activating "$6 million from seven public parking garages, sitting idle in the banks" strictly for the "protection" of bondholders.[146] The third option was something of a catch-22. The *SFBG* acknowledged that the city was "poorer," but mostly because "it banks at Wells Fargo, Crocker Citizens, and Bank of America." The consequence of depositing $250 million "at extraordinarily low interest rates" was twofold. First, "by obtaining the money at low rates, then loaning it out again at high rates, the banks stood to pick up millions from city funds." Second, the city missed the opportunity to invest inactive funds at higher interest rates. Oakland and Los Angeles saw returns of 7.24 percent and 7.1 percent, respectively, by splitting revenues between interest-bearing accounts and US government securities in 1970–71. By contrast, San Francisco saw a return of 5.5 percent. During a moment of "skyrocketing interest rates, the city could have done far better by putting the money in an ordinary short-term savings account." The point was not to nitpick returns; rather, the *SFBG* underscored that the opportunity costs of parking funds through sweetheart deals with commercial banks made for regressive parking fares and increased user utility rates.[147] The *SFBG*'s proposal was significant for another reason: it betrayed that debtor dependence on the bond market was not even challenged. Indeed, the idea of becoming still more dependent on financiers, and perhaps even improving budgetary fates through investment in debt, was cast as part of the natural order of things. The *SFBG* could at once critique the leverage of bondholders in shaping local governance and still see financial markets as a path toward greater municipal solvency.

Within the San Francisco Civil Grand Jury's forensic profile of the city's debt was a prescient observation about the "closed and privileged circle" of bankers, financial analysts, and municipal finance officers. The particular individuals changed over time, but the circle operated out of "tradition."[148] The circle might be taken as a particularly apt metaphor for the paradox of continuity and change during the 1970s. The basic outlines of offering, buying, and selling debt were largely the same; the moral strictures, assessments, and performances of creditworthiness part of a longer pattern of borrower-lender relations; the blaming of minorities a consistent narrative. Nevertheless, the 1970s marked the eclipse of the old fraternity of bondmen and the desiccation of New Deal financial solutions. Whereas San Francisco had sought to become the Wall Street of the West some twenty years earlier, its municipal officials now worked diligently to show that it was unlike New York. At the same time that the social ties among bondmen loosened and the old forms of municipal power weakened, up-and-coming bankers and credit analysts tightened their coercive grip.

San Francisco's governing officials could proclaim that the city was unlike New York. They could point to budgets to show it had spending under control. It remained to be seen, however, if bankers would believe it. Much like his predecessors, mayor George Moscone leaned heavily on bondmen to help San Francisco perfect a most consequential performance.[149] In early September 1976 Moscone embarked on his first real test in selling the city.

Along with his controller and chief budget officer, Moscone flew to New York City for lunch with the city's bankers at the World Trade Center's Windows on the World restaurant. The Moscone team hoped to drum up support for $60 million in "Various Purpose" bonds—a polished name for a package of unwanted debt.[150] Although the general obligation bonds for San Francisco's water, sewer, and street lighting were not authorized under his watch, to build a market for older debt was symbolic.[151] It would show that San Francisco was no problem borrower.

The mayor could count on an essential audience. He hoped to convince Edwin A. Bueltman of Bache Halsey Stuart, Leonard S. Allen of Chase Manhattan Bank, Arnold H. Happeny of Salomon Brothers, Herman R. Charbonneau of Chemical Bank, Sandra Reiners of Morgan Guaranty Trust Company, and George G. Fleig of the Continental Illinois National Bank and Trust Company of Chicago.[152] Hopefully, the statements of Terrence E. Comerford of Blyth Eastman Dillon & Co., a member of Moscone's BSC who was also in attendance, would affirm, clarify, and persuade these financiers.[153] The names had changed, but the basic purpose of the BSC remained the same.

If members of the Moscone team were lucky, they'd have time to practice their selling points before lunch. They might rehearse answers to potential follow-up questions about material only hinted at in the "Official Statement" to prospective bondholders. What about possible increases in sewer service rates? How did the city plan to deal with construction slowdowns brought about by "high interest rates and cost escalations," which delayed new housing opportunities in Hunters Point, the Western Addition, and Yerba Buena? What were the lingering consequences of the public sector strike wave of March 1974 and August 1976?[154] What, in other words, was San Francisco's plan for insulating itself from the kinds of bad behaviors that plagued other borrowers?

Moscone and his team convinced some bankers, but their success betrayed a few fundamental changes. By late September, a syndicate headed by the United California Bank underwrote and reoffered the various-purpose bonds to investors. Blyth Eastman Dillon & Co. and Smith, Barney, Harris Upham & Co., the investment banks whose employees met with Moscone, were syndicate members. But more notable than the participation of such commercial banks as the National Bank of North Carolina and the Bank of Oklahoma was the absence of Chase Manhattan Bank and First National City Bank. Even more striking, Bank of America, which had proven a reliable buyer, seller, and investor in San Francisco's debt, either did not bid or was not part of the winning syndicate. Moody's and S&P still rated the city's bonds "Aaa" and "AA," respectively.[155] But the strength of older relationships had diminished. The conspicuous absence of once-dependable banking institutions was perhaps the clearest indication that San Francisco and other cities would have to navigate an extractive market and dramatic shifts in urban governance.

9. Pinched

In the spring of 1980, Standard & Poor's (S&P) downgraded San Francisco's general obligation and revenue bond ratings.[1] Moody's Investors Service quickly followed suit. City finance officers responded to the major blows from the nation's leading rating agencies the only way they could. Instead of paying a higher interest penalty, they delayed a revenue bond sale for the Municipal Railway. What the city saved in interest charges through postponed bond sales, San Franciscans paid for in service delays. Some observers expected the general obligation downgrade to push up borrowing costs from 8.6 to 8.8 percent. If the city elected to issue this tried-and-tested debt instrument, it would guarantee further burdens on taxpayers.[2] San Francisco, which had maintained its strong credit reputation throughout the long, hot summers of the 1960s and the turbulent 1970s, now joined Cleveland, Chicago, and St. Louis, among other cities, in having its ratings cut.[3]

The national pattern of downgrades was a partial reflection of a very real urban fiscal crisis. When rating analysts highlighted the gap between revenues and expenditures to downgrade Philadelphia in November 1979, for instance, they echoed what many—from conservative economists to Marxist political economists—saw as a general fiscal crisis of the state.[4] In the throes of deindustrialization, hamstrung by a weakened tax base, and with "virtually no flexibility to raise additional revenues and virtually no flexibility to reduce expenses," Detroit found its general obligation bonds downgraded by S&P in August 1980.[5] Ohio and Michigan were downgraded because of Detroit and Cleveland's decline.[6] Greater demands for infrastructure and services, along with greater expenditures pledged for debt-service payments, were real structural constraints on cities.

All of this made San Francisco's downgrade even more curious. The city might score high in the genre of fiscal strain, but it managed to maintain its tenuous position in the top of a two-tiered municipal bond market.[7] Never an industrial powerhouse, San Francisco was insulated from deindustrialization. Nor was the city battered, like Buffalo, by inclement weather that might strain aging infrastructure and a retrenched public sector.[8] Even Moody's found San Francisco's "debt position bolstered by a diverse local revenue structure and growing tax base," both of which offered "margins of protection" in the face of financial difficulties.[9] San Francisco appeared to check off many of the quantitative metrics used to penalize other cities.

To some extent San Francisco's downgrade was the culmination of two older moral strictures. If, after World War II, analysts stressed the benefits of voluntarily submitting information, by the late 1950s, analysts for S&P told municipal finance officers they had no choice. Raters were like the parents of a child who hid failing report cards: they would "find out all about it anyway." Even if a city did not have problems, finance officers who failed to submit information did their "community incalculable harm." S&P's Walter H. Tyler held that without information, rating analysts had to "assume the worst."[10] Thus, when one city finance officer learned of San Francisco's downgrade, he admitted that the city had shot itself in the foot by failing to submit audited information.[11]

That S&P failed to reinstate the city's bond rating once the information finally arrived suggested that other terms and conditions applied. Moody's downgraded San Francisco due to purported financial difficulties "in a climate of uncertain voter support" for both local and statewide referenda.[12] Approved in June 1978, Proposition 13 had already created numerous borrowing problems for California and its cities. Two years later, Moody's hinted that it was unclear whether voters would again make decisions that impinged on investors' holdings. Bond rating analysts worked across past, present, and future to determine the quality of a bond. They used quantitative and qualitative metrics to navigate these three temporalities, but it was the incalculability of democracy, the second moral stricture, that proved vexing. Moody's rationale for downgrading San Francisco betrayed a long-standing ambivalence toward democracy. On the one hand, the *Daily Bond Buyer* once editorialized that the national passage of some but not all local bond issues in November 1966 "should reassure bond distributors. It means, first, that a big supply of new bonds will be coming along in due course for pricing and underwriting; it means, too, that the public's borrowing decisions spring from prudence, not recklessness."[13] Voting against some bonds but not others also suggested an even greater commitment to pay. Taxpayers might be in revolt, but not against debt-service payments. On the other hand, the referendum was still a means by which ordinary residents could directly participate in shaping spending priorities and, as such, create uncertainty for bond buyers and bondholders.[14] Voters might strike down issues deemed essential by local bond screening committees. They might also support issues deemed excessive, extravagant,

202 : CHAPTER NINE

and wasteful. Together, lenders and municipal technocrats had developed quantitative metrics to evaluate the risk of default and measure the proper ratios between fixed operating costs and revenues, tax collections, and debt-service charges. But the incalculability of democracy, the uncertainty of elections, continued to provoke mixed feelings. Lenders might rely on high voter thresholds, property qualifications, and the utter absence of voter input on certain classes of debt to mediate the unpredictability of democracy. Yet this did not fully resolve the problem.

The practice of penalizing state and local governments in advance of bond referenda was not new. From the late 1930s onward, bankers and their industry allies warned of the political and economic costs—costs they would impose—of propositions that would expand social welfare provisions beyond orthodox boundaries. Nor were the expectations of bond raters radically different. Cities were still expected to choose the interest of bondholders over the social welfare of the citizenry. But these practices, norms, and expectations took on greater force as local, state, and federal retrenchment pushed cities deeper into an extractive, punitive market. Restrictions on local property taxes and dramatic cuts in federal financial support came at a time of escalating interest rates. In the context of the urban fiscal crisis, and with cities ever more dependent on the market for public infrastructure and services, the older strictures of bond finance took on new force. The older, seemingly benign and symbiotic circulation of information had now become a way to punish borrowers. And if democracy caused a blemish, some municipal officials avoided asking the public altogether.

Tax Revolts Revisited

A generation of urban historians has shown that the postwar tax revolts were not simply acts of resistance against sovereign entities and collection authorities but were often a defense of white middle- and upper-class racial prerogatives. In some instances, white flight was at once a search for suburban living and a deliberate withdrawal of financial support for cities that followed court orders in desegregating public facilities. In other instances, white Americans responded to higher tax bills by demanding tax reductions across the board to protect illicit privileges achieved through New Deal housing reforms.[15] Likewise, though in ways previously underappreciated, the racial politics of tax resistance was also intimately linked to the redistributive dynamics of municipal debt. This was confirmed when, in the 1960s, black San Franciscans revolted against bond measures and opposed the use of their tax dollars while they lacked political representation and infrastructural equality. It was on display when racists in San Francisco opposed the channeling of their tax dollars to build schools for so-called black militants. These concurrent progressive and conservative tax revolts sought to withdraw social, economic, and political support for city government. But whereas black folks did so only momentarily in order to expand the provisions, rights, and benefits that they helped pay for, racist conservatives worked to place permanent limits around a racial welfare state that had, to their mind, expanded beyond acceptable limits.

Proposition 13 was the capstone of these earlier battles, though the macroeconomic context heightened the stakes. Escalating tax bills were now compounded by inflation. Higher interest payments on municipal debt crowded out other budgetary priorities. And the strengthened position of creditors who advocated discipline and budget cuts tipped the scale in favor of white homeowners equally committed to retrenchment.

The *San Francisco Bay Guardian* (*SFBG*) sympathized with owners burdened by rising property taxes. On the surface, supporters of Prop. 13 contended it would limit property taxes to no more than 1 percent of the "real cash value" of real property, assess property at older values, and require a two-thirds majority for increases in state tax rates and local special taxes.[16] However, Prop. 13 "would benefit the wrong people," the *SFBG* declared. The measure would especially benefit business property owners and utility companies such as Pacific Gas & Electric and Pacific Telephone. According to William M. Bennett, a member of the California Board of Equalization, by cutting the property taxes of corporations by some 65 percent, Prop. 13 was "the biggest giveaway in the history of California." Whereas homeowners received "only one-third of the benefits," Prop. 13 would throttle the public sector. The *SFBG* put the choice in plain terms: vote for the measure "only if you favor increased unemployment and drastically reduced government services . . . and are fond of half-baked measures that favor the rich."[17]

That the measure would be of tremendous consequence for homeowners, renters, and businesses was understood. But longtime municipal bond financier Alan K. Browne was worried that not enough attention was being paid to how lenders would react. How would bondholders and government borrowers fare if the measure passed? As throughout his career, Browne used his (declining) stature to warn against political experiments that infringed on stability. He began with something of a tutorial on public finance. Local governments placed revenues in one pot, earmarked for bondholders, and revenues for general expenditures in another. With less property tax revenue flowing into the second pot, and absent other revenue support, guaranteed interest payments necessarily meant that many expenditures would be "reduced or eliminated."[18]

Existing holders of California municipal bonds had some reason to worry. For years they had largely relied on the power of the issuer to levy and collect property taxes. The patchwork of local tax limits became a way to distinguish between borrowers, and lenders folded those differences into their evaluations of municipal creditworthiness. Prop. 13 raised the question, if not from property taxes, where would cities get the money to service debt? And what would happen if cities came up short? The courts had proven a friend to bondholders. Nevertheless, Browne thought borrowers had the upper hand in one crucial respect. If in the event of municipal bankruptcy a city was forced to choose between paying employees and operating vital services, on the one hand, and servicing debt, on the other, "the priority claim of a bondholder will find the courts unsympathetic if the municipality is to survive."[19]

The promise of borrowers to service debt come rain, hail, sleet, or snow would be tested. Nevertheless, bondholders could count on an additional layer of protection. Although Prop. 13 placed strict limits on annual tax increases, it also ensured enough funds to retire outstanding debt.[20] Should they sell, existing bondholders might even command a premium.[21] The potential windfall for bondholders was further confirmation that what appeared to redress the problems facing white middle-class homeowners ultimately benefited America's white upper class.

Alan K. Browne was unequivocal about the consequences for borrowers; they "had to bear the brunt of loss of investor confidence, lowered or suspended credit ratings and higher borrowing costs." This, in turn, would dramatically undermine the built environment and urban democratic processes. Borrowers would find it prohibitively expensive to fix collapsed roads, cracked sewage pipes, and the basic brick-and-mortar infrastructure on which so many city services relied. One financial consultant explained, "Things will begin to wear out faster, and new construction to handle growth and orderly replacement of old facilities won't take place. . . . The eventual day of reckoning will be that much worse."[22] With the general obligation bond severely weakened, Browne predicted officials would issue bonds for infrastructure that did not require voter approval. At the same time, not every school or park could be financed through circumvention. Other projects would deteriorate, "which means ultimately a capital replacement or a shutdown."[23] The cost of improvements, the cost of delays, and the budgetary pressures that flowed from declining investor confidence, reduced bond ratings, and higher borrowing costs would also trigger a new wave of cuts whereby only the most "essential" of services would be maintained.[24]

Burdens and brunts, though, would never be felt equally. Prop. 13 created disproportionate harms downstream. "Those who will be hurt,"

Browne concluded, "will be public employees, senior citizens, minority disadvantaged and the handicapped."[25] Those who relied on bus routes, who worked for public transit, and who depended on paratransit were not archetypes but actual human beings slotted into racial and class hierarchies who had long been on the wrong side of the infrastructural investment in whiteness and neglect of the poor. Even Browne acknowledged that retrenchment threatened to deepen those inequalities.[26]

The results of Proposition 13 exposed a number of fault lines throughout California. Whether in parts of the state with a high concentration of single-family homeownership or where rental housing was dominant, the racial and class structure of housing markets was not incidental to, but profoundly shaped the outcome of, Prop. 13. Across California, close to 65 percent voted in favor of the measure.[27] San Francisco was one of only three counties to reject it.[28]

San Francisco was not only a city of renters but also a major site of tenant organizing.[29] In the Western Addition, Tenderloin, Upper Market, and Haight-Ashbury neighborhoods, residents defeated the measure 2 to 1. In the Mission District, South of Market, and Hunters Point, Latino, white, and black renters handily defeated it, too.[30] We have seen how black homeowners were forced to make choices quite distinct from their white counterparts. It is unsurprising, then, that African American homeowners from the "substantially black Ingleside district" joined renters in opposition.[31] Faced with the choice between minimizing their tax burdens and contracting the public sector, they effectively voted for protecting a sector into which they had begun to make inroads, and the essential infrastructure and services on which so many depended.[32]

Support for Prop. 13 from more than 92,000 San Franciscans came from many of those neighborhoods that had proven a bulwark against infrastructure and services for black people. As one journalist remarked, Prop. 13 "was very popular among voters in the city's predominantly white, single-family neighborhoods." Elite residents in the Pacific Heights and Marina neighborhoods sought to minimize their tax bills and capitalize further on their appreciating home values. In the Presidio Heights, Crocker-Amazon, Excelsior, Visitacion Valley, Sunset, and Parkside districts, neighborhoods "characterized by a preponderance of white voters living in single-family residences," Prop. 13 won a majority.[33] Many of the residents in these neighborhoods had slammed the door on black futures through the rejection of earlier bond measures. Prop. 13 afforded these tax revolters the chance to bolt the door shut.

If people like Browne were right in their predictions, the remaining question was who would shoulder the burdens of widened revenue gaps. San Francisco was dotted with groups that proposed alternatives to hiring freezes, massive layoffs, service cuts, higher fares, and shuttered libraries, parks, and schools. People Opposed to Waste, "a coalition of community groups, labor unions, and taxpayers," insisted that "bureaucrats" should face layoffs instead of city "workers." Revenues, the group suggested, could be found by taxing housing speculators and increasing airport landing fees.[34] Parents involved with the All School Coalition charged that "large corporations and other beneficiaries of the tax breaks" should do more to ensure quality public education.[35] The *SFBG* went back to the fount, urging the city to "municipalize PG&E," referring to Pacific Gas and Electric. Why not redirect spending from building the controversial Yerba Buena Convention Center, appropriate funds earmarked for the Performing Arts Center and its garage, increase "taxes paid by commuters," opt against increasing debt through yet another airport bond, or tax banks and insurance companies expected to secure "a huge windfall"? These measures would save money "without increasing Muni fares, without throwing the city's poorest out onto the streets," the *SFBG* maintained.[36] The question was not whether revenue could be found but whether city officials would demand that the beneficiaries of Prop. 13 pay their fair share, or continue to place burdens on those well familiar with austerity. There is no doubt that these positions championed by local groups, which challenged the recourse to regressive extraction, helped push supervisors Harvey Milk and Carol Ruth Silver to defeat attempts to raise MUNI fares to 35¢, and 45¢ during rush hours.[37]

Preempting fare hikes was no small thing for users of public transit, but this victory paled in comparison to the spoils achieved by the city's corporations and utility companies. Nor did it redress the budget realities of declining property tax revenues. By the fall of 1978, the California legislature provided a lifeline. The state bailout was a massive rescue package that kept San Francisco and other cities afloat for the upcoming fiscal year, although municipal officials would soon have to follow up with more enduring measures.[38]

New Urban Realities

Structural adjustment is sometimes naturalized, imagined as emerging, from the very beginning, as a cohesive and immediate remaking of the social contract between the state and citizenry. However, structural adjustment, which weakened long-term obligations to ordinary Americans and preserved obligations to long-term bondholders, proceeded neither at the same pace nor in the same ways across the United States and beyond. In New York, financial aid was conditioned on budget cuts. In California and Massachusetts, statewide propositions accelerated the drive toward privatization and regressive fees and fares. In other states, voters turned down similar "radical tax cut initiatives," the *Wall Street Journal* remarked.[39] The means by which structural adjustment advanced— voter decisions, the carrot of conditional aid—was contingent. But with a playbook handed down by lenders, and from which municipal officials had to work, the general trend toward spending cuts, protections for long-term bondholders, and the desperate search for revenues was clear.

For years, bankers and the guardians of public finance articulated ideas around regressive revenue generation.[40] In the wake of Proposition 13, Alan K. Browne cautioned that city finance officers would have to strike a delicate balance between the imaginative search for revenues and ensuring that "levies are not counter-productive, chilling economic growth and employment." Fearful of a corporate tax revolt, he advised accelerating the trend toward "fees and charges for various municipal services" and suggested that cities look to "having the user pay for benefits received."[41] The *San Francisco Chronicle* told its readers to expect higher admission fees to the city's museums and its zoo.[42] The *Los Angeles Times* captured the fervent search: "From sewer services, building permits and the gross receipts of businesses to garage sales, paramedic services and even drinks served at local bars," local governments would resort to new or increased taxes and fees.[43] And indeed, throughout California, they did.[44]

Alan K. Browne now saw in the passage of Prop. 13 yet another "unique opportunity" to resolve the welfare state syndrome (see chapter 8).[45] Public infrastructure and social services, Browne contended, should be tied further to market logics. Whatever remained of the view of infrastructure as public works was thoroughly eclipsed by the idea of maximum revenue generation. The new litmus test for an infrastructure project was whether it would contribute to depleted municipal coffers. The older New Deal idea of self-liquidation had been decoupled from full employment and taken to its fullest conclusion.[46] Projects not "fully self-supporting" through user charges—that could not operate without minimizing expenditures, reducing subsidies, and maximizing revenues— should be discontinued or put up for "sale or shutdown."[47]

Investors lost confidence in California and its political subdivisions. General obligation bonds were placed on the endangered species list, with one analyst calling them "deader than a dodo bird."[48] The nation's two leading bond rating firms downgraded select California borrowers.[49] Moody's severely jeopardized redevelopment projects throughout the Golden State when the firm suspended its rating on tax allocation bonds.[50] As one financier for Blyth, Eastman Dillon explained, "Many analysts and institutions view California as a bad place to buy bonds," a startling remark given the dominant position of the state and its political subdivision in the expansion of the postwar municipal bond market.[51]

Doubtless, some investors jettisoned California municipal debt. However, the more revealing phenomenon was that their concerns (diminished municipal revenues, infrastructural deterioration, declining services) and penalties (suspended ratings and reputational blemishes) became a further means of extraction. During the late 1960s, bankers and long-term bond buyers had grown wary of investing in debt issued by cities. The economic crisis and fears of a financial contagion during the 1970s amplified this concern. Government retrenchment added another strike and, with it, a potentially profitable one.

Pinched by local and statewide cuts on one side, cities were squeezed further by the cutting of the federal financial lifeline.[52] President Ronald Reagan's "New Federalism," a beefed-up version of Richard Nixon's program, devolved decision-making to localities while also slashing Community Development Block Grants, aid for public transportation, and support for public housing.[53] Having budgeted federal funds in support of sewer projects, MUNI transit operations, and crime prevention, for instance, San Francisco officials trembled at the thought of these funds being placed in limbo.[54] Years earlier, bond promoters had insisted that sewage disposal was as essential to the city as plumbing was to a home, but now, federal cuts threatened to irritate the olfactory nerves and placed the city's public health at risk. Economic productivity declined when MUNI patrons were late to work. And tourism might suffer if San Francisco were imagined as too dangerous.

For years, bankers, raters, bond attorneys, and the financial press remained some of the loudest critics of federal grants-in-aid and direct loans to cities. Ironically, the very thing for which lenders clamored—reduced direct federal aid—prompted concerns over the quality of municipal debt. In the wake of reductions in federal financial assistance, bondholders worried that cuts might impact sectors vital to a local economy. Would declining federal financial support reduce the likelihood of "an increase in their bond rating"? Would a static bond rating diminish the opportunity for investors to resell debt on more favorable terms?[55] Like the riots and the doomsday scenarios of Proposition 13, these doubts ultimately worked in the interests of creditors. An elongating list of concerns about investing in municipal debt translated into greater leverage for creditors in the bond market.

The municipal bond market increasingly resembled a lion's den. It was through that once-dependable market that cities were now charged

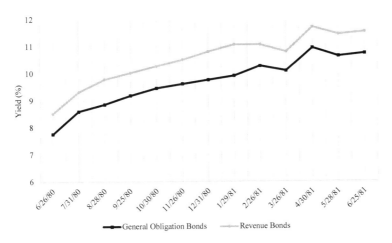

FIGURE 9.1 Average municipal bond yields, June 1980–June 1981.

Source: The Bond Buyer Indices, June 1980–June 1981, contained in "Chaos in the Municipal Bond Market," Joint Economic Committee, 97th Cong., 1st sess., September 26, 1981, 76.

astronomically high interest rates. The flip side of high rates was high yields for investors, and the opportunities to profit through municipal debt were especially vast for individual investors. On February 21, 1980, average yields reached 8 percent. On March 13 of that year, the Bond Buyer's 20-Bond Index rose to 10 percent. December 11, 1980, saw yields hit 11 percent. Finally, on September 3, 1981, municipal bond investors could count on astonishing tax-exempt yields of 13 percent.[56] When Congress lowered the top federal marginal tax rate from 70 to 50 percent in August 1981, some investors may have decided that shielding their capital was not as appealing as snatching up other financial assets. Those who thought otherwise could count on 12 percent tax-exempt interest income *and* a dramatically reduced federal tax burden.[57] Even when the index fell from an "all-time high" of 13.4 percent on January 14, 1982, it still hovered just below 10 percent in 1983.[58]

Municipal borrowers also confronted a gaping mismatch between their preference for fixed interest rates and the flexible rates investors desired. As historian Jon Levy has observed, high interest rates between 1979 and 1982 slayed the inflationary dragon, threw the world's economies into recession, and recruited short-term capital into the United States. The Volcker Shock also spurred the shift in capital investment away from long-term fixed capital such as factories and industrial plants, and toward asset price appreciation. This new political economy of American capitalism was marked by an "increasing preference . . . among the owners of capital to *not* hold illiquid investments and thus *not* to be burdened by fixed, heavy commitments in place. . . . Short-term speculation and hoarding became more attractive."[59] Lured by adjustable rate mortgages, commercial banks reentered the mortgage market.[60] Investors' pursuit of short-term asset appreciation ran up against the needs of stable urban governance, namely, long-term financial plans and fixed interest rates. Municipal borrowers, explained Roger C. Altman of Lehman Brothers, Kuhn, Loeb, "have not been willing, or in some cases able, to issue floating rate securities. As a result, banks and other depository institutions have been increasingly reducing the percentage of their assets in municipal bonds." In the 1970s large commercial banks had scaled back their annual purchases of municipal debt. Now, when they participated in the municipal bond market, they increasingly opted for maturities of five years or less. In 1980, for instance, 42 percent of commercial bank holdings of municipal debt matured in five years or less, while 27 percent had maturities of ten years or more. Likewise, other institutional investors such as insurance companies found "that investing in very short term instruments has been the most rewarding strategy."[61] Municipal borrowers had been penalized for the reliance on short-term debt. But in a new political economy, twenty- to thirty-year bonds at fixed interest rates proved unattractive. Borrowers had to either get with the program of short-term extraction or risk paying astronomical rates for the mere privilege of securing long-term funds.

July 1981 presented a stark dilemma: borrowers could issue a "good grade" ("Aa" to high "A") long-term bond maturing in thirty years and pay above 10 percent. They might also issue a similar quality bond maturing in five years and pay a shade below 9 percent. Paying 10 percent on a general obligation bond would prove disastrous for a city with an already weakened tax base. The shortened maturity might save thousands in interest payments, but it also truncated political horizons. Borrowers who opted for the five-year bond faced even greater pressures to generate immediate revenues. This perhaps explains why so many municipal borrowers effectively lent their tax-exempt status to commercial activities. Indeed, the postwar borrowing activities of housing authorities, redevelopment agencies, and nonprofit corporations proved a harbinger of things to come. If these entities emerged in part as a way to circumvent voter input, over time they had been hijacked to aid commercial and private development. As the National League of Cities explained, states and their political subdivisions were no longer the major issuers of municipal debt: "Half of all bond volume is issued by special districts and various statutory authorities, many of which are governed by bodies not

directly elected by the voters." By the early 1980s, the tax-exempt municipal bond market was being used not to upgrade public schools, roads,
sewers, and bridges, among other vital infrastructure: "About 60 percent of all long-term bonds issued last year were for single-family home
mortgages, industrial and commercial development, hospitals, pollution
control devices for private industry, public power, and student loans."[62]
The appropriation of the municipal bond market in service of revenue-
generating activities would have important long-term ramifications for
aging infrastructure. And dependence on a short-term extractive bond
market greatly curtailed the long-term commitment of borrowers to the
citizenry.

Like high borrowing costs and high yields, profits and expenditures
moved in tandem. The structural dependence on an extractive market
forced San Francisco to devote a greater chunk of expenditures to interest payments. Despite talk of the disappearance of the general obligation
bond, finance officers relied on them throughout the 1980s and into the
1990s.[63] In 1979–80, for instance, San Franciscans paid $36.7 million in
interest on general obligation debt, or roughly 3 percent of the city's total
expenditures.[64] By 1984–85, interest had jumped to $105.7 million, or close
to 8 percent of total expenditures.[65] With more funds going to bondholders, the nearly threefold increase in expenditures effectively meant fewer
funds for services throughout the city.

Revenue bonds offered no reprieve. For more than seventy years, San
Francisco had issued debt to deliver water to its residents. By the 1980s,
filtration plants and modern water treatment and holding facilities had
become incredibly expensive. Before San Franciscans ultimately approved a $104 million revenue bond to finance water system improve-
ments in November 1984, controller John C. Farrell did the usual work of
explaining to voters how much the bond would cost and how debt would
be covered. "In my opinion," Farrell proclaimed, the debt "will not affect
the tax rate . . . provided that there are sufficient revenues from Water
Department sources to cover operating and all debt service costs." The
conditionality was suggestive, but Farrell was explicit about the ways in
which the bond would morph into something more expensive. Assuming
a maturity of thirty years, Farrell estimated that interest payments would
total a whopping $169.2 million.[66] Water had become another conduit for
delivering millions of dollars to revenue bondholders.

Cities were already reeling from the exodus of commercial banks.
Within a shallower market, and in the face of federal cuts, borrowers
were at an even greater disadvantage. Lenders operated with greater leverage over borrowers to demand a new set of conditions. Borrowing was
always possible, but a successful bond sale was predicated on remaking

the social contract to prioritize bondholder interests. That this was done not through parasitical tactics but through liberal democratic procedures only sharpened the deep and wide contradictions between capitalism and democracy.

Supremacy

San Francisco still had to finance projects. Revenue bonds were costlier, but with a lower voter threshold (50 percent plus one vote) than general obligation bonds (two-thirds), revenue bond supporters faced much better odds. But even this degree of voter input was questioned. Beginning in the late 1970s, the Board of Supervisors asked the electorate to approve measures that would no longer require their approval in the future. When they did, they betrayed the desperation behind borrowing cheaply, how important it was to respond to the rhythms of the municipal bond market, and how the logics of the market took precedence over electoral democracy. Ironically, the antidemocratic thrust of this thinking was expressed through the referenda.

As the Board of Supervisors explained in November 1986, democracy took too long. In order to save money by refunding debt at lower interest rates, the city had to strike while the iron was hot. Because the process of securing voter input could "take more than a year," the chance to refinance would be "lost" if and when interest rates rose again.[67] In November 1990, the city went further. By approving Proposition C, voters would allow the city's port "to take advantage of favorable bond markets by not having to wait for an election."[68] Although that measure was handily defeated, the increased reliance on revenue bonds symbolized the older tension between creditor interests and democratic input. In effect, the turn to revenue bonds triggered new ways of insulating bond finance from popular mobilization. This was not lost on prescient onlookers. As one group fighting for greater democratic control over the city's spending priorities explained, the request for "special exemption[s] from voter approval" was simply a way to circumvent the wishes of the electorate who insisted on "voter control of City revenue bonds."[69] Ostensibly a way to lower fares and user charges, the attempt to avoid voters to refinance debt at lower interest rates brings into focus a strange irony: cities used democratic procedures to disenfranchise urban residents. That this occurred in a predominantly white, wealthy city suggests the need to view race and the contingent mechanics of municipal debt as concomitant variables in the broader trend toward urban disenfranchisement. By the early 1980s, even the liberal social contract between the state and middle-class whites was compromised by capital's undue leverage over public spending.

When the unencumbered ability of borrowers to levy and collect property taxes enhanced the security of a bond, rating analysts built an analysis of tax delinquency, the tax collection machinery, and possible threats to tax limits into their evaluations of general obligation debt. But as cities relied on bonds backed by revenues, fares, and fees, analysts incorporated different criteria into their schema. Should the decisions of the electorate clash with the interests of revenue bondholders and bond buyers, Moody's and S&P would refuse to improve city bond ratings, or worse, would downgrade a city's bonds.

Not long after San Francisco's downgrade in the spring of 1980, the city's chief administrative officer, Roger Boas, explained the uphill battle he and his colleagues faced. Sky-high interest rates, blighted big-city names, and a prevailing sense of caution among rating agencies meant it would not "be easy to regain" the city's sterling credit rating. "We'll have to run a tight ship."[70] Upon talking with Moody's analysts, controller John C. Farrell concluded an upgrade was conditional on two outcomes. First, San Franciscans had to approve Mayor Dianne Feinstein's revenue package.[71] Second, voters across California would have to strike down Proposition 9, an attempt to cut state personal income taxes. One out of two was insufficient; Feinstein's revenue package could not offset the annual loss of $100 million in state revenues.[72] Once again, an electoral decision at the state level, which impinged on local finances, made San Francisco hostage to the whole. San Franciscans might entirely oppose Prop. 9, but they would still have to pay a penalty if it passed.

Feinstein and the Board of Supervisors wove together matters of dollars and cents with moral imperatives. Rhetorically, at least, she sought to prioritize residents over suburban commuters, homeowners over corporations. Not only would the package respond to the urban fiscal crisis, but passage of a hotel tax would also shift the tax burden "away from its residents" and onto visitors, Feinstein explained.[73] Increasing the gross payroll tax, moreover, would ensure that "big business pays its fair share of our City budget."[74] A tax surcharge on parking garages and lots, as well as implementing a tax on nonprofit garage corporations, would augment the pot of funds badly depleted by Proposition 13.[75] The city embraced a postwar political economy partially predicated on touristic consumption. By the 1980s, its governing officials sought to adapt the consumer playground to meet the revenue targets expected by credit rating analysts.

When Prop. 9 was defeated, the city's municipal finance officers breathed a sigh of relief. But the results of Mayor Feinstein's revenue package were mixed: "Three wins, one definite loss and one seeming loser that may possibly be cured in court," the *San Francisco Chronicle* editorialized. The more regressive measures cleared the necessary hurdle;

the chance to secure $17 million annually by increasing the payroll and gross taxes on businesses was short of the two-thirds threshold needed to implement new taxes required by Prop. 13.[76] Prospective lenders might look more favorably at San Francisco, though that did the city little good: despite, or perhaps because of, the partial victory, Moody's refused to budge on the city's bond rating.[77]

The older forms of municipal economic power and the turn to the federal government for help were largely things of the past. Instead, city officials could only showcase evidence of a healthy urban political economy, which really meant pointing to regressive revenue streams and the adaptation of the Keynesian playground to new forms of consumption.

The postwar intraracial, cross-class infrastructural investment in whiteness had collapsed. What emerged was a very different kind of investment geared toward an emergent ideology of consumption, one that prioritized high style and high prices instead of the postwar emphasis on low prices and functionality.[78] Likewise, the infrastructural investment in whiteness was softened. In general, "blacks-as-a-race" did not have an economic role in the new political economy. Nevertheless, the proliferation of black images to facilitate this new ideology of consumption, and the rise of black athletes, entertainers, and executives, meant African Americans of means could also facilitate economic growth and contribute much-needed revenues.[79] Put simply, San Francisco's infrastructural investment was increasingly targeted toward upper-class residents, tourists, and suburbanites. This was less color-blind than it was a reification of older forms of racial inequality with a new class component. By definition, this meant that a relatively small number of nonwhites would feature prominently, if at all, as part of this new infrastructural investment.

In March 1983, San Francisco Mayor Dianne Feinstein did the usual duty of traveling with her treasurer, controller, and deputy city attorney to New York City. She sought "to assure analysts at Moody's and at Standard & Poor's that San Francisco's finances are in good shape," one journalist explained. The mayor pointed to a treasury surplus as evidence "that our next two budgets will be balanced. They liked that."[80] Given the rationale behind Standard & Poor's 1980 downgrade, controller John C. Farrell described new accounting systems designed to detail the quality of municipal financial information.[81] Treasurer Mary Callanan explained that although "tourism is off, sales tax revenues are up by 5 percent." Under Feinstein, she continued, San Francisco "has been able to maintain all its services despite cutbacks in state and federal assistance." Perhaps more exciting, "Our chances look very good for the Democratic National Convention to come here next year."[82] In this new constrictive environment, municipal officials hoped that their shiny bag of convention centers and sports stadiums would impress rating officials. Congress had put clamps on the issuance of municipal debt "for massage parlors, racetracks, hot tubs, and golf courses," among other forms of quick revenue-generating commercial activities in 1982, so stadiums and multipurpose convention centers were all municipal officials really had.[83]

Recourse to cuts and layoffs were also signs of a healthy urban political economy. Whether under Mayor George Moscone, Dianne Feinstein, or Art Agnos, retrenchment had become the default. Given the pressures to assure analysts, the timing of cuts, service reductions and layoffs was perhaps not coincidental. In May 1988, for instance, mayor Agnos announced another dose of retrenchment just as credit rating analysts reviewed the city's general obligation bond ratings, and two months before a scheduled bond offering. "We're waiting for the (budget) process to get further along," stated Joseph Rosenblum, vice president and manager of western regional ratings for Moody's.[84] If San Francisco could get a detailed picture to Moody's before July, the firm might upgrade the city's bond rating. Of course, the opposite could also occur—and did in June 1988. Despite San Francisco's "sound economic position and substantial tax base," Moody's explained, the firm downgraded its general obligation bonds "because of the city's recent history of general fund operating deficits."[85]

San Francisco was one of the lucky ones. Compared to Detroit, Cleveland, and many other Rust Belt cities, San Francisco's postwar embrace of economic growth through elite consumption, tourism, and finance, insurance, and real estate protected it from the ravages of deindustrialization. Nevertheless, that its bond rating was contingent on electoral decisions, regressive revenue measures, and the performance of sound fiscal management made San Francisco the exception that proved the rule of creditor supremacy. San Francisco's elected officials and municipal technocrats anticipated the broader shift away from manufacturing employment toward growth through high-end services. But in subsidizing the expansion of corporate offices in which bankers worked, and relying on those bankers' advice and services, city officials empowered a group of financiers, raters, and bondholders who, by the 1980s, wielded the undisputed power to extract guarantees, charge higher interest rates, and compel accordance with their rules and norms. This was a remarkable departure from the period of bondholder losses and banker failures just fifty years earlier. Perhaps more than the ability to extract and charge, the very fact that city officials continued to leverage the exceptionality of San Francisco despite its failures underscored the rule of bondholder supremacy.

By the 1980s, the layers of local, state, and federal retrenchment, as well as the lopsided dependence on lenders for urban necessities, had executed the dramatic shift in the nature of urban governance. At one level, the shift was expressed through the accommodation of cities to the rhythms of an extractive market, prioritizing bondholders over the electorate. At another level, the shift was signified by the very ability of raters to discipline borrowers and to penalize cities for electoral decisions beyond their control. Both expressions, though, were extensions of dependence on creditors, a dependence made through New Deal banking reform and built up over the postwar period. By the 1980s, city officials—from Los Angeles to San Francisco, from Boston to Chicago—were compelled to adopt similar programs of draconian cuts, higher fares and fees, sell-offs, and infrastructural scale-backs, without structurally adjusting their indebtedness to bondholders. This project was aided by populist-conservatives, the intellectual progeny of the Mont Pelerin Society, among others, but creditors gave the attack on the racial welfare state its real force.

During the twenty years or so after World War II, federally guaranteed mortgages, the baby boom, and rising incomes pushed and pulled middle-class whites to the suburbs, leading to greater demands for debt-financed schools, parks, and playgrounds. That flight also mandated not only new highways but also parking facilities and new streets and roads. Municipal debt delivered wealth upward, created profits for stockholders, and protected capital from high federal marginal tax rates. The tragic flip side of the infrastructural investment in working-class, middle-class, and upper-class whiteness was that during a moment of historically low interest rates, black neighborhoods were routinely deemed unworthy of debt. Similarly, other nonwhite neighborhoods like Chinatown became playgrounds for white consumers and tourists but often lacked amenities, such as recreational space, for their own poor and working-class residents.

The politics of municipal debt also circumscribed urban democracy, ironically, through such liberal democratic institutions as the referendum. Debt policy was always insulated; the rise of technocracy during the early twentieth century, and the insistence from bond rating analysts that city finance officers minimize popular input, made it so. Over the postwar period San Francisco and other municipal borrowers issued debts without voter approval, and in so doing, they established the precedent as well as the borrowing apparatus to jettison voter approval entirely. The Board of Supervisors asked voters to disenfranchise themselves. That even the left-leaning *San Francisco Bay Guardian*, which had once insisted on greater input, agreed on the need to prioritize the rhythms of the bond market over the local citizenry signaled a transition from insulation with little voter input to outright urban disenfranchisement.[86]

Epilogue

During the early twentieth century, progressive reformers looked to the bond market to resolve the infrastructural ills of urbanization and industrialization. Borrowing to finance water systems, underground sewage networks, and fire departments contributed, in turn, to the maturation of an industry of debt. The increased reliance of local government on this industry was severely tested by the Great Depression. Throughout the 1930s, large owners of real estate refused to pay taxes, and voters rejected bond issues that would have improved aging infrastructure. After the Second World War was won, Americans asserted their rights to housing, employment, recreational space, quality schools, and convenient transportation. Thus, the immediate postwar years proved a historic opportunity. Up until that point, well-regarded issuers of long-term municipal debt paid somewhere between 2.5 and 4.5 percent interest. In 1946, the cost to borrow on similar issues was slightly more than 1 percent. Borrowers were drawn to the municipal bond market, further embedding the delivery of new and improved infrastructure in the calculus of investors and evaluations of lenders. Investors, meanwhile, weighed these yields against the imperative to shield their capital from federal taxation.

New issues of general obligation and revenue bonds trended upward. Across the country, the issuance of new state and local long-term municipal debt seemed to set new records each year. If this was the golden age of American capitalism, it was so in part because of a municipal bond market that facilitated the flow of massive savings into municipal debt, in turn generating tax-exempt interest income and unlocking funds to build public schools, parks, airports, and stadiums, among countless other capital improvement projects that could directly and indirectly lead to economic growth.

But the postwar expansion of municipal debt in cities like San Francisco is largely a story of tragedy. Black neighborhoods were continuously deemed unworthy of debt. Officials desperate to retain and attract white middle-class residents used debt to tear down black neighborhoods. And indeed, debt offered far greater guarantees and protections to bondholders than to poor and increasingly black tenants living in debt-financed

public-housing projects. The seemingly color-blind ideology of municipal officials directed borrowed funds into white neighborhoods, while
requiring people of color to service debt through various taxes. The civil
rights revolution, urban riots, and other political revolts compelled city
and state officials to invest in underfunded schools and to deliver parks
and playgrounds to racially segregated neighborhoods. But by then it
was too late. The escalating cost to borrow and the attendant tax revolts
collided with the attempt to atone for a twenty-year infrastructural investment in whiteness. From that point, municipal officials would have
to resolve various crises under the gaze of suspicious lenders, many of
whom claimed that the city had lost the battle to minorities and labor
hell-bent on reckless spending.

Gaps between revenues and expenditures, the stresses of deindustrialization, and other difficulties were layered atop the fundamental problem: dependence on the market. Fears of a financial contagion became
an alibi for a political project that entailed retrenchment, while protecting the structural commitment to bondholders. Put simply, structural
adjustment emerged out of the contingencies of municipal debt and
entailed cuts for ordinary people and guaranteed rents and protections
for bondholders. In addition, municipal borrowers truncated long-term
political horizons. Paying the next bill took precedence over addressing
the social crisis of austerity.

San Francisco fared well compared to many other cities. Nevertheless,
it was still subjected to many of the same pressures, some of which
emerged, ironically, out of the planned course of postwar development.
When the progrowth coalition worked with city planners to anchor the
city's economy in financial services, they embraced a redevelopment program that displaced industrial development further from the city center.
They used reclaimed land to build high-rise commercial office buildings
for an expansive, white, white-collar workforce. To maintain this model
of development, in 1983 mayor Dianne Feinstein thought it wise to destroy the sports stadium Candlestick Park. That, she reasoned, would allow the city to sell off the land to cover outstanding Candlestick debt and
to place its coveted acreage in the hands of real estate developers. The
plan implied an added benefit of building a new stadium, perhaps near
downtown. Without it, "we will lose the San Francisco Giants," Feinstein
explained, and with it would come the much-needed revenue sources on
which bond buyers focused.[1]

The pressure to keep the Giants proved even greater in the face of a
corporate exodus. Facing their own financial strains, in the mid-1980s
some of the leading financial firms left San Francisco for Los Angeles.

In 1984 Merrill Lynch consolidated its California trading operations and closed its San Francisco offices. Kidder, Peabody & Co., as well as Paine Webber, did the same. Such consolidation, explained one vice president with Paine Webber, would lead to annual cost savings of between $200,000 and $250,000 on machinery, communications equipment, and real estate expenditures. San Francisco had once stood as the Wall Street of the West; now, "whether anyone wants to admit it," explained one vice president and manager with Merrill Lynch, "Los Angeles is the financial capital of the West."[2] The earlier decision to anchor the local economy in finance, insurance, and real estate was bearing unwelcome fruit. From mergers and closed firms to diminished profits and reduced underwriting spreads, the FIRE sector was undergoing dramatic changes that threatened municipal coffers. San Francisco was not a single-industry town, but the centrality of financial services and the reconfiguration of that industry harmed it, nonetheless.

The 1990s "new era of fiscal surpluses" at both the federal and state levels brought an end to the fiscal crisis.[3] But tell that to the everyday residents and governing officials of major American cities. As Connecticut senator Christopher J. Dodd said in the spring of 1991, "Our children attempt to learn in inner-city schools that, in some cases, resemble prisons." Workers, many of them enmeshed in low-wage service-sector employment, "commute[d] to jobs over collapsing bridges and deteriorating roads." In the midst of the AIDS crisis and homelessness, it seemed the only thing for which the state had money was police and public safety— "the single biggest item in municipal budgets across the country," Dodd maintained. Nor did bond raters relent. Indeed, the earlier wave of bond downgrades proved a harbinger. As Philadelphia's African American mayor Wilson Goode observed, "1990 set a record for the number of municipal credit rating downgrades. According to S&P, 474 ratings were lowered last year, surpassing the previous record of 362 downgrades in 1986."

There were, however, two monumental changes—which could have been foretold. Not long after the passage of Proposition 13 in 1978, many San Franciscans demanded corporations pay their fair share. They did not. Thus, state and local corporate tax receipts declined dramatically.[4] The second change was arguably more consequential. With the Tax Reform Act of 1986 (TRA), Congress enacted "the most sweeping restrictions on tax-exempt bonds in history." It curbed so-called private activity bonds—attempts to use tax exemption to finance things like "stadiums, convention centers, industrial parks, pollution control, and parking facilities." The TRA also imposed taxes on the interest of certain bonds held by individuals and corporations.[5] In March 1991, Ralph Horn, chairman of the Public Securities Association, explained how the TRA affected commercial banks, for years the institutional backbone of the municipal bond market: they could no longer "deduct 80 percent of the interest expense that they incurred to purchase municipal bonds." They were "virtually eliminated from this marketplace." Indeed, commercial bank holdings fell from more than one-third of all outstanding municipal debt to 15 percent. The municipal bond market, Horn argued, had basically become "a one sector market, and that is individuals." When commercial banks looked to off-load $100 billion in municipal debt, municipal borrowers "found themselves competing with banks for buyers."[6]

Municipal officials continued to reflect the conservative logic of financialization, leaving untouched the question of why cities should be dependent on an extractive and capricious market in the first place. Government retrenchment had made cities more dependent on the market. In bad times, borrowers were charged high interest rates and susceptible to changes in the financial sector. The stock market crash in 1907 was just one turbulent moment for the municipal bond industry, as "many dealers were closed down or their identities blurred as municipal departments were merged into other areas of a firm." And although the decline in bond volume and gross underwriting spreads, from $23 per $1,000 par value in 1983 to $10 in 1990, gave cities some flexibility, structural dependence was not challenged.[7] When interest rates fell, the response was to issue more debt.[8] The political lesson was clear: if you believe that finance is key to resolving distributionary conflicts, as municipal officials did, the only answer is to create or eliminate financial instruments, to regulate or deregulate financial markets. You even go so far as Orange County treasurer Bob Citron, who invested funds secured through the municipal bond market in derivatives, soon bankrupting his county.[9] The TRA highlighted the limits of reform. By that point, political economic alternatives to finance were not even considered. Cities were now thoroughly on the terrain of lenders.

And the state-backed power of bondholders was immense. By the 1980s, the surveillance apparatus, layers of contractual guarantees, and steep penalties if borrowers defaulted made bondholders supremely confident. Indeed, many bankers and analysts believed that the likelihood of a municipal bond default was "next to nothing."[10] But what of civil disobedience or labor strikes, which might disrupt revenues? The prioritization of bondholder concerns was no longer rooted in the whims and promises of elected officials, but it was given force by legal protections.[11]

When players for the National Football League went on strike in 1982, the portfolios of holders of stadium bonds were hardly "thrown for a loss." As the *Bond Buyer* explained, "nearly all their stadium bonds [were] secured by something more than ticket, parking and concession revenues." Bondholders could count on "special municipal taxes." In some cases, "the full faith and credit of the state or local government [stood] behind the bonds." The guarantees might, in turn, exacerbate budgetary pressures. Some local governments were "forced to use their general funds to cover debt service on their bonds."[12] To these local guarantees and liens were added federal protections. Alan K. Browne once observed that the courts would not be sympathetic to bondholders in the event of a municipal bankruptcy. Throughout the 1980s, revenue bondholders drew on lawyers and friends within the National League of Cities to make sure their claims would be honored. By the fall of 1988, this provision was written into the bankruptcy code itself. As Chicago lawyer James Spiotto explained, "If cities get into trouble and have to file for bankruptcy, that pledge of revenues to pay off the bondholders won't be terminated."[13] Ironically, the device used to address unemployment during the Great Depression had become a key means of deepening bondholder control over cities. Revenue bondholders had the best of both worlds: they could depend on non–property tax revenues to service debt, rendering irrelevant prospects of a tax revolt. They also had confidence that they would be protected if regressive revenues proved insufficient.

It was perhaps their supreme confidence, combined with an emergent racial regime, that triggered a shift in how creditors comprehended the links between race, debt, and governance. Throughout the 1970s, racial minorities entered the formal political arena in greater numbers.[14] Slowly, the older argument that, as a race, black people plundered and mismanaged public spending began to fade. Slowly, lenders made the distinction between minorities as municipal officials and minorities as disruptors of soundly managed cities. For lenders, the key question was how black mayors and appointees would manage the purse. In January 1996 the financial press expected an increase in debt under San Francisco's first black mayor, Willie Brown, whom the *Bond Buyer* described as "debt friendly." Provided that the new administration borrowed to finance the right projects (transportation and entertainment complexes, among other infrastructure deemed acceptable), bond financiers would prove receptive.[15] The financial press wondered, though, how Brown would "manage the conflicting demands of the many activists for different causes." As one banker asked, would he be "able to hold the line on social service spending"?[16] The declining numbers of black San Franciscans made the test easier. But independent of demographics, white and black municipal officials remained compelled by creditors to prioritize specific projects and service demands.

San Francisco has been the focal point of our story. What of other parts of the country and beyond? Briefly, the developmental trajectories of very different places in and outside the United States were also deeply rooted in the municipal bond market and shaped by the broader tensions between democracy and capitalism.

Discrimination

When we think about cities today, we really mean broad metropolitan areas. Yet rural areas, as well as smaller towns and municipal units, are often ignored. The story of development, inequality, and governance through debt offers a way to devote greater attention to these smaller, seemingly inconsequential governmental units. We can see this by returning to the problem of credit discrimination against non-big-city "names" in the 1960s.

In 1963, one student of municipal debt commented that "small banks without formal dealer departments" often purchased the bonds of issuers without name recognition and those of smaller municipalities more generally. What counted as small, which borrowers had "name" recognition, and how the answers congealed in the assessments of lenders were moving, and contingent, targets. Nevertheless, smaller municipalities tended to pay higher interest rates on long-term debt. If borrowers sought, say, $500,000 to finance improvements to a jail, they could not secure an endorsement from the leading bond rating services; $600,000 and $1 million were the minimum dollar amounts for which Moody's and Standard & Poor's would rate a bond, respectively. This disinterest often confused the issue. It was not that the absence of a rating caused higher interest rates. Rather, the question was why smaller municipalities were made dependent on a market and creditors who extracted concessions based on their own lack of knowledge, or what Moody's officials described as "a lack of marketability." Bond raters claimed that smaller borrowers were not necessarily at a disadvantage. Sometimes local banks bid out of a sense of civic pride. Other times, they did so to use the very funds they supplied by underwriting a bond as a depository asset for other investments. Placed, at best, in a lower tier of the municipal bond market, these borrowers might pay a premium, offering a yield approximating that offered by taxable investments.[17] What were the costs of being confined to this lower-tiered market? How did reliance on local investment capital affect infrastructural development and social welfare in these communities? The regional and scalar politics of municipal debt, in other words, might help us better integrate histories of social, political, and economic life in these smaller communities into our understandings of urban and metropolitan history.

Property vs. Democracy

As we have seen, the relationship between debt and property, and between capitalism and democracy, is not necessarily antagonistic, but it is defined by bondholders' ambivalence to democracy and their many efforts to protect their investments. Here, too, region matters, but not necessarily in the established ways. Do concepts like the Rust Belt and the Sun Belt take on different meanings when we focus on debt and democracy?

In San Francisco, the two-thirds voter threshold to approve a general obligation bond measure was routinely derided as elevating the veto power of a minority over the majority. The *San Francisco Examiner* pierced the veil in November 1968. The wishes of San Franciscans were being checked by an "archaic" rule established in the late nineteenth century to protect real property owners fearful that the "penniless masses" would burden them by approving "extravagant bonded debts."[18] But in many ways, the two-thirds rule was a far less flagrant elevation of the rights of property over the franchise. As late as July 1970, fourteen states (Alaska, Arizona, Colorado, Florida, Idaho, Louisiana, Michigan, Montana, New Mexico, New York, Oklahoma, Rhode Island, Texas, and Utah) restricted "the franchise to property owners or property taxpayers in some or all general obligation bond elections." Even if not uniformly imposed throughout these states, the explicit limit on democracy was more severe than the two-thirds threshold or the insulation of debt administration from popular input in California. Well into the twentieth century, property ownership was a precondition for voting on bond measures in large parts of the country.

The Supreme Court case *City of Phoenix v. Kolodziejski* (1970) appeared to settle the score, with the court holding that such restrictions violated the equal protection clause of the Fourteenth Amendment. As Justice Byron White explained, "The Constitution does not permit weighted voting or the exclusion of otherwise qualified citizens from the franchise." Moreover, property owners and non–property owners alike had a vested interest in quality public infrastructure and services in their communities. Besides, "more than half of the debt service requirements" on the specific bond measures at the center of the case would be derived from non–property tax revenues, and real property taxes would be passed down from owners to renters.[19] The impact of the decision was soon felt.

In Miami, administrators raced to change the city charter in time for an upcoming bond referendum, but the polling scene reflected their haste. "Two separate lines were formed at the polls, one for the freeholders and one for the general electorate," the *Daily Bond Buyer* noted.[20] Arizona, Louisiana, New York, and Rhode Island, among the other states with property qualifications on general obligation bond elections, have a lot more in common than many have thought. This history undoubtedly stretches back to the late nineteenth century, but it remains unexplored. What did these state restrictions on democracy mean for the credit profiles of municipal borrowers? How did class-biased and racially inflected restrictions on the franchise shape the investment profiles of their municipalities?

Racial Terrorism and Uninhibited Markets

The profound insulation of municipal debt from popular awareness conditioned the forms of political engagement among residents fed up with the burdens of debt. In San Francisco, at least, this produced popcorn politics: revolts in different directions that never hit the pressure points of the borrower-creditor arrangement. The long civil rights movement in the South and North came awfully close, yet it still underscored bondholder power.[21]

Four years after *Brown v. Board of Education*, in October 1958, *Daily Boston Globe* journalist Frederick McCarthy observed, "Despite the screaming headlines about the Little Rock crisis, there apparently has been no serious effect up to the present on the bonds of the troubled Arkansas community." Drawing on conversations with New England investors who were "reluctant" to purchase southern debt, McCarthy spoke with Arkansas bankers and editors of local newspapers, most of whom affirmed that the violent attempts to preserve segregation, and the attempts to desegregate public schools in the South, neither drove up the cost to borrow nor shrunk the market. Even if a school "were burned down by a mob, bond men point out that the entire credit of the city would be pledged to rebuild the schools," McCarthy remarked. This consensus can be read in two ways. On the one hand, these were honest reflections of bondholder confidence. On the other hand, denial could prove strategic. As with the silence surrounding a default, no borrower, financier, or bondholder wanted to acknowledge a problem with a batch of bonds. Whether changes in bond prices were due to the stain of segregation or because of Federal Reserve policy, those who traded in southern debt had to dismiss segregation and civil rights protests out of fear that the former, the latter, or both might reduce the market value of southern debt.[22]

By December 1962, the civil rights movement had entered a new phase of struggle. With an eye toward the municipal bond market, James Farmer, national director of the Congress of Racial Equality (CORE), "sent a letter to ten leading investment banking houses announcing the intention to start legal action at state and Federal levels to prevent Southern states from issuing tax-exempt municipal bonds," the *New York Times* reported.

According to Farmer, "the original idea for this new campaign came from someone in one of the larger houses in Wall Street." These origins perhaps explain why the letter did not pull on the heartstrings of bond buyers and bondholders. CORE spoke directly to bondholder fears. A legal challenge would undermine bondholder investments. CORE maintained that these bonds should be restricted from legal investment lists "on the grounds that . . . they are used for unconstitutional purposes—segregated schools and facilities." Because the bonds were tax-exempt, the federal government effectively provided a subsidy "for the act of breaking Federal law" through the construction of "illegal parks, schools, and other facilities." One bond dealer noted, "With no shortage of good municipals on the market, any legal action—even a nuisance action, as we believe it to be—on any issue could make it difficult to move."[23] With so many bonds from which to choose, many of which offered a litany of protections and guarantees, why should bond buyers be bothered with the validity of southern debt?

Not long after the Civil Rights Act of 1960, but before the passage of the Civil Rights Act of 1964, defenders of Jim Crow segregation were in a catch-22. In May 1963, officials in Jackson, Mississippi, could accept federal aid on the condition that they desegregate hiring practices at the airport. They could also forsake federal aid, turning instead to the bond market and risk investors either spurning the bonds entirely or extracting higher yields and other concessions to accommodate potential legal action by civil rights groups.[24] Some southerners attempted to fortify the borders of an "authoritarian enclave."[25] They chose to turn to the bond market.

The civil rights movement not only secured important legal victories in crushing Jim Crow governance; participants in the South and the North also ratcheted up financial pressure. In June 1964, the Jamaica, Queens, branch of the National Association for the Advancement of Colored People (NAACP) in New York urged "45 securities firms, five commercial banks and seven insurance companies" against bidding on bonds issued by Mississippi or its political subdivisions. Where CORE had focused on tax exemption and the material threat to bond buyers, the NAACP added a powerful dose of moral suasion. Executive director Roy Wilkins insisted that buying the bonds "morally commits the (securities) companies to support of a state government which permitted the denial of human rights, burning of churches, bombing of homes and beating, shooting and killing of civil rights workers." On December 14, 1964, the investment bank F. S. Smithers & Co. declined to bid on bonds issued in support of a water system in Jackson.[26]

By the spring of 1965, the NAACP's moral arguments, and the viciousness of white racial terrorism in Alabama, had effectively pushed Childs Securities Corp. to act. The New York–based dealer in federal and municipal debt, a subsidiary of one of the nation's oldest investment banks, C. F. Childs & Co., decided against purchasing Alabama state bonds and those of its cities and counties. Vice President Donald E. Barnes sent a scathing letter to racist governor George Wallace that made undeniable the links between racial terrorism and debt. Barnes highlighted the abdication of the Wallace administration's responsibility "to protect the citizens of Alabama in their exercise of Constitutional rights." This was a moral failure on its own, but Barnes used the language of law and order against Wallace, noting, "You have added alarming statements to the effect that Alabama has insufficient funds for use in maintaining law and order." The diversion of funds away from activities that supported "industrial growth" and toward the already "brutally excessive restraints by the Alabama State Police," Barnes continued, would "have grave effects upon the availability of credit to the state and to its municipalities."

Bankers were divided on the Childs decision. Some quietly supported it. Some investment banks "conceded they [had] reduced their purchases of Southern municipal bonds in recent years because of doubts about their marketability as a result of civil rights strife." Chicago's Baxter & Co. had not purchased Mississippi bonds "for some time because of the moral issue" and had recently added Alabama to the list of states to avoid. Meanwhile, Wallace H. Meyer, vice president of the municipal bond department with San Francisco's Crocker Citizens National Bank, revealed his firm "just plain avoided Southern bonds for the past 5 or 10 years." For him, racial segregation and desegregation had come to define the entire South, and the region "could blow up and cause trouble for the bonds." The "trouble" was in what CORE had recognized: if federal tax exemption subsidized the construction of segregated public facilities, then the bonds ran afoul of the equal protection clause of the Fourteenth Amendment. Holders of southern debt might be left with badly devalued bonds if civil rights groups were successful in eradicating "the tax-exempt privilege in these states."

Other bondmen thoroughly disagreed with Childs Securities Corp. Bondmen liked to assume that theirs was a business structured not by moral claims but by bond prices, yields, and other cold, calculative assessments. Thus, it required no major leap for one Toledo banker to insist that the Childs announcement went "pretty far afield from what our business is. We're not set up to establish moral principles." A Boston banker concurred: "The motivation may be excellent, but the move is ill-conceived and immature." Other bondmen made clear the divide between capitalism and democracy, between the supremacy of markets over the right to live and participate as equal citizens. Alan K. Browne declared, "You can't in effect say because you disagree with some officials you should deny them the right to find a market for public securities to carry out needed improvements to benefit the entire community." This was, of course, exactly what bondmen did all the time. Browne left unaddressed just who was part of the "entire community," but he made clear that no matter how violent a political regime, markets should not be restricted. He would have thoroughly disagreed with Roy Wilkins, who implored other firms to apply "economic sanctions against terroristic states" like Alabama.

In between those who supported and opposed the boycott of southern debt were smaller dealers, perhaps some of the same firms who profited from credit discrimination against smaller municipalities. These firms welcomed the Childs decision, though not for ethical reasons. A. Duncan Williams, vice president and manager of the bond department of First National Bank of Memphis, voiced what many surely thought: "I'd love to see all the Northern dealers quit bidding down here." Duncan mixed southern nationalism—"Southern dealers can take care of the needs of the South"—with profit seeking. If the civil rights movement succeeded in blighting southern bonds and more and more financial institutions refused to bid on southern debt, southern dealers would have a chance to purchase higher-yielding securities for their investors.[27]

Williams was pugnacious, though he spoke to the strength of bondholder power and the ironies of success. We have seen that the revolt that mattered most was not the one against bond referenda in San Francisco during the 1960s but the one in the imaginaries of lenders. Ironically, creditors could profit off the successes of CORE and the NAACP, adding further to the burdens of debt servicers, many of them black. The *DBB* punctuated the point: the boycotts had the effect of "enlarged profits for bankers, enlarged yields for investors, and greater tax burdens for the issuing districts. There is nothing wrong with such objectives, but is this what the boycotters really want?"[28]

The United States and Beyond

Finally, the ongoing struggle in Puerto Rico against creditors who use the idea of a debt crisis to extract still more concessions, and to exercise outsized political authority over spending decisions, reminds us that the politics of municipal debt extend beyond the continental United States. During the 1920s, officials from Aguadilla, Puerto Rico, solicited bids for improvement bonds. In return, buyers could collect semiannual interest payments "exempt from the payment of taxation in the United States and Porto Rico."[29] Historian Peter James Hudson has argued that these kinds of debts were integral to colonialism.[30] This history stretches well into the postwar period and into ongoing debates about statehood. In 1955, the United Statistical Association tracked the municipal debt holdings of insurance companies, some of which were issued by "the Territories of Alaska and Hawaii and the government of Puerto Rico and the Philippine Islands."[31] We might ask: How did municipal debt figure into statehood? As sellers of financial information encouraged municipal technocrats to become better salesmen, in June 1958 the *DBB*'s George Wanders noted:

> Puerto Rico has been in the vanguard of the movement, with a sort of 'Come and See' attitude. A group in Hawaii has taken a leaf from that book. Groups of municipal bond underwriters, institutional investors and occasionally some newsmen are taken on brisk tours of the areas. They are shown anything and everything, good or bad, that they want to see. All questions are answered candidly and criticisms are invited.

Meanwhile, the Government Development Bank of Puerto Rico (GDBPR) complemented the tours by "carrying its story aggressively to all investment areas." The bank did so by hiring "a competent public relations firm to foster the reputation of its securities" and posting slick notices of sale in the *DBB*.[32] As a nonresident member of the San Francisco Bond Club, Francis B. Bowen of GDBPR drummed up interest among West Coast financiers. In September 1966, Puerto Rico's public-housing authority secured a great deal of attention for its $9.2 million bond offering, exempt from both federal and state income taxes.[33] Although the government was "not legally liable" to pay the $55 million in moral obligation bonds outstanding as of 1975, as in the case of San Francisco's nonprofit bonds, ordinary residents of Puerto Rico were ultimately liable for the debt.[34] More than a few of these and other debt obligations stretched well into the 1990s.[35] As these examples suggest, similar questions about racial governance, inequality, and development raised in this book can—and must—be asked about US territories, past and present.

In Canada, communities in Ontario and Manitoba had long issued debt, with firms like Toronto's Municipal Bankers Corp., W. A. MacKenzie & Co., Dominion Securities Corp., and A. E. Ames & Co. active in underwriting funds for public improvements.[36] How did these debt deals work, and how did these bond offerings interact with the racial, spatial, and class politics of debt in Canada more generally? How did the methods of floating a bond interact with voter input?[37]

It was tax exemption that made bonds issued by American states, cities, counties, and territories distinct from other methods of financing infrastructure. Nevertheless, US municipal borrowers and financiers had to be aware of other offerings before issuing and reselling a bond. Thus, before San Francisco sold a $1.8 million bond for the Palace of Fine Arts approved in November 1959, its officials likely kept a watchful eye on the World Bank. On February 5, 1960, Eugene R. Black, bond salesman–turned–World Bank president, announced the upcoming sale of a $100 million issue, the bank's first in two years. Black hoped that the syndicate managed by Morgan Stanley & Co. and First Boston Corp. would bid on the batch of debt, which offered all kinds of slick provisions.[38] This was only one of the bevy of World Bank offerings in the 1950s, the study of which might enrich the global history of public debt—not least because of the revolving door of finance whereby commercial bankers who specialized in municipal debt underwrote and, in some cases, later guided the World Bank project of structural adjustment throughout much of the world.

The social crisis of austerity, the hollowing out of urban liberal democracy, the truncation of long-term commitments of local governments to the citizenry, and the deepening of inequality—social realities lazily treated as products of neoliberalism, financialization, or federal failure—are rooted in the politics of municipal debt. Yet rarely does anyone ask why the water systems on which we rely for daily hydration, the underground network of sewage systems that sort out toxins, and the recreational spaces in which our children play should be steeped in the municipal bond market in the first place; why it is that bondholders and raters should have so much influence over our collective social welfare. People like congressmen Wright Patman came close to detecting the problem with dependence on the market. Some African Americans and poor residents of Chinatown in San Francisco challenged the discriminatory use of bond funds by targeting the referenda and the financial institutions involved. They did not succeed. Nevertheless, detailing the mechanics of debt and revisiting some of those critiques might help the residents of tomorrow's Detroit and Puerto Rico—that is, all of us.

Acknowledgments

It is an honor to acknowledge the many people who helped make this book possible.

I want to first thank my teachers. When I was an undergraduate, Christopher L. Brown, Joshua Guild, Tera Hunter, and Samuel K. Roberts encouraged me to become a historian. Eric Foner taught me transformative writing habits. The Mellon Mays Undergraduate Fellowship helped make these and so many other mentorships possible. At Stanford University, Al Camarillo welcomed me into his wonderful family. He nurtured my ideas and demonstrated that the ability to do your best intellectual work is predicated on joy and laughter. Richard White helped me appreciate the surprises of history and the importance of patience when studying the seemingly dry yet ultimately revealing world of debt. For their warmth and whose questions continue to influence my thinking I thank Allyson Hobbs, Tom Mullaney, and Carolyn Winterer.

I have had the privilege of presenting early versions of chapters at numerous workshops, seminars, and conferences. I thank my colleagues at Stanford's Center for Comparative Studies in Race & Ethnicity for their early encouragement. For their many suggestions I thank participants in the US history workshops at Stanford University and the University of Chicago. Thanks to those who attended the Approaches to Capitalism workshop at Stanford. I am especially grateful to Branden Adams, Jennifer Burns, Benjamin Hein, Vivian Lu, Alastair Su, Richard White, Gavin Wright, and Sylvia Yanagisako. Fellow travelers who attended Harvard's History of Capitalism dissertation workshop forced me to sharpen my methodological assumptions, and a job talk of sorts at Harvard's Business History Initiative made me better equipped to defend the political stakes of my analysis. I made major headway on this project during an incredibly productive year at the Charles Warren Center for Studies in American History in Cambridge, Massachusetts. Thanks to Walter Johnson for his faith in my work, and to Megan Black and Christopher Clements for reading parts of the manuscript. I thank the participants and commentators at the Seminar in Capitalism Studies at Johns Hopkins University, the Mellon Initiative in Racial Capitalism at UC Davis, and Princeton University's Modern America Workshop. Conversations with colleagues at the Robert L. Heilbroner Center for Capitalism Studies pushed me to speak well beyond the parameters of this study. Thanks to William Milberg and Julia Ott for creating these and other opportunities. Finally, the Urban History Association's biennial conference has been the most generative space in which to present my work. I thank David Freund, Paige Glotzer, Noam Maggor, and Pedro Regalado for pushing me to confront an astonishing range of issues.

At the University of Chicago, I have benefited enormously from the advice and warmth of Leora Auslander, Mark Bradley, Matthew Briones, Paul Cheney, Jane Dailey, Brodie Fischer, Alice Goff, Faith Hillis, Thomas Holt, Matthew Kruer, Amy Lippert, Jonathan Lyon, Steven Pincus, Kenneth Pomeranz, Johanna Ransmeier, Michael Rossi, Julie Saville, Jim Sparrow, and Amy Dru Stanley. A special thanks to Kathleen Belew, Adam Green, Ramón Gutiérrez, and Jon Levy, whose generosity has extended well beyond the department, over dinners, drinks, and tea. I also wish to thank Dain Borges and Emily Osborn for their mentorship and Emilio Kourí, chair of the Department of History, for having my back from day one. I cherish my relationships with colleagues in other disciplines at the University of Chicago. I am grateful to Jessica Baker, Cathy Cohen, Edgar Garcia, Adom Getachew, Yanilda María González, Sarah Jessica Johnson, Kaneesha Parsard, Danielle Roper, and Robert Vargas for their friendship and solidarity. My deep gratitude extends to Vice Provost Melissa Gilliam for her enduring encouragement.

I have been supported by an astonishing number of friends and counselors. At different points Brent Cebul, Michael Glass, Louis Hyman, Andrew Kahrl, and Robin D. G. Kelley engaged with my work. Each of them affirmed early suspicions and contributed breathtaking insights that made this a better book. I am grateful to Jake Grumbach for our countless conversations about capitalism and democracy, and for making sure my graphs and tables were on point. For their excellent advice on a whole host of issues, I wish to thank Amna Akbar, Rudi Batzell, Vincent Brown, Megan Ming Francis, Evelyn Brooks Higginbotham, Peter James Hudson, Alison Issenberg, Manu Karuka, Shannon King, Jessica Levy, Allan Lumba, K-Sue Park, Michael Ralph, Leah Wright Rigueur, Robert O. Self, Amanda Seligman, Shauna Sweeney, Brandon Terry, Victor Thompson, and Caitlin Zaloom.

There is not enough space to thank my big brother and dear friend, N. D. B. Connolly. I have been fortunate to build with and learn from Michael Dawson. Our conversations about race and capitalism in Italy and Mexico have been among my greatest professional highlights. First my TA, Elizabeth Hinton has since become a terrific friend. Ryan Jobson has become my right-hand man. He has observed, inspired, and affirmed. I am grateful to Justin Leroy for our many collaborations. Thanks to Keeanga-Yamahtta Taylor for setting the bar so high.

It is my pleasure to thank the archivists and library curators without whom this book would not be possible. At the San Francisco Public Library, Christina Moretta and Tami Suzuki alerted me to new collections and gave me access to essential materials. Thanks to Columbia University's Catherine T. Parker-Thomas for handling the massive volumes of the *Daily Bond Buyer*. I am indebted to the helpful people at UC Berkeley's Bancroft Library. Of late, the specialists at the University of Chicago's Research Computing Center have been of immense help. The dexterous Brooke Luetgert, the visionary H. Birali Runesha, and the imaginative Parmanand Sinha deserve special praise. They have literally helped me visualize the business of debt.

During a stimulating book manuscript workshop, Mark Bradley, Jane Dailey, Brodie Fischer, David Freund, Adom Getachew, Adam Green, Ryan Jobson, Jon Levy, Jim Sparrow, and Thomas Sugrue offered an extraordinary round of comments. I hope they'll agree that I took many of their brilliant suggestions to heart. Special thanks go to my editor at the University of Chicago Press, Timothy Mennel. Since 2014, he has been a fervent believer in this project, and I am grateful to have had such an advocate. At the press I also thank Susannah Marie Engstrom and Tamara Ghattas. Two anonymous reviewers for the Press, one of whom has since become known to me as Kimberly Philips-Fein, offered clarifying distillations and productive research leads.

Finally, I want to thank my ancestors for their incredible sacrifices, some of which were coerced and others made by choice. The success of this book is theirs to claim, and the errors all my own. To my sister, aunts, uncles, and grandparents for sustaining me. Neither words nor deeds can express my appreciation for the love and sustenance from my mother and father, Tatrina and Gary Jenkins. It is fitting that as I was finishing these acknowledgments, the brilliant Dr. Rhea Boyd texted me, "You can do it, baby!" My partner and comrade, she has read countless versions of this story, helped me find the right words, encouraged me to dream more, and reminded me why we do this work.

Notes

Introduction

1. "Yes on A, Please," pamphlet (November 1968), folder "Vertical File (VF): S.F. Elections. November 1968," San Francisco Ephemera Collection, San Francisco History Center (SFH), San Francisco Public Library (SFPL).

2. City and County of San Francisco, "Proposition B: A $5 Million Bond Issue to Provide for Hunters Point Schools. Information for Speakers and Others Interested in Passage of Proposition B," undated, box 18, folder "Proposition B, 2 of 2, 1969–1970," Joseph L. Alioto Papers, 1958–1977, SFH 5 (SFPL), n.p.

3. Will Stevens, "Prop. B. Target: The Shabby School," *San Francisco Examiner*, October 30, 1969.

4. "Yes on A, Please."

5. Proposition A: Airport Bonds, "Propositions, Arguments and Statements of Controller relating to Costs to be Voted on at General Election and Consolidated Special Elections to be Held November 8, 1966" (1966), https://sfpl.org/pdf/main/gic/elections/November8_1966.pdf, 18.

6. Marx had national debt in mind, but the point that public debt reflects the claims of a "class of state creditors" holds true for municipal debt as well. Karl Marx, *Capital: A Critique of Political Economy*, vol. 3, reissue (New York: Penguin Classics, 1993), 607.

7. Barry Bluestone and Bennett Harrison, *The Deindustrialization of America: Plant Closings, Community Abandonment, and the Dismantling of Basic Industry* (New York: Basic Books, 1984); Thomas J. Sugrue, *The Origins of the Urban Crisis: Race and Inequality in Postwar Detroit* (Princeton, NJ: Princeton University Press, 1996); Andrew Highsmith, *Demolition Means Progress: Flint, Michigan, and the Fate of the American Metropolis* (Chicago: University of Chicago Press, 2015).

8. H. Paul Friesma, "Black Control of Central Cities: The Hollow Prize," *Journal of the American Institute of Planners* 35, no. 2 (1969): 75–79; James B. Lane, "Black Political Power and Its Limits: Gary Mayor Richard G. Hatcher's Administration," in *African-American Mayors: Race, Politics, and the American City*, ed. David R. Colburn and Jeffrey S. Adler, 70 (Champaign: University of Illinois Press, 2001).

9. Kim Phillips-Fein, *Fear City: New York's Fiscal Crisis and the Rise of Austerity* (New York: Metropolitan Books, 2017); Daniel T. Rodgers, *The Age of Fracture* (Cambridge, MA: Harvard University Press, 2011); Jason Hackworth, *The Neoliberal City: Governance, Ideology, and Development in American Urbanism* (Ithaca, NY: Cornell University Press, 2006).

10. Alberta M. Sbragia, *Debt Wish: Entrepreneurial Cities, U.S. Federalism, and Economic Development* (Pittsburgh: University of Pittsburgh Press, 1996), 13–14.

11. Charles W. Mills, *Black Rights, White Wrongs: The Critique of Racial Liberalism* (New York: Oxford University Press, 2017), xv, 4, 39, 47.

12. William Issel, "Liberalism and Urban Policy in San Francisco from the 1930s to the 1960s," *Western Historical Quarterly* 22, no. 4 (November 1991): 431–50; Christopher Lowen Agee, *The Streets of San Francisco: Policing and the Creation of a Cosmopolitan Liberal Politics, 1950–1972* (Chicago: University of Chicago Press, 2014).

13. Robert O. Self, *American Babylon: Race and the Struggle for Postwar Oakland* (Princeton, NJ: Princeton University Press, 2003).

14. Robert H. Dahl, *Who Governs?: Democracy and Power in an American City* (New Haven, CT: Yale University Press, [1961] 2005), 3, 7, 34, 51, 62, 63, 85.

15. Fraser Brown, *Municipal Bonds: A Statement of the Principles of Law and Custom Governing the Issue of American Municipal Bonds with Illustrations from the Statutes of Various States* (New York: Prentice-Hall, 1922), 183.

16. Harvey Molotch and John R. Logan, *Urban Fortunes: The Political Economy of Place* (Berkeley: University of California Press, [1987] 2007); Chester Hartman, *City for Sale: The Transformation of San Francisco* (Berkeley: University of California Press, 2002).

17. David Judge, "Pluralism," in *Theories of Urban Politics*, ed. David Judge, Gerry Stoker, and Harold Wolman, 13–32 (Thousand Oaks, CA: Sage, 1995).

18. Michael B. Katz, *Why Don't American Cities Burn?* (Philadelphia: University of Pennsylvania Press, 2010), 155–61.

19. Here and subsequent references to the ACNB drawn from Anglo California National Bank of San Francisco, "San Francisco: A Credit Study of Its Municipal Bonds." See also Sidney P. Allen, "Brochure Analyzes Strength behind San Francisco Credit," *San Francisco Chronicle*, September 15, 1936, 18.

20. John Joseph Wallis, "American Government Finance in the Long Run: 1790 to 1990," *Journal of Economic Perspectives* 14, no. 1 (Winter 2000): 69–70.

21. Terrence J. McDonald, *The Parameters of Urban Fiscal Policy: Socioeconomic Change and Political Culture in San Francisco, 1860–1906* (Berkeley: University of California Press, 1987), 21, 40, 47, 138, 146, 149, 156, 172.

22. A. M. Hillhouse, *Municipal Bonds: A Century of Experience* (New York: Prentice-Hall, 1936), 32–34.

23. McDonald, *The Parameters of Urban Fiscal Policy*, xi, 159, 177–89.

24. "Running into Debt," *San Francisco Chronicle*, December 25, 1897.

25. "Why the Taxpayers of San Francisco Should Vote against the Charter," *San Francisco Chronicle*, May 26, 1898.

26. McDonald, *The Parameters of Urban Fiscal Policy*, 20, 33.

27. "Why the Taxpayers of San Francisco Should Vote Against the Charter."

28. McDonald, *The Parameters of Urban Fiscal Policy*, 206; ACNB, "San Francisco: A Credit Study," n.p.

29. San Francisco Board of Freeholders, "The Charter of the City and County of San Francisco" (1899), https://archive.org/details/charterofcitycou1899 sanf, 343–44; William Issel, "'Citizens outside the Government': Business and Urban Policy in San Francisco and Los Angles," *Pacific Historical Review* 57, no. 2 (May 1988): 117–45.

30. Philip J. Ethington, *The Public City: The Political Construction of Urban Life in San Francisco, 1850–1900* (Berkeley: University of California Press, [1994] 2001), 389.

31. Rodman W. Paul, "After the Gold Rush: San Francisco and Portland," *Pacific Historical Review* 51, no. 1 (February 1982): 3–4, 10–15.

32. McDonald, *The Parameters of Urban Fiscal Policy*, 66.

33. Paul, "After the Gold Rush," 10–15; Richard Walker, "Industry Builds Out the City: The Suburbanization of Manufacturing in the San Francisco Bay Area, 1850–1940" (2004), http://geog.berkeley.edu/PeopleHistory/faculty/R_Walker/IndustryBuildsOut.pdf, 4.

34. James E. Vance Jr., "Geography and Urban Evolution in the San Francisco Bay Area," in *The San Francisco Bay Area: Its Problems and Future*, ed. Stanley Scott (Berkeley: University of California Press, 1964), 18.

35. Vance, "Geography and Urban Evolution," 20.

36. Montgomery Rollins, *Municipal and Corporation Bonds: Terms, Customs, and Usages. A Reference for the Investor and Banker* (Boston: Financial Publishing Co., 1919), 113–14.

37. "Power Bond Propositions Lose 3 to 1," *San Francisco Chronicle*, August 27, 1930, 1; William Issel and Robert W. Cherny, *San Francisco, 1865–1932: Politics, Power, and Urban Development* (Berkeley: University of California Press, 1986).

38. Greta R. Krippner, *Capitalizing on Crisis: The Political Origins of the Rise of Finance* (Cambridge, MA: Harvard University Press, 2011), 61.

39. Charles Geisst, *Wall Street: A History* (New York: Oxford University Press, 1997), 243.

40. John Connor, "Municipal Bond Regulation Bill Cleared for Senate Panel's Action," *Daily Bond Buyer* [DBB] 229, no. 24414 (July 24, 1974): 289, 304; John Connor, "Senate Banking Committee Approves Bill Regulating Municipal Bond Industry," *DBB* 229, no. 24426 (August 9, 1974): 513, 527. Here and throughout most of this book, page numbers from *DBB* correspond to those in the bound volumes at Butler Library, Columbia University. For more on regulation of the municipal bond market, see John Petersen, "Changing Conditions in the Market for State and Local Government Debt: A Study," Congress, Joint Economic Committee, 94th Cong., 2nd sess., April 16, 1976, 44–46; John J. Doran, "How the Dealer's Bible Came to Be;

Warding Off 'Pests' and Selling Ads," in *The Bond Buyer: 100 Anniversary Edition: A Salute to the Municipal Bond Industry, 1891–1991* (1991), 72; Robert J. Cole, "Holding Municipal Bonds Up to the Light," *New York Times*, October 26, 1975, 173.

41. Although commercial banks could *hold* revenue bonds issued by states and their political subdivisions as investment securities, they could not underwrite, or purchase with the intent to sell. For the exceptions to the Banking Act of 1933, see Geisst, *Wall Street: A History*, 222–23; Vincent P. Carosso, *Investment Banking in America: A History* (Cambridge, MA: Harvard University Press, 1970), 356; For exemption from SEC regulation of the over-the-counter market, see Geisst, *Wall Street: A History*, 243. For the ability to invest in but not underwrite the revenue bonds of municipal borrowers, see Roland I. Robinson, *Postwar Market for State and Local Government Securities*, (Princeton, NJ: Princeton University Press, 1960), 17.

42. Benjamin J. Klebaner, *Commercial Banking in the United States: A History* (Hinsdale, IL: Dryden Press, 1974), 153.

43. William J. Novak, "The Myth of the 'Weak' American State," *American Historical Review* 113, no. 3 (June 2008): 769–71.

44. John E. Petersen, *The Rating Game: Report of the Twentieth Century Fund Task Force on Municipal Bond Credit Ratings* (New York: Twentieth Century Fund, 1974), 52.

45. Statements of Brenton W. Harries and Robert C. Riehle, in Joint Economic Committee, Subcommittee on Economic Progress, "Financing Municipal Facilities: Volume II," 90th Cong., 2nd sess., July 9–11, 1968, 199, 213–14.

46. Sugrue, *The Origins of the Urban Crisis*, 10.

47. Becky M. Nicolaides, "The Neighborhood Politics of Class in a Working-Class Suburb of Los Angeles, 1920–1940," *Journal of Urban History* 30, no. 3 (March 2004): 445.

48. Robinson, *Postwar Market for State and Local Government Securities*, 12, 158, 161.

49. San Francisco Housing Authority [SFHA], *Fifth Annual Report* (April 1943); SFHA, *Sixth Annual Report* (1944).

50. Joint Economic Committee, Subcommittee on Economic Progress, "State and Local Public Facility Needs and Financing: Volume II," 89th Cong., 2nd sess., December 1966, 54, 148–49.

51. Susan B. Carter, Scott Sigmund Gartner, Michael R. Haines, Alan L. Olmstead, Richard Sutch, and Gavin Wright, eds., *Historical Statistics of the United States* (Cambridge, UK: Cambridge University Press, 2006), Series Ea, 758–72.

52. "State and Local Public Facility Needs and Financing: Volume II," 8, 58, 105–6.

53. "Profit Squeeze Called Symptom of Change at Opening of Third Municipal Conference," *DBB*, 190.21962 (October 9, 1964), 125, 140.

54. Robin L. Einhorn, *Property Rules: Political Economy in Chicago, 1833–1872* (University of Chicago Press, 1991, 2001), 15, 17, 103; McDonald, *The Parameters*, 136.

55. "State and Local Public Facility Needs and Financing: Volume II," 43.

56. Issel, "Liberalism and Urban Policy," 434–47.

57. Robinson, *Postwar Market for State and Local Government Securities*, 30, 158, 161.

58. "State and Local Public Facility Needs and Financing: Volume II," 347.

59. To be clear, higher fares, rates, and fees were not a direct function of the cost to borrow. In 1975, for instance, Pacific Gas & Electric attributed the need for a rate increase to rising gas and oil costs, escalating due in no small part to the 1973 oil crisis. In this case, proposed higher electric bills and user rates were due to shifts in the broader global political economy and intended to offset increased "interest rates on borrowed money." Most often the link between municipal debt and user charges was less explicit. San Franciscans saw "an increase of 10 percent on [water] rates and charges" on August 1, 1984. A few months later they were offered the chance to approve a $104 million revenue bond, which the San Francisco Public Utilities Commission averred would not affect the city tax rate. But if interest and principal payments on the proposed bond would be covered "entirely from Water Department revenues," and if interest rates remained high, this would almost certainly mean an increase in water rates. How else could the city pay for the $104 million revenue bond sold in October 1985 at an average interest rate of 8.86 percent "for various periods ranging up to 30 years"? "Pacific G&E Asks a Boost in Rates of $140 Million," *Wall Street Journal*, February 26, 1975, 74; San Francisco Public Utilities Commission, *Annual Report, 1968–1969*, n.p.; San Francisco Public Utilities Commission, *Annual Report, 1983–1984*, 13, 17; San Francisco Public Utilities Commission, *Biennial Report, 1984–1985 & 1985–1986*, 14; Tom Berkley, "On the Sidewalk," *Oakland Post*, July 9, 1978, 1.

Chapter One

1. David Kennedy, *Freedom from Fear: The American People in Depression and War, 1929–1945* (New York: Oxford University Press, 1999), 58–59, 162–63; Charles P. Kindleberger, *The World in Depression, 1929–1939* (Berkeley: University of California Press, 1978).

2. James D. Phelan, quoted in Terrence J. McDonald, *The Parameters of Urban Fiscal Policy: Socioeconomic Change and Political Culture in San Francisco, 1860–1906* (Berkeley: University of California Press, 1986), 195.

3. A. M. Hillhouse, *Municipal Bonds: A Century of Experience* (New York: Prentice-Hall, 1936), 18, 35, 475.

4. John E. Petersen, *The Rating Game: Report of the Twentieth Century Fund Task Force on Municipal Bond Credit Ratings* (New York: The Twentieth Century Fund, 1974), 51; "$8,403,859 Sought by Municipalities," *New York Times*, October 3, 1931, 25; "Municipal Bonds Sales Delayed Pending Gains," *New*

York Herald Tribune, October 20, 1931, 30; "Bond Offerings Slated Despite Poor Market," *New York Herald Tribune*, December 24, 1931, 22.

5.   Hillhouse, *Municipal Bonds*, 475; C. A. Dykstra, "New Tasks for Public Administrators," in *Municipal Year Book 1934*, ed. Clarence E. Ridley and Orin F. Nolting (Chicago: International City Managers' Association, 1934), 24–25; George Wanders, "Cities Waging Campaign to Collect Taxes," *New York Herald Tribune*, May 22, 1933, 18.

6.   The *Municipal Year Book* provided a state-by-state overview of "defaults on bonds, notes, certificates of indebtedness, etc. This summary does not embrace defaults of special assessment obligations. Many defaults are from unofficial sources." "Table 5—Summary of Municipal Debt Defaults" in *Municipal Year Book 1939*, ed. Clarence E. Ridley and Orin F. Nolting (Chicago: International City Managers' Association, 1939), 394–95; Hillhouse, *Municipal Bonds*, 18, 29.

7.   Dykstra, "New Tasks for Public Administrators," 19, 24–25.

8.   W. A. Lyon, "Coast Meeting of Bankers Set for Tomorrow," *New York Herald Tribune*, October 2, 1932, C1, "Cut in Government Expenditures Urged by A.B.A.," *Bankers' Magazine*, February 1932, n.p.; "The A.B.A. and the Glass Bill," *Bankers' Magazine*, April 1932, n.p.; "Los Angeles Prepares for A.B.A. Convention," *Bankers' Magazine*, June 1932, n.p.

9.   Hillhouse, *Municipal Bonds*, 354–55, 415.

10. Jason Scott Smith, *Building New Deal Liberalism: The Political Economy of Public Works, 1933–1956* (New York: Cambridge University Press, 2006); Gail Radford, *The Rise of the Public Authority: Statebuilding and Economic Development in Twentieth-Century America* (Chicago: University of Chicago Press, 2013), 14, 128–29.

11. Testimony of Carl H. Chatters, Committee on Manufactures, "Federal Aid for Unemployment Relief," 72nd Cong., 2nd sess., January 3–17, 1933, 172.

12. Carl H. Chatters, *Municipal Bond Defaults, Their Prevention and Adjustment* (Chicago: Public Service Administration Service, 1933); A. M. Hillhouse, *Defaulted Municipal Bonds, 1830–1930* (Chicago: Municipal Finance Officers' Association, 1935).

13. A. M. Hillhouse, *New Sources of Municipal Revenue* (Chicago: Municipal Finance Officers' Association, 1935).

14. Israel Rafkind, *Manual of Accounting and Financial Procedure in the Office of the Controller of the City and County of San Francisco, California* (July 1938), foreword.

15. H. D. Ross, "Financing Airport Operations," *Municipal Finance* 21, no. 1 (August 1948): 21–23; "Possible Tax on Municipal Bonds, S.F. Official Warns," *San Francisco Chronicle*, June 18, 1952, 20; "City Officials Conference Starts Today," *San Francisco Chronicle*, May 24, 1954, 34.

16. Hillhouse, *Municipal Bonds*, 240, 445, 452.

17. Frederick M. Wirt, *Power in the City: Decision Making in San Francisco* (Berkeley: University of California Press, 1974), 114–20.

18. Rafkind, *Manual of Accounting*, 2–4.

19. Rafkind, *Manual of Accounting*, 125–27.

20. Harold J. Boyd, "A Finance Officer's Responsibilities," *Municipal Finance* 11, no. 1 (August 1938): 20–23.

21. Frederick L. Bird, "The Basis of Municipal Credit," *Municipal Finance* 11, no. 1 (August 1938): 14, 19–20.

22. Frederick L. Bird, "A Municipal Policy for Postwar Public Works and Public Borrowing," *Municipal Finance* 19, no. 1 (August 1946): 16.

23. Bird, "The Basis of Municipal Credit," 14, 19–20.

24. "Ex-S.F. Controller Harry Ross Dies," *San Francisco Chronicle*, December 22, 1970, 14.

25. Victor H. Green, *The Negro Motorist Green-Book, 1941 Edition* (New York: Victor H. Green & Co., 1941), http://digitalcollections.nypl.org/items/cc8306a0-83c4 -0132-cc93-58d385a7bbd0, 11, 17–18, 7; Albert S. Broussard, *Black San Francisco: The Struggle for Racial Equality in the West, 1900–1954* (Lawrence: University of Kansas Press, 1993), 175, 135; Wirt, *Power in the City*, 33.

26. Roger W. Lotchin, *The Bad City in the Good War: San Francisco, Los Angeles, Oakland, and San Diego* (Bloomington: Indiana University Press, 2003), 66, 182, 185, 186, 188; Lotchin, *Fortress California, 1910–1961: From Warfare to Welfare* (Champaign: University of Illinois Press, 1992).

27. San Francisco Planning and Housing Association, "San Francisco Public Housing: A Citizens' Survey of Five Permanent Projects—Holly Courts, Potrero Terrace, Sunnydale, Valencia Gardens and Westside Court" (San Francisco: San Francisco Planning and Housing Association, 1946).

28. "Will Connolly Says: Where Can Father Crowley Park Kids Play Next?" *San Francisco Chronicle*, May 30, 1948, 35.

29. Carolyn Anspacher, "The Need Is Great—The Time Is Late," *San Francisco Chronicle*, November 1, 1948, 10.

30. Harold J. Boyd, "The Finance Officer and the Public," *Municipal Finance* 12, no. 2 (November 1939): 7–8.

31. Thomas J. Sugrue, *The Origins of the Urban Crisis: Race and Inequality in Postwar Detroit* (Princeton, NJ: Princeton University Press, 1996), 10; Robert O. Self, *American Babylon: Race and the Struggle for Postwar Oakland* (Princeton, NJ: Princeton University Press, 2003), 23.

32. Bird, "A Municipal Policy for Postwar Public Works and Public Borrowing," 15.

33. "City and County of San Francisco Bonded Debt Limit at June 30, 1947," in *Annual Report of the Controller of the City and County of San Francisco for the Fiscal Year Ended June 30, 1947* (San Francisco, CA: Office of the Controller, 1947–48), 26, https://archive.org/details/annualreportofco1947sanf; Joseph P. Crosson, "Municipal Bond Problems Today," *MFOA Annual Conference* 25, no. 1 (August 1952): 55.

34. San Francisco Redevelopment Association [SFRA], "Program of San Francisco Redevelopment Agency for Eighteen Months Beginning January 1,

1949 and Ending June 30, 1950"; SFRA, *Annual Report 1962*, 33; Theodore Gould Robinson, "Coordinating the Technical and Administrative Aspects of an Urban Redevelopment Project," (Ph.D. diss., University of Southern California, 1948), 19–26. Mohamed Omar Hefni, "A Comparative Organizational Analysis of Selected Community Redevelopment Agencies in California," (Ph.D. diss., University of Southern California, 1969), 16.

35. For the debt-issuing powers of the SFRA, see, e.g., SFRA and the Department of City Planning, "A Report to the Board of Supervisors: Redevelopment in Diamond Heights" (March 1950), 16. For the federal government's encouragement that redevelopment agencies borrow through the municipal bond market, see Housing and Home Finance Agency, "A Handbook of Information on Provisions of The Housing Act of 1949 and Operations Under the Various Programs" (Washington, DC: HHFA, July 1949), 4; Urban Renewal Administration. "Urban Renewal Manual: Policies and Requirements for Local Public Agencies," book II: 1960–1962, 1.

36. Frank Marini, *Local Bond Elections in California: The Two-Thirds Majority Requirement* (Berkeley:, University of California Institute of Governmental Studies, 1963), 15–16.

37. "Annual Bond Interest and Redemption Requirements Based upon Bonded Indebtedness as at June 30, 1948," in *Annual Report of the Controller of the City and County of San Francisco for the Fiscal Year Ended June 30, 1948*, 27.

38. Proposition 26: Sewer Construction and Reconstruction Bonds, "City and County Bond Propositions and Charter Amendments to be voted on at Election," (November 7, 1944), n.p., https://sfpl.org/pdf/main/gic/elections/November7_1944.pdf.

39. Earl C. Behrens, "State Taxes: Governor's New Advisory Group Meets Today," *San Francisco Chronicle*, February 2, 1943, 24; "Archbishop Presides at Rites for S.F. Leader," *San Francisco Chronicle*, November 5, 1953, 3.

40. Proposition 26: Sewer Construction and Reconstruction Bonds, n.p.

41. "Local Bond Issues and Amendments," *San Francisco Chronicle*, November 9, 1944, 9.

42. "City Granted Priorities for Sewer Work," *San Francisco Chronicle*, March 3, 1945, 5.

43. "Clerk to Advertise Sale of $4,000,000.00 City and County of San Francisco Sewer Bonds—1944, Series A and $5,000,000.00 City and County of San Francisco Airport Bonds—1945, Series A," *San Francisco Chronicle*, December 1, 1945, 6.

44. Rudiger Dornbusch, "Dealing with Debt in the 1980s," *Third World Quarterly* 7, no. 3 (July 1985): 532–33.

45. "2 Bond Issues Sold by San Francisco," *New York Times*, January 8, 1946, 27.

46. Crosson, "Municipal Bond Problems Today," 55.

47. "Declarations of Candidacy . . . Candidates and Propositions to be voted on at General Municipal Election," November 4, 1947, 52–54, https://sfpl

.org/pdf/main/gic/elections/November4_1947.pdf. The results are derived from the San Francisco Public Library's Ballot Propositions Database.

48. "Vote Yes on 7" in "City and County Propositions . . . To be Voted on at Primary Election," June 1, 1948, n.p., https://webbie1.sfpl.org/multimedia /pdf/elections/June1_1948.pdf.

49. Elaine Tyler May, *Homeward Bound: American Families in the Cold War Era* (New York: Basic Books, 1988), 6, 130; Sugrue, *The Origins of the Urban Crisis*, 74.

50. Rodger W. Valentine, "The Municipal Bond Market—1944," *Municipal Finance* 17, no. 2 (November 1944): 7.

51. Valentine, "The Municipal Bond Market—1944," 7–11; Roland I. Robinson, *Postwar Market for State and Local Government Securities* (Princeton, NJ: Princeton University Press, 1960), 158, 161; Steven H. Jaffe and Jessica Lautin, *Capital of Capital: Money, Banking, and Power in New York City, 1784–2012* (Columbia University Press, 2014), 151–52; George T. Conklin Jr., "The Bond Market, 1962 and 1963," *Journal of Finance* 18, no. 2 (May 1963), 418–19.

52. "Who Buys Municipals?" *Daily Bond Buyer* [*DBB*] 85, no. 9952 (February 18, 1922): 366–67; "The 'Tax-Exempt Refuge,'" *Wall Street Journal*, July 22, 1922, reprinted in *DBB* 86, no. 10087 (July 29, 1922): 1874.

53. Robinson, *Postwar Market for State and Local Government Securities*, 72–77.

54. Robinson, 97, 214–15.

55. John S. Linen, "What Factors Make the Bond Market?" *Municipal Finance* 20, no. 1 (August 1947): 21; Robinson, *Postwar Market for State and Local Government Securities*, 7, 69, 84–6; Benjamin J. Klebaner, *Commercial Banking in the United States: A History* (Hinsdale, IL: Dryden Press, 1974), 174–75.

56. Linen, "What Factors Make the Bond Market?," 25; Valentine, "The Municipal Bond Market—1944," 7–8.

57. David M. Wood, "Effect of Current Political Trends on Municipal Finance," *Municipal Finance Officers' Association* 23, no. 1 (conference issue, August 1950): 3.

58. "Why S.F. Hires That Bond Firm," *San Francisco Chronicle*, December 3, 1965, 2.

59. David M. Ellinwood, "Preparing Municipal Bonds for Sale," *Municipal Finance* 20, no. 1 (August 1947): 56.

60. David M. Wood, "Drafting Municipal Bond Proceedings," *Municipal Finance* 21, no. 4 (May 1949): 13–16.

61. "Municipal Bond Club Hits Maloney Bill," *New York Times*, February 15, 1938; David M. Wood, "Boren Bill Cures Unlawful Delegation of Power to SEC," *Bond Buyer*, February 27, 1943, carton 3, folder "Miscellaneous Corres. & Reference Material, 1954–1979," Alan K. Browne Papers (BANC MSS 91/6), Bancroft Library, University of California, Berkeley [AKBP], n.p.

62. David M. Wood, "Effect of Current Political Trends on Municipal Finance," 3–8.

63. Ellinwood, "Preparing Municipal Bonds for Sale," 56–59.

64. Alan K. Browne, Memorandum to Salesmen, "RE: Points to Consider in the Choice of Municipal Bonds (Continued)," August 4, 1937, carton 2, folder "BankAmerica Co. Municipal Market Letter, 1937–39," AKBP, 1–2.

65. Ellinwood, "Preparing Municipal Bonds for Sale," 56–59.

66. Linen, "What Factors Make the Bond Market?," 25.

67. David M. Ellinwood, "Municipal Financial Reports to Investors," *Municipal Finance* 19, no. 2 (November 1946): 3–6.

68. Moody's Investors Service, *Moody's Municipal & Government Manual: American and Foreign* (New York: Moody's Investors Service, 1955), 232–34.

69. William Cronon, *Nature's Metropolis: Chicago and the Great West* (New York: W. W. Norton, 1991), 268.

70. Moody's Investors Service, *Moody's Municipal & Government Manual*, 232–34.

71. Ellinwood, "Municipal Financial Reports to Investors," 4–5.

72. Frederick L. Bird, "A Comparison of the Financial Reports of Public and Private Corporations," *Municipal Finance* 13, no. 4 (May 1941): 10–14; "City and County of San Francisco Bonded Debt Limit at June 30, 1947," in *Annual Report of the Controller of the City and County of San Francisco for Fiscal Year Ended June 30, 1947*, 26.

73. Ellinwood, "Municipal Financial Reports to Investors," 3.

74. *Annual Report of the Controller of the City and County of San Francisco for Fiscal Year Ended June 30, 1947*, 92.

75. Crosson, "Municipal Bond Problems Today," 54–55.

76. Anglo California National Bank of San Francisco, "San Francisco: A Credit Study of its Municipal Bonds" (San Francisco: ACNB, 1936), n.p.

77. "Annual Bond Interest and Redemption Requirements Based Upon Bonded Indebtedness as at June 30, 1948," in *Annual Report of the Controller of the City and County of San Francisco for Fiscal Year Ended June 30, 1948*, 27.

78. Crosson, "Municipal Bond Problems Today," 54–55.

79. Crosson, "Municipal Bond Problems Today," 55; "Statement of Bonding Capacity at June 30, 1948," in *Annual Report of the Controller of the City and County of San Francisco for Fiscal Year Ended June 30, 1948*, 26.

80. Crosson, "Municipal Bond Problems Today," 55.

Chapter Two

1. Alan K. Browne, Memorandum to Salesmen, "RE: Municipal Bond Department," April 30, 1937, Carton#2, Folder "BankAmerica Co. Municipal Market Letter, 1937–39," Alan K. Browne Papers (BANC MSS 91/6), Bancroft Library, University of California, Berkeley [AKBP], 1; Benjamin J. Klebaner, *Commercial Banking in the United States: A History* (Hinsdale, IL: Dryden Press, 1974), 112, 119–20.

2. Alan K. Browne, "'Mr. Municipal Bond': Bond Investment Management, Bank of America, 1929–1971," oral history conducted in 1988 by Malca

Chall, Regional Oral History Office, The Bancroft Library, University of
California, Berkeley (1990), vii, x, 3–4, 21–22, 29, 31, 75, 115; Alan K. Browne,
"Bond Investment Department," May 23, 1955, carton 3, AKBP, n.p.

3. "Alan K. Browne, 78, A Banking Executive," *New York Times*, August 12,
1988, D18.

4. Browne, "'Mr. Municipal Bond,'" xi; "Alan K. Browne," *San Francisco
Chronicle*, August 11, 1988, B7.

5. "World Bank to Offer $100 Million Bonds in Week of February 8," *Daily
Bond Buyer [DBB]* 172, no. 20785 (February 5, 1960): 452. For more on World
Bank financing, see Jochen Kraske, *Bankers with a Mission: The Presidents
of the World Bank, 1946–91* (New York: Oxford University Press, 1996).

6. "Dealers' Bids Best for Housing Bonds," *New York Times*, July 18, 1951, 35;
Public Housing Administration, "Terms and Conditions Constituting Part
Two of an Annual Contributions Contract between Local Authority and
Public Housing Administration," Housing and Home Finance Agency, re-
vised 1951, 37; J. A. Livingston, "Competitors for Housing Bonds Must Bid
in 5 Places at Once," *Washington Post*, July 13, 1951, B3.

7. "Button to Visit East on California Bond Sale Mission," *DBB* 168, no. 20318
(March 28, 1958): 1458, 1478.

8. Kevin Starr, *Embattled Dreams: California in War and Peace, 1940–1955* (New
York: Oxford University Press, 2002); Kevin Starr, *Golden Dreams: California
in an Age of Abundance* (New York: Oxford University Press, 2009).

9. Alan K. Browne, Memorandum to R. A. Kent, "Underwriting of New Municipal Bond Issues," July 1, 1947, carton 3, AKBP, 7–8.

10. Emphasis in original. Alan K. Browne, "Trading Account," October 1, 1947,
carton 3, AKBP, 5.

11. Browne, "Trading Account," 1.

12. Investment Bankers Association of America, Quarterly Report, *IBA Statistical Bulletin: A Survey of the Municipal Bond Market* 7 (April 1958): 1–3.

13. Browne, "Underwriting of New Municipal Bond Issues," 1–3.

14. Alan K. Browne, "Bond Investment Department," May 23, 1955, carton 3,
AKBP, 3–6.

15. Browne, "Trading Account," 4–5.

16. "Bond Buyer's Index of Municipal Bond Values, January 1, 1917–1939," in
*The Municipal Yearbook 1939: The Authoritative Résumé of Activities and Sta-
tistical Data of American Cities*, ed. Clarence E. Ridley and Orin F. Nolting
(Chicago: International City Managers' Association, 1939), 393.

17. Roland I. Robinson, *Postwar Market for State and Local Government Securities* (Princeton, NJ: Princeton University Press, 1960), 178.

18. Browne, "Trading Account," 3; Alan K. Browne, Memorandum to L. H.
Prager, "Subject: Trading Section," August 22, 1947, in "Trading Account," 1.

19. Emphasis in original. Robinson, *Postwar Market for State and Local Government Securities*, 34.

20. Browne, "Subject: Trading Section," 5.

21. Susie J. Pak, *Gentlemen Bankers: The World of J.P. Morgan* (Cambridge, MA: Harvard University Press, 2013), 17–20.

22. "Results of Sales: Week of April 7, 1947," in Browne, "Underwriting of New Municipal Bond Issues," n.p.

23. "Five Issues Sold by San Francisco," *New York Times*, February 3, 1948, 37; "Syndicates Bid on $27,000,000 Issues of Bonds," *New York Herald Tribune*, February 3, 1948, 28.

24. "Tax Exempts: San Francisco Plans Sale of Two Issues Totaling $12 Million," *Wall Street Journal*, March 21, 1951, 10.

25. Browne, "Underwriting of New Municipal Bond Issues," 2, 4.

26. Bank of America National Trust and Savings Association, "Syndicate Agreement," November 1952, carton 2, folder "Memos & Reports: Investment Baking [*sic*], 1965–70," AKBP, 1–3.

27. Alan K. Browne, "Municipal Syndicate Agreements: Some Fresh Concepts Discussed," November 30, 1953, carton 2, folder "Memos & Reports: Investment Baking [*sic*], 1965–70," AKBP, 1, 2, 4, 6.

28. Browne, "Underwriting of New Municipal Bond Issues," 4.

29. Timothy J. Sinclair, *The New Masters of Capital: American Bond Rating Agencies and the Politics of Creditworthiness* (Ithaca, NY: Cornell University Press, 2005).

30. For instance, "of the rated bonds that plunged into default in the 1930s, 48 percent had been rated Aaa in 1929 and 78 percent had been rated either Aaa or Aa." John E. Petersen, *The Rating Game: Report of the Twentieth Century Fund Task Force on Municipal Bond Credit Ratings* (New York: Twentieth Century Fund, 1974), 52.

31. For one important take on how municipal bond financiers used Moody's ratings, see Alan K. Browne, Memorandum to Salesmen, "RE: Municipal Offering Lists," May 4, 1937, carton 2, folder "BankAmerica Co. Municipal Market Letter, 1937–39," AKBP, 1; Alan K. Browne, Memorandum to Representatives, "RE: California State and Municipal Bonds," August 16, 1940, carton 2, folder "BankAmerica Co. Memos & Sales Bulletins, 1937–1941," AKBP, 1.

32. John S. Linen, "What Factors Make the Bond Market?" *Municipal Finance* 20, no. 1 (August 1947): 23; Walter H. Tyler, "The Validity and Use of Bond Ratings," *Municipal Finance* 30, no. 1 (August 1957): 54.

33. Regulators would raise questions about bonds with anything lower than a "Baa" credit rating. Tyler, "The Validity and Use of Bond Ratings," 54; Petersen, *The Rating Game*, 65–67.

34. Browne, "Underwriting of New Municipal Bond Issues," 5.

35. Browne, "Subject: Trading Section," 3.

36. Browne, "Underwriting of New Municipal Bond Issues," 7.

37. Browne, "Subject: Trading Section," 1.

38. Browne, "Bond Investment Department," 3–6.

39. Alan K. Browne, "Comments on Proposals before California Voters at

Special Election," *Bond Buyer*, October 15, 1949, carton 2, folder "Misc. Press Clippings etc. S.F. Chamber. S.F. Bond Club," AKBP, 7.

40. Alan K. Browne, Letter to Mr. S. Clark Beise, June 24, 1959, carton 2, folder "BOA Corres . . . 1936–71," AKBP, 1–2.

41. R. A. Kent, "Space Problems. Bond Investment Department," November 9, 1953, carton 3, AKBP, 1.

42. The Bond Buyer, *Directory of Municipal Bond Dealers of the United States*, 1953 midyear ed. (New York: The Bond Buyer, 1953), 26, 28.

43. Browne, Letter to Beise, 1–2.

44. Kent, "Space Problems. Bond Investment Department," 1–3.

45. Browne, "Bond Investment Department," 3–6; Alan K. Browne, Letter to George B. Wendt, October 30, 1962, carton 2, folder "Corres . . . 1962–1974," AKBP, 3; "Albert E. Schwabacher Elected New Chairman of California Group of IBA," *DBB* 190, no. 21982 (November 10, 1964): 556.

46. "Colis Mitchum," *DBB* 190, no. 22002 (December 10, 1964): 1007.

47. "Broad Bond Survey by Bank of America Making Good Progress," *DBB* 168, no. 20268 (January 16, 1958): 218.

48. George Wanders, "Bank of America bond Survey Results Show Various Viewpoints," *DBB* 168, no. 20326 (April 9, 1958): 1636.

49. "$60,000,000 San Francisco Bay Area Rapid Transit District," *New York Times*, September 17, 1964, 63; "$20,000,000 Los Angeles County Flood Control," *Wall Street Journal*, October 18, 1967, 25; "$150,000,000 State of Illinois," *Chicago Tribune*, March 13, 1963, C9.

50. Municipal Bond Department, Bank of America, "Answers and Comments to the Underwriting and Bond Sale Survey," undated, carton 2, folder "Memos & Reports: Investment Baking [*sic*], 1965–70," AKBP, 2, 34, 38, 39, 45–47, 49–50, 52–53; Gene Smith, "Mutual Funds: Restrictions on Ads Abound," *New York Times*, July 9, 1962, 38.

51. This chapter treats the San Francisco Bond Club as a representative local organization. For the New York Municipal Bond Club, see "Municipal Bond Club Holds First Meeting," *New York Times*, March 2, 1932, 30. For the Bond Club and Municipal Bond Club of Philadelphia, see "Philadelphia Bond Club Holds Annual Outing," *Wall Street Journal*, June 13, 1936, 6; and "Municipal Bond Club Formed in Philadelphia," *Wall Street Journal*, April 18, 1941, 7; respectively. For Chicago, see "Kellogg States Case against Security Bids," *Chicago Daily Tribune*, April 18, 1940, 7. For the Milwaukee Bond Club, see "Banker Warns This Is No Time to Experiment," *Chicago Daily Tribune*, May 21, 1941, 29. On October 27, 1957, the National Traders Security Association published an advertisement in the *New York Times* (p. F5) listing among its affiliated groups the Bond Club of Denver, the Bond Club of Louisville, and the Bond Club of Syracuse, New York.

52. I draw inspiration from John Broderick's recurring column in the *Wall Street Journal*, "Bonds and Bond Men," in conceptualizing bond financiers as bondmen.

53. My synthesis is also derived from "Public Housing as Investment Rated Nation's Best by Post," *New York Herald Tribune*, October 8, 1937, 33; "Detroit's Finances Seen Now on Sounder Basis with Outlook Better," *Wall Street Journal*, March 17, 1938, 9; "Mayor Sees Bonds Kept Tax-Exempt," *New York Times*, March 8, 1941, 21.

54. Browne was also a member of the San Francisco Municipal Bond Club. Unfortunately, the sources for this organization have been difficult to locate. Nevertheless, the fact that municipal and corporate bond financiers were members of the same organization only bolsters my argument about social cohesion. See Browne, "'Mr. Municipal Bond,'" 312–13.

55. San Francisco Bond Club, "Founders and Past Presidents Anniversary Dinner, 1930–1955," October 26, 1955, carton 2, folder "Misc. Press Clippings etc. S.F. Chamber. S.F. Bond Club," AKBP, n.p.

56. For overlapping membership, see Browne, "'Mr. Municipal Bond,'" 312–13; "Richard D. Gordon Elected to Position of President by San Francisco Club," *DBB* 190, no. 21984, (November 13, 1964): 583. For the specialized function of the San Francisco Municipal Bond Club, see "San Francisco Club to Hold Conference for Municipal Field," *DBB* 190, no. 21991 (November 24, 1964): 764.

57. William G. Roy, "Institutional Governance and Social Cohesion: The Internal Organization of the American Capitalist Class, 1886–1905," in Donald J. Treiman and Robert V. Robinson, eds., *Research in Social Stratification and Mobility* (Greenwich, CT: JAI Press, 1984), 153, 164; E. Digby Baltzell, *The Protestant Establishment Revisited*, ed. Howard G. Schneiderman (New Brunswick, NJ: Transaction, 1991), 99, 108; Sven Beckert, *The Monied Metropolis: New York City and the Consolidation of the American Bourgeoisie 1850–1896* (New York: Cambridge University Press, 2001), 263–65.

58. Diana Kendall, *Members Only: Elite Clubs and the Process of Exclusion* (Lanham, MD: Rowman & Littlefield, 2008); Jeffrey A. Charles, *Service Clubs in American Society: Rotary, Kiwanis, and Lions* (Champaign: University of Illinois Press, 1993).

59. Like underwriting syndicates, the San Francisco Bond Club was cooperative, yet hierarchical. The club maintained a board of directors and charged officials with keeping tabs on its finances and documenting its history. "San Francisco Bond Club," December 1965, carton 4, loose material, AKBP, 42, 43, 45.

60. "San Francisco Bond Club," December 1965, 43.

61. Elizabeth Ellsworth Cook Papers, 1917–1970, Arthur and Elizabeth Schlesinger Library (A/C771), Harvard University; "San Francisco Sewer Bonds," *Wall Street Journal*, May 18, 1936, 9; "San Francisco Financial Women Elect Officers," *DBB* 168, no. 20283 (February 6, 1958): 620; "Marcia Wolfe Elected President of San Francisco Financial Women's Club," *DBB* 172, no. 20793 (February 18, 1960): 606; "San Francisco Financial Women to Hear Realtor," *DBB* 172, no. 20821 (March 30, 1960): 1122; "Women's Municipal Bond

Club Reelects Delia Iavazzo Pres.," *Daily Boston Globe*, December 29, 1959, 14; "Women's Municipal Bond Club Elects Elizabeth Dickinson," *Boston Globe*, January 5, 1961, 14; "New Orleans Women's Bond Club Organized," *DBB* 172, no. 20810 (March 15, 1960): 926; "President's Gavel Passed at Municipal Women's Club," *DBB* 197, 22449 (September 19, 1966): 990; "New York's Municipal Bond Women's Club Installs Its New Officers and Governors," *DBB* 197, no. 22449 (September 19, 1966): 1008.

62. Browne, "'Mr. Municipal Bond,'" ix, 30; "Conference of Texas Municipal Secretaries Holds Mock Bond Sale as Program Theme," *DBB* 198, no. 22461 (October 5, 1966): 51.

63. See the emphasis on being employed in a "senior capacity" as a prerequisite for membership in the Municipal Bond Women's Club of New York: Museum of American Finance, "Municipal Bond Women's Club of New York: Archival Finding Aid," https://www.moaf.org/publications -collections/museum-collection/mbwc_finding_aid.

64. "San Francisco Bond Club," December 1965, 55–56.

65. Emphasis in original. Browne, "'Mr. Municipal Bond,'" 13/.

66. "San Francisco Bond Club," December 1965, 43.

67. "San Francisco Bond Club," December 1965, 19, 20, 23, 24.

68. Browne, "Bond Investment Department," 3–6.

69. "San Francisco Bond Club," December 1965, 44.

70. "San Francisco Bond Club," December 1965, 42.

71. Names and professional affiliations derived "San Francisco Bond Club," December 1965, 18–20.

72. United Statistical Associates, *Municipal Holdings of Insurance Companies* (1955), 91.

73. United Statistical Associates, *Municipal Holdings of Insurance Companies* (1956), 97.

74. "San Francisco Bond Club," December 1965, 21, 23.

75. "Growing Federal Powers Dangerous, Davis Warns," *Wall Street Journal*, May 11, 1937, 10; "Defeat Roosevelt, Attorney Pleads," *Washington Post*, April 13, 1938, X2.

76. Browne, "'Mr. Municipal Bond,'" 61, 70–71. For the work of the municipal bond attorney, see Ronald David Greenberg, "Municipal Securities: Some Basic Principles and Practices," *Urban Lawyer* 9, no. 2 (Spring 1977), 361–62.

77. "San Francisco Bond Club," December 1965, 23; Browne, "'Mr. Municipal Bond,'" 70.

78. I cross-checked the names of the investment and commercial banking firms in the 1947 Joint Account statement with the SFBC's 1965 listing of its "Membership by Organization." I assumed that even with slight name changes between 1947 and 1965, these firms were largely the same. For original sources, see "Banks and Investment Dealers Associated with Us in Joint Accounts Managed by Us," in Browne, "Underwriting of New Municipal Bond Issues," 1–2; "San Francisco Bond Club," December 1965, 18–26.

79. "San Francisco Bond Club," December 1965, 59.

80. Rosemary Joyce characterized late-1970s financiers as "an occupational folk group" that shared "traditions that have been passed on orally over a period of time." Joyce presciently interpreted financial jokelore as "ice breakers": potential investors might be more willing to trust tellers of offensive jokes with their capital. Rosemary O. Joyce, "Wall Street Wags: Uses of Humor in the Financial Community," *Western Folklore* 41, no. 4 (October 1982): 302–3. On how contemporary financiers joke about their profession, see Daniel Souleles, "Don't Mix Paxil, Viagra, and Xanax: What Financiers' Jokes Say about Inequality," *Economic Anthropology* 4, no. 1 (January 2017): 107–19.

81. "The Tapeworm," *San Francisco Tapeworm* 1, no. 23 (May 3, 1952): 2, carton 4, binder "San Francisco Bond Club, 1955–56," AKBP.

82. Joyce, "Wall Street Wags," 300; "Bond Club of N.Y. to Revive Field Day, *Bawl Street Journal*," *Wall Street Journal*, April 8, 1946, 9. It was fitting that William S. Shanks, whose family founded the *Daily Bond Buyer* in 1891 and who ran it until 1949, was a committee member for the *Bond Crier*. On Shanks, see Joe Mysak, "The Bond Buyer After 100 Years," in *The Bond Buyer, 100 Anniversary Edition: A Salute to the Municipal Bond Industry, 1891–1991*, 9; *The Daily Bond Crier*, no. 16, June 14, 1957, carton 3, folder "Misc. Corres. 1972–79," AKBP, 2.

83. "Bawled Out," *San Francisco Tapeworm* 1, no. 26 (April 30, 1955): 1, carton 4, binder "San Francisco Bond Club, 1955–56," AKBP.

84. *San Francisco Tapeworm* 1, no. 27 (May 5, 1956): 3, carton 4, binder "San Francisco Bond Club, 1955–56," AKBP .

85. "Fulbright Group Hears Bankers Views Big Shots Air Ideas," *San Francisco Tapeworm* 1, no. 26 (April 30, 1955): 1, carton 4, binder "San Francisco Bond Club, 1955–56," AKBP. On Empey, see "San Francisco Bond Club," December 1965, 26.

86. "Browne in Schwab Out," *San Francisco Tapeworm* 1, no. 26 (April 30, 1955): 1, carton 4, binder "San Francisco Bond Club, 1955–56," AKBP; "San Francisco Bond Club," December 1965, 6, 37.

87. Browne, "'Mr. Municipal Bond,'" 2.

88. "Browne in Schwab Out," 1.

89. In 1974, G. William Domhoff provided an "Appendix of Heavies," or a list of the names and occupations of "the most prominent men" who were members of the Bohemian and Pacific Union clubs. I cross-checked those names with the 1965 SFBC membership roster, finding such men as Robert M. Bacon; Gerald F. Brush; Jean C., Thomas W., and Wendell W. Witter; John Inglis; and Arthur E. Pointing. G. William Domhoff, *The Bohemian Grove and Other Retreats: A Study in Ruling-Class Cohesiveness* (New York: Harper & Row, 1974).

90. *San Francisco Tapeworm* 1, no. 26 (May 21, 1960): 4, carton 4, binder: "San Francisco Bond Club, 1955–56," AKBP.

91. Abigail Vanilla, "Dear Abby," *San Francisco Tapeworm* 1, no. 26 (May 21, 1960): 2, carton 4, binder "San Francisco Bond Club, 1955–56," AKBP.

92. *San Francisco Tapeworm* 1, no. 23 (May 3, 1952): 2, carton 4, binder "San Francisco Bond Club, 1955–56," AKBP.

93. *San Francisco Tapeworm*, 1, no. 26 (May 21, 1960): 1, carton 4, binder "San Francisco Bond Club, 1955–56," AKBP.

94. Philip Deloria, *Playing Indian* (New Haven, CT: Yale University Press, 1998).

95. C. F. Childs & Co., *The Daily Bond Crier*, June 14, 1957, 2.

96. "No More Pee Pee in the Tee Pee," *San Francisco Tapeworm* 1, no. 23 (May 3, 1952): 1, carton 4, binder "San Francisco Bond Club, 1955–56," AKBP.

97. "Travel Notes," *San Francisco Tapeworm* 1, no. 23 (May 3, 1952): 2, carton 4, binder "San Francisco Bond Club, 1955–56," AKBP.

98. "$100,000,002 State of California Bonds," *San Francisco Tapeworm* 1, no. 26 (May 21, 1960): 4, carton 4, binder "San Francisco Bond Club, 1955–56," AKBP.

99. Joan W. Scott, "Gender: A Useful Category of Historical Analysis," *American Historical Review* 91, no. 5 (December 1986): 1069.

100. "Chash Manhattan Bank," *San Francisco Tapeworm* 1, no. 27 (May 5, 1960). 2, carton 4, binder "San Francisco Bond Club, 1955–56," AKBP.

101. "F.S. Smithers and Company," *San Francisco Tapeworm* 1, no. 26 (May 21, 1960): 4, carton 4, binder "San Francisco Bond Club, 1955–56," AKBP.

102. T. Hess, "For Sale," under "Classified Ads," *The San Francisco Tapeworm* 1, no. 23 (May 3, 1952): 2, carton 4, binder "San Francisco Bond Club, 1955–56," AKBP. To identify Hess's full name and firm, I cross-checked this "for sale" advertisement with the San Francisco Bond Club membership roster. See "San Francisco Bond Club," December 1965, 18.

103. Collins MacRae, "Classified," under "Classified Ads," *San Francisco Tapeworm*, 1, no. 23 (May 3, 1952): 2, carton 4, binder "San Francisco Bond Club, 1955–56," AKBP. To identify MacRae's full name and firm, I cross-checked this "classified" advertisement with the San Francisco Bond Club membership roster. See "San Francisco Bond Club," December 1965, 26.

104. Browne, "Trading Account," 6–7.

105. "A Part of the Investment Business," letter to the editor, *San Francisco Tapeworm* 1, no. 26 (May 21, 1960): 2, carton 4, binder "San Francisco Bond Club, 1955–56," AKBP.

106. "Miss Tapeworm of '52," *San Francisco Tapeworm* 1, no. 23 (May 3, 1952): 2, carton 4, binder "San Francisco Bond Club, 1955–56," AKBP.

107. Count Farco, "Be Private, Secretaries," *San Francisco Tapeworm* 1, no. 26 (May 21, 1960): 1, carton 4, binder "San Francisco Bond Club, 1955–56," AKBP.

108. "Abreast of the Market," *San Francisco Tapeworm* 1, no. 26 (May 21, 1960): 2, carton 4, binder "San Francisco Bond Club, 1955–56," AKBP. Bondmen perhaps drew inspiration from a frequent *Wall Street Journal* column that ran during the 1950s. See, for example, "Abreast of the Market," *Wall Street Journal*, April 20, 1953, 15. For another example of bondmen using "abreast"

252 : NOTES TO PAGES 68-71

as a double entendre to highlight their knowledge about bond markets and the breasts of their secretaries, see image of James B. Skinner of Schwabacher and Co. in *San Francisco Tapeworm* 1, no. 31 (June 12, 1965): 2, carton 4, binder "San Francisco Bond Club, 1955–56," AKBP. For the eroticism of Manpower Inc., see "High Speed STENO!" in the same issue, 2.

Chapter Three

1.   Robert A. Beauregard, ed., *Atop the Urban Hierarchy* (Totowa, NJ: Rowman & Littlefield, 1989), 2, 12, 33; Jefferson Cowie, *Capital Moves: RCA's Seventy-Year Quest for Cheap Labor* (New York: The New Press, 1999).

2.   San Francisco Planning and Urban Renewal Association [SPUR], "The Impact of Intensive High Rise Development on San Francisco: Detailed Findings" (June 1975), 3.

3.   San Francisco Department of City Planning, "Studies in the Economy of Downtown San Francisco" (September 1963), 13.

4.   SPUR, "The Impact of Intensive High Rise Development on San Francisco," 60, 85.

5.   Richard Lewis Nelson, Letter to Lapham Jr.; Real Estate Research Corporation and San Francisco Department of City Planning, "Summary of Market Analysis, Redevelopment Area 'E,' San Francisco, California," "Acknowledgements" section (May 1956).

6.   Emphasis in original. Real Estate Research Corporation, "Summary of Market Analysis," 7.

7.   Raymond W. Rast, "The Cultural Politics of Tourism in San Francisco," *Pacific Historical Review* 76, no. 1 (February 2007): 32, 37; Chiou-Ling Yeh, "'In the Traditions of China and in the Freedom of America': The Making of San Francisco's Chinese New Year Festivals," *American Quarterly* 56, no. 2 (June 2004): 401–5, 410; Christopher Lowen Agee, *The Streets of San Francisco: Policing and the Creation of a Cosmopolitan Liberal Politics, 1950–1972* (Chicago: University of Chicago Press, 2014), 249.

8.   David Harvey, *The Urban Experience* (Baltimore: Johns Hopkins University Press, 1989), 37–38.

9.   Frederick M. Wirt, *Power in the City: Decision Making in San Francisco* (Berkeley: University of California Press, 1974), 56–63, 131.

10. "San Francisco Mayor Approves $11,865,000 Bonds for June 3 Vote," *Daily Bond Buyer* [DBB] 168, no. 20274 (January 24, 1958): 380; Jack Burby, "Mayor, Board Head for Bond Clash," *San Francisco Chronicle*, February 7, 1958, 2; Wirt, *Power in the City*, 133–35; San Francisco Board of Supervisors, *Journal of Proceedings*, April 2, 1956, 187.

11. Thus, a bland emphasis on "business elites" misses the particular power wielded by municipal bond financiers and their outsized ability to shape debt administration.

12. Art Hoppe, "The Man Who Controls the City," *San Francisco Chronicle*, April 26, 1960, 28.

13. "Ex-S.F. Controller Harry Ross Dies," *San Francisco Chronicle*, December 22, 1970, 14. For bankers, see "Plan San Francisco Bond Issue for Giants' New Baseball Stadium," *DBB* 168, no. 20286 (February 11, 1958): 710; "Approve Financing Plans for San Francisco Giants Stadium," *DBB* 168, no. 20308 (March 14, 1958): 1244; "Private Funds to Supply Portion of San Francisco Stadium Financing," *DBB* 168, no. 20311 (March 19, 1958): 1291. For the mode of financing, see William R. Shapiro, "Special Report on City Debt Management," ca. 1975–76, box 028, "Office of the Mayor San Francisco . . . Program & Budget Office 1976–77," folder "Bond Information," George Moscone Collection (MSS 328), University of the Pacific, 324–25; Alan K. Browne, "'Mr. Municipal Bond': Bond Investment Management, Bank of America, 1929–1971," oral history conducted in 1988 by Malca Chall, Regional Oral History Office, Bancroft Library, University of California, Berkeley, (1990), 206.

14. "San Francisco Agency Approves Contract for $4,500,000 Garage," *DBB* 168, no. 20336 (April 23, 1958): 1859.

15. Madeline Nelson, "Found! Six Million Dollars in Public Revenues Lying Idle in SF Banks," *San Francisco Bay Guardian* [*SFBG*], March 14, 1973, 7–8.

16. John Mapel, "The Edict from the Elite Bond Screening Committee," *SFBG*, November 1, 1972, 21.

17. "Christopher Picks New Bond Screening Group," *San Francisco Chronicle*, February 7, 1956, 2.

18. "Christopher Picks New Bond Screening Group"; "2 Bond Plans Okayed, Four Turned Down," *San Francisco Chronicle*, July 8, 1958, 1, 5.

19. San Francisco Unified School District, "1948 School Bond Building Program. Final Report," box 86, folder "1948 School Bond Building Program Final Report, 1956," San Francisco Unified School District Records, 1854–2005, SFH 3, San Francisco Public Library [SFPL], 3–4, 6; "Proposition B: A $5 Million Bond Issue to Provide for Hunters Point Schools. Information for Speakers and Others Interested in Passage of Proposition B," undated, box 18, folder "Proposition B, 2 of 2, 1969–1970," Joseph L. Alioto Papers, 1958–1977, SFH 5, SFPL, 2.

20. "2 Bond Plans Okayed, Four Turned Down," *San Francisco Chronicle*, July 8, 1958, 1, 5.

21. "San Francisco Mayor Approves $11,865,000 Bonds for June 3 Vote," *DBB* 168, no. 20274 (January 24, 1958): 380.

22. "San Francisco Bonds Approved in Piecemeal for June 3 Ballot," *DBB* 168, no. 20287 (February 13, 1958): 746.

23. "2 Bond Plans Okayed, Four Turned Down."

24. Peter Hann, "Bond Experts Revolt, Block 3 Big Issues," *San Francisco Chronicle*, June 30, 1961, 1, 2.

25. "Christopher Picks New Bond Screening Group."

26. Mapel, "The Edict from the Elite Bond Screening Committee."

27. Bruce Johnstone, Letter to Mayor Christopher, "Rapid Transit-Financing," April 2, 1956, box 3, series 2, folder "Bay Area Rapid Transit (BART), 1 of 3, 1956," George Christopher Papers, 1950–2000, SFH 7, SFPL [GCP]; Mayor Christopher, Letter to Bruce Johnstone, April 9, 1956, box 3, series 2, folder "Bay Area Rapid Transit (BART), 1 of 3, 1956," GCP.

28. Marin E. Lewis, Letter to Charles R. Blyth, June 19, 1953, box 1, series 1, folder "Bay Area Rapid Transit (BART) Commission, 1951–56," Elmer E. Robinson Papers, 1935–1982, SFH 6, SFPL; San Francisco Bay Area Rapid Transit Commission [BARTC], "Report to the Legislature of the State of California," December 1957, box 3, series 2, Folder "BART Reference Materials 2 of 2, 1956–57," GCP; Richard Grefe and Richard Smart, *A History of the Key Decisions in the Development of Bay Area Rapid Transit: BART Impact Program* (San Francisco, CA: McDonald & Smart, 1975), 11–14, 22, 64.

29. Johnstone, Letter to Christopher, "Rapid Transit-Financing."

30. Christopher, Letter to Johnstone.

31. Chester Hartman, *City for Sale: The Transformation of San Francisco* (Berkeley: University of California Press, 2002), 8–11. For notable moments in the history of Blyth & Co., see *The Blyth Story: Fifty Years of Investment Banking, 1914–1964* (San Francisco: Blyth & Co., 1964), 1, 28, 30, 33, 51, 77.

32. "Dignitaries at Rites for Charles Blyth," *San Francisco Chronicle*, August 29, 1959, 13; Hartman, *City for Sale*, 9.

33. Alan K. Browne, Letter to E. R. Stallings, San Mateo County Manager, March 27, 1957, box 3, series 2, folder "BART, 2 of 3, 1956–57," GCP.

34. BARTC, "Report to the Legislature," 16–17.

35. Stone & Youngberg, "Rapid Transit for the Bay Area: A Summary of Engineering, Financial and Economic Reports Submitted to the San Francisco Bay Area Rapid Transit District," October 1961, 7.

36. Smith, Barney & Co. "Financial Report on Proposed San Francisco Bay Area Rapid Transit System," June 1961, folder "S.F. Transit, Rapid. Financial Report on Proposed BART System, 1961," Ephemera Collection, S.F. Transit, Rapid, SFPL, 50, 24.

37. Proposition B: Airport Bonds, "City and County Propositions to Be Voted on at the General Election," November 6, 1956, 8–13, https://sfpl.org/pdf /main/gic/elections/November6_1956.pdf.

38. San Francisco Redevelopment Agency and the Department of City Planning, "A Report to the Board of Supervisors: Redevelopment in Diamond Heights," March 1950, 4.

39. San Francisco Department of City Planning, "Census Tract Totals for San Francisco, 1960," Technical Monograph 61.1, February 16, 1961), 1–2.

40. Wirt, *Power in the City*, 19; Richard Walker, "Industry Builds Out the City: The Suburbanization of Manufacturing in the San Francisco Bay Area, 1850–1940" (2004), http://geog.berkeley.edu/PeopleHistory/faculty/R_Walker /IndustryBuildsOut.pdf.

41. San Francisco Department of City Planning, "Modernizing Downtown San Francisco," (January 1955), 5–7; Donald L. Foley, "The Suburbanization of Administrative Offices in the San Francisco Bay Area," Research Report 10, Real Estate Research Program, Bureau of Business and Economic Research, University of California (1957).

42. Wirt, *Power in the City*, 33.

43. San Francisco Department of City Planning, "Modernizing Downtown San Francisco," 2, 5.

44. "Store Sales Fell in Week," *Wall Street Journal*, April 11, 1961, 3.

45. "Macy's California Store," *Wall Street Journal*, September 7, 1962, 22.

46. San Francisco Redevelopment Agency [SFRA], "San Francisco Redevelopment Program: Summary of Project Data and Key Elements" (1977), 1–3.

47. SFRA and San Francisco Department of City Planning, "Diamond Heights: A Report on the Tentative Redevelopment Plan" (November 1951; revised March 5, 1952), 4, 61–62.

48. SFRA, "Commercial Development in the Golden Gateway, San Francisco" (May 1, 1963), 6.

49. San Francisco City Planning Commission, "New City: San Francisco Redeveloped" (1948).

50. "San Francisco Bonds to Complete Freeway Program Suggested," *Daily Bond Buyer* 168, no. 20268 (January 16, 1958): 218.

51. San Francisco Department of City Planning, "Modernizing Downtown San Francisco," 16, 30.

52. M. H. De Young Memorial Museum, Education Department, "Annual Report" (1959), 1–2.

53. "Official Report to the Bond Buyer: San Francisco, CAL.," *DBB* 172, no. 20806 (March 9, 1960): 850; "Plan San Francisco Bond Issue for Giants' New Baseball Stadium," *DBB* 168, no. 20286 (February 11, 1958): 710; "Cost of San Francisco Giant Stadium Higher Than Expected," *DBB* 168, no. 20319 (March 31, 1958): 1485.

54. Proposition B: Airport Bonds, "City and County Propositions," 8–13.

55. John J. Rosen, "Guardians of the Black Working Class: Labor and Racial Politics in Postwar San Francisco" (Ph.D. diss., University of Illinois, Chicago, 2014), 153–58, 173.

56. Editorial, *San Francisco Chronicle*, November 6, 1958, 36.

57. Earl C. Behrens, "City Row over Bond Loss; GOP Gloomy, Ike Confident," *San Francisco Chronicle*, November 5, 1953, 1.

58. Ray Leavitt, "Reaction to Bond Defeats: Muni May Abandon Conversion Plans," *San Francisco Chronicle*, November 5, 1953, 6.

59. John H. Maher, letter to the editor, *San Francisco Chronicle*, November 10, 1953, 18.

60. Jack Burby, "5 Lost Bond Projects Kept Alive," *San Francisco Chronicle*, November 6, 1958, 1, 5.

61. Editorial, *San Francisco Chronicle*, November 6, 1958, 36.

62. Scott was a researcher for the Bureau of Public Administration at the University of California, Berkeley. He provided a fascinating comparative example of local bond financing in Toronto, where, he said, officials "can float a bond issue without any election at all. The metropolitan council considers the question, and, if it approves, passes the bond proposals by a simple majority. The bonds are then given a searching scrutiny by the Ontario Municipal Board, a provincial (state) reviewing body. If the Ontario Municipal Board says yes, the bonds are ready for the market. Toronto has issued bonds to finance a subway, a new highway system, a new waterworks and a sewage disposal system. It has expanded its parks, initiated an urban development program and made many other public improvements." What's more, bondmen spoke highly of Toronto's credit profile. For Scott, the answer was not doing away "completely with electoral approval of bond proposals," but rather "reducing the 2-to-1 requirement to a simple majority vote." Stanley Scott, letter to the editor, *San Francisco Chronicle*, November 13, 1958, 38.

63. "'Hurry Up and Do It Wrong,'" *San Francisco Chronicle*, February 13, 1958, 34.

64. Mel Wax, "Mayor Maps Fight for Art Collection," *San Francisco Chronicle*, September 11, 1958, 4.

65. "Palace of Fine Arts as Investment in Beauty," *San Francisco Chronicle*, October 22, 1958, 30.

66. "Fix Up the Auditorium," *San Francisco Chronicle*, October 17, 1958, 32.

67. Proposition B: Palace of Fine Arts Bonds, "Propositions, Arguments, and Statements of Controller . . . to be voted on at General Election" (November 4, 1958), 13–14, https://sfpl.org/pdf/main/gic/elections/November4_1958.pdf.

68. John C. Becket, "San Francisco's Proposed Interurban Transit System," reprinted from *Electrical Engineering*, published by the American Institute of Electrical Engineers, June 1956, box 3, series 2, folder "Bay Area Rapid Transit (BART), 1 of 3, 1956," GCP, 1.

69. Becket, "San Francisco's Proposed Interurban Transit System," 1.

70. Alvin Guthertz, Letter to Mayor Christopher, April 2, 1957, box 3, series 2, folder "BART, 3 of 3, 1957," GCP.

71. Milton Raasch, Letter to Mayor Christopher, April 3, 1957, box 3, series 2, folder "BART, 3 of 3, 1957," GCP.

72. Douglas Hayward, Letter to Mayor Christopher, April 2, 1957, box 3, series 2, folder "BART, 3 of 3, 1957," GCP.

73. Marjorie Kelley, Letter to Mayor Christopher, April 3, 1957, box 3, series 2, folder "BART, 3 of 3, 1957," GCP.

74. Warren Northwood, Letter to Mayor Christopher, April 2, 1957, box 3, series 2, folder "BART, 3 of 3, 1957," GCP.

75. Proposition B: Palace of Fine Arts Bonds, "Propositions, Arguments, and Statements," 15.

76. Proposition C: Ferry Park Bonds, "Propositions, Arguments, and State-

ments of Controller . . . to be voted on at General Election" (November 4, 1958), 16–18, https://sfpl.org/pdf/main/gic/elections/November4_1958.pdf.

77. Roland I. Robinson, *Postwar Market for State and Local Government Securities*, (Princeton, NJ: Princeton University Press, 1960), 158, 180–89.

78. Proposition A: School Bonds, and Proposition B: Airport Bonds, "City and County Propositions," 7, 12; Sylvia Porter, "We Okayed Bond Issues but Will They Sell?" *San Francisco Chronicle*, November 14, 1956, 23.

79. Porter, "We Okayed Bond Issues but Will They Sell?".

80. Wade S. Smith, "Sound Financing for Sound Municipal Credit," *Municipal Finance* 29, no. 3 (February 1957): 121.

81. David M. Ellinwood, "Preparing Municipal Bonds for Sale," *Municipal Finance* 20, no. 1 (August 1947): 60.

82. For more, see Destin Jenkins, "Bonded Metropolis: Race, Infrastructure, and the Search for Capital in San Francisco, 1900–1976," (Ph.D. diss., Stanford University, 2016), especially chapter 1.

83. "Request $384 Million San Francisco Projects for Next Five Years," *DBB* 168, no. 20292 (February 20, 1958): 851.

84. "San Francisco, CAL. (City and County)" under "Proposed Bond Issues," *DBB* 168, no. 20298 (February 28, 1958): 1000.

85. "San Francisco May Consider $139 Million Bonds Next Four Years," *DBB* 172, no. 20781 (February 1, 1960): 365.

86. "Current Financial Reports and New Literature on Public Finance," *DBB* 168, no. 20274 (January 24, 1958): 399.

87. "San Francisco Plans Expansion Program at International Airport," *DBB* 172, no. 20762 (January 5, 1960): 18; "San Francisco Airport Traffic Up 26% in Dec.," *DBB* 172, no. 20787 (February 9, 1960): 483. For broader attempts by the *DBB* to convince lenders on the investment merits of revenue bonds and the financial feasibility of the projects themselves, see the reporting on Seattle's Department of Lighting, the Southeast Alabama Gas District, and the Dallas–Fort Worth Turnpike, among other examples, in "Revenue Bond Reports," *DBB* 172, no. 20822 (March 31, 1960): 1148.

88. "Cost of San Francisco Giant Stadium Higher Than Expected." See also "The Candlestick Swindle," *SFBG*, May 14, 1968, 1, 6, 10, 14.

Chapter Four

1. The first phase of the Western Addition project had multiple, overlapping designations. The SFRA referred to the project as "A-1," but the San Francisco Board of Supervisors and others referred to it as "Project No. UR Calif. 2-2." Joseph L. Alioto, "NOTICE OF SALE OF PRELIMINARY LOAN NOTES OF Redevelopment Agency of the City and County of San Francisco," *Daily Bond Buyer* [DBB] 168, no. 20447 (September 30, 1958): 1035. See also San Francisco Board of Supervisors, *Journal of Proceedings*,

January 17, 1955; Robert F. Oaks, *San Francisco's Fillmore District* (Charleston, SC: Arcadia, 2005), 90.

2. "Housing Authorities Notes (Preliminary) Sold," *DBB* 169, no. 20466 (October 28, 1958): 1340.

3. "Notice of Sale of Local Public Housing Agency Temporary Notes," *DBB* 172, no. 20782 (February 2, 1960): 393–95.

4. San Francisco Redevelopment Agency [SFRA], "Information for Residents of Western Addition Area 2" (April 1967), 1; SFRA, "You and Your Housing: Information for Residents of Western Addition A-2" (July 1968), 4–7. Both contained in "Western Addition Redevelopment Miscellaneous Documents," Volume II: 1965–1994, San Francisco Public Library; Chauncey Bailey, "Redevelopment's Squeeze on Fillmore Merchants," *Sun Reporter* [*SR*], September 29, 1973, 10.

5. Brian J. Godfrey, *Neighborhoods in Transition: The Making of San Francisco's Ethnic and Nonconformist Communities* (Berkeley: University of California Press, 1988), 95, 101–2.

6. Mark Brilliant, *The Color of America has Changed: How Racial Diversity Shaped Civil Rights Reform in California, 1941–1978* (New York: Oxford University Press, 2010), 143; *Banks v. San Francisco Housing Authority*, 120 Cal. App. 2d 1 (1953); *Housing Authority of City and County of San Francisco v. Banks*, 347 US 974 (February 8, 1954), 5; Richard Reinhardt, "S.F. Segregation in Housing to End," *San Francisco Chronicle*, May 25, 1954, 1.

7. Amy Lynne Howard, *More Than Shelter: Activism and Community in San Francisco Public Housing* (Minneapolis: University of Minnesota Press, 2014), 73, 164–65.

8. R. Joseph Monsen, "Who Owns the City? Data and Implications from San Francisco Experience," *Land Economics* 37, no. 2 (May 1961): 174–78.

9. Council for Civic Unity, *Open or Closed?* Daniel E. Koshland San Francisco History Center, San Francisco Public Library [SFPL], 9, 15, 21–29.

10. "'Goodbye Slums, Hello Corruption,'" *SR*, July 23, 1960, 5.

11. Albert S. Broussard, *Black San Francisco: The Struggle for Racial Equality in the West, 1900–1954* (Lawrence: University of Kansas Press, 1993), 132.

12. SFRA, "The Effect of Redevelopment on Residents and Property Owners in Western Addition Project Number One" (October 10, 1952), 5.

13. SFRA and San Francisco Department of City Planning, "The Tentative Plan for the Redevelopment of Western Addition Project Area Number One" (November 13, 1952), 7, 9.

14. John Baranski, *Housing the City by the Bay: Tenant Activism, Civil Rights, and Class Politics in San Francisco* (Stanford, CA: Stanford University Press, 2019), chapter 2.

15. "Tax Exempts: Terms of First Public Housing Bond Issue," *Wall Street Journal*, June 14, 1951, 10.

16. Public Housing Administration, "General Covenants and Conditions Comprising Part Two of Amended Contract for Financial Assistance between

Local Authority and Public Housing Administration (1947), 6; Moody's Investors Service, *Moody's Municipal & Government Manual* (New York: Moody's Investors Service, 1955), 1616–19.

17. Moody's Investors Service, *Moody's Municipal & Government Manual*, 1615–17.

18. San Francisco Housing Authority [SFHA], *Fourteenth Annual Report* (1952), 3.

19. United Statistical Associates [USA], *Municipal Holdings of Insurance Companies* (New York: United Statistical Associates, 1955), n.p. Columbia University's Lehman Library contains volumes of this series for 1955–58. *Municipal Holdings* listed the terms and holders of both *new* housing authority bonds and local housing authority debt issued under the Housing Act of 1937. I chose to focus on the former. I examined the par value, years of maturity, and yields secured by holders of new SFHA bonds. However, holdings from around the country are also illuminating.

20. USA, *Municipal Holdings* 1955, 99, and 1956, 98.

21. USA, *Municipal Holdings* 1956, 18, 43, 162.

22. USA, *Municipal Holdings* 1956, 98, 442.

23. USA, *Municipal Holdings* 1956, 98.

24. USA, *Municipal Holdings* 1957, 99.

25. USA, *Municipal Holdings* 1958, 114. The 1958 volume lists the Ohio Farmers Indemnity Company and Ohio Farmers Insurance Company as one and the same.

26. Keeanga-Yamahtta Taylor, *Race for Profit: How Banks and the Real Estate Industry Undermined Black Homeownership* (Chapel Hill: University of North Carolina Press, 2019), 75.

27. SFHA, *Second Annual Report* (1940), 15, and *Third Annual Report* (1941), 12.

28. San Francisco Area Description, D-15, Robert K. Nelson, LaDale Winling, Richard Marciano, Nathan Connolly, et al., "Mapping Inequality," in *American Panorama*, ed. Robert K. Nelson and Edward L. Ayers, https://dsl.richmond.edu/panorama/redlining/#loc=4/36.71/-96.93&opacity=0.8&text=intro.

29. Ocean Howell, *Making the Mission: Planning and Ethnicity in San Francisco* (Chicago: University of Chicago Press, 2015), 166–67.

30. Nathan Straus, *The Seven Myths of Housing* (New York: Knopf, 1944), 189.

31. Paul Heffernan, "Popularity Rises for Municipals," *New York Times*, May 31, 1959, F1.

32. "Long Term Issues Postponed by PHA," *Washington Post*, June 7, 1957, B4; "PHA Won't Sell Bonds This Summer Unless Market Gets Better," *Wall Street Journal*, June 7, 1957, 11.

33. Steven H. Jaffe and Jessica Lautin, *Capital of Capital: Money, Banking, and Power in New York City, 1784–2012* (New York: Columbia University Press, 2014), 194–202; "Public Housing Unit May Get Only One Bid for $104.8 Million Bonds," *Wall Street Journal*, May 20, 1959, 21.

34. Untitled document, April 26, 1965, carton 2, folder "BOA Corres . . . 1936–71," Alan K. Browne Papers (BANC MSS 91/6), Bancroft Library, University of California, Berkeley [AKBP], n.p.

35. SFHA, "Authority Short Term Notes to N.Y. Groups; Interest Rates Are Up," *San Francisco Housing Authority News* 4, no. 1 (January 1947), n.p.; SFHA, "HA Saves $9,357 on Short Term Notes," *San Francisco Housing Authority News* 2. no. 2 (January 1945): 1; SFHA, "Award SFHA Loan Notes to N.Y. Group at Premium," *San Francisco Housing Authority News* 3, no. 1 (January 1946), n.p.

36. "Local Renewal Agencies Sell $110,973,000 of Notes," *Wall Street Journal*, June 1, 1962, 17; Lizabeth Cohen, *A Consumers' Republic: The Politics of Mass Consumption in Postwar America* (New York: Vintage, 2003); Louis Hyman, *Debtor Nation: The History of America in Red Ink* (Princeton, NJ: Princeton University Press, 2011), 170.

37. To draw another contrast, the federal government placed a 6 percent interest ceiling on new housing authority bonds. Long-term debt for public housing came with interest rate caps; short-term debt did not. "Rate Restrictions on Urban Renewal Notes Limit Acceptable Bids to About $54 Million," *DBB* 197, no. 22427 (August 17, 1966): 581–82; Ivan Silverman, "The Bond Market: Housing Issue Breaks a Two-Year-Old Curse; All of It Is Bid For," *Wall Street Journal*, January 28, 1971, 21.

38. Alan K. Browne, Memorandum to T. A. Griffinger, "Municipal Bond Underwriting," July 23, 1965, carton 2, folder "BOA Correspondence, 1963–1973/Bank of America NT & SA," AKBP, 1; Michael H. Hopewell and George G. Kaufman, "Costs to Municipalities of Selling Bonds by NIC," *National Tax Journal* 27, no. 4 (December 1974), 532; Michael D. Joehnk and David S. Kidwell, "The Impact of Market Uncertainty on Municipal Bond Underwriter Spread," *Financial Management* 13, no. 1 (Spring 1984), 38.

39. Alan K. Browne, Memorandum to Bank Investment Securities Division, "December 31, 1965 Securities Holding Targets," September 30, 1965, carton 2, folder "BOA Correspondence, 1963–1973/Bank of America NT & SA," AKBP, n.p.

40. SFHA, "Twenty-Eighth Annual Report" (1965), 11, 14.

41. SFRA, "San Francisco Redevelopment Program: Summary of Project Data and Key Elements" (1977).

42. Project boundaries derived from "Finding Aid to the San Francisco Redevelopment Agency Records, 1948–2012," SFH 371, San Francisco History Center, San Francisco Public Library, 3–5, http://pdf.oac.cdlib.org/pdf/csf/sfpl/SFH_371_ead.pdf.

43. This description of preliminary/temporary loan note financing is derived from William L. Slayton, "The Operation and Achievements of the Urban Renewal Program," in *Urban Renewal: The Record and the Controversy*, ed. James Q. Wilson (Cambridge, MA: MIT Press, 1966), 200; "Officials of Urban Renewal Administration Await Big Note Sale with Uneasy Optimism,"

DBB 197, no. 22426 (August 16, 1966): 565, 580. As for the temporary loan notes, the notes stood at the center of a financial web of reimbursements. Redevelopment agencies entered into a contract with the federal government for a specific urban renewal project. The federal government mandated that the interest rates on notes be no higher than that specified in the contract. When redevelopment agencies issued notes, they borrowed from bond financiers who, in turn, supplied working capital. Through the redevelopment agency, the federal government guaranteed tax-exempt interest payments to the holders of notes. For the outlines of this financial web of reimbursements, see "New Watertown Renewal Agency May Borrow over Bond Limit," *DBB* 197, no. 22397 (July 6, 1966): 43; "Johnson Wants Congress to Check Interest War; Over-Limit Bids Curb Urban Renewal Financing," *DBB* 197, no. 22403 (July 14, 1966): 149, 151; Thomas J. Foley, "Housing Stymied: U.S. Halts Calif. Renewal Funds," *Los Angeles Times*, November 11, 1964, 1.

44. Housing and Home Finance Agency [HHFA], *Thirteenth Annual Report* (1959), 269.

45. Joseph C. [*sic*] Alioto, "NOTICE OF SALE OF PRELIMINARY LOAN NOTES OF Redevelopment Agency of the City and County of San Francisco," *DBB* 168, no. 20403 (July 29, 1958): 330–31.

46. Table VII-3, "Summary of Financial Assistance for Urban Renewal Projects, 1950–1961" in HHFA, *Fifteenth Annual Report* (1961), 301.

47. HHFA, *Twelfth Annual Report* (1958), 261.

48. SFRA and San Francisco Department of City Planning, "A Report to the Board of Supervisors: Redevelopment in Diamond Heights" (March 1950), 3, 4, 7, 9.

49. Real Estate Research Corporation and San Francisco Department of City Planning, "Summary of Market Analysis, Redevelopment Area 'E,' San Francisco, California" (May 1956), 8; SFRA, "Annual Report to Mayor George Christopher for the Fiscal Year for the Year July 1, 1960 to June 30, 1961," 7.

50. SFRA, "In the Golden Gateway: The Time Is Now: Residents, Business Men, Property Owners," (February 15, 1960).

51. San Francisco Board of Supervisors, *Journal of Proceedings* 50, no. 1 (October 10, 1955): 706.

52. SFRA, "In the Golden Gateway." Emphasis in original.

53. SFRA, "Annual Report to Mayor George Christopher for the Fiscal Year for the Year July 1, 1961 to June 30, 1962," 5, 6.

54. John H. Mollenkopf, *The Contested City* (Princeton, NJ: Princeton University Press, 1983), 153–54.

55. Comptroller General of the United States, "A Report to the Congress of the United States: Review of Slum Clearance and Urban Renewal Activities of the San Francisco Regional Office, Housing and Home Finance Agency" (July 1960), 5, 13–16.

56. *Take This Hammer*, directed by Richard O. Moore (San Francisco, CA: KQED-Film, 1964), https://vimeo.com/13175192; *The Negro and the American Promise*, produced by Henry Morgenthau III (Boston: WGBH, 1963).

57. Testimonies of John A. Hannah and Justin Herman, US Commission on Civil Rights, "Hearings before the United States Commission on Civil Rights, Los Angeles and San Francisco 1960" (Washington, DC: Government Printing Office, 1960) 2, 534–35. Hereafter, "CCR hearing."

58. N. D. B. Connolly, *A World More Concrete: Real Estate and the Remaking of Jim Crow South Florida* (Chicago: University of Chicago Press, 2014), 142.

59. Testimony of Justin Herman, CCR hearing, 538.

60. Testimony of Frank Quinn, CCR hearing, 549.

61. Testimony of Tarea Hall Pittman, CCR hearing, 701.

62. "'Goodbye Slums, Hello Corruption.'"

63. Elizabeth Pepin and Lewis Watts, *Harlem of the West: The San Francisco Fillmore Jazz Era* (San Francisco: Chronicle Books, 2005), 38, 51, 65, 72, 118.

64. Wade Woods, "The Decline of an Urban Community: What Happened to the Fillmore Center?" *SR*, March 3, 1977, 4.

65. Paul T. Miller, *The Postwar Struggle for Civil Rights: African Americans in San Francisco, 1945–1975* (New York: Routledge, 2010), 32–33, 40, 42.

66. "'Goodbye Slums, Hello Corruption.'"

67. Testimony of Justin Herman, CCR hearing, 534, 537.

68. Testimony of Frank Quinn, CCR hearing, 551–53.

69. Justin Herman, quoted in Richard Brandi, "San Francisco's Diamond Heights: Urban Renewal and the Modernist City," *Journal of Planning History* 12, no. 2 (2012): 144.

70. Testimony of Justin Herman, CCR hearing, 539.

71. "'Goodbye Slums, Hello Corruption.'"

72. Testimony of Tarea Hall Pittman, CCR hearing, 701–2.

73. SFRA, "Annual Report to Mayor George Christopher for the Fiscal Year July 1, 1959 to June 30, 1960," 16.

74. SFRA, "Annual Report to Mayor George Christopher for the Fiscal Year July 1, 1961 to June 30, 1962," 5.

75. SFRA, "San Francisco Redevelopment Program: Summary of Project Data and Key Elements," 15.

76. Connolly, *A World More Concrete*, 184.

77. SFRA, "San Francisco Redevelopment Program," 24–25.

78. Charles W. Mills, *Black Rights, White Wrongs: The Critique of Racial Liberalism* (New York: Oxford University Press, 2017), 127.

79. National Association of Real Estate Boards, "Practical Urban Renewal in San Francisco" (1962), 9, 10, 14.

80. Justin Herman, Letter to Harry D. Ross, July 3, 1961, box 2, folder "Hunters Point Redevelopment, 1961–1966," John F. "Jack" Shelley Papers, 1953–1967, SFH 10, SFPL, 1; Jim Leonard, "Hunters Point Public Auction Shellacked," *S.F. News Call Bulletin*, July 24, 1962.

81. San Francisco Board of Supervisors, "Declaring Policy Affecting Hunters Point War Housing Projects," December 13, 1965, box 2, folder "Hunters Point Redevelopment, 1961–1966," John F. "Jack" Shelley Papers, 1953–1967, SFH 10, SFPL, 1.

82. SFHA, *Twentieth Annual Report* (1958), 4.

83. Public Housing Administration, "Open Occupancy in Housing Programs of the Public Housing Administration," no. 9 as of March 31, 1960, iii, 9, 13, 22, 48.

84. Robert Moore Fisher, *20 Years of Public Housing: Economic Aspects of the Federal Program* (New York: Harper & Brothers, 1959), 257–58.

Chapter Five

1. Lyndon B. Johnson, "The Great Society," commencement address at the University of Michigan (May 22, 1964), 230–31; Robin Muncy, "Coal-Fired Reforms: Social Citizenship, Dissident Miners, and the Great Society," *Journal of American History* 96, no. 1 (June 2009): 72–98; Robert M. Collins, *More: The Politics of Economic Growth in Postwar America* (New York: Oxford University Press, 2000), 59; Mark Krasovic, *The Newark Frontier: Community Action in the Great Society* (Chicago: University of Chicago Press, 2016), 2–3.

2. Joint Economic Committee, Subcommittee on Economic Progress, "State and Local Public Facility Needs and Financing: Volume II," 89th Cong., 2nd sess., December 1966, 6–8.

3. Lyndon B. Johnson, Message from the President of the United States, "Problems and Future of the Central City and Its Suburbs," House of Representatives, 89th Cong., 1st sess., March 2, 1965, 1–4.

4. Testimony of Mayor Joseph Alioto before the Committee on Banking and Currency, Subcommittee on Financial Institutions, "Financial Institutions and the Urban Crisis," 90th Cong., 2nd sess., September 30 and October 1–4, 1968, 35–36.

5. Johnson, "Problems and Future of the Central City and Its Suburbs," 1–4.

6. Joint Economic Committee, Subcommittee on Economic Progress, "Financing Municipal Facilities: Volume I," 90th Cong., 1st sess., December 5–7, 1967, 2.

7. Statement of William B. Camp before the Joint Economic Committee, Subcommittee on Economic Progress, "Financing Municipal Facilities: Volume II," 90th Cong., 2nd sess., July 9–11, 1968, 304.

8. Collins, *More*, 59; James T. Patterson, *America's Struggle against Poverty in the Twentieth Century* (Cambridge, MA: Harvard University Press, 2000), 109–10; Maurice Isserman and Michael Kazin, *America Divided: The Civil War of the 1960s*, 4th ed. (New York: Oxford University Press, 2012), 181, 213; Collins, *More*, 72; Keeanga-Yamahtta Taylor, *Race for Profit: How Banks*

and the Real Estate Industry Undermined Black Homeownership (Chapel Hill: University of North Carolina Press, 2019), 60.

9. "U.S. Chamber Opposes CFA Expansion Senate Measure," *Daily Bond Buyer* [*DBB*] 168, no. 20318 (March 28, 1958): 1477.

10. Gordon L. Calvert, "Federal Loan Programs Not Needed," reprinted in *DBB* 168, no. 20368 (June 9, 1958): 4, 8, 10.

11. "U.S. Chamber Opposes CFA Expansion Senate Measure"; "Business Leaders Warned of Federal URBiculture Control," *DBB* 168, no. 20310 (March 18, 1958): 1270.

12. "IBA Opposes Federal Funds for Low Cost Local Financing," *DBB* 168, no. 20359 (May 26, 1958): 2439.

13. "HHFA Administrator Cole Calls Expanded CFA Bill Undesirable," *DBB* 168, no. 20352 (May 15, 1958): 2262, 2282.

14. Frederick M. Wirt, *Power in the City: Decision Making in San Francisco* (Berkeley: University of California Press, 1974), 277–89.

15. "Patman Seeks Law to Curtail Banks' Municipal Buying," *DBB* 172, no. 20791 (February 16, 1960): 553, 583.

16. "Patman Urges Federal Agency be Established to Purchase Municipals," *DBB* 172, no. 20821 (March 30, 1960): 1121–22. For Wright Patman's New Deal roots, see Earl Black and Merle Black, *The Rise of Southern Republicans* (Cambridge, MA: Harvard University Press), 196.

17. Wright Patman, statement before the Joint Economic Committee, Subcommittee on Economic Progress, "Financing Municipal Facilities: Volume I," 90th Cong., 1st sess., December 5–7, 1967, 103–4. In the late 1950s Patman proposed low-interest direct federal loans to cities to circumvent bankers. With the Municipal Capital Market Expansion Act of 1968 Patman sought to remedy the "limited supply of private capital" and "failings" of rating agencies. He struck a middle ground. On the one hand, the legislation would have turned the federal government into a clearinghouse for information for underwriting banks—implying a continued role for financiers. On the other hand, he did not entertain their concerns about the threat of federal grants, which municipal governments could use to keep down interest costs. Most controversial, the federal government would guarantee all municipal bonds, essentially lending its credit to all municipal borrowers. Patman sought to eliminate confounding price differentials between bonds of similar credit by granting all borrowers, regardless of size and credit reputation, the sterling credit rating of the US government. See Patman's bill, H.R. 15991, "a bill to establish a Government corporation to assist in the expansion of the capital market for municipal securities," 90th Cong., 2nd sess., March 14, 1968. Wisconsin Senator William Proxmire proposed a similar version (S. 3170) on the same date.

18. "IBA Municipal Conference: Federal Aid Surpasses Volume of Tax-free Municipal Financing," *DBB* 198, no. 22471 (October 20, 1966): 225, 256.

19. "Grants and Loans Approved by Federal Agencies for Public Works and

Urban Renewal Programs," *DBB* 190, no. 21976 (October 30, 1964): 418; "Grants and Loans Approved by Federal Agencies for Public Works and Urban Renewal Programs," *DBB* 190, no. 21987 (November 18, 1964): 670.

20. "Humphrey to Bring Some Novel Ideas into Financing of Anti-Poverty Program," *DBB* 190, no. 22005 (December 15, 1964): 1045, 1059.

21. Odette Lineau, *Rethinking Sovereign Debt: Politics, Reputation, and Legitimacy in Modern Finance* (Cambridge, MA: Harvard University Press, 2014).

22. "Browne Honored at San Francisco Bond Club Meeting," *DBB* 168, no. 20376 (June 19, 1958): 2038.

23. Investment Bankers Association of America, *IBA Statistical Bulletin: A Survey of the Municipal Bond Market*, no. 4 (July 1957), 10; no. 9 (October 1958), 7, 10.

24. Exhibit C—California Municipal Bond Underwriting—1960 General Obligation Bonds in Committee on Banking and Currency, "Increased Flexibility for Financial Institutions," 88th Cong., 1st sess., September 23–30, October 1–3, 7–11, November 6–7, and December 10–11 and 13, 1963, 883.

25. Bank Investment Securities Division, "Management Plan," August 14, 1967, carton 2, folder "BOA Corres . . . 1936–71," Alan K. Browne Papers (DANC MSS 91/6), Bancroft Library, University of California, Berkeley [AKBP], n.p.

26. "Men on $pot for Inve$tment$," *Finance Magazine* (August 1965), 4–5.

27. Alan K. Browne, Memorandum to T. A. Griffinger, "Municipal Bond Underwriting," July 23, 1965, carton 2, folder "BOA Correspondence, 1963–1973/ Bank of America NT & SA," AKBP, 1, 2.

28. Untitled document, April 26, 1965, carton 2, folder "BOA Corres . . . 1936–71," AKBP, n.p.

29. The handwritten note at the bottom dates the source to November 21, 1960, but this is a mistake: the panelists dealt with the fiscal troubles of 1966. Statement of Thomas L. Ray contained in Fourth Municipal Conference of the Investment Bankers' Association of America, "The Cost-Profit Squeeze," carton 2, folder "Misc. Paper Clippings, S.F. Chamber of Commerce, S.F. Bond Club," AKBP, 40. For Texas municipal bondmen, see John Racine, "Tinsley: A Force Behind Texas's Bond Industry," *in The Bond Buyer: 100 Anniversary Edition: A Salute to the Municipal Bond Industry, 1891–1991*.

30. Glenn Cremer, Memorandum to Arthur J. Micheletti, "History of Out-of-State Municipal Underwriting Commitments," December 6, 1967, carton 2, folder "Memos & Reports: Investment Baking [*sic*], 1965–70," AKBP, n.p.

31. Alan K. Browne, Letter to Mr. C. E. Pierson, July 8, 1965, carton 2, folder "BOA Correspondence, 1963–1973/Bank of America NT & SA," AKBP, 4.

32. Lisa McGirr, *Suburban Warriors: The Origins of the New American Right* (Princeton, NJ: Princeton University Press, 2001), 25–28.

33. Andrew Needham, *Power Lines: Phoenix and the Making of the Modern Southwest* (Princeton, NJ: Princeton University Press, 2014).

34. Bank Investment Securities Division, "Management Plan," August 14, 1967, carton 2, folder "BOA Corres . . . 1936–71," AKBP, n.p.

35. Greta R. Krippner, *Capitalizing on Crisis: The Political Origins of the Rise of Finance* (Cambridge, MA: Harvard University Press, 2011), 60–68; Louis Hyman, *Debtor Nation: The History of America in Red Ink* (Princeton, NJ: Princeton University Press, 2011), 224.

36. "Bonds and the Public: a Rediscovery," *DBB* 197, no. 22400, (July 11, 1966): 106.

37. George H. Hempel, *The Postwar Quality of State and Local Debt* (New York: National Bureau of Economic Research, 1971), 133.

38. Testimony of Walter H. Tyler, "Financing Municipal Facilities: Volume II," 382.

39. "Paul Heffernan to Join the *Daily Bond Buyer*," *New York Times*, August 2, 1962, 35.

40. Paul Heffernan, "War on the Short-Term Interest Rates: Escalation, Expostulation, Frustration," *DBB* 197, no. 22409 (July 22, 1966): 257, 272.

41. "Tax-Exempt Bond Interest," *DBB* 197, no. 22420 (August 8, 1966): 474.

42. "Is There a Secondary Market?," *DBB* 197, no. 22435 (August 29, 1966): 734.

43. *Annual Report of the Controller of the City and County of San Francisco for the Fiscal Year Ended June 30, 1967*, (San Francisco, CA: Office of the Controller, 1967–68), 41–42, https://archive.org/details/annualreportofco1967sanf.

44. "Average Net Interest Cost on Bonds Sold, (Chart) 1950–51 to 1966–67," in *Annual Report of the Controller of the City and County of San Francisco for the Fiscal Year Ended June 30, 1967*, 17.

45. US Bureau of the Census, "City Government Finances in 1965–1966" (Washington, DC: Government Printing Office, 1966), 14, https://www2.census .gov/govs/pubs/city_govt_fin/1966.pdf; US Bureau of the Census, "City Government Finances in 1967–1968" (Washington, DC: Government Printing Office, 1968), 13, https://www2.census.gov/govs/pubs/city_govt_fin/1968 .pdf.

46. "Bay Area Transit Sets 41.7 Cent Rate for District," *DBB* 197, no. 22436 (August 30, 1966): 737.

47. US Bureau of the Census, "City Government Finances in 1965–1966," 14; US Bureau of the Census, "City Government Finances in 1967–1968," 13.

48. US Bureau of the Census, "City Government Finances in 1965–1966," 14; US Bureau of the Census, "City Government Finances in 1967–1968," 13.

49. "$240,507,000 Notes Offered . . . Eighty Housing Authorities Invite Bids," *DBB* 197, no. 22411 (July 26, 1966): 301–3, 305.

50. San Francisco Housing Authority, *Twenty-Ninth Annual Report* (1966), 1, 3–4.

51. "Hunters Pt. Rent Strike Threatened," *San Francisco Chronicle*, October 18, 1966, 34; "A Plan for Better Housing," *San Francisco Chronicle*, November 18, 1966, 5.

52. "Housing Notes Totaling $61,683,000 Awarded at Record 4.1063%," *Wall Street Journal*, July 14, 1966, 19; "Urban-Renewal Units Sell $102,883,000 Notes," *Wall Street Journal*, June 16, 1966, 25; "Johnson Wants Congress to

Check Interest War; Over-Limit Bids Curb Urban Renewal Financing," *DBB* 197, no. 22403 (July 14, 1966): 151.

53. "Officials of Urban Renewal Administration Await Big Note Sale with Uneasy Optimism," *DBB* 197, no. 22426 (August 16, 1966): 565.

54. "Notice of Sale . . . Urban Renewal $135,841,000 Preliminary Loan Notes," *DBB* 197, no. 22416 (August 2, 1966): 393–96. The *DBB* refers to these urban renewal projects as "UR Calif. 2–1," "Calif. R-7," and "Calif. R-54," respectively. R-7 was the Embarcadero–Lower Market, Golden Gateway project; R-54 was the Western Addition Area-2 urban renewal project. See San Francisco Board of Supervisors, *Journal of Proceedings*, January 11, 1960, 17; January 20,1964, 28; April 19, 1965, 204; and June 6, 1966, 417.

55. "Rate Restrictions on Urban Renewal Notes Limit Acceptable Bids to About $54 Million," *DBB* 197, no. 22427 (August 17, 1966), 581–82.

56. "Results of Bond Sales . . . District of Columbia," *DBB* 197, no. 22435 (August 29, 1966): 722–73; "Notice of Sale . . . Urban Renewal $135,841,000 Preliminary Loan Notes," *DBB* 197, no. 22416 (August 2, 1966): 393–96.

57. "Officials of Urban Renewal Administration Await Big Note Sale with Un easy Optimism," *DBB* 197, no. 22426 (August 16, 1966): 580.

58. "Officials of Urban Renewal Administration Await Big Note Sale with Uneasy Optimism," 565, 580; "Borrowing Costs Houston 4.128%; 2 Deals Canceled," *DBB* 197, no. 22403 (July 14, 1966): 149, 162; "4 Per Cent Limit Rules Out Bidding for Tulsa Bonds," *DBB* 197, no. 22427 (August 17, 1966): 581, 592; "Cleveland City District Rejects All Bids; Will Borrow Short Within Three Weeks," *DBB* 197, no. 22432 (August 24, 1966): 665, 682; "Boston Borrows $5 Mil. For 2 Months at 4.49%," *DBB* 197, no. 22433 (August 25, 1966): 700; "4½% Cost Limit Rules Out Sale of Baltimore Bonds," *DBB* 197, no. 22437 (August 31, 1966): 761, 786.

59. "Urban-Renewal Units Sell $102,883,000 Notes," *Wall Street Journal*, June 16, 1966, 25.

60. "Results of Bond Sales . . . District of Columbia," *DBB* 197, no. 22406 (July 19, 1966): 216–17.

61. BISD, BOA advertisement in *DBB* 197, no. 22410 (July 25, 1966): 278. See also BISD, BOA advertisement in *DBB* 197, no. 22435 (August 29, 1966): 721.

62. Timothy Wolters, "'Carry Your Credit in Your Pocket': The Early History of the Credit Card at Bank of America and Chase Manhattan," *Enterprise and Society* 1, no. 2 (2000): 315–54.

63. Richard R. West, "Determinants of Underwriter Spreads on Tax Exempt Bond Issues," *Journal of Financial and Quantitative Analysis* 2, no. 3 (September 1967), 243–46; Michael D. Joehnk and David S. Kidwell, "The Impact of Market Uncertainty on Municipal Bond Underwriter Spread," *Financial Management* 13, no. 1 (Spring 1984), 40–41.

64. Joint Economic Committee, Subcommittee on Economic Progress, "State and Local Public Facility Needs and Financing: Volume II," 9, 197.

65. "Profit Squeeze Called Symptom of Change at Opening of Third Municipal Conference," *DBB* 190, no. 21962 (October 9, 1964): 125, 140.

66. "Investment Banking Drop Is Reported as Warning for IBA Membership,"
     DBB 190, no. 21995 (December 1, 1964): 860.
67. Statement of Alan K. Browne at Fourth Municipal Conference of the
     Investment Bankers' Association of America, "The Cost-Profit Squeeze,"
     carton 2, folder "Misc. Paper Clippings, S.F. Chamber of Commerce, S.F.
     Bond Club," AKBP, 36.
68. Statement of Lloyd Hatchers at ibid., 38.
69. Statement of Anthony E. Tomasic at ibid., 39.
70. Statement of Thomas L. Ray at ibid., 40.
71. Statement of Alan K. Browne at ibid., 37.
72. Alan K. Browne, Memorandum to Samuel B. Stewart, July 12, 1967, car-
     ton 2, folder "BOA Correspondence, 1963–1973/Bank of America NT & SA,"
     AKBP, 1.
73. "Is There a Secondary Market?," 734.
74. Mary R. Ciarlo, "Obligations of States and Political Subdivisions Held by
     100 Largest Banks," *DBB* 198, no. 22489 (November 17, 1966): 630–31.
75. "Is There a Secondary Market?," 734.
76. "85 Per Cent of State and Municipal Bonds in California Underwritten by
     Local Banks," *DBB* 198, no. 22484 (November 9, 1966): 481.
77. Bank Investment Securities Division, "Management Plan," n.p.
78. Ciarlo, "Obligations of States and Political Subdivisions," 630–31.
79. "Chicago Municipal Bond Club Holds 30th Annual Field Day," *DBB* 197,
     no. 22447 (September 15, 1966): 950.
80. "Costs Not Likely to Check Financing on Tax-Exempts, Halsey, Stuart
     Finds," *DBB* 197, no. 22399 (July 8, 1966): 87.

Chapter Six

1. "Two San Francisco Issues Of $192 Mil. Recommended By Screening Com-
    mittee," *Daily Bond Buyer* [*DBB*] 197, no. 22402 (July 13, 1966): 134; "Finance
    Panel OK's $192 Mil. Bond Vote for San Francisco," *DBB* 197. no. 22406
    (July 19, 1966): 201, 220; "San Francisco Vote on $192 Mil. Bonds Slated for
    Nov. 8th," *DBB* 197, no. 22408 (July 21, 1966): 241–42.
2. "'No' Vote by Negroes on Bond Issues Asked in San Francisco," *DBB* 198,
    no. 22478 (October 31, 1966): 357, 369.
3. See, for instance, "Boycott and Public Finance," *DBB* 190, no. 22009 (De-
    cember 21, 1964): 1138; "Two Civil Rights Groups Back Oct. 4th Bond Issue
    for Berkeley Subway Plan," *DBB* 198, no. 22461 (October 5, 1966): 37, 52.
4. Frederick M. Wirt, *Power in the City: Decision Making in San Francisco*
    (Berkeley: University of California Press, 1974), 56–60, 250.
5. For the politics of "rebellions," "riots," and "civil violence," see Kevin
    Mumford, "Harvesting the Crisis: The Newark Uprisings, the Kerner Com-
    mission, and Writings on Riots," in *African American Urban History Since*

World War II, ed. Kenneth L. Kusmer and Joe W. Trotter (Chicago: University of Chicago Press, 2009); Michael B. Katz, *Why Don't American Cities Burn?* (Philadelphia: University of Pennsylvania Press, 2012).

6. Justin Herman and Eneas J. Kane, Letter to Richard G. Mitchell and Louis Ambler, December 16, 1965, box 2, folder "Hunters Point Redevelopment, 1961–1966," John F. "Jack" Shelley Papers, 1953–1967, SFH 10, San Francisco Public Library [JFSP].

7. "Riot Creates Tensions in Troubled Bay Area," *Los Angeles Sentinel*, September 29, 1966, A1; "Rioting Hits S.F.," *Los Angeles Times*, September 28, 1966, 1.

8. John Laurence Rayon, "Hell in Hunters Point," *Sun Reporter* [*SR*], October 1, 1966, 3.

9. "The City's Troubled Night—Looting and Arson Erupt," *San Francisco Chronicle*, September 28, 1966, 1, 11.

10. "City Sore Spot That Erupted," *San Francisco Chronicle*, September 28, 1966, 10; Bill Robertson, "'Frisco Not Watts Yet,'" *Los Angeles Sentinel*, September 29, 1966, 1, 3.

11. "Trouble Spreads to the Fillmore," *San Francisco Chronicle*, September 28, 1966, 1, 10.

12. "San Francisco Negroes Attack Police after Boy Is Fatally Shot," *New York Times*, September 28, 1966, 24; Daryl E. Lembke, "Troops Move into 2 S.F. Riot Areas," *Los Angeles Times*, September 29, 1966, 1; "S.F. Trouble Spots Calm," *San Francisco Chronicle*, September 30, 1966, 1; "S.F. Ends State of Emergency," *San Francisco Chronicle*, October 3, 1966, 1.

13. Lawrence E. Davies, "Calm Is Restored in San Francisco," *New York Times*, September 30, 1966, 1; "S.F. Ends State of Emergency," 1.

14. Lawrence E. Davies, "Racial Violence Breaks Out Again in San Francisco," *New York Times*, September 29, 1966, 1.

15. Arthur E. Hippler, *Hunter's Point: A Black Ghetto* (New York: Basic Books, 1974), 207–10.

16. Daryl E. Lembke, "S.F. Riot Area Force Reduced," *Los Angeles Times*, October 1, 1966, 1.

17. Ray Zeman, "Officials Operated by Blueprint in S.F. Riot," *Los Angeles Times*, September 29, 1966, 24.

18. Mayor John Shelley, Western Union telefax to Dr. Robert C. Weaver, October 3, 1966, box 5, folder "Hunters Point, 1965–1967," JFSP.

19. "Mayor's Committee Lists Poverty Needs," *SR*, October 8, 1966, 2.

20. S. C. Pelletiere, "When the Chinese Clamor," *San Francisco Bay Guardian* [*SFBG*], December 1, 1966, 1, 8.

21. Table P-1, census tracts 401–2, 451–52, and 476–79 in US Department of Commerce, Bureau of the Census, *Census of Population and Housing: San Francisco-Oakland, Calif., Standard Metropolitan Statistical Area* (Washington, DC: Government Printing Office, 1970).

22. Pelletiere, "When the Chinese Clamor."

23. "A Suit to Block Park Bond Issue," *San Francisco Chronicle*, August 30, 1969, 4.

24. Proposition A: Recreation and Park Bonds, "Arguments and Statements of Controller . . . General Municipal Election" (November 4, 1969), 26–27, https://sfpl.org/pdf/main/gic/elections/November4_1969.pdf.

25. "Mary Rogers Elected," *SR*, January 30, 1971, 15; Emory Curtis, "The Political Game," *SR*, October 30, 1971, 10; "See How She Runs . . . and Runs . . . and Runs," *SR*, May 27, 1972, 17; John H. Mollenkopf, *The Contested City* (Princeton, NJ: Princeton University Press, 1983), 187–88.

26. See the variously titled endorsements and guides in *Sun Reporter*, November 1, 1952, 1; June 5, 1954, 1; October 30, 1954, 10; November 3, 1956, 10; May 31, 1958, 1; November 1, 1958, 10; June 4, 1960, 2; June 4, 1960, 6; November 5, 1960, 16; June 2, 1962, 1; November 3, 1962, 1; November 3, 1962, 3; May 30, 1964, 22; and October 31, 1964, 1.

27. "Vote No on Props. A and B," *SR*, November 5, 1966, 8.

28. "A Bid for a PUC Member," *SR*, October 22, 1966, 4; "Vote No on 'A' Vote No on 'B,'" *SR*, October 22, 1966, 28.

29. "Sun-Reporter Recommendations," *SR*, November 5, 1966, 1.

30. Jay Winston Driskell Jr., *Schooling Jim Crow: The Fight for Atlanta's Booker T. Washington High School and the Roots of Black Protest Politics* (Charlottesville: University of Virginia Press, 2014); Glenda Gilmore, *Gender and Jim Crow: Women and the Politics of White Supremacy in North Carolina, 1896–1920* (Chapel Hill: University of North Carolina Press, 1996).

31. "Vote No on Props. A and B," 8.

32. "Vote Yes on City Propositions 'A' and 'B,'" *SR*, October 29, 1966, 10.

33. "A Letter Condemning Proposition B," *SR*, November 5, 1966, 4.

34. "Vote No on 'A' Vote No on 'B,'" 28.

35. "An Effective Voting Instrument," *SR*, December 3, 1966, 10.

36. "San Francisco Mayor Urges New Vote on $192 Mil. Airport and Railway Bonds," *DBB* 198, no. 22487 (November 15, 1966): 561, 586.

37. Sydney Kossen, "Rumford Comeback?" *San Francisco Chronicle*, November 20, 1966, 34.

38. For the "muted" discussion of wealth and presence of the mid-century bourgeoisie, see Sven Beckert, *The Monied Metropolis: New York City and the Consolidation of the Bourgeoisie, 1850–1896* (New York: Cambridge University Press, 2003), 332.

39. San Francisco Public Utilities Commission, "1966 Bond Issue: San Francisco Municipal Railway" (April 26, 1966), 1–3.

40. Richard Grefe and Richard Smart, *A History of the Key Decisions in the Development of Bay Area Rapid Transit: BART Impact Program* (San Francisco: McDonald & Smart, 1975), 55, 59, 141.

41. Propositions B: Municipal Transit Bonds, "Propositions, Arguments and Statements of Controller .Relating to Costs to be Voted on at General Election" (November 8, 1966), 18–22, 24–25, https://sfpl.org/pdf/main/gic/elections/November8_1966.pdf,.

42. J. Knight Allen and Morgan Sibbett, *Organizational and Financial Aspects of the Proposed San Francisco Bay Area Rapid Transit System* (Menlo Park, CA: Stanford Research Institute, 1956), 82, 106. Paginations correspond with the San Francisco Bay Area Rapid Transit Commission, *Report to the Legislature of the State of California*, December 1957, box 3, series 2, folder "BART Reference Materials 2 of 2, 1956–57," George Christopher Papers, 1950–2000, SFH 7, San Francisco Public Library [SFPL], 87, 104, of which the former was a part.

43. San Francisco Bay Area Rapid Transit District, "Special Report to Bond-holders" (September 1972), Wallace Mersereau Collection of Bay Area Rapid Transit (2016–18 unprocessed), San Francisco History Center, SFPL, 16.

44. Proposition A: Airport Bonds, "Arguments and Statements of Controller Relating to Costs to be Voted on at General Municipal Election" (November 7, 1967), https://sfpl.org/pdf/main/gic/elections/November7_1967.pdf, 78.

45. Propositions B: Municipal Transit Bonds, "Propositions, Arguments and Statements," 18.

46. Proposition A: Airport Bonds, "Arguments and Statements," 80.

47. "We Approve," *SFBG*, May 10, 1968, 8.

48. Caitlin Zaloom, *Indebted: How Families Make College Work at Any Cost* (Princeton, NJ: Princeton University Press, 2019).

49. "We Approve," 8.

50. "The San Francisco Propositions," *SFBG*, November 1, 1968, 8.

51. "Public vs. Private Financing," *SFBG*, March 9, 1967, 8.

52. "The Candlestick Swindle," *SFBG*, May 14, 1968, 1, 6, 10, 14.

53. "Guilty Firms Wriggle on Taxes," *SFBG*, April 20, 1967, 1, 2; Bruce B. Brugmann, "O'Connor Odd Stand Can Cost the City Plenty," *SFBG*, May 19, 1967, 1, 5.

54. Grefe and Smart, *A History of the Key Decisions*, 124–25.

55. Senate bill no. 850, June 11, 1957, box 3, series 2, folder "BART, Senate Report and Bills, 1949–1957," George Christopher Papers, 1950–2000, SFH 7, SFPL, 33–45.

56. Mrs. Elmer A. Weden Jr., "Position Statement: Bay Area Citizens to Save BART," January 13, 1969, box 2, folder "Transportation, 1968–1969," Jack Morrison Papers, SFH24, SFPL [JMP].

57. Testimony of Robert Tideman, Prepared for Presentation before the Board of Directors of the Bay Area Rapid Transit District, San Francisco, California, January 23, 1969, box 2, folder "Transportation, 1968–1969," JMP, 1.

58. Weden, "Position Statement."

59. Art Carter, Letter to Board of Directors of the Bay Area Rapid Transit District, January 23, 1969, box 2, folder "Transportation, 1968–1969," JMP.

60. Testimony of Robert Tideman, 1.

61. Lawrence E. Davies, "Transit Tunnel Is Completed under San Francisco Bay," *New York Times*, April 4, 1969, 66.

62. San Francisco Bay Area Rapid Transit District, "Special Report to Bond-holders," 14–15.

63. Elizabeth Hinton, *From the War on Poverty to the War on Crime: The Making of Mass Incarceration* (Cambridge, MA: Harvard University Press, 2016); Keeanga-Yamahtta Taylor, *Race for Profit: How Banks and the Real Estate Industry Undermined Black Homeownership* (Chapel Hill: University of North Carolina Press, 2019); Russel Rickford, *We Are an African People: Independent Education, Black Power, and the Radical Imagination* (New York: Oxford University Press, 2016).

64. "Riot Fear Impact: Ghetto Firms Are Hit by Canceled Insurance, Higher Rates; Some Forced out of Business," *Wall Street Journal*, July 11, 1968, 30.

65. John H. Allan, "Will the Riots Hurt Municipal Bond Sales?," *New York Times*, August 13, 1967, section 3, 1; Joint Economic Committee, Subcommittee on Economic Progress, "Financing Municipal Facilities: Volume I," 90th Cong., 2nd sess., December 5–7, 1967, 63.

66. John H. Allan, "Bonds: Prices Decline as Uncertainty Mounts in Gold Market," *New York Times*, March 5, 1968, 56.

67. John E. Petersen, *The Rating Game: Report of the Twentieth Century Fund Task Force on Municipal Bond Credit Ratings* (New York: Twentieth Century Fund, 1974), 126.

68. Statement of Robert C. Riehle in reply to statements by Finance Administrator Roy M. Goodman before the Joint Economic Committee, Subcommittee on Economic Progress, "Financing Municipal Facilities: Volume II," 90th Cong., 2nd sess., July 9–11, 1968, 240.

69. "Text of Award Winning Paper Analyzing Ratings of Municipals," *DBB* 198, no. 22507 (December 14, 1966): 1013.

70. Peter Kihss, "Wagner Defends the City's Credit; Moody's Scores It," *New York Times*, July 19, 1965, 1.

71. Destin Jenkins, "Ghosts of the Past: Municipal Debt and Racial Governance in the New South," in *Histories of Racial Capitalism*, ed. Destin Jenkins and Justin Leroy (New York: Columbia University Press, 2021).

72. Statement of Robert C. Riehle, "Financing Municipal Facilities: Volume II," 240.

73. Statement of Robert C. Riehle, "Financing Municipal Facilities: Volume II," 238, 246.

74. Statement of Brenton W. Harries, "Financing Municipal Facilities: Volume II," 293.

75. Statement of Robert C. Riehle, "Financing Municipal Facilities: Volume II," 239, 294.

76. Statement of Robert C. Riehle, "Financing Municipal Facilities: Volume II," 217.

77. Petersen, *The Rating Game*, 82, 101–6.

78. Statement of Walter H. Tyler, "Financing Municipal Facilities: Volume II," 381, 383.

79. "Calif. Banker Wins Contest," *Washington Post*, November 28, 1966, D8.

80. "Text of Award Winning Paper," 1013, 1031.

81. "Final Installment: Text of Award Winning Paper Analyzing Ratings of Municipals," *DBB* 198, no. 22508 (December 15, 1966): 1047, 1051.

Chapter Seven

1. There were 176,874 supporters and 93,195 opponents of Proposition A. "Proposition 'A' Vote Count," undated, box 18, folder "Yes on Proposition A, 1 of 2, 1968," Joseph L. Alioto Papers, 1958–1977, SFH 5, San Francisco Public Library [JLAP].

2. "Propositions," *San Francisco Chronicle*, November 5, 1969, 1B. For support from labor, see "'More Jobs; Better Schools': Union Chief Backs Prop. B," *San Francisco Examiner*, October 31, 1969; for ethnic groups, see "Ethnic Groups for Passage of Proposition 'B,'" *Philippine News*, October 30, 1969; for religious support, see "New Support for Prop. B," *San Francisco Chronicle*, October 30, 1969. For an exhaustive list of the many endorsers of Proposition B, see Proposition B: School Bonds, "Arguments and Statements of Controller Relating to Costs to be Voted on at General Municipal Election," (November 4, 1969), 32–35, https://sfpl.org/pdf/main/gic/elections/November4_1969.pdf. For an analysis of voter turnout, see Jerry Burns, "The Pattern of Voting in the City," *San Francisco Chronicle*, November 6, 1969, 1.

3. Jon C. Teaford makes a similar point, though he blandly attributes urban fiscal woes to "depleted city treasuries" and "insufficient funds." In San Francisco, at least, it wasn't the *absence* of funds so much as a question of distribution: who would pay for municipal infrastructure and services, through what means, and how bondholders would benefit from property and regressive sales taxation. Jon C. Teaford, *The Rough Road to Renaissance: Urban Revitalization in America, 1940–1985* (Baltimore: Johns Hopkins University Press, 1990), 168–69.

4. John H. Allan, "Yields Set Record for Tax-Exempts," *New York Times*, May 15, 1970, 51.

5. John Getze, "No End Seen to Municipal Bond Price Collapse," *Los Angeles Times*, May 25, 1970, D10.

6. "Municipals Reach Lowest Prices Ever," *Los Angeles Times*, May 24, 1970, H5.

7. Charles W. Mills, *Black Rights, White Wrongs: The Critique of Racial Liberalism* (New York: Oxford University Press, 2007), 39.

8. Nicholas von Hoffman, "'Programs' Stifle a Lofty Ghetto: View of San Francisco is Great but Three Years of Aid Leave Hunters Point Unchanged," *Washington Post*, August 28, 1966, E1.

9. Arthur E. Hippler, *Hunter's Point: A Black Ghetto* (New York: Basic Books, 1974), 3, ix, 5–6, 7, 10, 210, 223. For an excellent critique of ghetto studies,

see Arnold R. Hirsch, *Making the Second Ghetto: Race & Housing in Chicago, 1940–1960*, 2nd ed. (Chicago: University of Chicago Press, 1998); and Joe W. Trotter Jr., "Black Migration in Historical Perspective: A Review of the Literature," in Trotter, ed., *The Great Migration in Historical Perspective: New Dimensions of Race, Class, and Gender* (Bloomington: Indiana University Press, 1991).

10.   For one definition, see the San Francisco Conference on Religion, Race and Social Concerns, "Housing," *San Francisco: A City in Crisis* (1968), 18. The pagination is highly inconsistent but roughly corresponds to the particular chapter subject.

11.   Philip Shinoda, "The Impact of the Bay Area Rapid Transit on Hunters Point Residents Seeking Industrial Jobs" (San Francisco: PACT, 1968), 6.

12.   Hippler, *Hunter's Point*, 5.

13.   Shinoda, "The Impact of the Bay Area Rapid Transit," 6.

14.   As of 1960, "permanent" housing projects in the area included Harbor Slope, Hunters Point, and Hunters View. The SFHA counted as "temporary" the massive, 2,049-unit Ridge Point public-housing project. SFHA, *Road to the Golden Age: A Report on the First Twenty Years of Operations, 1940–1960* (1960), 32–33.

15.   Hippler, *Hunter's Point*, 14–16.

16.   Eneas J. Kane, Letter to Mayor John F. Shelley, undated, box 5, folder "Hunters Point, 1965–1967," John F. "Jack" Shelley Papers, 1953–1967, SFH 10, San Francisco Public Library [JFSP], 1.

17.   The San Francisco Conference on Religion, Race and Social Concerns. "Housing," *San Francisco: A City in Crisis* (1968), 4, 26–7.

18.   Shinoda, "The Impact of the Bay Area Rapid Transit," 15, 20–22, 27–30.

19.   San Francisco Planning and Urban Renewal Association, "Proposition 'A,'" *SPUR Report*, no. 32, September 1968, box 18, folder "Yes on Proposition A, 1 of 2, 1968," JLAP, 2.

20.   Hippler, *Hunter's Point*, 188–89.

21.   "Major Dates Relating to the Hunters Point Project," August 19, 1963, box 2, folder "Hunters Point Redevelopment, 1961–1966," JFSP; SFRA, "Hunters Point," June 30, 1969, box 18, folder "Proposition B, 2 of 2, 1969–1970," JLAP.

22.   Allan B. Jacobs and William Becker, Memorandum to John F. Shelly, May 9, 1967, box 9, folder "HUD, Hunters Point, 1968–1969," JLAP, 1–2. For the powers of the SFRA, see SFRA, "Proposed Redevelopment Plan for Hunters Point Redevelopment Project," November 22, 1968, box 9, folder "HUD, Hunters Point, 1968–1969," JLAP, 28. For conflicts between the Department of City Planning and SFRA, see John H. Mollenkopf, *The Contested City* (Princeton, NJ: Princeton University Press, 1983), 168; Allan B. Jacobs, *Making City Planning Work* (Chicago: American Planning Association, 1980).

23.   Richard A. Walker, "Industry Builds Out the City: The Suburbanization of Manufacturing in the San Francisco Bay Area, 1850–1940," 3, 6–7,10, http://geog.berkeley.edu/PeopleHistory/faculty/R_Walker/IndustryBuildsOut

.pdf; Andrew Robichaud, *Animal City: The Domestication of America* (Cambridge, MA: Harvard University Press, 2019); San Francisco Area Description, D-16, Robert K. Nelson, LaDale Winling, Richard Marciano, Nathan Connolly, et al., "Mapping Inequality," in *American Panorama*, ed. Robert K. Nelson and Edward L. Ayers, https://dsl.richmond.edu/panorama/red lining/#loc=13/37.7485/-122.4118&opacity=0.8&city=san-francisco-ca&area =D16&sort=20&adimage=3/63/-120; SFRA, "San Francisco Redevelopment Program; Summary of Project Data and Key Elements," (January 1977), 4, 62–67.

24. San Francisco Planning and Urban Renewal Association, "Proposition "A," 1; "Summary of Recreation and Park Proposals in November, 1968 Bond Issues,"; both in box 18, folder "Yes on Proposition A, 1 of 2, 1968," JLAP.

25. Citizens for Proposition A, "Prop. 'A' Appeal," folder "Vertical File (V.F.): S.F. Elections. November 1968 Propositions," San Francisco Ephemera Collection, San Francisco Historical Collection, SFPL [SFEC].

26. "Yes on A, Please" pamphlet, folder "Vertical File (V.F.): S.F. Elections. November 1968 Propositions," SFEC.

27. See such mini-articles as "Business, Clubs Back Playground Proposal for Kids," "Downtown Assn. Gives Okay: Little Effect on Taxes," "Top Veterans Group Supports Park Bond," and "Labor Council Says Yes on 'A,'" in Citizens for Proposition A, "Prop. 'A' Appeal."

28. Edward McDevitt, Letter to Frank Moitoza, October 4, 1968; "Council Approves the Proposition "A" to Improve Recreation," *Neighborhood Merchants News*, October 1968; both in box 18, folder "Propositions A and B, 1 of 2, 1968–1969," JLAP.

29. "Yes on A—No on 9," *Sun Reporter* [*SR*], October 26, 1968, 18.

30. Joe Johnson, Memorandum to Mr. Jerry Flam and Revels H. Cayton, October 31, 1968, box 18, folder "Yes on Proposition A, 1 of 2, 1968," JLAP.

31. Compare the "Black Letter" to the Labor Letter," both contained in box 18, folder "Yes on Proposition A, 1 of 2, 1968," JLAP.

32. San Francisco Planning and Urban Renewal Association, "Proposition 'A,'" 1; Sydney Worthington and Terry Francois, Letter to Father Pierre Dumaine, October 18, 1968, box 18, folder "Propositions A and B, 1 of 2, 1968–1969," JLAP.

33. Thomas N. Saunders, Letter to Hadley Roff, August 13, 1968, box 18, folder "Yes on Proposition A, 2 of 2, 1968," JLAP, 1.

34. John Lee Mikesell, "An Analysis of Municipal Sales Taxation" (Ph.D. diss., University of Illinois, 1969), 30–37. For the specific projects serviced through sales taxation see Tom Ross, "Bond Priorities," *San Francisco Progress*, October 27–28, 1968; San Francisco Unified School District, "Proposed 1964 Building Program," May 28, 1964, box 86, folder "Proposed 1964 Building Program, 1964," San Francisco Unified School District Records, 1854–2005, SFH 3 (SFPL), 2; San Francisco Planning and Urban Renewal Association, "San Francisco Shopping List—The Capital Improvement Program," *SPUR Newsletter*, no. 16 (July 1964): 2.

35. "Yes on A, Please"; Sydney Worthington and Terry Francois, Letter to Father Pierre Dumaine, October 18, 1968, 1.

36. San Francisco Fire Department, "Press Release," October 31, 1968, box 18, folder "Yes on Proposition A, 1 of 2, 1968," JLAP.

37. Jerry Flam, Letter to Al Hyman, October 29, 1968, box 18, folder "Yes on Proposition A, 1 of 2, 1968," JLAP.

38. Thomas M. Saunders, Letter to Proposition "A" Campaigners, November 7, 1968, box 18, folder "Yes on Proposition A, 2 of 2, 1968," JLAP, 1.

39. "An Archaic Rule on Bond Votes," *San Francisco Examiner*, November 27, 1968.

40. Frank Marini, *Local Bond Elections in California: The Two-Thirds Majority Requirement* (Berkeley: University of California Institute of Governmental Studies, 1963), 1, 2.

41. Nathan Cohn, Letter to Friends, October 16, 1968, box 18, folder "Propositions A and B, 1 of 2, 1968–1969," JLAP.

42. Contributions derived from A. F. Derre Letter and Attachments to County Clerk, City and County of San Francisco, December 2, 1968, box 18, folder "Propositions A and B, 1 of 2, 1968–1969," JLAP, 1–10.

43. Flam, Letter to Al Hyman, 2.

44. "Vote on Bond Issues Is Challenge to City," *Argonaut*, November 13, 1968, 9.

45. Saunders, Letter to Proposition "A" Campaigners, 1.

46. Mark Brilliant, *The Color of America Has Changed: How Racial Diversity Shaped Civil Rights Reform in California* (New York: Oxford University Press, 2010); Ronald Formisano, *Boston against Busing; Race, Class, and Ethnicity in the 1960s* (Chapel Hill: University of North Carolina Press, 1991); Matthew D. Lassiter, *The Silent Majority: Suburban Politics in the Sunbelt South* (Princeton, NJ: Princeton University Press, 2006).

47. Proposition B: School Bonds, "Arguments and Statements of Controller," 31.

48. Gerald R. Flam, Letter to Joseph T. McGucken, October 20, 1969, box 18, folder "Proposition B, 1 of 2, 1969," JLAP.

49. Guy Wright, "Bonds or Bused," *San Francisco Sunday Examiner and Chronicle*, November 2, 1969.

50. Brilliant, *The Color of America Has Changed*, 227–56; Parents and Taxpayers, "Speak to the Issue!" newsletter, vol. 2, no. 6 (March 1967), box 4, folder "City Demonstration Program, Parents and Taxpayers Newsletters, 1966," JFSP.

51. Citizens for Proposition "B," news release, October 13, 1969, box 18, folder "Proposition B, 2 of 2, 1969–1970," JLAP, 2.

52. Daniel E. Koshland and John A. Sutro, "Citizens for Proposition B—News Release," October 6, 1969, box 18, folder "Proposition B, 2 of 2, 1969–1970," JLAP.

53. "Draft," October 20, 1969, box 18, folder "Proposition B, 1 of 2, 1969," JLAP, 1–3.

54. Russell Rickford, "Integration, Black Nationalism, and Radical Democratic Transformation in African American Philosophies of Education, 1965–74,"

in *The New Black History: Revisiting the Second Reconstruction*, ed. Manning Marable and Elizabeth Kai Hinton (New York: Palgrave Macmillan, 2011).

55. Wright, "Bonds or Bused."

56. Gail Roberts, Letter to Milton Reiterman, November 12, 1969, box 18, folder "Proposition B, 1 of 2, 1969," JLAP.

57. Mrs. Stanley M. Friedman, Letter to John A. Sturo, October 10, 1969, box 18, folder "Proposition B, 1 of 2, 1969," JLAP.

58. Milton Reiterman, Letter to Jack Harrington, October 10, 1969, box 18, folder "Proposition B, 1 of 2, 1969," JLAP.

59. "Yes on B," ephemera, undated, box 18, folder "Proposition B, 1 of 2, 1969," JLAP.

60. Wright, "Bonds or Bused,"

61. "Draft," October 20, 1969, 2–3.

62. City and County of San Francisco, "Proposition B: A $5 Million Bond Issue to Provide for Hunters Point Schools. Information for Speakers and Others Interested in Passage of Proposition B," undated, box 18, folder "Proposition B, 2 of 2, 1969–1970," JLAP, 4–5.

63. "Butchertown Property Owners Fight Prop. B," *San Francisco Examiner*, October 27, 1969.

64. Joel Twmak, "Bayview Homeowners—Black and Furious," *San Francisco Examiner*, November 3, 1969.

65. "Butchertown Property Owners Fight Prop. B."

66. "Butchertown Property Owners Fight Prop. B"; "Bayview Group Opposes Prop. B," *San Francisco Examiner*, November 3, 1969.

67. Hunters Point Citizens Committee Against Proposition "B," "Vote 'No' on Proposition 'B,' flyer, October 18, 1969, box 18, folder "Proposition B, 2 of 2, 1969–1970," JLAP.

68. Twmak, "Bayview Homeowners—Black and Furious."

69. Michael C. Dawson, *Behind the Mule: Race and Class in African-American Politics* (Princeton, NJ: Princeton University Press, 1994).

70. "Butchertown Property Owners Fight Prop. B."

71. Emory Curtis, "The Political Game," *SR*, August 21, 1971, 6.

72. Thomas W. Hanchett, "Financing Suburbia: Prudential Insurance and the Post–World War II Transformation of the American City," *Journal of Urban History* 26, no. 3 (March 2000): 322.

73. SFRA, "San Francisco Redevelopment Program; Summary of Project Data and Key Elements," (January 1977), 65, 67.

74. Emory Curtis, "The Political Game," *SR*, February 6, 1971, 8, and April 22, 1972, 8.

75. "The Key Votes . . . San Francisco Propositions," *San Francisco Chronicle*, June 7, 1972, 1, 2.

76. William Issel, "'Land Values, Human Values, and the Preservation of the City's Treasured Appearance': Environmentalism, Politics, and the San

Francisco Freeway Revolt," *Pacific Historical Review* 68, no. 4 (November 1999): 611–46.

77. Numbers calculated by the author. Proposition A: Public School Building Bonds, "City and County Propositions to be Voted on at the Direct Primary Election" (June 2, 1970), 6, 10–11, https://sfpl.org/pdf/main/gic/elections/June2_1970.pdf.

78. Proposition A: Public School Building Bonds, "City and County Propositions," 7–8.

79. See also the attempt to use sales taxes to service a $14.8 million park and recreation bond measure. Proposition B: Recreation and Park Bonds, "Arguments and Statements of Controller Related to Costs to be Voted on at Consolidated Primary and Special Election" (June 4, 1968), 13–14, https://sfpl.org/pdf/main/gic/elections/June4_1968.pdf.

80. Lassiter, *The Silent Majority*, 13.

81. Proposition A: Public School Building Bonds, "City and County Propositions," 10.

82. Proposition A: Public School Building Bonds, "City and County Propositions," 10. For a positive appraisal of the Board of Education's bond performance, see Tom Ross, "Bond Performance," *SR*, May 16, 1970, 4.

83. For the eviction letters to those displaced by the Board of Education, see box 9, folder "HUD, Model Cities, Acquisition of Bayview School Property, 1969–1971," JLAP.

84. Proposition A: Public School Building Bonds, "City and County Propositions," 9–10.

85. For the progressive impulse of the neighborhood movement, see Chester Hartman, *City for Sale: The Transformation of San Francisco* (Berkeley: University of California Press, 2002), esp. chapter 11; Manuel Castells, *The City and the Grassroots: A Cross-Cultural Theory of Urban Social Movements* (Berkeley: University of California Press, 1983).

86. Jeffrey J. Drapel, "Citizens of San Francisco," *Committee for Safe and Decent Schools Newsletter*, October 21, 1969, folder "Vertical File (V.F.): S.F. Associations. Committee for Safe and Decent Schools," SFEC.

87. Drapel, "Citizens of San Francisco."

88. Proposition A: Public School Building Bonds, "City and County Propositions," 8–9.

89. "Trouble for School Bonds," *San Francisco Progress*, November 5, 1969.

90. Mary R. Ciarlo, "June Elections Show 31.3% of Bonds Approved," *Daily Bond Buyer [DBB]* 213, no. 23399 (July 2, 1970): 21, 44.

91. Joel Tlumak, "Taxpayers Defeat S.F. Cash Issues," *San Francisco Examiner*, November 5, 1969.

92. Frederick Wirt, *Power in the City: Decision Making in San Francisco* (Berkeley: University of California Press, 1974), 60.

93. Editorial, "The Mood Shown by the Voters," *San Francisco Chronicle*, November 6, 1969, 40.

94. Wirt, *Power in the City*, 59–60.

95. "A Challenge of S.F. Bond Voting Rule," *San Francisco Chronicle*, November 7, 1969, 5.

96. "Calif. High Court Upsets Need for Two-Thirds Vote," *DBB* 213, no. 23400 (July 6, 1970): 45–46; "Calif. School Districts, Agencies May Seek New Bond Elections," *DBB* 213, no. 23406 (July 14, 1970): 169, 184.

97. "Recent Calif. Court Ruling Leaves Future Bond Issues Clouded in Doubt," *DBB* 213, no. 23414 (July 24, 1970): 349–50.

98. "A Cloudy Bond Victory," *San Francisco Chronicle*, November 5, 1970, 11.

99. "Simple Majority Bill for Bond Issues Stalled in California Assembly," *DBB*, 213.23427 (August 12, 1970), 645.

100. Proposition B: School Bonds—Hunters Point Redevelopment Project, "Arguments and Statements of Controller Relating to Costs to be Voted on at General Election" (November 3, 1970), 17–19, https://sfpl.org/pdf/main/gic/elections/November3_1970.pdf.

101. Robert O. Self, *American Babylon: Race and the Struggle for Postwar Oakland* (Princeton, NJ: Princeton University Press, 2003), 291.

102. US Bureau of the Census, *City Government Finances in 1965–66* (Washington, DC: Government Printing Office, 1966), 14, https://www2.census.gov/govs/pubs/city_govt_fin/1966.pdf; US Bureau of the Census, *City Government Finances in 1967–68* (Washington, DC: Government Printing Office, 1968), 13, https://www2.census.gov/govs/pubs/city_govt_fin/1968.pdf.

103. Proposition B: School Bonds—Hunters Point Redevelopment Project, "Arguments and Statements of Controller," 19.

104. "A Cloudy Bond Victory," 11.

105. *Gordon v. Lance*, 403 US 1 (1971); Louis M. Kohlmeier, "Justices Uphold 'Super Majority' Voting on Bond Issues in 'Conservative' Ruling," *Wall Street Journal*, June 8, 1971, 6.

106. Editorial, "United States Supreme Court Decision," *Oakland Post*, June 10, 1971.

107. "Negotiated Sales Soar; Drop Seen in Competitives," *DBB* 221, no. 23929 (August 14, 1972): 666; Denis F. McFeely, "Week in Advance: Note Offerings Total Record $1.82 Billion," *DBB* 229, no. 24446 (September 9, 1974): 839.

108. SFRA, "San Francisco Redevelopment Program; Summary of Project Data and Key Elements," 62. The school was likely financed out of the SFRA's $3,075,000 offering in November 1972. "Tax-Exempts: New Jersey Schedules $75 Million of Bonds," *Wall Street Journal*, November 24, 1972, 13.

109. During the early 1960s, many anticipated that if a California borrower issued a $7 million lease-revenue bond, the interest rate would register at nearly 4.6 percent, compared to between 3.25 and 3.45 percent on general obligation bonds. Thus, lease-revenue bonds cost taxpayers and paid bondholders more than $2.65 million in interest. Indeed, "lease-purchasing [was] the most expensive method of long-term financing." Marini, *Local Bond Elections in California*, 15–16.

110.   Paul Heffernan, "The Editor's Corner," *DBB* 213, no. 23454 (September 21, 1970): 1217, 1239.

Chapter Eight

1.   Testimony of Joseph Alioto before the Committee on Finance, Subcommittee on Financial Markets, "The Growing Threat of a Domestic Financial Crisis," 93rd Cong., 2nd sess., August 7–8, 1974, 3–4.

2.   "HUD Plans $130 Million Bonds for Oct. 28 Sale; First Since Nov., 1969," *Daily Bond Buyer* [*DBB*] 213, no. 23459 (September 28, 1970): 1345, 1366; "$550,499,000 Notes Offered Seventy-Two Authorities Invite Bids," notice of sale in *DBB* 221, no. 23920 (August 1, 1972): 459–60; "$275.4 Mil. New Housing Bonds of 35 Authorities Slated by HUD for Sept. 13 Competitive Bidding," *DBB* 221, no. 23932 (August 17, 1972): 717, 735; "$694,918,000 Notes Offered: One Hundred Three Authorities Invite Bids," *DBB* 229, no. 24413 (July 23, 1974): 277–78.

3.   Merrill Lynch, Pierce, Fenner & Smith, Inc., "The Market Digest: Dealers Seen Keeping Low Profile Position Until Signs Reflect Short-Term Rate Peak," *DBB* 229, no. 24403 (July 9, 1974): 112.

4.   Merrill Lynch, Pierce, Fenner & Smith, Inc., "The Market Digest"; Greta Krippner, *Capitalism in Crisis: The Political Origins of the Rise of Finance in the United States Economy* (Cambridge, MA: Harvard University Press, 2010), 60–68; Louis Hyman, *Debtor Nation: The History of America in Red Ink* (Princeton, NJ: Princeton University Press, 2011), 224; Monica Prasad, *The Land of Too Much: American Abundance and the Paradox of Poverty* (Cambridge, MA: Harvard University Press, 2012).

5.   James T. Patterson, *Grand Expectations: The United States, 1945–1974* (New York: Oxford University Press, 1996), 785–86; Robert M. Collins, *More: The Politics of Economic Growth in Postwar America* (New York: Oxford University Press, 2000), 153, 155.

6.   John Connor, "Beame Proposes a Taxable Municipal Bond Option and a Federal Agency to Lend Funds to Local Bodies," *DBB* 229, no. 24425 (August 8, 1974): 493.

7.   "Nation's Mayors Urge Swift Action on House Revenue Sharing Bill," *DBB* 221, no. 23916 (July 26, 1972): 380.

8.   Alioto testimony, "The Growing Threat of a Domestic Financial Crisis," 23.

9.   Alioto testimony, "The Growing Threat of a Domestic Financial Crisis," 4.

10.   Statement and Testimony of Hubert H. Humphrey before the Joint Economic Committee, "State and Local Government Credit Problems," 94th Cong., 1st sess., June 20, 1975, 2, 15.

11.   Joint Economic Committee, Subcommittee on Economic Progress, "Financing Municipal Facilities: Volume II," 90th Cong., 2nd sess., July 9, 10, 11, 1968, 346, 305, 304, 298.

12. John Petersen, "Changing Conditions in the Market for State and Local Government Debt: A Study," Joint Economic Committee, 94th Cong., 2nd sess., April 16, 1976, 34, 36.

13. "Banks Will Be Net Sellers of Municipals Over Next 12 Months, Dr. Kaufman Says," *DBB* 197, no. 22445 (September 13, 1966): 913, 928.

14. "Morris Foresees Decline in Support of Tax-Free Market by Commercial Banks," *DBB* 221, no. 23953 (September 18, 1972): 1170.

15. Krippner, *Capitalism in Crisis*; Roland I. Robinson, *Postwar Market for State and Local Government Securities*, (Princeton, NJ: Princeton University Press, 1960), 84–86; For the new investment avenues, see Kim Phillips-Fein, *Fear City: New York's Fiscal Crisis and the Rise of Austerity Politics* (New York: Metropolitan Books, 2017), 75; Petersen, "Changing Conditions," 31, 37.

16. Statement of Gedale Horowitz in "State and Local Government Credit Problems," 35.

17. Petersen, "Changing Conditions," 2, 9–10. For attempts to aid the revitalization of parts of San Francisco through tax-exempt municipal bond finance, see Thomas J. Black, "Private Market Housing Renovation in Older Urban Areas," *Urban Land Institute* 26 (1977): 32; "Redevelopment's New Home Loan Program," *Sun Reporter*, May 15, 1976; Proposition A, Housing Revenue Bond Issue, "San Francisco Voter Information Pamphlet," (June 3, 1980), 20–23, http://sfpl.org/pdf/main/gic/elections/June3_1980short.pdf.

18. James C. Cobb, *The Selling of the South: The Southern Crusade for Industrial Development, 1936–1990* (Champaign: University of Illinois Press, 1993).

19. Petersen, "Changing Conditions," 2, 8, 18.

20. "$445,400,000 Project Notes of Local Housing Authorities," notice of sale in *DBB* 213, no. 23455 (September 20, 1970): 1255–58; "$550,499,000 Notes Offered Seventy-Two Authorities Invite Bids," notice of sale in *DBB* 221, no. 23920 (August 1, 1972): 459–60.

21. "$263.5 Mil. HUD Notes for Urban Renewal Sold at 2.8311%," *DBB* 221, no. 23926 (August 9, 1972): 581.

22. Ivan Silverman, "The Bond Market: Housing Issue Breaks a Two-Year-Old Curse; All of It Is Bid For," *Wall Street Journal*, January 28, 1971, 21.

23. Petersen, "Changing Conditions," 9.

24. Denis F. McFeely, "Week in Advance: Note Offerings Total Record $1.82 Billion," *DBB* 229, no. 24446 (September 9, 1974): 839.

25. United Virginia Bank, "The Market Digest: Gloomy Fundamental Picture Augurs Higher Long-Term Rates for Summer," *DBB* 229, no. 24399 (July 2, 1974): 40.

26. Bank of America, "The Market Digest: Mini-Rally Cheers Some, but Caution Remains Prevailing Mood in Market," *DBB* 229, no. 24408 (July 16, 1974): 200.

27. Trust Co. of Georgia, "The Market Digest: Mini-Rally Cheers Some, but Caution Remains Prevailing Mood in Market," *DBB* 229, no. 24408 (July 16, 1974): 200.

28. Thomas Piketty, *Capital in the Twenty-First Century* (Cambridge, MA: Harvard University Press, 2014), 544, 453.

29. Statement of Wade S. Smith in "Financing Municipal Facilities: Volume II," 262.

30. Numbers derived from "Table 7: Selected Measures of Commercial Bank Demand," Joint Economic Committee, "Chaos in the Municipal Bond Market," 97th Cong, 1st sess., September 28, 1981, 78.

31. BankAmerica Corporation, *Annual Report 1974*, 6, 14. By the end of 1977, BOA stepped up its purchases of municipal securities, earning profits of $16 million. More interesting, BOA now held debts overwhelmingly issued by states rather than cities, districts, or authorities. See "Table 9: Bank of America NT&SA Consolidated—Ten Largest Holdings of State, County, and Municipal Bonds at December 31, 1977—Par Values" in BankAmerica Corporation, *Annual Report 1977*, 43.

32. Citicorp, *Annual Report 1976*, 20.

33. As fears of a financial contagion intensified, and with greater yields on short-term debt available, big commercial banks essentially off-loaded debt onto smaller banks and individual investors. By the mid-1970s, the "household sector" retuned with a great appetite for municipal bonds. In response, the architects of San Francisco's 1976 "various purpose" bond package denominated some of the bond issues in lower amounts in an effort to reach these creditors. Petersen, "Changing Conditions," 34–35, 37; "Official Statement, City and County of San Francisco Relating to $59,983,000 Various Purpose General Obligation Bonds," August 30, 1976, box 028, "Office of the Mayor San Francisco . . . Program & Budget Office 1976–77," folder "Bond Screening Committee 1976–77," George Moscone Collection (MSS 328), University of the Pacific [GMC], 3.

34. Wallace Turner, "Bank of America Officer Quits in Protest," *New York Times*, June 16, 1971, 61. See also the letters to Alan K. Browne from Gardner Frost of Chase Manhattan Bank; Theodore L. Haff Jr. of Smith, Barney & Co.; and James S. Saffran of Stone & Youngberg, included in Alan K. Browne, "'Mr. Municipal Bond': Bond Investment Management, Bank of America, 1929–1971," oral history conducted in 1988 by Malca Chall, Regional Oral History Office, Bancroft Library, University of California, Berkeley (1990), xi, xii, 281, 282, 286. "Joins Drexel Firestone," *DBB* 221, no. 23908 (July 14, 1972): 197.

35. Michael Keenan and Lawrence J. White, eds., *Mergers and Acquisitions: Current Problems in Perspective* (Lexington, MA: Lexington Books, 1982); "Eastman Dillon Plans Merger with Blyth," *DBB* 221, no. 23900 (July 3, 1972): 17; "Blyth Eastman Dillon, Created from Merger, Capitalized at $90 Mil.," *DBB* 221, no. 23904 (July 10, 1972): 103; "Merger Discussions between Paine, Webber, Shearson, Hammill Ended," *DBB* 221. no. 23917 (July 27, 1972): 407; Blyth Eastman Dillon & Co. merger announcement in *DBB* 221, no. 23929 (August 14, 1972): 654.

36. Alan K. Browne, Letter addressed "Dear Pfef," July 12, 1973, carton 3, folder "Miscellaneous Corres. & Reference Material, 1954–1979," Alan K. Browne Papers (BANC MSS 91/6), University of California, Berkeley [AKBP], 1, 11.

37. Browne, Letter addressed "Dear Pfef," 1, 11.

38. "A Conversation with John Mitchell," interview conducted in November 1984 and reprinted in *The Bond Buyer, 100 Anniversary Edition: A Salute to the Municipal Bond Industry, 1891–1991*, 62.

39. Turner, "Bank of America Officer Quits in Protest."

40. Francis R. Schanck, Letter to Alan K. Browne, September 24, 1975, carton 3, folder "Misc. Corres. 1974–1978," AKBP, 2.

41. Martin Shefter, *Political Crisis, Fiscal Crisis: The Collapse and Revival of New York City* (New York: Basic Books, 1987), xxii–xxiii, 106–7.

42. Phillips-Fein, *Fear City*, 6, 35, 41.

43. Alan K. Browne, Letter to Francis R. Schanck, September 15, 1975, carton 3, folder "Misc. Corres. 1974–1978," AKBP, 1.

44. Alan K. Browne, Letter to Mr. L. William Seidman, September 3, 1975, carton 3, folder "Misc. Corres. 1974–1978," AKBP, 1.

45. Browne, Letter to Seidman, 1. For the kinds of complicated financing techniques used by New York City municipal officials, see . Roger E. Alcaly and David Mermelstein, eds., *The Fiscal Crisis of American Cities: Essays on the Political Economy of Urban America with Special Reference to New York* (New York: Vintage Books, 1977), 30–33.

46. Alan K. Browne, Rejected Letter to the Editor, *New York Times*, October 28, 1975, carton 3, folder "Misc. Corres. 1974–1978," AKBP, 1.

47. Browne, Letter to Seidman, 2.

48. Alan K. Browne, Letter to Henry S. Reuss, October 3, 1975, carton 3, folder "Misc. Corres. 1974–1978," AKBP, 3.

49. Philip Revzin, "Big-Apple Blight: Other Big Cities Hurt by New York Bond-Sale Woes," *Wall Street Journal*, June 19, 1975, 1.

50. Petersen, "Changing Conditions," 28.

51. Petersen, "Changing Conditions," 23–24.

52. Ben Weberman, "At Least 8 Cities Besides New York City in Cash Bind, Run Risk of Suspensions of Credit Ratings," *American Banker*, May 9, 1975.

53. Revzin, "Big-Apple Blight," 1.

54. Martin Tolchin, "U.S. Mayors Fear Default Here; Say it would Injure Bond Sales," *New York Times*, September 6, 1975, 1, 9.

55. Alan K. Browne, Letter to Joseph L. Alioto, June 6, 1975, carton 3, folder "Misc. Corres. 1974–1978," AKBP, 2.

56. Frederic A. Moritz, "San Francisco Mayoral Race Swings on Cutting Local Costs," *Christian Science Monitor*, December 10, 1975, 4.

57. By this I mean San Francisco's general obligation, public service enterprise, and nonprofit debt. The San Francisco Civil Grand Jury report is attached to Lloyd D. Luckmann, Memorandum to All City Officials, September 27, 1976. William R. Shapiro, "Special Report on City Debt

Management," ca. 1975–76, box 028, "Office of the Mayor San Francisco . . .
Program & Budget Office 1976–77," folder "Bond Information," GMC, 328.

58. *Annual Report of the Controller of the City and County of San Francisco for
the Fiscal Year Ended June 30, 1975* (San Francisco: Office of the Controller,
1975–76), 4, https://archive.org/details/annualreportofco1975sanf.

59. City Government Finances, US Department of Commerce, Bureau of Census,
1974–75, 18, 48, https://www2.census.gov/govs/pubs/city_govt_fin/1975.pdf

60. Marshall Kilduff, "Bond Debt Taking Almost Half of S.F. Port Budget," *San
Francisco Chronicle*, January 26, 1978, 18.

61. On fiscal strain generally, see David T. Stanley, "Cities in Trouble,"in *Na-
tional Urban Policy Roundtable* (Columbus, OH: Academy for Contemporary
Problems, December 1976); Philip M. Dearborn, *City Financial Emergencies:
The Intergovernmental Dimension* (Washington, DC: Government Printing
Office, 1973); Terry Nichols Clark, "How Many New Yorks? The New York
Fiscal Crisis in Comparative Perspective," report no. 72 of Comparative
Study of Community Decision-Making, University of Chicago (April 1976);
Continental Illinois National Bank and Trust Company, "Comparative
Analysis of City Credits: A Guide for Municipal Bond Investors," (1978).

62. Alan Merridew, "Chicago Does Well in Bankruptcy Test," *Chicago Tribune*,
April 29, 1976, F1, copy in box 013, "Untitled," folder "Schedule of Budget
Hearings and Budget Matters 1975–76," GMC. Someone, perhaps Moscone,
circled in red ink San Francisco's disturbing score.

63. Testimony of William Proxmire before the Joint Economic Committee,
Subcommittee on Economic Progress, "Financing Municipal Facilities:
Volume II," 90th Cong., 2nd sess., July 9–11, 1968, 289–90. Tabulating the
number of defaults was difficult. According to the Public Securities Association, 1950–1969 actually witnessed the default of over four hundred
municipal bond issues. *The Bond Buyer, 100 Anniversary Edition, 1891–1991*
(1991), 36.

64. Jackson Phillips and Roger Baum, "Postwar Default Experience of Municipal Bonds," in Joint Economic Committee, Subcommittee on Economic
Progress, "State and Local Public Facility Needs and Financing: Volume II,"
244–45.

65. Shapiro, "Special Report on City Debt Management," 322–25.

66. "San Francisco Board Approves $7.5 Mil. For New Welfare Building," *DBB*
221, no. 23955 (September 20, 1972): 1214.

67. Shapiro, "Special Report on City Debt Management," 326.

68. Madeline Nelson, "Found! Six Million Dollars in Public Revenues Lying
Idle in SF Banks," *San Francisco Bay Guardian [SFBG]*, March 14, 1973, 7–8.

69. Shapiro, "Special Report on City Debt Management," 325, 327.

70. Shapiro, "Special Report on City Debt Management," 331, 333.

71. For discussions of "Manhattanization," see Alison Isenberg, *Designing San
Francisco: Art, Land, and Urban Renewal in the City by the Bay* (Princeton,
NJ: Princeton University Press, 2017), 344–53.

72. John Mapel, "The Edict from the Elite Bond Screening Committee," *SFBG*, November 1, 1972, 21.

73. Proposition P: Revenue Bond Elections, "San Francisco Voters Information Pamphlet" (November 2, 1976), 15, https://sfpl.org/pdf/main/gic/elections /November2_1976short.pdf.

74. For protests against nonprofit debt, see Chester Hartman, *City for Sale: The Transformation of San Francisco* (Berkeley: University of California Press, 2002), 50, 146–54; *Duskin v. Alioto et al.*, Superior Court City and County of San Francisco, No. 641-88; *Williams v. City and County of San Francisco et al.*, Superior Court City and County of San Francisco, No. 644-426; Carol Kroot, "Non-profit Corporations: Millions for Public Works without Vote," *San Francisco Progress*, April 2, 1976; and "Voter Approval Sought for Non-profit Bonds," *San Francisco Progress*, July 28, 1976.

75. San Francisco Community Congress (June 7–8, 1975), 1, 6–7, 13.

76. "The New York Domino Theory," *Wall Street Journal*, September 30, 1975, 24.

77. Hobart Rowen and Don Oberdorfer, "Financiers Deeply Divided on Effects of N.Y. Default," *Washington Post*, November 9, 1975, A1–A2.

78. Note, for instance, Browne's criticism of the Public Works Administration in Alan K. Browne, "Financial Illiteracy," n.d., carton 2, folder "Bank America Co. Municipal Market Letter, 1937–39," AKBP, 2.

79. Alan. K. Browne, Letter to Gerald Ford, October 14, 1974, carton 3, folder "Miscellaneous Corres. & Reference Material, 1954–1979," AKBP, 1.

80. Alan K. Browne, Letter addressed "Dear Pfef," 5, 9.

81. Alan K. Browne, Letter to Ronald Reagan, November 20, 1975, carton 3, folder "Misc. Corres. 1972–79," AKBP, 3. For attempts by commercial bankers to cut away at Glass-Steagall, see Karen W. Arenson, "Revenue Financings Tempt Bankers," *New York Times*, June 27, 1979, D1.

82. Joint Economic Committee, Subcommittee on Economic Progress, "Financing Municipal Facilities: Volume I," 90th Cong., 1st sess., December 5, 6, and 7, 1967, 103–4.

83. "Financing Municipal Facilities: Volume I," 107; H.R. 15991, cited in "Financing Municipal Facilities: Volume II," 171, 189.

84. "Financing Municipal Facilities: Volume I," 112.

85. "Bank Underwriters of Tax-Free, Public Debt Form New Group to Foster Special Interests," *DBB* 221, no. 23902 (July 6, 1972): 48, 65.

86. Alioto testimony, "The Growing Threat of a Domestic Financial Crisis," 4.

87. "Financing Municipal Facilities: Volume I," 96.

88. John J. Winders, "The Editor's Corner," *DBB* 229, no. 24427 (August 12, 1974): 543.

89. Alan Bautzer, "The Municipal Market: Chicago Rejects Sole Bid for $40 Million," *DBB* 229, no. 24405 (July 11, 1974): 133.

90. "Higher Ceilings, Callable Bonds Seen as Key to Interest Squeeze," *DBB* 229, no. 24423 (August 6, 1974): 461, 474. For earlier calls to remove interest

rate ceilings, see John J. Winders, "Statutory Interest Rate Ceilings Shift; 27 States Now Have No Lids on GOs," *DBB* 213, no. 23405 (July 13, 1970): 145, 166.

91. Kim Phillips-Fein alludes to this in her rich discussion of bond financier William E. Simon's prominence within President Gerald Ford's cabinet. Phillips-Fein, *Fear City*, 180–88.

92. Winders, "The Editor's Corner," 529, 543.

93. Revzin, "Big-Apple Blight."

94. Schanck, Letter to Browne, September 24, 1975, 1.

95. Alcaly and Mermelstein, *The Fiscal Crisis of American Cities*, 300–302; Charles R. Geisst, *Wall Street A History* (New York: Oxford University Press, 2012), 307.

96. David E. Keefe, "Governor Reagan, Welfare Reform, and AFDC Fertility," *Social Science Review* 57, no. 2 (June 1983): 234–53.

97. Browne, Letter to Reagan, November 20, 1975, 1–3.

98. Browne, Letter to Schanck, September 15, 1975, 2.

99. Browne, Letter to Reagan, November 20, 1975, 1–2.

100. Herman H. Kahn, "To Extirpate Our City's 'Rooted Cancer,'" Letters to the Editor, *New York Times*, August 22, 1975, 30.

101. Alan K. Browne, Letter to Thomas M. Rees, October 30, 1975, carton 3, folder "Misc. Corres. 1974–1978," AKBP, 2; Browne, Rejected Letter to the Editor, 2.

102. Browne, Letter to Reagan, November 20, 1975, 2.

103. Browne, Rejected Letter to the Editor, 1.

104. Bob Levering, "City Strike: Revolt of the New Rank and File," *SFBG*, March 14–27, 1974, 12.

105. For public-sector employee strikes, see Leroy F. Aarons, "Alioto Overrides Board to End Strike," *Washington Post*, August 22, 1975, A1; Daryl Lembke, "S.F. Supervisors Hit Back, Attempt to Trim Back Benefits," *Los Angeles Times*, August 23, 1975, 1; San Francisco Planning and Urban Research Association, "Curbing Public Employee Demands in San Francisco," *SPUR Report*, no. 114 (October 1975), 1–5. For the organizing efforts of people of color in San Francisco, see Eduardo Contreras, *Latinos in the Liberal City: From San Francisco's Big Strike to Gay Liberation* (Philadelphia: University of Pennsylvania Press, 2019); Martin Meeker, "The Queerly Disadvantaged and the Making of San Francisco's War on Poverty, 1964–1967," *Pacific Historical Review* 81, no. 1 (February 2012): 21–59; and Tomás F. Summers Sandoval Jr., *Latinos at the Golden Gate: Creating Community & Identity in San Francisco* (Chapel Hill: University of North Carolina Press, 2013), esp. chapter 5.

106. Browne, Letter to Alioto, June 6, 1975, 2.

107. For material to craft a much-needed social history of landlord-tenant relations in San Francisco, see examples from *Haight Action* (San Francisco), esp. vol. 2, no. 2 (April 1972) and vol., no. 2 (June 1973), housed at the San Francisco Public Library (SFPL), Special Collections, 1970–1974.

108. Clark Howard, *Zebra: The True Account of the 179 Days of Terror in San Francisco* (New York: R. Marek, 1979).

109. Hartman, *City for Sale*, 293, 227–28.

110. Daryl Lembke, "5 Major Candidates in S.F. Mayoral Race," *Los Angeles Times*, October 28, 1975, A3.

111. Wallace Turner, "An Antipolitician Almost Makes It in San Francisco," *New York Times*, December 14, 1975, 62.

112. Lembke, "5 Major Candidates in S.F. Mayoral Race."

113. "Vote for Mayor on December 11, 1975," *Sun Reporter* [*SR*], November 8, 1975, 7.

114. Daryl Lembke, "Liberal, Conservative in S.F. Mayor Runoff," *Los Angeles Times*, November 6, 1975, 3.

115. Rowland Evans and Robert Novak, "San Francisco: Warnings of a Voters' Revolt," *Washington Post*, November 19, 1975, A15.

116. "Moscone Says He'll Tighten S.F. Spending," *Los Angeles Times*, December 12, 1975, A3; Jim Finefrock, "The Weatherman was a Democrat," *Chicago Tribune*, December 17, 1975, B4.

117. Frederic A. Moritz, "San Francisco Needs 'Message of New York,'" *Christian Science Monitor*, January 12, 1976, 4.

118. Daryl Lembke, "Politicians Get the Message in S.F. Vote," *Los Angeles Times*, December 13, 1975, 30.

119. Daryl Lembke, "Moscone Sworn In as S.F. Mayor, Pledges Frugality," *Los Angeles Times*, January 9, 1976, C1–2.

120. "Moscone Says He'll Tighten S.F. Spending," A3.

121. Lembke, "Politicians Get the Message in S.F. Vote," 30.

122. Phillips-Fein, *Fear City*, 5.

123. Robert Lindsey, "In the West, More Scrutiny," National Economic Survey, *New York Times*, January 4, 1976, Part II, Section 3, 37.

124. George Moscone, untitled document, April 15, 1976, box 013, "Untitled," folder "Schedule of Budget Hearings and Budget Matters 1975–76," GMC, 1.

125. Office of the Mayor, "Mr. Chairman and Members of the Finance Committee," n.d., box 013 "Untitled," folder "Schedule of Budget Hearings and Budget Matters 1975–76," GMC, 1.

126. Office of the Mayor, Press Release, March 24, 1976, box 013, "Untitled," folder "Schedule of Budget Hearings and Budget Matters 1975–76," GMC, 3.

127. Moscone, untitled document, April 15, 1976, 2.

128. Moscone, untitled document, April 15, 1976, 3–4.

129. "Possible Sources of Revenue," March 17, 1976, box 013, "Untitled," folder "Schedule of Budget Hearings and Budget Matters 1975–76," GMC, 1.

130. Moscone, untitled document, April 15, 1976, 6. References to the Asian Art Museum of San Francisco, Fine Art Museum of San Francisco, San Francisco General Hospital, and methadone maintenance derived from the attached document, "Grand Recapitulation."

131. Emphasis in the original. Rudy Nothenberg, Memorandum to All Department Heads, "RE: Summary of Remarks Regarding Budget, By Mayor

Moscone Today," March 22, 1976, box 013, "Untitled," folder "Schedule of Budget Hearings and Budget Matters 1975–76," GMC, n.p.

132. Office of the Mayor, Press Release, March 24, 1976, 2–4.

133. John J. Barbagelata, "Budget Statement of Supervisor John J. Barbagelata on Behalf of the Finance Committee," May 19, 1976, box 013, "Untitled," folder "Schedule of Budget Hearings and Budget Matters 1975–76," GMC, 1–9.

134. Barbagelata, "Budget Statement," 1–9.

135. Leroy F. Aarons, "Alioto Overrides Board to End Strike," *Washington Post*, August 22, 1975, A1; Daryl Lembke, "S.F. Supervisors Hit Back, Attempt to Trim Back Benefits," *Los Angeles Times*, August 23, 1975, 1.

136. Barbagelata, "Budget Statement," 1–9.

137. George R. Moscone to Frances Hicks, June 1, 1976, box 013, "Untitled," folder Schedule of Budget Hearings and Budget Matters 1975–76, GMC, n.p.

138. Frances Hicks, Telegram to Mayor Moscone, May 24, 1976, box 013, "Untitled," folder "Schedule of Budget Hearings and Budget Matters 1975–76," GMC, n.p.

139. Stefanie Steinberg, Telegram to Mayor Moscone, May 22, 1976, box 013, "Untitled," folder "Schedule of Budget Hearings and Budget Matters 1975–76," GMC, n.p.

140. Alessandro Baccari, Letter to George Moscone, May 13, 1976, box 013, "Untitled," folder "Schedule of Budget Hearings and Budget Matters 1975–76," GMC, 1.

141. Peter A. Balestreri and James P. Zerga, Letter to George Moscone, May 10, 1975, box 013, "Untitled," folder "Schedule of Budget Hearings and Budget Matters 1975–76," GMC, n.p.

142. "A Hatchet Job on City Budget," *SR*, May 29, 1976, 7. For more on the relationship between African Americans and the SFPD, see Christopher Lowen Agee, *The Streets of San Francisco: Policing and the Creation of a Cosmopolitan Liberal Politics, 1950–1972* (Chicago: University of Chicago Press, 2014), 196–204.

143. Roger Cornut, Letter to Robert H. Mendelsohn, March 1976, box 013, "Untitled," folder "General Files—Supervisors, Board of 1975–76," GMC, n.p.

144. Community Advisory Board of The Prisoner Medical Program of the San Francisco Health Department, Telefax to Mayor Moscone, undated, box 013, "Untitled," folder "Schedule of Budget Hearings and Budget Matters 1975–76," GMC, n.p.

145. Carlton Jones, "Aftermath of Community Relations Cut," *SR*, June 5, 1976, 3; Peter Magnani, "SF Supervisors Going After Social Services," *SR*, June 19, 1976, 13; Abe Mellinkoff, "The Bleeding Budget," *San Francisco Chronicle*, September 3, 1976, 36.

146. Nelson, "Found!" 7–8.

147. "San Francisco Isn't Broke—But the City Is Poorer because It Banks at Wells Fargo, Crocker Citizens, and Bank of America," *SFBG*, June 7, 1971, 2, 4.

148. Shapiro, "Special Report on City Debt Management," 329–33.

149. James J. Lowrey, Letter to George R. Moscone, June 3, 1976, box 028, "Office of the Mayor San Francisco . . . Program & Budget Office 1976–77," folder "Bond Screening Committee Citizens. Citizen's Bond Screening Committee (Mayors Financial Advisory Committee) '75-'76" (this folder is nestled in the "Bond Screening Committee 1976–77" folder), GMC, 1.

150. "Luncheon Guest List," September 3, 1976, box 028, "Office of the Mayor San Francisco . . . Program & Budget Office 1976–77," folder "Bond Screening Committee 1976–77," GMC, 1.

151. "Official Statement, City and County of San Francisco Relating to $59,983,000," 1, 3.

152. "Luncheon Guest List," September 3, 1976, 1.

153. George R. Moscone, Memorandum to Gilbert Boreman, May 17, 1976, box 028, "Office of the Mayor San Francisco . . . Program & Budget Office 1976–77," folder "Bond Screening Committee Citizens. Citizen's Bond Screening Committee (Mayors Financial Advisory Committee) '75-'76" (this folder is nestled in the "Bond Screening Committee 1976–77" folder), GMC, 1–2.

154. "Official Statement, City and County of San Francisco Relating to $59,983,000," 1, 9, 19.

155. United California Bank syndicate, "$59,983,000," *Los Angeles Times*, September 23, 1976, D13.

Chapter Nine

1. "San Francisco Bonds Lose Rating by S&P in Statement Delay," *Wall Street Journal*, March 31, 1980, 27.

2. "2nd Outfit Downgrades S.F. Bonds," *San Francisco Chronicle*, April 18, 1980, 18.

3. Joint Economic Committee, "Chaos in the Municipal Bond Market," 97th Cong., 1st sess., September 28, 1981, 23, 88.

4. "Rating for Philadelphia Downgraded by S&P," *Wall Street Journal*, November 30, 1979, 36; Iver Peterson, "New Mayor to Confront Philadelphia's Fiscal Ills," *New York Times*, February 3, 1980, 22. For ideological agreement on the urban fiscal crisis, see statements of Herbert Stein and Milton Freidman in *The Fiscal Crisis of American Cities: Essays on the Political Economy of Urban America with Special Reference to New York*, ed. Roger E. Alcaly and David Mermelstein (New York: Vintage, 1977), 7–8; and James O'Connor, *The Fiscal Crisis of the State* (New York: St. Martin's Press, 1973).

5. "Detroit's Bond Rating Cut by S&P, Reflecting 'Potential Fiscal Crisis,'" *Wall Street Journal*, August 7, 1980, 4.

6. "Chaos in the Municipal Bond Market," 88; Iver Peterson, "Michigan Aides Shaken as Bonds are Downrated," *New York Times*, June 12, 1980, A17.

7. Philip Revzin, "Big-Apple Blight: Other Big Cities Hurt by New York Bond-Sale Woes," *Wall Street Journal*, June 19, 1975, 1.

8. "Buffalo, N.Y.'s Plan for Offering Is Test of Its 'Respectability,'" *Wall Street Journal*, March 2, 1977, 25.

9. "2nd Outfit Downgrades S.F. Bonds," 18.

10. Walter H. Tyler, "Debt Management and Municipal Credit," *Municipal Finance* 29, no. 3 (February 1957), 130.

11. "San Francisco Bonds Lose Rating by S&P in Statement Delay."

12. "2nd Outfit Downgrades S.F. Bonds," 18.

13. "Discrimination in Borrowing," *Daily Bond Buyer* [*DBB*] 198, no. 22486 (November 14, 1966): 558.

14. Winston W. Crouch, "Municipal Affairs: The Initiative and Referendum in Cities," *American Political Science Review* 37, no. 3 (June 1943): 491–504. To be clear, there was nothing inherently progressive about the bond referendum. Direct democracy could give way to undemocratic outcomes. Lloyd Sponholtz, "The Initiative and Referendum: Direct Democracy in Perspective, 1898–1920," *American Studies* 14, no. 2 (Fall 1973): 43–64.

15. Kevin M. Kruse, "The Politics of Race and Public Space: Desegregation, Privatization, and the Tax Revolt in Atlanta," *Journal of Urban History* 31, no. 5 (July 2005): 610–33; Andrew W. Kahrl, "Capitalizing on the Urban Fiscal Crisis: Predatory Tax Buyers in 1970s Chicago," *Journal of Urban History* 44, no. 3 (May 2018): 382–401.

16. Robert O. Self, *American Babylon: Race and the Struggle for Postwar Oakland* (Princeton, NJ: Princeton University Press, 2003), 317–23; Stephen J. Sansweet, "Capital Crisis: California's Tax Revolt Slashes Local Spending by Blocking Bond Sales," *Wall Street Journal*, November 27, 1979, 1.

17. "The Guardian Endorses . . . ," *San Francisco Bay Guardian* [*SFBG*], May 18–26, 1978, 6; Robert Levering, "Prop. 13: PG&E, PT&T, and SP Will Get a 65% Reduction in Property Taxes," *SFBG*, June 1–9, 1978, 7.

18. Alan K. Browne, Letter to Leo McCarthy, May 10, 1978, carton 3, folder "Miscellaneous Corres. & Reference Material, 1954–1979," Alan K. Browne Papers (BANC MSS 91/6), Bancroft Library, University of California, Berkeley [*AKBP*], 2.

19. Browne, Letter to McCarthy, May 10, 1978, 2, 4.

20. Jack H. Beebe, "Proposition 13 and the Cost of California Debt," *National Tax Journal* (June 1979): 243–59.

21. Barbara Bry, "State Bond Holders Could Collect Bonus," *Los Angeles Times*, July 10, 1978, E10.

22. Sansweet, "Capital Crisis," 1.

23. Browne, Letter to McCarthy, May 10, 1978, 1, 3.

24. Browne, Letter to McCarthy, May 10, 1978, 2.

25. Alan K. Browne, "Proposition 13: The Aftermath," June 22, 1978, carton 2, folder "Misc. Paper Clippings, S.F. Chamber of Commerce, S.F. Bond Club," *AKBP*, 2.

26. Self, *American Babylon*, 317–23.

27. Ron Javers, "Two Families Revisited: What It All Means to Them Now," *San*

Francisco Chronicle, October 6, 1978, 4; Larry Kraemer, "Rent Adjustments, Largess Aftermath of Proposition 13," *Washington Post*, July 14, 1978, D1.

28. "Big Win for Number 13," *San Francisco Chronicle*, June 11, 1978, 5.

29. Chester Hartman, *City for Sale: The Transformation of San Francisco* (Berkeley: University of California Press, 2002), 340; "Hotline to Coax Landlords," *San Francisco Chronicle*, August 10, 1978, 17.

30. Jerry Burns, "Where Prop. 13 'Won' in S.F.," *San Francisco Chronicle*, June 22, 1978, 7.

31. Burns, "Where Prop. 13 'Won' in S.F."; Richard Brandi and Woody LaBounty, "San Francisco's Ocean View, Merced Heights, and Ingleside (OMI) Neighborhoods, 1862–1959," 40–42, http://www.outsidelands.org/OMI-small-feb2010.pdf.

32. "Black Candidates Win Big—Prop 13 Damage Assessments," *Sun Reporter* [*SR*], June 8, 1978, 3; "Proposition 13 Shuts Door on Blacks," *SR*, June 22, 1978, 7.

33. Burns, "Where Prop. 13 'Won' in S.F.," 7.

34. Peter Magnani, "Aftermath of Jarvis-Gann: Layoffs, Cutbacks, Price Hikes," *SR*, June 15, 1978, 3; Jerry Roberts, "Protest at Standard Oil Over Prop. 13," *San Francisco Chronicle*, August 1, 1978, 8.

35. "Parents Blast School Cutbacks," *SR*, July 20, 1978, 13.

36. "Jarvis-Gann Is Out of Hand: 10 Ways to Save the City," *SFBG*, June 22–30, 1978, 2.

37. Robert Levering, "Moscone Moves to Raise Muni Fare," *SFBG*, July 6–14, 1978, 2; Robert Levering, "The Inside Story of How the 25 Cent Muni Fare Was Saved," *SFBG*, July 6–14, 1978, 5.

38. Tom Benet, "Moscone Lets Board Cancel the Tax Rise," *San Francisco Chronicle*, August 4, 1978, 1, 14; Ron Javers, "The First 100 Days of Proposition 13," *San Francisco Chronicle*, October 6, 1978, 4–5; Jackson Rannells, "State Supreme Court Urged to End Prop. 13 Pay Freeze," *San Francisco Chronicle*, December 5, 1978, 12.

39. For New York, see Kim Philips-Fein, *Fear City: New York's Fiscal Crisis and the Rise of Austerity Politics* (New York: Metropolitan Books, 2017), 125. For Proposition 2½ in Massachusetts and the alleged end to the tax revolts, see Martin and Kathleen Feldstein, "Examining the Main Points in Tax Cut Proposition 2½," *Boston Globe*, September 30, 1980, 34; "Beyond the Tax Revolt," *Wall Street Journal*, November 7, 1980, 26.

40. See, e.g., Calvin A. Kent, "Users' Fees for Municipalities," *Governmental Finance* 1, no. 1 (February 1972): 7. *Governmental Finance* was the successor to *Municipal Finance*, an official publication of the Municipal Finance Officers' Association.

41. Browne, "Proposition 13: The Aftermath," 3.

42. "Fees to Rise at Museums, S.F. Zoo," *San Francisco Chronicle*, June 30, 1978, 1.

43. Ronald L. Soble, "Dozens of Cities, Counties Move Swiftly to Enact New Fees to Recover Lost Funds," *Los Angeles Times*, July 3, 1978, A4.

44. Michael A. Shires, *Patterns in California Government Revenues since Proposition 13* (San Francisco: Public Policy Institute of California, 1999).

45. Browne, "Proposition 13: The Aftermath," 5.

46. Alan K. Browne, Letter to John Knox, February 8, 1979, carton 3, folder "Miscellaneous Corres. & Reference Material, 1954–1979," AKBP, 1.

47. Browne, "Proposition 13: The Aftermath," 3.

48. Sansweet, "Capital Crisis," 1; Kent Pierce, "Property Tax Rate in San Francisco Expected to Fall," *Bond Buyer*, September 1, 1983, 3

49. David Lampe, "Moody's, S&P Restoring Rating to Bonds in State," *Los Angeles Times*, September 20, 1978, E15.

50. "Moody's Won't Rate Bonds in California Due to Tax-Cut Bid," *Wall Street Journal*, April 12, 1978, 36.

51. Sansweet, "Capital Crisis," 1.

52. Testimony of John E. Petersen in "Chaos in the Municipal Bond Market," 23–24.

53. Thomas J. Sugrue, *Sweet Land of Liberty: The Forgotten Struggle for Civil Rights in the North* (New York: Random House, 2008), 523–24; Robert M. Collins, *Transforming America: Politics and Culture During the Reagan Years* (New York: Columbia University Press, 2007), 72.

54. Reginald Smith and Carl Nolte, "How Reagan Budget Plan Will Affect the Bay Area," *San Francisco Chronicle*, December 6, 1984, 19.

55. Petersen testimony, "Chaos in the Municipal Bond Market," 88.

56. Matthew Kreps, "Ups and Downs of Municipal Bonds' Volume and Yield in the Past Century," in *The Bond Buyer: 100 Anniversary Edition: A Salute to the Municipal Bond Industry, 1891–1991*, 21.

57. Collins, *Transforming America*, 71.

58. Kreps, "Ups and Downs of Municipal Bonds' Volume and Yield in the Past Century," 21.

59. Jon Levy, *Ages of American Capitalism* (New York: Random House, 2021).

60. Louis Hyman, *Debtor Nation: The History of America in Red Ink* (Princeton, NJ: Princeton University Press, 2011), 236.

61. Statement of Roger C. Altman in "Chaos and the Municipal Bond Market," 10–13, 59.

62. "Chaos in the Municipal Bond Market," 36, 101–2.

63. Witness the general obligation bonds proposed and, in some instances, passed in support of San Francisco's parks, libraries, and correctional facilities.

64. "General debt" as distinct from "utility debt," which was defined as that issued to "finance city-owned and operated water, electric, gas, or transit utility facilities." US Bureau of the Census, "City Government Finances in 1979–80," Table 8: "Finances of Individual City Governments Having 300,000 Population or More, in Detail, 1979–80," 109–10, https://www2.census.gov/govs/pubs/city_govt_fin/1980.pdf.

65. US Bureau of the Census, "City Government Finances in 1984–85," Table 5:

"Finances of Individual City and Selected Urban Town and Township Governments Having 50,000 Population or More: 1984–85," 17, https://www2 .census.gov/govs/pubs/city_govt_fin/1985.pdf.

66. Proposition B: Water Revenue Bonds, "Voter Information Pamphlet," General Election (November 1984), 52–53, https://sfpl.org/pdf/main/gic /elections/November6_1984short.pdf.

67. Proposition C: Refund Revenue Bonds Without Voter Approval, "Voter Information Pamphlet," General Election (November 4, 1986), 48, https:// sfpl.org/pdf/main/gic/elections/November4_1986short.pdf.

68. Proposition C: Port Revenue Bond Procedure, "San Francisco Voter Information Pamphlet & Sample Ballot," General Election (November 6, 1990), 71–72, https://sfpl.org/pdf/main/gic/elections/November6_1990short.pdf.

69. San Francisco Tomorrow, "Argument Against Proposition A," in San Francisco Voter Information Pamphlet, Municipal Election (November 3, 1981), 19, https://sfpl.org/pdf/main/gic/elections/November3_1981short.pdf.

70. "2nd Outfit Downgrades S.F. Bonds," 18.

71. For the package of revenue proposals, see propositions I, O, Q, R, and S in "San Francisco Voter Information Pamphlet," Primary Election (June 3, 1980), 43–4, 51–3, 57–60, 61–3, 64–66, http://sfpl.org/pdf/main/gic/elections /June3_1980short.pdf.

72. "2nd Outfit Downgrades S.F. bonds," 18.

73. Proposition O: Hotel Tax, "San Francisco Voter Information Pamphlet," Primary Election (June 3, 1980), 52, http://sfpl.org/pdf/main/gic/elections /June3_1980short.pdf.

74. Proposition. Q: Payroll and Gross Receipts Tax, "San Francisco Voter Information Pamphlet," Primary Election (June 3, 1980), 58, http://sfpl.org/pdf /main/gic/elections/June3_1980short.pdf.

75. Proposition R: Parking Tax Surcharge and Proposition S: Nonprofit Parking Revenue, "San Francisco Voter Information Pamphlet," Primary Election (June 3, 1980), 61, 64, http://sfpl.org/pdf/main/gic/elections/June3 _1980short.pdf.

76. "The City Package," San Francisco Chronicle, June 5, 1980, 60; Marshall Kilduff, "S.F. Rejects Corporate Tax," San Francisco Chronicle, June 4, 1980, 1.

77. Harry Jupiter, "Moody's Upgrades San Francisco Bond Rating," San Francisco Chronicle, March 24, 1983, 29; Thomas G. Keane, "S.F. Municipal Bond Rating Downgraded," San Francisco Chronicle, June 21, 1988, 2.

78. Saskia Sassen, The Global City: New York, London, Tokyo (Princeton, NJ: Princeton University Press 1991, 2001), 284–89.

79. Thomas C. Holt, The Problem of Race in the 21st Century (Cambridge, MA: Harvard University Press, 2000), 97–102.

80. Jupiter, "Moody's Upgrades San Francisco Bond Rating," 29.

81. Kent Pierce, "Moody's Raises San Francisco Rating Prior to $18.1 Million GO Offering," Bond Buyer, March 23, 1983, 3.

82. Jupiter, "Moody's Upgrades San Francisco Bond Rating," 29.

83. Joan Pryde, "The Ongoing Battle: Almost 70 Years of Assaults on Tax-Exempt Municipals," in *The Bond Buyer: 100 Anniversary Edition: A Salute to the Municipal Bond Industry, 1891–1991*, 89.

84. Dennis Walters, "Revenue Increases, Budget Cuts Proposed to Prevent Deficit in San Francisco," *Bond Buyer*, May 12, 1988, 5.

85. "Moody's Downgrades San Francisco's GO Debt to Aa from Aa1, Citing General Fund Deficits," *Bond Buyer*, June 21, 1988, 2.

86. "The Bay Guardian's Election Endorsements," *SFBG*, May 29 through June 5, 1980, 9.

Epilogue

1. Kent Pierce, "San Francisco's Mayor Will Ask for Construction of New Stadium," *Bond Buyer*, October 12, 1983, 3; Task Force to the Mayor, "Stadium Feasibility Analysis" (October 1983), 3–5.

2. Kent Pierce, "Merrill Lynch Joins Other Firms Moving Units to Los Angeles from San Francisco," *Bond Buyer*, November 5, 1984, 4.

3. James O'Connor, *The Fiscal Crisis of the State* (New York: St. Martin's Press, 1973, 2001), xviii, xxv.

4. Testimony of Christopher J. Dodd and Wilson Goode before the Committee on Banking, Housing, and Urban Affairs, Subcommittee on Securities, "State and Local Governments Under Stress: The Role of the Capital Markets," 102nd Cong., 1st sess., March 13, April 24, 1991, 2–3, 13–14.

5. Joan Pryde, "The Ongoing Battle: Almost 70 Years of Assaults on Tax-Exempt Municipals," *The Bond Buyer: 100 Anniversary Edition: A Salute to the Municipal Bond Industry, 1891–1991*, 89–90; Albert M. Sbragia, *Debt Wish: Entrepreneurial Cities, U.S. Federalism, and Economic Development* (Pittsburgh: University of Pittsburgh Press, 1996), 188–200.

6. Testimony of Ralph Horn in "State and Local Governments Under Stress: The Role of the Capital Markets," 44–45. The question of just *who* these individual investors were is intriguing: they were long presumed to be wealthy individuals. But in 1981, the *New York Times* revealed the blurred boundaries between the formal and illicit economies. Funds derived from organized crime and "the so-called underground economy" were being invested in tax-exempt municipal bonds. Municipal debt helped launder income from connections to specific public-housing projects; by the 1980s, no longer just a metaphor, municipal debt was "a vehicle for laundering tainted funds," a charge to which investment bank E. F. Hutton & Co. pled guilty in April 1988. Steve Lohr, "Municipal Bond Market: Means to Launder Funds," *New York Times*, March 27, 1981, D1; Howard Kurtz, "E.F. Hutton to Plead Guilty," *The Washington Post*, April 2, 1988, A3.

7. John J. Doran, "How the Dealer's Bible Came to Be; Warding Off 'Pests' and Selling Ads," *The Bond Buyer: 100 Anniversary Edition: A Salute to the Municipal Bond Industry, 1891–1991*, 72.

8. Deborah Verna, "San Francisco Expects Sewer Refunding to Pare Fee Increases Planned for Users," *Bond Buyer*, August 19, 1992, 5.

9. Testimony of Christopher Cox before the Committee on Banking and Financial Services, Subcommittee on Capital Markets, Securities, and Government Sponsored Enterprises, "Debt Issuance and Investment Practices of State and Local Governments," 104th Cong., 1st sess., July 26–27, 1995, 3.

10. "Figuring the Odds of Default," *Bond Buyer*, April 28, 1982, 23.

11. Nathaniel S. Preston, "The Bondholder and the Public Authority: Financial Control," *Municipal Finance* 35, no. 3 (February 1963): 129–47.

12. Howard Gleckman, "Even with the Football Strike, NFL Stadiums Can Cover Debt," *Bond Buyer*, October 5, 1982, 19.

13. Jan Paschal, "Congress Approves Bankruptcy Code Amendment to Shield Muni Bondholders," *Bond Buyer*, October 24, 1988, 4.

14. Michael B. Katz, *Why Don't American Cities Burn?* (Philadelphia: University of Pennsylvania Press, 2012), 86–89.

15. Joe Bel Bruno, "Issuance Expected to Increase During New San Francisco Mayor's Term," *Bond Buyer*, December 18, 1995, 1.

16. "Analysts Forum: San Francisco Enters the Debt-Friendly Age of Brown," *Bond Buyer*, January 30, 1996, 6.

17. Committee on Banking and Currency, "Increased Flexibility for Financial Institutions," 88th Cong., 1st sess., 1963, 489; Joint Economic Committee, Subcommittee on Economic Progress, "State and Local Public Facility Needs and Financing: Volume II," 89th Cong., 2nd sess., December 1966, 11–12, 250; Joint Economic Committee, Subcommittee on Economic Progress, "Financing Municipal Facilities: Volume II," 90th Cong., 2nd sess., July 9–11, 1968, 212, 406–7.

18. "An Archaic Rule on Bond Votes," *San Francisco Examiner*, November 27, 1968.

19. "Complete Text of High Court Ruling in Today's '*Bond Buyer*,'" *DBB* 213, no. 23401 (July 7, 1970): 65; "Text of High Court Ruling on Non-Freeholder Vote in Arizona," *DBB* 213, no. 23401 (July 7, 1970): 68–69.

20. "Miami Voters Approve $81.4 Million, Reject $47.5 Million of New Bonds," *DBB* 213, no. 23399 (July 2, 1970): 21.

21. For starters, see Jacqueline Dowd Hall, "The Long Civil Rights Movement and the Political Uses of the Past," *Journal of American History* 91, no. 4 (March 2005): 1233–63.

22. Frederick McCarthy, "Is Integration Issue Hurting School Bonds?" *Daily Boston Globe*, October 5, 1958, 32.

23. H. J. Maidenberg, "CORE Attacking Southern Bonds," *New York Times*, December 6, 1962, 52.

24. James C. Tanner, "Jackson, Miss., Plans Tough Stand Against Desegregation Drive," *Wall Street Journal*, May 29, 1963, 1.

25. David A. Bateman, Ira Katznelson, and John S. Lapinski, *Southern Nation: Congress and White Supremacy after Reconstruction* (Princeton, NJ: Princeton University Press, 2018), 15, 18.

26. John H. Allan, "Brokers Shun Mississippi Bonds Attacked in Plea by N.A.A.C.P.," *New York Times*, December 15, 1964, 48.

27. "Childs Securities to Shun Alabama Bonds," *Wall Street Journal*, April 1, 1965, 4.

28. "Boycott and Public Finance," *DBB* 190, no. 22009 (December 21, 1964): 1138.

29. "$185,000 Municipality of Aguadilla Porto Rico," *DBB* 86, no. 10106 (August 21, 1922): 2059.

30. Peter James Hudson, *Bankers and Empire: How Wall Street Colonized the Caribbean* (Chicago: University of Chicago Press, 2017).

31. United Statistical Associates, *Municipal Holdings of Insurance Companies* (1955), n.p.

32. George Wanders, "The Finance Officer Is Also a *Salesman*," reprinted in *DBB* 168, no. 20370 (June 11, 1958): 1, 6, 9. Page numbers correspond to reprint.

33. "The Fuss and the Outcome," *DBB* 197, no. 22449 (September 19, 1966): 1009.

34. "Changing Conditions in the Market for State and Local Government Debt," prepared for the Joint Economic Committee, 94th Cong., 2nd sess., April 16, 1976, 11.

35. "$40,000,000 Commonwealth of Puerto Rico Public Improvement Bonds of 1970, Series A," *DBB* 213, no. 23455 (September 22, 1970): 1258.

36. "Canadian Bond Market Trend 1910–1921," *DBB* 85, no. 9931 (January 24, 1922): 181; "Bond Sales Reported During the Week Ending Saturday, January 28, 1922," *DBB* 85, no. 9936 (January 30, 1922): 227.

37. "A Friendly Warning to Canada," *DBB* 85. no. 9970 (March 13, 1922): 553; Stanley Scott, "Letter to the Editor," *San Francisco Chronicle*, November 13, 1958, 38.

38. "World Bank to Offer $100 Million Bonds in Week of February 8," *DBB* 172, no. 20785 (February 5, 1960): 452. See also Jochen Kraske, *Bankers with a Mission: The Presidents of the World Bank, 1946–1991* (New York: Oxford University Press, 1996); Davash Kapur, *The World Bank: Its First Half Century* (Washington, DC: Brookings Institution, 1997).

Index

Wirt, Frederick M., 131
Witkowski, Leonard W., 128
women in bond finance, 58, 66
Woo, George, 134–35
Wood, David M., 39
Woods, Wade, 106
World Bank, 45, 229
Worthington, Sydney G., 155

W. P. Fuller Co., 72
Wright, Guy, 161, 162

Zellerbach, Harold L., 83
Zellerbach, J. D., 74
Zerga, James P., 196
Zurich General Accident and Liability
Company, 96

Made in the USA
Columbia, SC
16 February 2024